LIFECLOCK

For over thirty years Louise and Bruno Huber have been working with astrological psychology—teaching, training, and writing. They are the founders of the internationally recognized Astrological Psychology Institute (API) in Adliswil/Zürich, Switzerland, and the English Huber School in Devon, England. In addition to personal counseling practices, the Hubers teach at both schools, and lecture all over the world. They have been keynote speakers at the American Federation of Astrologers Convention and since 1981 they have been co-organizers of the now-famous International World Congress in Astrology held every year in Lucerne, Switzerland. They are the authors of several books including *Astrology and The Spiritual Path* as well as the forthcoming *Moon Node Astrology.*

Bruno and Louise Huber

LIFECLOCK

The Huber Method of Timing in the Horoscope

Complete in One Volume

Volume 1
Life Clock: Age Progression in the Horoscope

Volume 2
Life Clock: Practical Techniques for Counseling
Age Progression in the Horoscope

SAMUEL WEISER, INC.

York Beach, Maine

Revised edition published in one volume in 1994 by
Samuel Weiser, Inc.
Box 612
York Beach, Maine 03910-0612

99 98 97 96 95 94
9 8 7 6 5 4 3 2 1

Library of Congress Cataloging-in-Publication Data

Huber, Bruno.
    (Lebensuhr im Horoskop. Band 1-2. English)
    Lifeclock : the Huber method of timing in the horoscope / by Bruno and Louise
Huber.
    P.   cm.
    Originally published: York Beach, Me. : S. Weiser, c1982-c1986.
    Includes bibliographical references.
    1. Horoscopes. 2. Progressions (Astrology) 3. Age (Psychology)— Miscellanea. 4.
Life cycle, Human—Miscellanea. I. Huber. Louise. II. Title. III. Title: Life clock.
    [BF1708.1.H8313 1994]
    133.5'4—dc20   93-46228
                                                                             CIP
ISBN 0-87728-803-8
MV

This book was previously published as two separate volumes—*Life Clock: Age
Progression in the Horoscope,* and *Life Clock: Practical Techniques for Counseling Age
Progression in the Horoscope.* The original German edition was published by Verlag
Astrologisch-Psychologisches Institut, Zurich, Switzerland in 1980, 1983.

We wish to extend our appreciation to Haloli Q. Richter for her translation of
Volume 1, to Transcript, Ltd. for Volume 2, and to Agnes Shellens for her help
with the revised material.

Typeset in Baskerville

Printed in the United States of America

The paper used in this publication meets the minimum requirements of the
American National Standard for Permanence of Paper for Printed Library
Materials Z39.48-1984.

LIFECLOCK

Volume 1
Life Clock: Age Progression in the Horoscope

Bruno and Louise Huber

Translated by Haloli Q. Richter

SAMUEL WEISER, INC.

York Beach, Maine

*A wise man contributes to the
heavenly happenings as much as the
farmer, who, by planting or cleansing
the earth, contributes to the bounty of nature.*

The 100 stanzas by Claudius Ptolemy

Contents

Symbols of the planets

Sun	☉	♂		Mars
Moon	☽	♃		Jupiter
Saturn	♄	♅	(♅)	Uranus
Mercury	☿	♆		Neptune
Venus	♀	♇	(♇)	Pluto
Dragon's Head	☊			

Symbols of the Signs

Aries	♈	♎	Libra
Taurus	♉	♏	Scorpio
Gemini	♊	♐	Sagittarius
Cancer	♋	♑	Capricorn
Leo	♌	♒	Aquarius
Virgo	♍	♓	Pisces

Abbreviations

AC = Ascendant   AP = Age Point
IC = Imum Coeli   HC = House Cusp
DC = Descendant   LP = Low Point
MC = Medium Coeli   IP = Invert Point

Synonyms: Age Progression, Hand on the Life Clock, Age Point (AP)

Foreword

Dear Reader,

This book presents a method for using astrology as a diagnostic tool in the study of human psychology. It will help beginners to gain a better attitude toward life, and help experts to work faster and more securely with other people's problems.

For several years, the age progression technique has been used by students of astrology in counselling work; it has been tested and applied successfully. Now, this work is offered to the public.

In our last book, *Man and His World* (Samuel Weiser, York Beach, 1978), we discussed the spatial division of the horoscope, describing the human being in relationship to his environment. This book discusses the time element in the horoscope. We call this time element the *age progression* or *age point*. It moves through the houses like the hands of a clock and indicates the unfolding life of the human being.

We have divided the broad subject of age progression into two volumes. This first volume discusses the structural and qualitative elements of the age point method. It includes the calculation techniques and methods for understanding individual life phases. We consider both short and long astrological cycles as well as crisis points at different ages.

The second volume will cover the practical application of age progression in daily life, as well as in the realm of personality development. Example horoscopes will be used to show the reader how to apply this method for clients.

While working with this first volume, you will be able to apply and examine the age point method (the big hand on your life clock) in your own horoscope. This will give you an overview of the cyclic unfolding of your life and will most likely convince you of the effectiveness and value of this surprisingly simple method of astrological forecasting.

In case you are a beginner in the study of astrology, you will find a short introduction to the basics of astrological psychology in the appendix.

Bruno and Louise Huber

Part I

Structure, Effectiveness and Technique of Age Progression

Chapter 1

Basic Observations

Most people's acquaintance with astrology is through the newspaper, and this has led many to believe that astrology is fortune telling. Astrology has always been concerned with much more for it really deals with the human psyche and the paths to self-awareness. Astrology is not only the oldest science but also the oldest psychology in the world. Few people are aware of this fact. Serious astrologers work to develop new, useful, and reliable methods for using the horoscope as a diagnostic tool in psychological counseling. This book presents one such method, developed through long years of research and practical application.

In our times, many seemingly new professions (i.e., the helping professions) have developed in pursuit of creative solutions to existing human problems. Old approaches are no longer satisfactory. Often, psychologists find themselves at a dead end; they are looking for new ways to understand the human psyche in order to offer effective help to their patients. In this light, more and more psychologists, social workers and educators are turning to astrology and its reservoir of wisdom for insight into the human condition. Conversely, more and more astrologers are eager to integrate modern psychological knowledge with traditional astrological thinking.

The synthesis of astrology and psychology is of benefit to all parties concerned. The combination offers a complete and whole portrait of the human being and is useful in finding solutions to psychological problems and conflicts.

Over the centuries, many great thinkers have involved themselves with astrology. Among them were such men as Ptolemaeus, Albertus Magnus, Paracelsus, Melanchton, Kopernikus, Kepler, Galilei, Shakespeare, Goethe and others. They recognized the connection between human fate and the movement of heavenly bodies, and translated cosmic laws into basic rules. Astrology changed with the times and in recent decades it has experienced a renaissance. Based on modern psychological knowledge, a clear concept of man was again developed, putting the emphasis on inner energy fields and related external behavioral processes. These ideas are really centuries old, but they are now presented with new terminology.

While traditional astrology still works with the observation of events and bases its interpretations upon such events, modern astrological psychology addresses itself to the issue of *causation*. The combination of astrology and psychology has nothing to do with the dualistic, predetermined "black and white" thinking of the past, when "bad" was opposed to "good" and the world was separated from God. In modern astrology, we no longer speak of good or bad aspects or good or bad horoscopes for our psychological awareness demands more complex definitions. We can recognize the shades and nuances, and therefore the causes, the reasons, and purposes of good or bad indications.

Today the trend is toward uncovering dynamic causes. People now resent being judged by behavior alone. People want to be recognized and understood in their innermost beings. They want to know *why* they are a certain way and *why* they are successful or unsuccessful in different areas of life.

Astrological psychology, based on the individual horoscope and on newly developed and psychologically influenced interpretive methods, can determine the reasons for defeats as well as for extraordinary accomplishments. It is possible to understand a person as a holistic being and bring to consciousness many subconscious patterns. Astrology can and should judge the human being by his inner attitude, as evidenced by the horoscope. The goal is to lead humanity to the point where we can become master of our fate, of ourselves and of our stars. Psychological astrology is contrary to any form of determinism or of negative interpretations that are utilized to make a business out of fear.

Astrological psychology encompasses the complete individual because it allows for a three-fold personality. The integration of this personality—physical, emotional and mental—is called psychosynthesis, and the process of integration leads us toward a new and creative rebirth of the real inner human being. Through astrological psychology, it is possible to offer new guidelines and ethical principles for a natural and meaningful life.

Psychological astrology is still based on the traditional symbolism of planets, aspects, signs and houses. These factors can be adapted rather easily to a psychological approach. The horoscope, calculated for the exact time of birth, is a symbolic picture of man and his subjective world. Personal characteristics and the path of individual development can be deduced from the natal horoscope.

The connection between heavenly mechanics and character is as yet not explainable in terms of science. However, the connection can be proved through the diagnostic tools of psychology. We cannot prove nor explain the operational effects of astrology; we cannot say how and why astrology functions. These facts make for a contested science. The fact that we are indeed dealing with a science is not in doubt because we work with exact measuring methods and with known criteria. The results are precise statements of psychological values that can be checked and repeated by anyone.

In the same way that a voltmeter functions as a measuring device for electricity, the planets work as indicators of individuality. The voltmeter does not produce electricity; it only measures it. The horoscope is a similar instrument. Its components do not form our character nor do they determine our actions. They function as a kind of measuring instrument which clocks the biological, psychological, and spiritual make-up of a human being in very precise ways.

Knowing that the horoscope is such a measuring device or diagnostic instrument is invaluable in psychological practice. The trained eye can identify the current problems and offer possible solutions. Not only does this knowledge save time but, with the help of age progression, a remedial program within time is possible.

Age progression is a relatively new concept. Through long years of research and twenty years of counseling and teaching, we have developed and successfully applied this system. It is not a hypothesis; the method has been used by many psychologists and astrologers in their practices. It is a kind of time mechanism within the horoscope, an individual life clock. This clock can indicate where we are in life and how we can make the best of current influences in the light of problems past, present, or future. Age progression refers to psychological processes, not to outer events.

As we demonstrate this new method of progression in this book, it is not to determine events but rather to understand the psychological structure of a given life period in order to apply that basic energy properly. To transform diagnostic studies from materialistic thought into psychological insight is the important challenge and demand of our time. If we want to practice progressive astrology without danger, then we must not fixate upon future events. We must learn to see life not only in terms of the obvious, but also in terms of the psychological qualities, energies, and levels of consciousness that are a part of the human experience. Psychology infiltrates all spheres of daily life and we astrologers need to incorporate these psychological dimensions into our work. Without these psychological dimensions, modern astrology is not credible.

Chapter 2

Prognosis and Psychological Problems

What is prognosis?—Astrological prediction—Differences between age progression and other progression methods—The significance of age levels in prediction—Life cycles versus "magnifier effects"—The compulsion to fulfillment: dangers of prognosis—Freedom of will and choice—Practical example of freedom of choice—Tesing the self: the "I" as a reference point for the will function—Self-determination and the individuation process—Responsibility, ethics, and free will.

● **What is Prognosis?**

Prognosis in astrology generally embraces all methods by which we determine the timing of planetary aspects which influence our actions or our attitude in the present and past, as well as in the future. Many people believe that astrology deals only with future-oriented prognosis. They consult an astrologer to look for a positive period ahead or to learn when something terrible will come their way. Many make use of astrology in order to avoid making decisions on their own; many want to rid themselves of existential anxieties.

In reality, the question of the future is only a small aspect of the astrological concept. Astrological psychology avoids a deterministic emphasis on the future because the prediction of events can easily hinder the self-development of the human being. It can even do real psychological damage.

• Astrological Prediction

Astrological predictions are often made by astrologers who have no psychological background and no real understanding of their fellow human beings. These astrologers may judge clients only through outward appearance and measure astrological symbolism only through events.

Unfortunately, there are still many astrology books which are exclusively event-oriented. All kinds of events are descriptively assigned, and in great detail, to specific transits. Beginning students in astrology often read these books without discrimination, seeking interpretations of upcoming aspects. Many become so dependent that no day goes by without consulting an ephemeris for the day's transits. We call this disease "Transititis." These people literally believe what they read and do not realize that every aspect, every transit, every direction will work differently for each human being and can only be correctly interpreted in connection with the individual horoscope. Each progressed aspect will be modified according to the natal base. Ever new variations develop for which there are no recipes, no pat answers.

To understand a human being, it takes more than reading what a book says about a certain aspect. We need our mental and intuitive faculties as well. We must consider, in the case of a transiting Saturn square or opposition to natal Mars, for example, that the whole horoscope, with its individual signs, houses and aspects, is a part of that transit and must be treated as such. In addition, the individual's familial, social, and mental background must be part of the overall consideration.

Of course, it could easily happen that an astrologer makes the observation that, for example, a tension aspect (a square or opposition) forming between a transiting planet and the natal Moon and Mercury appears to have some connection with physical injury—such as different kinds of traffic and/or bungling accidents—even if nothing like this was previously read in any textbook. And just as easily, these kinds of isolated observations could be formulated into rules. In reality, such rules apply only in a few cases, mainly when the natal horoscope shows a hard aspect between the Moon and Mercury. It may be that this advice only works when the natal aspect is also in a mutable sign or in an angular house. This combination indicates a tendency toward accidents, a weakness which could be activated through some transitory irritation.

In principle, we feel that the following rule of thumb should apply to all prediction work: *The individual horoscope, as a reflection of our inner psychological structure, does not indicate events. Rather, it indicates stimulation and effects upon our psyche.* The manner in which a person will react to such stimulation is dependent upon the person's level of development and personal circumstance. Each human being reacts differently to the same planets, aspects or transits. His reaction also changes with age and maturation. That is the main reason why astrological prediction only has a 20-40 per cent accuracy.

With sensitivity to psychological astrology, we can at any time ascertain the qualitative effects of aspects. For example, an aspect could suggest that we tend toward nervous energy and therefore act hastily and without caution. This is a psychological observation and the knowledge of it allows us to counteract this inner restlessness and control it. In this sense, we are able to prepare mentally and emotionally for coming influences, recognize subconscious energies, and render them harmless. We not only develop our own will power but are also in control when we want to react to internal or external stimulations or when we want to reject them because they do not represent our real intentions. The goal is to have a certain inner maturity and self-knowledge. This puts us in touch with the need to improve ourselves in order to fulfill personal ideals. Much growth can come from such knowledge.

● Differences between Age Progression and Other Progression Methods

Age progression is based upon the time mechanism within the horoscope's *house system* (not within the zodiac). A horoscope is not only a self-portrait fixed at the moment of birth, but it is also a kind of "life clock" that shows where we are at any moment in our development. The age progression or age point (AP) is the hand on this life clock moving through life and through the twelve houses of the horoscope. With its help, we can gain a detailed overview of the course of life.

All other methods of progression concentrate on certain periods or days when an aspect is exact as an indication of when that aspect will "trigger" stimulation and events. Age progression differs totally from these methods. The practice of considering single transit elements without seeing the chart as a whole is questionable, because coherence is lost. An attempt to overcome this problem was first made by Dane Rudhyar when he published *The Astrology of Personality* in 1936. Alex Ruperti expanded on this idea in his book *Cycles of Becoming,* where he described the movements of the planets within the context of the solar system.

In contrast to the general methods of progression, the age progression has the advantage, technically speaking, of being only one process and also being indicative of an entirely individualized dimension. To understand this fully, we have to change our traditional concepts regarding astrology. It is a psychological and more synthesized way of observing the human being and his life. It does not speculate about detailed effects deduced from isolated planetary positions, but rather suggests fundamental emotions which affect active and passive phases in life. With age progression, there is always a line of development, a motion within time. The details, the individual points, are links in the whole developmental process. With age progression, we can stop at any time in this developmental process and learn what psychological theme is basically at work at that moment. All other influences are seen to be secondary to the basic theme of that period.

When we work with age progression or age point (AP), the purpose is not to ascertain when something happens but why, what meaning it has for our development. Through the AP, we recognize how consciousness changes through time and what is important at certain times in terms of interest or conflict. The AP reflects psychological processes within the human being that, in reality, actually create events. These processes, then, are the source of symptoms and outer activities, and events are not necessarily relevant because they are but the symptoms of mental-spiritual processes.

The usual "event thinking" in astrology, the attempt to arrive at the exact dates of events through calculation of transits and progressions, can become the major oversight of astrology. To seek out causes through events is very difficult and easily leads to totally inaccurate assumptions. We can see parallels of this in other disciplines, such as medical oversight when only surface symptoms are treated rather than searching for the "cause" of the symptoms.

The astrology of the past could only base knowledge on such event-symptoms. It was not yet possible to connect psychological conditions with outer events as we can today. Our consciousness has changed significantly. We are now able to recognize the underlying causes of our actions. The AP gives us this information and indicates our psychological attitude during different life phases.

Within the human psyche, constant processing takes place that is only conditionally related to outer events. On the one hand, we have deep-seated and, therefore, often sub-conscious individual motivations that push us in certain directions. On the other hand, life takes its course and constantly produces stimuli that demand a reaction. We are supposed to comply, but often we are not in agreement or only partially so. We then tend to block or falsify reality. At other times, these stimuli may correspond with our wishes; we consider them as opportunities which we urgently have to take.

Such processes are shown in the horoscope through the AP. They become visible as the AP transits over planetary positions, changes signs, or makes aspects to planets in other parts of the horoscope. The AP takes six years to move through each house and establishes our inner attitude to the outer world according to the psychological theme of that house.

The AP is therefore a primary element in progression study. The progression of planets is a secondary element. The planetary transits are third. The AP can be compared with the hour hand on our life clock; progressed planets then are the minute hand; and transits track the seconds.

It can even be said that transits and progressions can only be judged correctly if they are seen within the AP concept—or in terms of age and maturity. We have researched transit and progression activity in many horoscopes over a long period of time, and we have come to the conclusion that transits and progressions only have a measurable effect when they are thematically related to the age point. The AP sensitizes other elements of progression because it represents the main element of the living horoscope. It also undermines many astrological predictions because the individual can work with underlying causes rather than events.

People do not have a direct individualized relationship to progressed planets and angles, but they do have such an individualized relationship through the AP. The AP is very close to us. It is part of the horoscope as well as ourselves. It is the built-in life clock within our being. We can read the AP in the horoscope at any time without complicated calculations of progressed planets, angles, and transits. The AP is easily used for it is like the hand of a clock, moving along the house system, touching all the positions of the natal planets, aspects and signs. It is easy to determine when the AP reaches a certain planet or house cusp in life. It interacts in time in certain points in the horoscope, bringing that area of life into focus for a certain period of time. (See calculations for the AP in Chapter 3, Part I.)

• The Significance of Age Levels in Prediction

When judging a progressed position, it is of utmost importance to consider the age of the human being. This is one of the most important points of modern prognostic evaluation of a horoscope. A transiting planet affects a twenty-year-old differently than it does a fifty-year-old. That is why all planetary influences must be considered within the framework of age and the consciousness existing at that age.

Through the age point method, we can recognize and identify the basic theme and orientation of consciousness at every age level. From this basic observation point, it is possible to anticipate effects in the outer world although concrete events can not be determined in advance.

To reiterate: the age progression shows our basic inner attitude, the psychological tendencies which change and which are dependent upon inner and outer factors. In reality, the age point is our own consciousness travelling through time. This constantly changing consciousness affects emotions that push outward for action. All outer events have their roots within us. All events develop within us long before they are recognized and reflected in the outer world.

Major events usually manifest when a new cycle is starting within us as our attitude towards life changes. This is clearly shown in the age progression when the age point enters a new house or new sign. We automatically change, according to the theme of the house, the quality of the sign, and our present age. In the unfolding of life, we put on different eyeglasses through which we view the world; we make certain choices. We feel an inner change that colors outer experiences and we are never separated from outer events. Everything that happens to us begins not only in ourselves but as part of ourselves. This is the journey of our life.

● Life Cycles versus "Magnifier Effects"

In traditional methods of progressions that incorporate transits, the usual technique is to view single points through an analytic magnifying glass. The danger is that we easily lose sight of coherence through the "Magnifier Effects."

Commonly, we see one, two, or three aspects as separate from the whole texture. We become disproportionately preoccupied with them and are subject to anxiety. Our field of vision can be distorted. We lose psychological balance because we lose sight of true orientation and proportion. We must then attempt to reach a higher level of observation in order to gain a bird's-eye view over a greater span of time and space. When the correct balance is again established, anxiety disappears and we recognize ourselves as the causative factor. If balance is not achieved, anxiety and insecurity keep growing and we tend to fear the worst. We are unduly focused on a detail and are unable to direct our view toward a bigger segment of life.

The age progression method incorporates separate single points of astrological life, but it also relates such aspects and times to a bigger life frame and to the total development of the human being. This perspective allows coherent situational judgement. When using the AP, it is almost impossible to get lost in details because it describes the whole life development within interlocking steps or cycles of time. The AP forces us to view man and his horoscope holistically and in relation to the whole birth picture. This means, in practical terms, that we must always recognize the human being first as a distinct individual (and interpret the natal horoscope in such terms) before we can allow ourselves to study life prognosis.

● The Compulsion to Fulfillment— Dangers of Prognosis

From overevaluation of single components in the natal as well as in the progressed horoscope, we easily develop a fear of "bad aspects" or "bad transits." How often we hear, "Right now, I've got bad aspects; that's why things are tough."

In astrological psychology and in the evaluation of the age point, we can no longer speak of bad or good aspects. Through the appreciation of psychological determinants we can recognize the nuances of an aspect: the opportunities offered within challenge, growth potential through the use of inner strength. Such measuring devices are psychological and wise. Passing difficulties are much more easily accepted because we realize they lead us to greater growth. The AP helps bring us back to a basic understanding that we develop by understanding the greater connections, the larger picture.

The tendency in predictive astrology, to place the blame for personal failure somewhere else, is widespread—be it on Mars, Saturn or some other planetary situation. Sometimes such a projection is helpful in overcoming fears for the time being, but major life problems are simply not solved in that way. People also fear supernatural forces which might control them. These and other fears are deeply implanted in man's subconscious. That is why some people interested in astrology or magical activity seek a way to protect themselves against unknown dangers, to learn the secrets of fate, or to influence this fate to their advantage.

This attitude has an atavistic heritage. It makes us weak, fatalistic, and vulnerable to all kinds of prophecies. If an astrologer tells someone certain things based on his astrological knowledge and this information confirms the client's subconscious fears, that astrologer has played a role in prohibiting the development of a healthy, strong personality in his client.

If we say to someone, "You will have an accident at such and such a time," we may make a deeper impression on that person than he or she may care to admit. Such statements can trigger in the subconscious of most people the compulsion to fulfillment. With such event prognosis, we can inadvertantly take away someone's freedom of choice. What gives us the right to interfere with the free will of another human being? It is especially irresponsible and dangerous to predict events when someone is in a crisis or weakened situation. The same occurs when we choose only to see positive happenings in the horoscope and hope for a client's carefree and happy future: the client ends up living in a fantasy and believes that nothing negative can happen to him. He does not see reality any longer and becomes unstable. A heavy blow will affect that person that much harder. Although positive thinking is preferable to negative projection, either may diminish our perception of reality. In any case, as responsible astrologers, we must always be aware of the effects that our statements have on others, as well as on ourselves. This is especially so when astrology is viewed by many as mysterious and deterministic.

To avoid this compulsion to fulfillment, we must be willing and able to work on ourselves, to try to see reality as it is: opportunities for individual development offered to us at different times of our lives. We must mature into reality with an awareness which is free of deception, free of protective illusions and fearsome prophecies.

● Freedom of Will and Choice

In dealing with the subject of predicting the future, we need to clearly understand that we are actually manipulating the freedom, or lack of freedom, in our lives or in the lives of others. Thus, before studying the age point further, we must examine the problem of freedom of will and choice. When we realize that a horoscope with all its elements is the expression of our psychological and mental qualities and abilities, we can then work to free ourselves from compulsions, negative thinking, and false reactions. We have to decide for ourselves if we want to do something or not. Without will, it is not possible to be in control of life. In any situation, we have a power of choice to the extent that we are aware of ourselves and our horoscopes and have active wills. We want to demonstrate this thought in a simple example.

Practical Example
of Freedom of Choice:

I am downtown doing errands. I should be home for dinner at seven o'clock, as usual. I still have some time and sit for a while in a cafe. Suddenly, an old school friend appears. We are thrilled to see each other again after such a long time. There is much to talk about; the time flies by and soon it is 7 o'clock. My friend says, "Let's enjoy the evening together and catch up on our lives." I know that I should be home and find myself in a decision-making situation. My nature will determine how I will react, what I will decide.

There are three possibilities:

1. I am by nature responsive and spontaneous in such a situation. If so, this sudden stimulation will be the determining factor. I will spend the evening with my friend. Therefore, I cannot be home at seven for dinner.

2. I love order and must follow a preset routine, otherwise I feel that life is unruly. I will not accept my friend's invitation, and I will go home.

3. The third possibility is to call home and discuss the circumstances with my family. This adds additional pressure because I have to ask others how to behave in this situation. It helps me avoid making a decision because others are making it for me.

These are three possible reactions. As long as I blindly react, everyone who knows me can predict how I will behave in a given situation. The same can be said for astrology. Prognosis is more often correct with clients who reject the idea of free choice or who have not yet realized and exercised it. Every time we react automatically we ignore the opportunity to exercise free choice.

● Testing the Self—the "I" as a Reference Point for the Will Function

Freedom of choice always begins with the act of self-probing, self-observation, self-questioning, "Why do I want to make this choice? Why do I decide this way and not another? Do I usually want to react in a spontaneous fashion? Do I react to new opportunities flexibly, or will I be kept from doing something by other considerations? Why do I have to stick to a certain schedule, to a routine? Can't I break through these routines to make life more interesting, especially if I recognize that they have lost their meaning?"

At the moment of testing one's Self, all the questions are focused on the "I." Free will assumes a focal point, the "I," the reference point for awareness and orientation. He who can not refer to himself as "I," because he does not know who he is, cannot use his will effectively. Without "I" one cannot think independently and cannot exercise self-responsibility. Such a person often blames external circumstances on other people for his own personal failures. He is looking for the "I" in the outer world, in anything he deems an authority. Astrology can be used as that authority.

We need the "I" as a reference point in order to observe, recognize, and judge circumstances. The less we are aware of this "I," the more we are dependent upon the environment, the given situation. We need an "I" that is sufficiently strong to prevail and assert itself. The "I" must be informed, must know, understand, and wish, in order to gain from experience the ability to influence the development of events. This is the definition for an individual freedom which allows free will to function. The degree to which we are capable of self-determination is a measure of the effectiveness of our free will.

In this self-determination process, we are confronted with a great number of inner and outer pressures. We must clearly recognize and analyze them. We need to critically confront our usual reaction patterns. It is best to go back to the starting point, the origin of such behavior patterns. The root will tell us if these patterns make sense or not. Only then can we decide freely if those behavior patterns are part of the past or if they still have validity in the present. We can then consciously adopt another reaction that corresponds to the reality of life and allows for greater life fulfillment. If we want to be honest with ourselves, we have to admit that these opportunities do exist for all human beings. For Self-development only requires the will.

• Self-Determination and the Individuation Process

This process of self-testing and self-education serves the development of character and will. It leads eventually to individuation, the integration of personality forces. That process can be aided by a psychologist or an astrological-psychological counselor. With the help of the individual horoscope, the necessary knowledge, and the right motivation, we can also do it by ourselves.

The weighing, reflecting, struggling, and awakening of our natures not only develops our own understanding and thinking but also strengthens our self-awareness. Ultimately, our ability to think and judge depends on the freedom of will and the opportunity for self-determination. We know what we want from our innermost self, and we can consciously initiate corresponding changes. When we begin to live more consciously, we are happier because we know what we do; we have gained, as it were, full possession of our power.

● Responsibility, Ethics, and Free Will

It is obvious that a more aware life brings greater freedom as well as greater responsibility. By gaining a greater influence on the environment and upon events, personal responsibility grows accordingly. We can say that free will develops in direct proportion to how ready we are to *use* our abilities, our interests, and goals in the service of the whole evolution of the personality.

Our development depends essentially upon motivation. A healthy will can only be directed toward the good, toward growth and value development. This motivation is dependent upon individual ethical development. The capacity for self-determination, the ability to chose among different possibilities and even act against one's own vital needs and interests for the good of the whole, leads to a cleansing of motives and to the development of a spiritually oriented personality.

Chapter 3

Structure and Technique of Age Progression

Age progression and the Koch house system—Time dimensions in the horoscope—The age point and its direction—Development dynamic—The effects of age progression—The cyclic passage of the age point through the houses—Six and seven year cycles—The cosmic number 72—The number six: key to age progression—Age progression and cosmic cycles—Research results—The horoscope as life clock—Determination of age—Simple calculation of the age point—Age progression as a method for rectification.

● Age Progression and the Koch House System

Before we discuss the application of age progression, two points need clarification: 1) Age progression is measured by the houses, not the zodiac. 2) Age progression can only be used with the Koch house system for other systems don't yield mathematically precise results.

After much study of the age progression using three different house systems—Campanus, Placidus and Koch—we found that only the Koch system furnished time calculations which were precise in regard to the fixed houses (2, 5, 8, 11). Most of the house systems use a spherical-trigonometric space division of the half-day arc (with the exception of equal house systems that are nonspherical geometic divisions) while the Koch system is based on a time division. The half-day arc is consequently divided, according to Ptolemaic direction, into temporal houses. It therefore seems natural that the age progression—a time mechanism in the chart—works best with the Koch system.

The Age Theory of the houses evolved out of our work with age progression because it applies to life. The definitions given for the twelve houses are formulations of real life conditions as we grow through the twelve stages of life. Knowing that house meanings also symbolize phases of life can be of great help in a wide range of therapeutic situations, as long as exact timing is not needed for the process of therapy. Regardless of the house system one uses, the meanings of the twelve houses as we discuss them here remains constant.

• Time Dimensions in the Horoscope

The age progression method is based upon the assumption that the natal horoscope must be viewed not only in terms of static space but in terms of emergent time as well, embracing the wholeness of life development. We can see the horoscope as a life clock that indicates personal dispositions which are activated at various times in the life. The house system, as a reference point to the environment, offers a space orientation as well as a time orientation with the help of age progression. (Our book, *Man and His World,** dealt in detail with the former.) When we view the twelve houses in the age

---

*Publisher's Note: *Man and His World* is now published as *The Astrological Houses: A Psychological View of Man & His World* (York Beach, ME: Samuel Weiser, 1978).

progression process as a spatial unit and as a time sequence, we can recognize a developmental dynamic that concerns a whole life. What follows is a step-by-step explanation of this new method of progression.

• The Age Point and Its Direction

We call age progression the "age point" as well because we see the concept as a point that progresses, with age, through the twelve houses and activates everything they

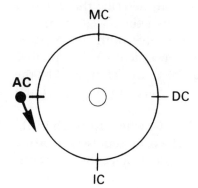

Figure 1.3.1. The counterclockwise movement of the age point, beginning at the ascendant.

symbolically represent. It starts at the ascendant and moves counterclockwise through the houses until it returns to the ascendant. (See figure 1.3.1.)

The Sun's motion, the greatest timing mechanism of the year, also moves through the zodiac against the clock. Astrologically, this is the direction followed by the zodiac, the planets, the houses, and the AP measurement.

• Development Dynamic

There is a certain developmental dynamic when we move from the ascendant to the lowest point (IC), then to the point opposite the ascendant (DC), then to the highest point (MC), and then back again to the AC.

At the ascendant, the human being is born. The AC is the rising sign in the east at the moment of birth. At the IC, the human being becomes an adult and normally leaves the childhood home. At the descendant, or "you-space," he is confronted with the environment or with a partner. At the MC he matures to full individuality and finally returns to the ascendant and to himself.

Throughout this journey, we can describe the different stations of life depending upon whether we divide the horoscope into two, three, four, six, twelve, or thirty-six parts. From these divisions we gain a general picture of life phases. Specific opportunities for development are determined by the signs and planets occupying these spaces in the individual horoscope.

Life symbolically begins at the AC, when, through birth, we thrust ourselves into the material world (represented by the AC/DC axis). After birth, the age point descends below the

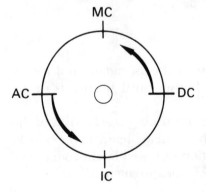

Figure 1.3.2. The descent into unconscious life, as represented by the movement from AC to IC. The ascent into consciousness as represented by the movement from DC to MC.

horizon, into the unconscious sphere of the horoscope. We dive into life. From the IC on, we aim again at the surface and reach daylight at the DC, the beginning of the conscious space. (See figure 1.3.2.)

The first eighteen years of life are times of formation. Man is in a passive phase of life; he descends "down" into the world in order to be shaped, to be formed. When we can free ourselves from the crowded collective space below the horizon, we come up for the air at the descendant. That's when life starts to get interesting.

At the IC—the polar axis of the MC—a person receives a substantial impulse that urges him to seek his own individuality. Whenever anyone reaches an angle, he always strives for the opposite pole. The life impulse carries one from the AC, toward the goal of the DC. From the IC to the DC that momentum can still be used, but it is a mental force that now carries us upward.

Some people, prepared for an extroverted successful life, think that reaching the DC is the end. They are at a loss as to what to do with the dimensions of life which follow the DC. If they continue seeking only success in outer life, then there is often a breakdown when they reach the eighth and ninth houses. If we prepare for the higher zones of life, then we will reach the MC unimpaired, and we will live on harmoniously. At the MC, individuality should be in full bloom in order that the return to the ascendant can be lived with consciousness.

● The Effects of Age Progression

The unfolding of life as it is depicted in the horoscope is similar to the spotlight that follows an actor through the different scenes of a play. Like the actor, our consciousness travels through time meeting individual aspects of our character and environment. This is indicated in the horoscope by the positions of the planets in the signs and houses.

When the age point crosses over a planet, the abilities represented by this planet come into consciousness, into the spotlight. In the period in which this passage is taking place, we encounter situations that confront us with the qualities and energies symbolized by this planet. We now can experience and use these qualities consciously.

In addition, when the age point passes though a house the qualities associated with that house are activated. New psychological energies that have been dormant within us are developed. Those energies cause definite attitudes toward the environment, toward friends and acquaintances, which are sometimes positive and active, sometimes passive or even rejecting. The quality of the signs in the houses also plays a role which we will discuss in detail later.

● The Cyclic Passage of the Age Point Through the Houses

The age point travels through a house in six years (as shown in figure 1.3.3) regardless of the size of that house.

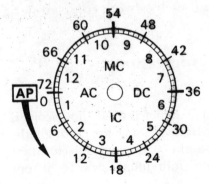

Figure 1.3.3. Schematic drawing of the six year passage of the age point through each house.

Every six years we experience a change in our basic attitude toward life, not abruptly but gradually. The passage of the age point through the houses suggests an evenly regulated life plan. In contrast to the aspects and the sign changes within the houses, which are individual, the six-year rhythm is common to everyone. This rhythm divides our life into twelve essential themes, representing a natural process of order and development. These themes confront us with new life challenges which help us to grow.

We can look directly to the meanings of the individual house for a sense of the effect of the six-year divisions. The first house deals with self-development. In the second, from age six to twelve, the child develops his own space. In the third house he expands and fortifies his knowledge. In the fourth, he is confronted with home life and wants to become independent. In the fifth, the growing person goes out into the world to test the self. In the sixth, the human being looks for adequate work to secure existence. In the seventh, he encounters partnership. In the eighth, status and the recognition of the personality come into being. In the ninth, one's own life philosophy develops. In the tenth, one reaches the top and gains authority. In the eleventh, the person relies on a small circle of people and friends. In the twelfth, he or she finds the way back to the self after the life's work is fulfilled.

This is only a brief dicussion of the developmental tendencies of the twelve houses. We will discuss them in great detail in the following chapters.

● Six and Seven Year Cycles

We are repeatedly asked why age progression is based upon a six-year cycle rather than the more widely recognized seven-year cycle. The six-year cycle grew out of our research in which we test different possibilities. Only the six-year cycle brought dependable results.

The number six is related to the cosmic number seventy-two. (We will discuss the cosmic significance later.) The number six allows a division of the 360° circle by two, three, four, six, and twelve. A circle of 360 degrees cannot be divided evenly by seven.

The numbers seven and 84 are secondary astronomical cycle numbers. They are derived only from the motion of the planet Uranus, which orbits the Sun every 84 years. Some astrologers also count the motion of Saturn and the Moon, but the Moon needs 29 days to circle the Earth and Saturn circles the Sun in 29 years. The number 29 cannot be divided by seven.

The seven-year rhythm, based upon the motion of a single planet, has no space-or time-dividing function for the overall life. That is why we also do not use the number seven as a progression tool. Since the number seven has been used repeatedly as a biological cycle number, the number six could in comparison be seen as a psychological rhythm number.

• The Cosmic Number 72

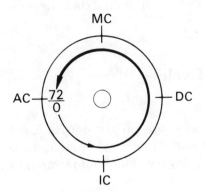

Figure 1.3.4. In age progression, one revolution of the horoscope takes seventy-two years.

In the age progression method, the number 72 plays an important part. One complete passage of the age point through the houses represents 72 years. (See figure 1.3.4.) That does not mean that at age 72 life is over; when this age is reached, the circle starts again as a spiral.

Within the 360-degree circle of the horoscope, the number twelve is most closely related to the numbers six and 72 (12×6=72). The number 12 represents the cosmos as a whole entity. Through the division of the horoscope into twelve individual spheres, we develop six pairs of polarities (axes). If we divide the number 72 by 12 (number of houses) we get the number six. This schema then emerges:

One house in the horoscope	72÷12 =	6 years
One quadrant of the horoscope (3 houses)	72÷ 4 =	18 years
One-third of the horoscope (4 houses)	72÷ 3 =	24 years
One-half of the horoscope (6 houses)	72÷ 2 =	36 years

● The Number Six: Key to Age Progression

For Pythagoras, the number six had the meaning "world." The world was always symbolized by a circle. The circle is determined by its radius, which is half of its diameter. When we draw a six-pointed star within the circle as shown in figure 1.3.5., the distance from one point to the next is exactly the same as the radius. The number six measures the circle, the symbol of life. So the number six becomes the basic unit of the number system, the measurement of the cosmos and the key number to age progression.

Figure 1.3.5. The six-pointed star inscribed within the circle. *R* equals radius.

● Age Progression and Cosmic Cycles

In astronomy, the number 72 is also very important. The precession of the equinoxes takes 71.7 years to move through one degree of the zodiac. Seventy-two years therefore represent also 1/360 of the precession. To put it differently: in the period of 72 × 360 years or 25,920 years (astronomically 25,816 years), the 0° Aries point returns to its original position. This period is called a cosmic or Ptolemaic year. Correspondingly, a period of 2,160 years (2151.33 to be exact, or 30° of precession movement) is called a cosmic month, and a period of 72 years is a cosmic day.

To illustrate this astronomical data, we use rounded-off time units:

72 years × 360°	= 25,920 years	= a cosmic year
72 years × 30°	= 2,160 years	= a cosmic month
2,160 years ÷ 30°	= 72 years	= a cosmic day

The 72 years in which the equinoctial point moves through one degree represents exactly 25,920 days, the year calculated at 360 days (72 × 360). This number is a unique expression of the macro/microcosmic relationship and explains why the Bible establishes the normal life span of man at 72 years. The average life expectancy of Western man has also evolved to 72 years. Man, viewed cosmically, is indeed a "one-day fly" in the vast scheme of nature.

Age progression is in harmony with the time cycles which correspond to Sun and Earth motions. Our life is dependent upon our Sun, upon the rhythmic development of seasons, of day and night that affects all living beings. The motion of the Sun is marked in yet another way by the cosmic number 72. For instance, the human heart beats at a rate of 72 times per minute. In one minute, 72 heart beats pump the whole blood supply through the body. We breathe 24 times per minute or $72 \div 3$. There are many more correspondences that show us the astonishing human harmony that reflects the cosmic order.

● The Five Degree Steps

The number 72 is also connected to the pentagram, the five-pointed star symbol of Venus or Ishtar. If we draw the pentagram within a circle, then the distance between the points of the star measures 72 as in figure 1.3.6. The resulting division relationship is the basis for the golden mean, which we described in *Man and His World*, page 96. When we divide

Figure 1.3.6. The distance along the circle between each point of the star measures seventy-two degrees.

360° by 72 we get 5°. These five degrees are, in a way, the one-year steps of the age point measured by the house system.

Five and six are key numbers that have a relationship to circular harmonics as well as to numerology. In the theory of harmonics, the fifth harmonic is connected with the concept of individual development, with an intelligent and powerful personality that has gained freedom of choice as a result of a well-developed power of discrimination.* Age progression, based upon the numbers five and six, indicates the possibilities for self-realization, for the development of latent talents, and for mental growth.

In relationship to the circle division, age progression is also based on the numbers seventy-two, six and five. See figure 1.3.7 for an illustration of what we discuss here. That is, 360

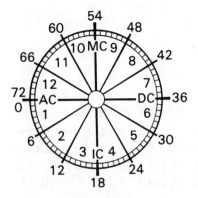

Figure 1.3.7. The 360° circle divided into 72, 12, 6, and 5. Each one year step in age progression equals 5 degrees in the 360° circle.

degrees divided by seventy-two years = 5° per year (with 30° houses). Seventy-two years divided by 12 houses = 6 years per house. This means that six yearly steps of five degrees will add up to thirty degrees and 30° = one house or one twelfth of a circle. To carry our cycle symbolism further, age point motion through a house will last one fifth of a year or 73 days.

*See *Harmonics in Astrology* by John M. Addey, Fowler, London, 1976.

● **Research Results**

Apart from agreement with cosmic laws, the best evidence for the accuracy of the age progression method is repeated application of the age point in astrological calculation. In countless horoscopes, we have applied the six and seven rhythms as well as the secondary five and nine cycles within the houses progressively and regressively. We compared the resulting planetary contacts and aspects with life events. Results were clear-cut: the six rhythm was 90 per cent correct while the other rhythms hit home only 15-20 per cent of the time or sometimes not at all.

With the age progression method and the six year steps, precise life timing can be obtained so that within a short time a person's birth hour can be rectified down to the second.

● **The Horoscope as Life Clock**

We can compare the age progression to a life clock. The hand of this life clock starts to move at the ascendant and proceeds through the house system like the hand of a clock that measures time as in figure 1.3.8. The age point shows us

Figure 1.3.8. The age progression method as life clock.

with one glance the exact time, the present point in life. With the help of Table 1.31 (on pages 38 and 39) we can locate the exact aspects and planetary contacts (past and future) to the week and even to the day. This can be done only by using the Koch table of houses and precisely interpolated house cusps and if we work with an exact birth time.

As already mentioned in an earlier chapter, the age point in its progress through the twelve houses touches all planetary positions, aspects, and points of sign change. At any time, we can recognize what psychological, mental, and physical processes are at work. We can also view this moving hand as the timely motion of our focus of consciousness through the horoscope just as an actor changes his stance during the development of drama.

When the AP touches a planet, the qualities represented by this planet come fully into consciousness, as if a strong light were focused upon the planet. Depending upon the position and integration of that planet within the horoscope and the overall aspect picture, psychodynamic effects will be noted. Such planetary contacts always offer the opportunity to confront and cultivate our psychological make-up.

● Determination of Age

With the age point method, we can examine any particular time in life at *any* time. When we slice into time at age forty, for example, we can immediately recognize the problems connected to that year. At age forty, the age point is in the seventh house, a few months after the low point.* (See figure 1.3.9.) We can see immediately if any planets are positioned there, which could make important statements

*The "low point" in a house is a turning point and corresponds to the golden mean of the size of a house. More about this is explained in *Man and His World*.

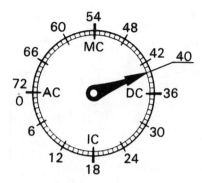

Figure 1.3.9. Using the age point to slice into time at age forty.

about the psychological situation, or if AP aspects are formed to any planets within the horoscope. Since the seventh house is connected to the "you" concept, to partnerships, we can offer insights for consciousness changes in this area.

Our reaction pattern to present life situations can be analyzed in different ways, but our reactions are dependent upon psychological factors from our past and how we coped with them then, upon our mental attitude, and upon our individual freedom of consciousness.

In this connection, it may be significant to determine, for example, why a person made a certain mistake at age twenty that has brought unpleasant results at a later age. The age point can do this easily. That's why it is important to observe past behavior patterns in order to understand the present and to create a better future.

• Calculation of the Age Point

As we have seen, the passage of the age point through a house lasts six years. To ascertain the motion for one year the following simple steps are necessary.

Table 1.3.1. The AP-LP-IP Table.

Per Month	Per Year	House Size	Low Point	Invert Point
′ ″	° ′	°	° ′ ″	° ′ ″
09 10	1 50	11	6 47 54	4 12 06
10 00	2 00	12	7 24 59	4 35 01
10 50	2 10	13	8 02 04	4 57 56
11 40	2 20	14	8 39 09	5 20 51
12 30	2 30	15	9 16 14	5 43 46
13 20	2 40	16	9 53 19	6 06 41
14 10	2 50	17	10 30 24	6 29 36
15 00	3 00	18	11 07 29	6 52 31
15 50	3 10	19	11 44 34	7 15 26
16 40	3 20	20	12 21 38	7 38 22
17 30	3 30	21	12 58 43	8 01 17
18 20	3 40	22	13 35 48	8 24 12
19 10	3 50	23	14 12 53	8 47 07
20 00	4 00	24	14 49 58	9 10 02
20 50	4 10	25	15 27 03	9 32 57
21 40	4 20	26	16 04 08	9 55 52
22 30	4 30	27	16 41 13	10 18 47
23 20	4 40	28	17 18 18	10 41 42
24 10	4 50	29	17 55 23	11 04 37
25 00	5 00	30	18 32 28	11 27 32
25 50	5 10	31	19 09 33	11 50 27
26 40	5 20	32	19 46 38	12 13 22
27 30	5 30	33	20 23 42	12 36 18
28 20	5 40	34	21 00 47	12 59 13
29 10	5 50	35	21 37 52	13 22 08
30 00	6 00	36	22 14 57	13 45 03
30 50	6 10	37	22 52 02	14 07 58
31 40	6 20	38	23 29 07	14 30 53
32 30	6 30	39	24 06 12	14 53 48
33 20	6 40	40	24 43 17	15 16 43
34 10	6 50	41	25 20 22	15 39 38

Minutes

″	′ ″	′	′ ″	′ ″
08	1 40	10	6 11	03 49
17	3 20	20	12 22	07 38
25	5 00	30	18 32	11 28
33	6 40	40	24 43	15 17
42	8 20	50	30 54	19 06

Table 1.3.1. The AP-LP-IP Table (cont.)

Per Month	Per Year	House Size	Low Point	Invert Point
′ ″	° ′	°	° ′ ″	° ′ ″
35 00	7 00	42	25 57 27	16 02 33
35 50	7 10	43	26 34 32	16 25 28
36 40	7 20	44	27 11 37	16 48 23
37 30	7 30	45	27 48 42	17 11 18
38 20	7 40	46	28 25 46	17 34 14
39 10	7 50	47	29 02 51	17 57 09
40 00	8 00	48	29 39 56	18 20 04
40 50	8 10	49	30 17 01	18 42 59
41 40	8 20	50	30 54 06	19 05 54
42 30	8 30	51	31 31 11	19 28 49
43 20	8 40	52	32 08 16	19 51 44
44 10	8 50	53	32 45 21	20 14 39
45 00	9 00	54	33 22 26	20 37 34
45 50	9 10	55	33 59 31	21 00 29
46 40	9 20	56	34 36 36	21 23 24
47 30	9 30	57	35 13 41	21 46 19
48 20	9 40	58	35 50 45	22 09 15
49 10	9 50	59	36 27 50	22 32 10
50 00	10 00	60	37 04 55	22 55 05
50 50	10 10	61	37 42 00	23 18 00
51 40	10 20	62	38 19 05	23 40 55
52 30	10 30	63	38 56 10	24 03 50
53 20	10 40	64	39 33 15	24 26 45
54 10	10 50	65	40 10 20	24 49 40
55 00	11 00	66	40 47 25	25 12 35
55 50	11 10	67	41 24 30	25 35 30
56 40	11 20	68	42 01 35	25 58 25
57 30	11 30	69	42 38 40	26 21 20
58 20	11 40	70	43 15 45	26 44 15
59 10	11 50	71	43 52 49	27 07 11
60 00	12 00	72	44 29 54	27 30 06

Age Progression (AP) = 6 years per house
Invert Point (IP) = 2 years 3 months 15 days = 836 days
Low Point (LP) = 3 years 8 months 15 days = 1354 days
    (After passing house cusp)
Number of Golden Mean: 0.381966 + 0.618034 = 1

1. Count the degrees in a house;
2. divide that number by 6;
3. mark the yearly progressions within the house.

Or, after determining the house size (which could be anywhere from 20 to 50 degrees or more) find the corresponding number in Table 1.3.1, middle column. Read the AP motion per year and month from the table. With the help of this table, it is easy to determine the yearly steps in all houses and to mark them on the horoscope. See figure 1.3.10 for an illustration of these ideas. For a more detailed discussion of how to do these calculations with a calculator, see the next section.

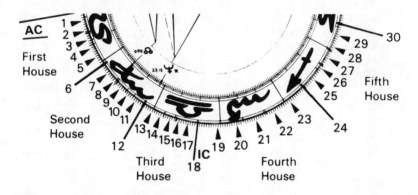

Figure 1.3.10. One year steps from age one to thirty. The size of the house affects the placement of the steps; note the difference between the first house markers and those in the fourth.

● Short System for Calculators

If you are familiar with pocket calculators, the following three-step method is very easy to use. It calculates the AP with precision. You'll need a sexagesimal date calculator set to calculate the number of days between any two dates. The following data will be needed:

One House (6 years)   = 2,191.5 days
Low Point of a House = 1,354 days
One Year (exact)   = 365.25 days
72 years   = 26,298 days

In order to make the necessary calculations you will always use a combination of the following three rules. Each calculation will be a combination of 1 and 2, or 1 and 3.

1. To find the daily progression of the AP through a house: Divide the house size (degrees) by 2,191.5. This equals the *degrees per day* motion.

2. To determine when the AP reaches a certain point (e.g., a planet): a) Determine the planet's distance in degrees from the former house cusp, then divide that degree distance by the daily degree progression of that house. The answer will equal *days of motion*. b) Days motion plus the date of the house cusp will equal the AP date.

3. To determine where the AP will be at a certain date: a) Subtract the specific date from the date of the house cusp. The answer will be in *days*. b) Multiply your answer above (days) by the degree progression to get the specific degree.

● Age Progression as a Method for Rectification

As we have seen, we can locate any particular time in life using the age point. In the case of rectification, we first make a list of events that were psychologically important to the person such as birth, physical and psychological crises, the beginnings and endings of relationships, marriages, divorces, deaths in the family, births of children, operations, accidents, sicknesses, changes of job, etc. The date noted in terms of the month suffices. Of particular help are the actual circumstances of birth: a difficult birth is indicated by planetary positions near the ascendant or through tension aspects to the ascendant. Mars, Saturn, or Neptune on the ascendant often indicate difficulties during birth. Also, prenatal influences absorbed through the mother may be indicated when a strong planet (for example, Pluto) rises just before the ascendant. This will be discussed more fully in Part II, Chapter Five.

After calculating a horoscope for the approximate birth time, ascertain the corresponding age point positions in the horoscope from the list of events. Mark these points outside the horoscope and write a key word next to it. See Jimmy Carter's horoscope on page 182 as an example.

If the events do not correspond with the aspects, cut the horoscope out in a neat circle and then turn planets and aspect pictures until the marked events and planetary configurations coincide. In this fashion, we can swiftly determine the new ascendant to the degree. We can correct the birth time by calculating the difference forward or backward.

A detailed explanation of this rectification method and practical instruction with examples will appear in Volume 2 of *Life Clock.*

Chapter 4

The Function of the Life Clock

Psychological effects and the advantages of age progression—Process of recognition—The age point: focus of consciousness—Visualization exercise —The age point and the intensity curve—The low point—The invert point.

● Psychological Effects and the Advantages of Age Progression

The age point (the hand of our life clock), when passing through a house, activates our psychological readiness to react to the qualities of that sphere of the horoscope. It sensitizes us to the individual houses or spheres of life and indicates the individuated life plan that we can read from this life clock.

To make this clearer, let us look at the life spheres—the houses of the horoscope—as practical manifestations of certain psychic functions within ourselves. The psychological energies are the primary expression of these psychic functions; the material correspondences are secondary and can be expressed in different ways. Challenges, problems, difficulties, clear-cut experiences and events are nothing but the effect of our psychological and mental energies. Every change and every new life cycle begins within us.

From this point of view, we can learn to recognize our own responses to the theme of the house through which the age point is passing. We can use what we know of the houses to energize our lives during each six-year period. This helps us see the field of vision we have of our own lives.

● Process of Recognition

Depending upon the position of the age point at a given moment, several things become clear to me:

1. I recognize how one-sidedly I view the world; to what degree I decide in advance what I'll accept and what will interest me; to what degree other subjects are neglected.
2. I recognize my present attitudes and the concomitant difficulties which proceed from them. I also recognize the opportunities now presented to overcome challenges and reach my goals.
3. I experience an intensity of development when the hand of my life clock reaches a planet and I can identify myself for this special planetary quality.
4. I know when the age point crosses over a house cusp or over a sensitive point (low point or invert point, see pages 49-52) in a house. There is an increased willingness to react the house cusp; to make long-term plans at the invert point; and to stand still and reorient myself at the low point.

There are tension and development points, or variable energy gradations, everywhere in the horoscope. They correspond to mental and psychological crises. There could be transformations at the low point, at planetary concentrations or aspect contacts, holes in the aspect pattern, or at certain sign positions—for example, strong points in the signs on a weak point of a house or vice versa (positions in the sign center at the low point of a house, or at the beginning or end of a sign at a house cusp). We can determine when the age point will come in contact with these positions and when it will activate these sensitive points in our consciousness.

This collection of energy and tension points in the horoscope can be ascertained with modern astrological-psychological interpretative methods. During a person's developmental journey, it is of great help to know when special qualities or characteristics can be put to positive use, when they will be held back, or when certain problems will confront the individual and call forth all his energies.

It is also important to know when the energy cycle is at a peak: when the age point is crossing an angle or a house cusp; when it changes signs; when it makes a conjunction or another strong aspect with a planet in another house. All this can be determined to the day.

We should not only examine the timing of such specific high points but also examine pertinent periods before and after for indications of related psychological development. The passage of the age point reveals how a situation slowly develops toward a high or low point, how it fades away, and how it transforms into a new phase.

With the help of the life clock, we can view and understand the present, the past, and the future. We learn not only about ourselves, our tendencies, environmental influences, dependencies, blockages, but also about our own freedom, about the next step to be taken. With this method we recognize our abilities as well as our limitations. We can prepare for future opportunities and, at the same time, understand which mistakes in the past have caused a present situation.

The investigation of individual problems—the study that takes psychologists many long sessions—can be approached with the help of the life clock. The individual horoscope can be understood with one careful look. Since we can immediately identify the position of the age point, we can be aware of the problems that are present, which planets are involved, and which opportunities are indicated. It is vital for modern man to find out why certain events happen, which psychological forces within his own constitution are responsible for one reaction or another in a given situation. With the age progression method, it is possible to understand one's own reaction pattern more fully as it is expressed through the symbolism of the houses, planets, and aspects.

• The Age Point: Focus of Consciousness

The age point position is the focus of our present consciousness. We identify ourselves with it because it is part of us. The age progression concept strongly affects our own identity. It assists us in living life fully and consciously. For the human being who wants to live life in consciousness, this is the progression method that goes deepest and stimulates us mentally and spiritually. The AP helps us relate to all levels of our being.

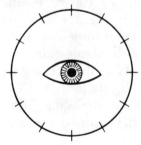

Figure 1.4.1. The age point as the eye of the inner self.

From this perspective, we can also view the age point as our consciousness point or as the eye of our inner self (see figure 1.4.1.) through which we perceive the world and react to it. This allows us the opportunity to experience the "here and now," because, at this moment, we feel the connection between the inner self and outer reality. It is important that we realize the possibility of union between consciousness and reality and recognize the moment in which space and time come together as well. That is why the psychological and spiritual interpretation of age progression requires a heightened state of awareness, a psychological understanding, and a flexible responsiveness to the life energies that flow from within to the outside world.

The age point is identical with the developmental dynamic that is inherent in all of nature and active within the center of man's being. The understanding of this factor is extremely important for proper evaluation. Let's approach it through a visualization exercise.

• Visualization Exercise

Imagine yourself in the center of the horoscope. On your forehead, between the eyebrows, visualize a light similar to a spotlight. Turn around slowly and focus the spotlight throughout the circle of the horoscope. The beam illuminates a sign, a cusp, a low point, a planet with its aspects.

When we hit upon a planet we can become fully conscious of its essence by directing the light of our consciousness on this planet. In this way all related opportunities, problems, and psychological factors come to the foreground. This allows us to absorb the special faculties of this planet and to use these in accordance with the powers at our command. Often, without our involvement, opportunities come our way from the environment, because this light of consciousness also affects the houses, the practical life spheres.

If we are frightened or blinded by the sudden appearance of planetary qualities or if we try to block them, we can anticipate unpleasant age point manifestations.

It is useful to keep in mind that rewards come through labor. That labor needs to be harnessed to awareness if we are to grow.

Within the framework of this book, we define consciousness as an awareness or as an ability to confront and deal with life situations openly and sincerely. At first there is a recognition: of an object, a human being, a thought, or feeling. We become aware and we direct our interest, thoughts, and feelings fully at the target. Symbolically speaking, we come closer, take the focus into ourselves, assimilate, and identify ourselves with it; we become as one. Only then do we know. This is a well-known meditative process, through which we can learn much about ourselves and others in relation to the age point.

When we experience ourselves as the focus of consciousness in the center of the horoscope and in the passage of the age point through the houses, we become aware that there are forces within us that want to be externalized and allowed free development. We often think, "When I have time, I want to do this or that; I want to live then; I want to develop an interest in such a subject or idea."

Basically, all potential is always within us. It is a part of us. We can at any time manifest full individuality because our unconscious always contains the entire horoscope, with all its signs, houses, and planets. But everything has its time! Our inner abilities must mature in order for them to be used for the benefit of others. The maturation process develops by its own laws and rhythms, according to its own life plan. This is what age progression is all about.

● The Age Point and the Intensity Curve

The intensity curve shows the strong and weak positions of the planets within the house system. It is a wavy line that

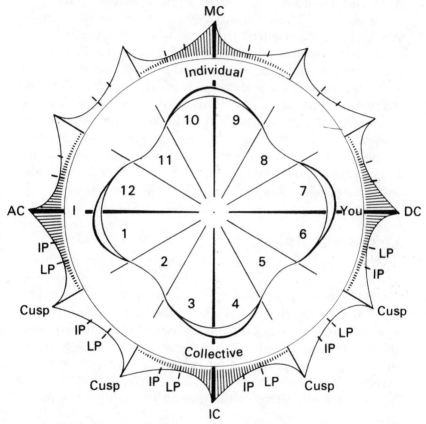

Figure 1.4.2. The intensity curve. The six year cycles are shown on the outside of the wheel. The high point in the curve occurs at the cusps of the houses, the depths are shown at the low points (LP) and the stage between is the invert point (IP). The inner wheel indicates the twelve houses in the natal chart.

encircles the whole house system and peaks at house cusps and has the least energy at the low points. This flow of energy is also reflected in age progression.

In every life there are psychological and mental low points as well as peaks when everything works smoothly. After a period of stability, we can begin to perceive a change in our goals and plans, in a way never believed possible before. We have all experienced this, and when we examine these cycles and rhythms in life, we find an amazingly constant correlation between these cycles and the intensity curve. The high and low tides repeat themselves with great reliability so that we can recognize the rhythms not only in the past but also in the present and future. These tides are connected with the six-year cycles as well as with smaller cycles which are also visible in the house system and can be measured along the intensity curve as shown in figure 1.4.2. These cycles have also been described in *Man and His World,* page 94.

● The Low Point

The point of greatest activity is each house cusp. This emphasis slowly diminishes toward the LP (low point) which is at the golden mean point of the house. The intensity curve reaches bottom at the LP (see figure 1.4.3). This point of minimum outer expression (or environmental activity) occurs three years and eight months after the age point crosses a house cusp. We perceive this period in life as an apparent

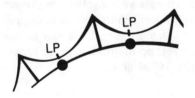

Figure 1.4.3. The low point (LP) of the intensity curve is reached three years and eight months after the AP enters the house.

standstill. Certain things just cannot be accomplished easily. We get depressed when we try too hard for outer-directed successes. At these points in time, a new orientation and a turn toward inner values is in order. These are times for reflection. After this time of curtailed activity, the intensity curve begins its ascent toward the next house cusp and energy flows again.

● The Invert Point

In addition to the low point, each house also has what we call the invert point (IP). This point is also measured by the golden mean, but in reverse: we measure the golden mean clockwise through the houses. The age point reaches the invert point, about two years and four months after it crosses over the last house cusp.

For example, the age point crosses the eighth house cusp at age forty-two and reaches the invert point at age forty-four and four months. The IP is not as clearly defined in effect as the house cusp or the LP. Many people are not aware of having reached the invert point.

The invert point is the turning point, however, between the house cusp focus and the low point focus. A house cusp is the expression of maximum expansion; vital energies are available for successful outward application. The LP is the expression of maximum contraction; energies going inward. There is an interaction between inward and outward energies,

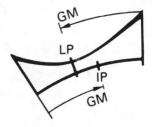

Figure 1.4.4. The invert point (IP) of the curve is reached two years and four months after the AP enters the house. A change in direction doesn't occur until after the AP has reached the LP. GM = the Golden Mean.

similar to breathing in and out. The IP is the turning point between these two directions.

After crossing the house cusp, the energy curve descends to the invert point, the turning point between expansion and contraction. From there, the motion is inward until the low point. (See figure 1.4.4.) Expanding and contracting forces are in balance at the invert point. At this time, we should look for the right balance in order to apply our energies to long-term plans. Projects started at the invert point are usually of long duration if they are done with care and deliberation.

Chapter 5

Rules for Application of the Age Point

*(This chapter written by
Michael-A. Huber, our son)*

The first steps—Extent of age point effectiveness—Points in time—Further
rules for interpretation—Duration of low point effect—Problem positions
—Five important factors in the evaluation of age progression.

● The First Steps

When we apply the age progression method in any
horoscope, we do it systematically. First, we ask the following
questions for any specific period in time:

Where is the age point located? By ascertaining the house
position of the AP, we can discover the psychological outlook
or mental attitude the person brings to his life. We can
understand the basic mood and the external stimuli to which
all other influences are subordinated.

Through which sign is the age point passing? The sign indicates the basic attitude—the inner central yearning in life. The house indicates the environment, the possibilities, and opportunities offered us to master our tasks. The sign indicates the inner striving and yearning which may or may not be in alignment with the possibilities and challenges of the environment. This happens when the signs and houses are different in quality. You will see this in figure 1.5.1. When inner promptings and outer possibilities are out of sync with each other, this can lead to tension. (See the correspondences between sign and house in the appendix.)

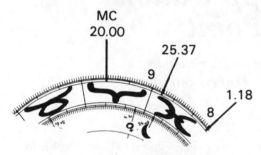

Figure 1.5.1. Here we see Aries, a cardinal sign, in the mutable ninth house which is ruled by Sagittarius in the natural zodiac. The passage of the AP will bring out the tension here.

Is a planetary contact or aspect imminent? A planet symbolizes an ability, a psychological force which we can apply in life. Each human being has ten such basic faculties that can be used to cope with all life situations. See *Basic Functions of the Planets* in appendix. When the age point comes into contact with such a faculty by aspect, this specific facility will be activated and brought into consciousness.

Is the age point at the house cusp or the low point? This inspection tells us something about the intensity of the external experience, which is strongest at a house cusp and weakest at the LP. As discussed in an earlier chapter, there is always a new impulse born at the house cusp. Here we reach the high point of a phase or cycle and things go our way. For about two years after the AP crosses the cusp of a house, things run smoothly and we are relatively successful.

When we approach the LP, activity decreases markedly. At the end of this activity cycle, not quite four years after the cuspal impulse, we reach the LP of a house. At the low point, a pause is necessary because this is a time of inner change, of new attitudes. If we continue at this point to seek external success, disappointment will be the result. The LP in the fixed houses is especially sensitive and meaningful. For example, at age sixty-four, we reach the low point in the eleventh house, where heavy upsets in connection with retirement are often felt. We will describe the specific crises associated with the low points in the individual houses in the second volume of *Life Clock*.

After the low point, the AP goes upward again to the next house cusp. Sometimes, this phase can be experienced as a very stressful one. This seems especially true in the short period before the angles (AC, IC, DC, MC). The approach to that angular cross can create stress, burdens and the feeling that circumstances are too much to handle. It can feel like climbing to the peak of the mountain.

● Extent of Age Point Effectiveness

It is not possible to give a rule for the orb and extent of effectiveness of the age point's relationship to a planet. This depends upon the person for whom we calculate the age point aspects. If someone is consciously working on himself, the quality of events and experiences will be far different than, say, with a child. The same holds true with the classic elements of progression that have an effect apart from the age point. We live in a field of intermingled energies that keep life moving in a highly complicated rhythm. It is unthinkable that one human being could recognize and judge all influential forces within their full context! There are not only a great number of energies but they also vary in strength.

We find an applicable parallel in everyday life: there are many small influences, through words, advertisements, and in personal contacts, that we are not aware of because they have little meaning for us. Our consciousness concentrates on things in life that are really important. What is important is decided by our consciousness through an awareness that selects among all the environmental stimuli available.

As already mentioned, the effect of the age point is of a basic nature. It can be seen in all the striving energies of the personality. The progressive elements, especially the transits, are stimulations that can cause difficulties or opportunities in our present life situation. The effectiveness of these influences is logically dependent upon the circumstances in life or where the AP is at that time. That's why we speak about an overlay of progressed elements through the AP and also of the sensitizing effect represented by the AP.

● Points in Time

With traditional methods of progression, a certain date—when the aspect is exact—is often given as a time for an event. We then expect a specific event on the given day. Sometimes it even happens, but perhaps only because we expected it (compulsion to fulfillment). When an event doesn't happen, the predictive work is viewed as being silly, or unnecessarily frightening. With age progression, this kind of valueless forecasting doesn't happen because we work with a time orb of four to six weeks. Within this period, the consciousness is in strong contact with the aspected planetary qualities.

If I block the forces that want to enter my consciousness because they have not been a part of me so far, an event will happen that will force a confrontation with myself. That experience can be of a purely inner nature. It can also be brought about by an event. The event will always happen as a result of stored-up energies from the repressed parts of myself. Such displacement of dynamic energies is not necessary. If I am aware of what is in store for me, if I confront the age point consciously and prepare, then there is no room for anxiety. (Fear waits behind anxiety and leads to blockage.)

Orbs and Time

Conscious self-preparation may begin three to five months before the time span of greatest intensity of any aspects of the AP. The focus of consciousness will gently shift to the areas that were previously unknown. The effect accelerates evenly and reaches a high point during the exact aspect period (approximately two to four weeks). Afterwards, there is a period of two to three months before the effect vanishes. (See figure 1.5.2.)

The length of the effect cannot be determined exactly for each individual. It depends upon the person's capacity for reaction and response. The length of the time spans depends upon three criteria: consciousness and intensity, the nature of the aspect itself, and the size of the house involved.

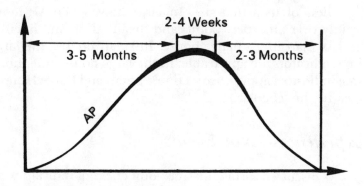

Figure 1.5.2. The effect of the AP changes in intensity according to its proximity to the point of contact.

Consciousness and Intensity

Awareness plays an important role. The more aware we are, the earlier we will feel aspect stimulation, and the sooner we can get control of connected factors and prevent unwanted events.

Aspects

For age progression the seven basic aspects are divided into two groups:
  a) Conjunction and opposition
  b) Semi-sextile, sextile, square, trine, and
     quincunx.
The duration of the aspect effect is one and one-half times as long with group A as with group B. For conjunctions and oppositions between the AP and the planets, the duration of effect is approximately eight to twelve months.

House Size

The age point takes six years to pass through a house, regardless of its actual size. In large houses, the AP moves rapidly over an aspect point, and the duration and intensity are less than in a smaller house. In small houses, the larger time indicators are applicable; in the large houses, the shorter time indicators apply. (See section, "Small and Large Houses" later in this chapter.)

Experiences—Not Events

As discussed earlier, the age point does not indicate events as much as experiences which have impressed us. Events, seen in a daily context, often impress us not at all. When we take a two week vacation, for example, some events occur that we quickly forget. Other events can blossom into a special experience. Such experiences form and change us. Age progression only stresses those events which will indeed change us.

There are also events which are externally generated that we cannot influence. For example, when a father dies, the age point will indicate what impression such a death made upon each of us. For some people it means a separation from the father influence; others stay relatively untouched because this separation occurred a long time ago. Outer events always have meaning; they serve our development, whether we understand them or not. We can ascertain the meaning of a particular event and its connection with other meanings through the use of the age progression method—but only if we are aware that the age point indicates experiences rather than events. The outer happening is only an expression of inner reality and experiences.

The Triggering of Events

Events always happen in connection with psychological processes and are therefore arbitrary to a certain extent. Although we cannot expect an event with every transit, events are often triggered by planetary progressions or transits. Progressions and transits are the "second hand" on the clock, so to speak, and indicate the timing of events. For example,

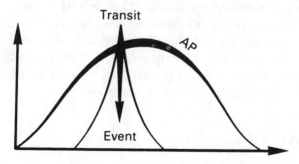

Figure 1.5.3. The transit of a planet to the age point often triggers an event.

when the age point aspects a planet in my natal chart, a certain quality of my character wants to express itself intensively. If I don't pay attention to the quality forming within me, and if at the same time a transit touches off the planet symbolizing this quality, an event may be triggered as symbolized graphically in figure 1.5.3. In a way, I may need this event, for it will awaken latent energies within myself. The event, then, helps me to learn how to use these energies. In this case, the outer event reinforces the theme already suggested by the AP. This in turn spurs me toward greater awareness of that portion of the self which has been hidden until now.

However, when working with the age point on a regular basis, we can learn to express the energies forming and changing within in a different way. If we work with this energy consciously, the outer events may no longer occur.

● Further Rules for Interpretation

Early Planetary Effects

A planet that is approaching the age point by conjunction or opposition can be considered active as much as eighteen months ahead of the exact aspect. Although we are not yet confronted with its significance at this early time, we become aware of its existence subconsciously. We may feel a restlessness and are not able to pinpoint the reason. For other aspects, an early effect of up to eight months applies if the respective planet holds a particularly important position in regard to factors in the natal horoscope.

Planetary Passages

The intensity of planetary transits depends upon the planets' positions in the horoscope. Planets that are positioned strongly by aspect or that are at a cusp or low point of a house are particularly important. These planets have a tremendous effect when in conjunction or opposition to the age point. They also have a greater time orb. This can mean problem planets or special qualities. For example: if, in a male chart, the age point makes a conjunction or opposition to Mars, his consciousness is geared toward subjects that have to do with his masculinity. Opportunities to experience the masculine traits are much more easily realized. Naturally, problems existing in connection with that masculine nature also come into focus. This is an opportunity to understand one's Mars better and to come into control of that quality. The more deeply a planet is understood, the fewer the difficulties we will experience with it in life. For more information, see our introduction to psychological astrology in the appendix.

Planetary Stelliums

When the age point passes through a house occupied by several planets, we experience a very active and intensive period. This growth-affording life period begins with the entrance of the age point into the house or even the sign that is so heavily occupied, regardless of whether the planets are at the end of that sign or house.

If a house is unoccupied, the psychological processes and the outer life experiences are less intense. The only significant aspects will be made to planets in other houses. Therefore, the passage of the age point over the house cusp, as well as the low point, are the main events of that life period.

Unaspected Planets

A planet without aspects is a life force without clear direction from our consciousness. It is a faculty that functions separately from our personality and tends to react to environmental stimulation automatically.

Each age point aspect, but especially the conjunction with such a separately functioning planet, offers a superb opportunity to observe certain characteristics in ourselves that were never fully understood. Suddenly it becomes very clear how we function with these personality quirks.

Dynamic Direction of Aspect Structure

If the AP enters a house in which many aspects are involved and the whole aspect structure suggests a specific goal, a special developmental dynamic is indicated. We often become very stimulated by and sensitive to our environment. We react with greater awareness because this sensitivity is part of our destiny and offers special opportunities for the development of our personality. For more information, see "Aspect Configurations or Structures of Consciousness" in the appendix.

Small and Large Houses

The age point takes six years to pass through a house, regardless of size. Therefore, the AP takes longer to pass over an aspect or a planet in a small house than it would in a larger one. That is why we experience the age point more intensely in a small house. The effect is more superficial in a larger house. An old astrological rule says: the slower the motion, the deeper the impression.

In a small house, things may seem boring on the surface, but much goes on under the skin. We are more preoccupied with issues associated with this house and cannot get rid of them easily. Of course, much depends upon the individual: people who are quick and flexible can deepen their awareness without too much trouble. Others, who have a more ponderous nature and are less adaptable, have a difficult time dealing with so much activity. In our judgement, it is important to consider whether the characteristic mode of reaction is mainly cardinal, fixed, or mutable. The strength of the quadruplicities and triplicities are the most essential astrological indicators of character and must be considered in this context.

● Duration of the Low Point Effect

The effect of AP passage over the low point in a house begins about eight months ahead of exactitude and can last four months afterwards. The effect is easily felt by everyone, even by people who are relatively unaware. The aftereffects depend partly upon the proximity of a planet to the LP. If a planet is close to the low point, the process is prolonged. If the planet is important (for example, if it is the tension point of an aspect structure) the low point phase naturally will be active longer and felt more deeply. A long aftereffect can also be an indication that the individual has not been able to accept those introverted energies and perhaps has a persistent feeling of loneliness. We must always judge the age point relative to the particular situation, listen to our psychological intuition, and not simply try to apply a rule.

Normally, as soon as the low point is passed, we feel a renewed sense of energy, optimism, and hope. We know where and how life is to continue. The two years before the AP passes the next house cusp should be viewed as a period of new orientation and preparation. In this period, we look for the right direction without being able to translate it into activity. For new activity, we should wait for the impulse of the next house cusp. Often, however, things really take about a year after the passage of the house cusp before there is smooth sailing.

● Problem Positions

When the age point reaches a position in the horoscope that suggests severe psychological problems, it is important to be psychologically prepared and to cultivate the correct mental outlook. We should clearly recognize that we are encountering problems designed to further the growth of our personality and that events (or people) are not out "to get us." It is up to us to react with awareness of the balance between the different factors, qualities, genetic influences, weaknesses, and strengths of the situation and to avoid any debilitating anxiety or compulsion to fulfillment.

● Five Important Factors in the Evaluation of Age Progression

Under the following circumstances, the age point always indicates a reorientation, an awareness of a problem, or a period of special opportunities and life development:

1. When it crosses a house cusp and enters another house with a new psychological theme.
2. When it approaches the low point of a house and requires a new orientation and change in consciousness.
3. When it enters a new sign. Normally, the basic outlook and motivation change according to the new sign qualities.
4. When in conjunction or opposition with a planet. These aspects are considered constructive because they allow optimal opportunities for consciousness expansion, problem solving, and personality development.
5. When making exact aspects to other planets in the natal horoscope.

Chapter 6

The Course of Life through the Twelve Houses

The houses—Horoscope showing the 36 phases of life—Keywords for the 36 life stations—36 age levels and their crisis points.

This chapter outlines the house meanings and the phases that we use when determining the energy that is activated in the life of an individual during the passage of the age point. First, we list the house meanings. Then we move on to the keywords for the houses and ages of life. And in the last section we describe the various phases that take place during the course of our lives.

● The Houses

1st House: Formation of the "I"
2nd House: Creation of life and possessions sphere
3rd House: Learning and educational sphere
4th House: Parental home and detachment
5th House: Experience and testing phase

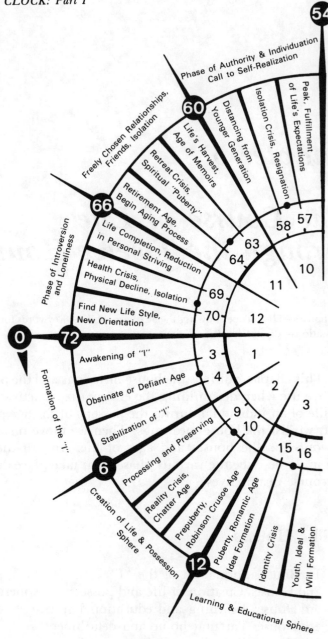

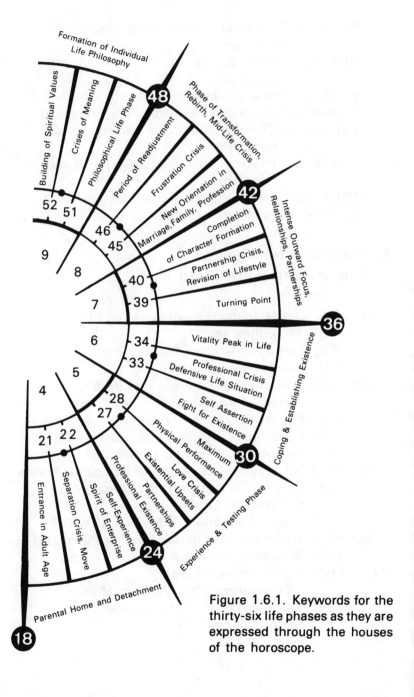

Figure 1.6.1. Keywords for the thirty-six life phases as they are expressed through the houses of the horoscope.

6th House: Coping and establishing existence and livelihood

7th House: Intensive outward focus, relationships, partnerships

8th House: Phase of change, process of rebirth

9th House: Formation of individual life philosophy

10th House: True vocation and calling to self-realization

11th House: Freely chosen relationships, friends, isolation

12th House: Phase of introversion and loneliness

The Ascendant: Phase of rebirth

● Keywords for the Houses and Ages of Life

Age   0-6   (1st House)—Formation of the "I"
 0-3   Awakening the "I"
 3-4   Low Point—The Obstinate Age
 4-6   Stabilization of the "I"

Age   6-12 (2nd House)—Creation of Life & Possessions Sphere
 6-9   Processing and Preserving
 9-10 Low Point—Reality Crisis, Chatter Age
 10-12 Prepuberty, Robinson Crusoe Age

Age 12-18 3rd House—Learning and Education Sphere
 12-15 Puberty, Idea Formation, Romantic Age
 15-16 LP, Identity Crisis
 16-18 Youth, Formation of Ideals and Will

Age 18-24 4th House—Separation from the Parental Home
 18-21 Beginning the Adult Age
 21-22 LP, Separation Crisis, Detachment from Parental Home
 22-24 Years of Travel, Self-Experience, Spirit of Enterprise

Age 24-30 5th House—Experience and Testing Phase
24-27 Building of Professional Existence,
Partnerships, and Love Relationships
27-28 LP, Existential Upsets, Love Crisis
28-30 Maximum Physical Performance

**Age 30-36 6th House—Coping with Living and
Finding One's Place in Life**
30-33 Fight for Existence, Self-Assertion
33-34 LP, Defensive Life Situation, Professional Crisis
34-36 Vitality Peak in Life

**Age 36-42 7th House—Intensive Outward Focus,
Relationships, Partnerships**
36-39 Turning Point
39-40 LP, Revision of Life Style, Partnership Crisis
40-42 Completion of Character Formation

**Age 42-48 8th House—Phase of Transformation, Process
of Rebirth, Mid-life Crisis**
42-45 New Orientation in Marriage, Family,
and Profession
45-46 LP, Frustration Crisis
46-48 Period of Readjustment

**Age 48-54 9th House—Formation of Individual
Life Philosophy**
48-51 Philosophical Life Phase
51-52 LP, Crisis of Meaning
52-54 Building of Spiritual Values

**Age 54-60 10th House—Calling to Self-Realization,
Phase of Authority and Individuation**
54-57 Peak, Fulfillment of Life's Expectations
57-58 LP, Isolation Crisis, Resignation
58-60 Distancing from the Younger Generation

**Age 60-66 11th House—Freely Chosen Relationships,
Friends, Isolation**
60-63 Life's Harvest, Age of Memoirs
63-64 LP, Retreat Crisis, Spiritual "Puberty"
64-66 Retirement Age, Beginning of Aging Process

**Age 66-72 12th House—Phase of Introversion
and Loneliness**

66-69 Life Completion, Reduction in
Personal Striving

69-70 LP, Decline of Physical Power, Health Crisis,
Isolation

70-72 Finding New Life Style, New Orientation

**Age 72-78 1st House—Phase of Rebirth,
New Life Sources**

72-75 New Appearance of Life Joys (Childhood "I")

75-76 LP, Obstinate or Defiant Phase Against Own
Children (Disinheritance Threats)

76-78 New Awakening of the Nesting Instinct

Age 78-84 2nd House—Memories, Dreams, Thoughts

78-81 Working through Childhood Memories

81-82 LP, Putting Distance between Possessions,
Separation Crisis

82-84 Decline of Vital Forces

● Explanation of the Phases

If we divide the horoscope into phases, we should be
aware that the phases are general in nature—they do not have
clear-cut limits. Some phases overlap, and when this happens,
the influence may start earlier or last longer than the periods
indicated here. The overlap would depend upon the individual positions of signs and planets in relation to the life cycle
or phase under consideration.

The first year of life begins with the birth of the child at
the Ascendant. The first year of life ends at the first birthday.
The baby is then one year old. (See figure 1.6.2). When we
have completed the first year, we celebrate the first birthday,
but we are beginning our second phase of life.

The first phase in the first house (or in any of the twelve
houses) lasts for three years. It begins with the birthday at the

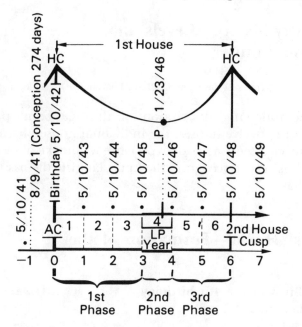

Figure 1.6.2. The three life phases within each house. The figures here are based on a chart calculated for birth on May 10, 1942. The complete chart is shown in the Appendix, page

cusp of the first house (the ascendant) and ends with the third birthday in that house.

The second phase lasts from the third birthday until the fourth (a low point year). The LP transit lasts exactly 258 days, which is eight months and two weeks after the third birthday.

The third phase lasts for two years, from the fourth birthday until the sixth.

This time rhythm (3-1-2 years) repeats itself in each house. It is what we call the golden mean.

● Thirty-Six Age Levels and Crisis Points*

*Adapted from lectures by Beat Imhof, Ph.D., Educational Psychologist.

The following description of the age point passage through the twelve houses, the individual house phases, and the connected tendencies of experience will make observation easier. It is easy to recognize the important life themes within each phase.

● First House—Formation of the "I"

From Birth to the 4th birthday   *Awakening of*
Ascendant to LP 1   *the "I"*

This sphere covers the period of the subconscious and preconscious existence of the child. It is a period of slow awakening for the "I." Psychomotor development is in the foreground: learning to sit, stand, walk, speak, and control body functions. The inherited physical constitution begins to develop, but the child is not yet differentiated from its environment.

4th Year of Life   *Obstinate Age*
LP 1 in the Cardinal Fire House

Low point 1 occurs in the angular fire house. At the stubborn age, which occurs at the fourth year, the child becomes conscious of his uniqueness and begins to differentiate himself from the environment. The recognition of the will comes with the awakening of the "I." It is the crisis time of the first obstinate or defiant cycle.

Low point 1 represents the first crisis point. The child realizes that he is not absolutely secure within his known environment and life situation. He recognizes that the environment does not always cooperate with his will. He begins to confront will power different than his own. The first reactions to defiance are formed.

5th and 6th Years of Life   *Stabilization*
LP 1 to the 2nd House Cusp   *of "I"*

During this time of life, the qualities of the second house begin to manifest as directions for growth. There is awareness of others and an awakening of environmental consciousness. Unconsciously, the first impulsive relationships are formed: Oedipus and Electra phase, identification process, separation process from the opposite sex parent around the sixth year, and the beginning of the super-ego formation.

• Second House—Creation of Personal Life and Possessions Sphere

7th to 10th Year of Life   *Utilization and*
House Cusp 2 to LP 2   *Preservation,*
      Creation of Personal
      Possession Sphere

Around the sixth year, the first physical changes take place (permanent teeth, change of body proportions). The child slowly gets ready for school and at the same time prepares for separation from the family. This is the time for the psychological delivery (or separation) from the mother. The child begins to define his own territory and to defend it against the environment. A personal sense of possession is created, and the accumulated personal possessions are individualistically distinguished.

Typical second house behaviors (possessiveness, inherited behavior, talents) also determine the behavior toward possessions in later life and, in this context, the social attitude in general.

Difficult or disharmonious aspects involving the second house can express themselves with great complexity: for example, as an overcompensatory block or aggressiveness regarding the defense of one's possessions.

10th Year of Life   *Crisis of Reality,*
LP 2 in the Fixed Earth House   *Chatter Age*

Now, the child begins to turn away from the subjective and often surrealistic private world toward the reality-bound environment. The age of magical-mystical thinking (fairy tales) is over. The crisis precipitated by LP 2, connected with the destruction of previously held illusions, makes the child physically restless and active, talkative and changeable. A new urge for verbal exchange and banter is awakened. The developmental phase associated with the tenth year is also known as the "Age of Chatter."

At the fixed low point 2 (called fixed because it takes place in the 2nd house), the child recognizes the fact that material possessions are subject to loss and change and that there is no long-term security in them. The child will seek out new possibilities for self-establishment in the collective environment.

11th and 12th Years of Life   *Prepuberty,*
LP 2 to the 3rd House Cusp   *Robinson Crusoe Age*

From the tenth year on, the child turns more and more toward the qualities of the fatherly third house: the sphere of recognition, observation, and experience. The child is eager for new learning experiences. He wants to discover and explore the unknown and bring it into his own frame of reference. This developmental phase is also called the "Robinson Crusoe Age."

This is also a time for learning and accumulating knowledge. At no other time of life do we gain as much knowledge as between our tenth and twelfth years. The urge and enthusiasm for knowledge, learning, and exploring are fully awakened now. The interest in school is gaining. Since the child is moving toward the collective sphere (third and fourth houses), it desires knowledge of the collective. The actual experience of learning in the strictly educational sense is the province of the third house, where we gain and integrate intellectual possessions.

• Third House—Learning and Education Sphere

13th to 16th Year of Life
House Cusp 3 to LP 3

Puberty,
Idea Formation,
Romantic Phase

Puberty begins around the twelfth year, normally a little earlier with girls than boys. A second physical change takes place which involves a thrust in growth and the formation of secondary sexual organs. The genital phase beings with the development of the libido in the Freudian sense. The first friendships and love relationships are sought out, and through them the child develops contacts in an expanded personal environment. Through the enormous accumulation of knowledge and education, including tests for higher education and/or vocational abilities, collective thought forms are accepted. (In Europe, young people can choose a profession at fourteen and continue in a vocational school while working. Ed.) During this period, the child pushes out from the intimate sphere of the parental home and feels most in harmony with the peer group collective.

16th Year of Life   *Identity Crisis*
LP 3 in the Mutable Air House

The crisis at this point often has considerable repercussions, mainly in connection with difficulties in school or vocational development. Usually the crisis is focused upon difficulties with parents and authority figures. The danger of suicide occurs. The constructive side of this third phase is that larger connections with life are made and assimilated which stimulate the youth to a new awareness and new orientation.

17th and 18th Years of Life   *Youth, Formation*
LP 3 to 4th House Cusp   *of Ideals and Will*

This developmental phase often brings the first valid indication of professional and life direction. Vocational choice comes to maturity in these years. Intuition is added to the "I-function." The need for freedom and independence is awakened in the youth.

The *individuality axis* (IC, MC) begins to be felt toward the end of the third house. We can observe the awakening of higher, spiritual and intellectual interests (philosophy, sociology, theology, ethics, etc.) and, with them, the beginning of actual intellectual self-realization (formation of ideals and goals).

● Fourth House—Separation from the Parental Home

19th to 22nd Year of Life
House Cusp 4 to LP 4

Beginning of Adult Age

This is the phase when the young human being becomes a full member of the collective and, at the same time, separates himself from the collective to become independent. Often, marriage or communal living is chosen in order to overcome the familial influence. The youth finds independent living quarters, and begins to support himself in order to develop an independent life style. Normally, these acts strengthen self-worth considerably.

22nd Year of Life
LP 4 in the Angular Water House

Separation Crisis from Parental Home

At this low point the youth phase and the developmental years are ended. Vocational preparation is usually over, and the necessary separation from parents or guardians follows. The tendency to move out and away leads the young person into new and different life situations. A new adjustment is made and attitudes are established at this fourth point of change since it becomes necessary to truthfully examine all that has been known, accepted, or believed.

23rd and 24th Years of Life
LP 4 to 5th House Cusp

Years of Travel, Self-Experience, Spirit of Enterprise

This phase is already influenced by the 5th house. It is the house of self-experience in the larger world. The young person behaves in an increasingly expansive manner. He wants to win the world, to make a big impression, to be on the offensive in human interaction, and to be victorious in the professional and private spheres.

● Fifth House—Experiment and Testing Phase

25th to 28th Year of Life   *Building of Professional*
House Cusp 5 to LP 5   *Existence, Partnerships,*
          Love Relationships

This is one of the great phases of experience and learning. The fifth house is an active, dominant house in which an offensive-aggressive approach is made to the environment. When the age point moves through this fifth house, the human being will experience his most aggressive time. He courageously and energetically pursues the organization of professional and family goals.

28th Year of Life   *Existential Upset,*
LP 5 in the Fixed Fire House   *Love Crisis*

In a fixed house, the characteristics of the low point are intensely activated. Low point 5 is reached three months before the twenty-eighth birthday. Often, marked professional pressures are felt that demand an introverted or withdrawn period of reflection which later leads to a new orientation. The first disappointments in the professional and private sector manifest now and are typical of this crisis point in the fifth house. It is important now to find one's own measure, one's own limitations, and to determine the balance between inner and outer values. Appearance and identity must be clearly distinguished. If this is not accomplished, there is the real danger that the human being in self-overestimation expects too much of himself, of the environment, and the future.

29th and 30th Years of Life   *Maximum*
LP 5 to 5th House Cusp   *Physical Performance*

The apex of intellectual and physical ability is reached and passed. This is the time for highest power, speed and dexterity. Achievements are critically evaluated by others. All efforts are strategically planned to show how well life demands have been met. Here are the first results of individual striving in the professional and private sectors.

• Sixth House—Coping with Living and Finding One's Place in Life

31st to 34th Year of Life   *Fight for Existence,*
House Cusp 6 to LP 6   *Self-Assertion*

This house confronts the human being with a sombre challenge: there are no more games to play. The sixth house is a passive serving house. The human being becomes defensive. Much has to be accepted as unalterable fact. He must find his own place in life and bring what is wished for into balance with what can be accomplished in order to find a secure life situation. He must find the correct groove in his future life path. This phase, therefore, is a time of assertion, especially in the physical sphere.

34th Year of Life
LP 6 in the Mutable Earth House

Defensive Life
Situation,
Professional Crisis

Anyone who has not found his life's form at age thirty-four often find himself in a seriously depressed phase. The person thinks, "I can't make it. I am not needed." This can lead to very defensive life and career situations.

At low point 6, we see our own limitations. We admit, with resignation, that the world does not wait around for us. Projections and dreams often prove to be illusions, born out of naive or unreal wishful thinking. Large and small blows of fate, rejections, defeats, and setbacks can dislodge self-belief. The tendency toward illness (mainly for employees) rises sharply in this critical time. One flees into an illness and gives up. Suicide may be an alternative. According to K. H. Waggerl, those who live and react calmly and with common-sense during this crisis point will gain the insight that "we think we direct but instead, we are directed," and "we live not; we are lived."

35th and 36th Years of Life
LP 6 to 7th House Cusp

Vital Peak in Life

After the feelings of resignation and reorientation which are often the results of low point 5, the human being slowly comes back to life. Under the advance influence of the seventh house cusp, new hope and courage is felt. It is of utmost importance that the right decisions be made during this phase, that true life opportunities are recognized. This phase, which can be in effect for two years into the seventh house, is normally not as problem free and successful as the fifth house. One cannot expect that spectacular success and triumphs are within easy reach. Yet, we can call this phase in time a "vital peak in life" because we are changing from the unconscious realm of the chart, by passing the DC, into the consciousness realm.

● Seventh House—Intensive Outward Focus, Relationships, Partnerships

37th to 40th Year of Life   *Turning Point*
House Cusp 7 to LP 7

The first effects of the seventh house are mostly felt during the thirty-seventh year of life; some people, however, begin to feel the effect at thirty-five. Jung calls the thirty-sixth year the "deciding year" or a turning point in life. Suddenly opportunities are offered for self-realization, and these opportunities reflect the true inner being. Decisive turns are made with regard to the future. In this life phase, we gain acceptance from others (the DC). Significant relationships and commitments take place and the consequences of these commitments will be seen in the eighth house. These new relationships cause a phase of success in the professional and personal spheres. That is why the most successful years of a whole life may occur between thirty-six and forty.

40th Year of Life   *Revision of Life Style,*
LP 7 in the Cardinal Air House   *Crisis in Partnership*

Low point 7 represents a new point of self-realization. At age forty, we wonder whether we have lived our lives fully so far. Past challenges are now a nuisance. Commitments are viewed as constraints, and responsibilities become burdens. The first signs of aging appear, and chronic illnesses and weakness can announce themselves ever so lightly. At this seventh crisis point, we take account of ourselves and often adopt new goals and begin a new and healthier life style. Henry Ford rightly said, "Life begins at forty."

41st and 42nd Years of Life   *Completion of*
LP 7 to 8th House Cusp   *Character Formation*

We have now passed life's halfway mark and the shadows grow taller. Secretly, for the first time, we confront the problems of aging and death. At first we may try to avoid the facts of life, death and the aging process. With all kinds of hectic activities and youthful cosmetics, we try to avoid the unavoidable. This is also true of certain obligations or engagements that remain from the past. With the advanced influence of the eighth house, the crises multiply in the private, family, social, and professional sphere. The completion of character formation takes place around age forty-two.

● Eighth House—Phase of Transformation —Process of Rebirth—Mid-Life Crisis— Responsibilities Toward Others and Toward Society

Between ages 42 and 48 the phase corresponds to what we call "mid-life crisis."

43rd to 46th Year of Life   *New Orientation*
House Cusp 8 to LP 8   *in Marriage,*
          Family, Profession

This period often brings decisive changes in the personal and professional sectors. One's children slowly become independent. The mother is not needed by her childen for physical sustenance any longer; the father's influence on his sons and daughters is often not the guiding force any more; the parents are delivered from their responsibilities toward their children. Suddenly, intellectual and spiritual energies are freed and they press for attention. Many women go back to their former careers; many men become active in clubs or politics. Also, for the first time the serious question of the meaning of life becomes important and manageable.

46th Year of Life   *Frustration*
LP 8 in the Fixed Water House   *Crisis*

If we consider the average life span to be 72 years, and then consider a circle of 70° as a symbol of that life span, and also work with the concept that 1 degree equals 1 year of life, the low point of the life span will be between 44 and 45 degrees—or the forty-fifth year of life. This turning point occurs in the eighth house. *Low point 8 is therefore the low point of the whole life.* The traditional description of the eighth house as the death house indicates that it is the most difficult of the twelve houses. Low point 8 often brings the most massive crises and shake-ups of an entire lifetime. At this point on the life clock, some things that were stable for a long time just die. At times, this may express drastically in, for example, a radical change of profession or the divorce of a long-time partner. In many cases, we wish for the change, but its realization is made difficult by psychological or environmental pressures. It can be a very frustrating time.

47th and 48th Years of Life   *Period of*
LP 8 to 9th House Cusp   *Readjustment*

The human being becomes painfully aware of the confinement and hopelessness which he believes he has created over the years. Many feel stuck and want to break out of their supposed prison. Some may consider suicide. The urge for freedom is stimulated as the AP approaches the ninth house. Those who feel themselves railroaded in life and who do not recognize a future for themselves consider the possibility of making an early end to it all.

In the period between the forty-seventh and the forty-eighth year, the last favorable opportunity to aim for higher, spiritual, permanent, and timeless values takes place. Now, the human being may begin to recognize that there are more important values in life than money, possessions, and status. At best, these are guarantees for existence but not necessarily guarantees for fulfillment.

• Ninth House—Formation of Personal Life Philosophy

49th to 52nd Year of Life   *Philosophical*
House Cusp 9 to LP 9   *Phase of Life*

In this phase, it is essential for the human being to find true values for his existence. Everyone, at this point in life, is challenged to form his own philosophy, his views on life and the world. In this mutable ninth house, we grapple with questions about the meaning of life, about the "where from and where to." Some people develop their own philosophy of happiness. The essential theme of this ninth house is self-determination and the consciousness of true destination. Those who can successfully reach this plateau will transcend petty everyday problems, turn toward the horizons of a liberating world philosophy, and divine the deeper meaning of life. We often see an interest in occult, magical, esoteric, or religious disciplines as means for gaining an understanding of life.

52nd Year of Life *Crisis of*
LP 9 in the Mutable Fire House *Meaning*

If the human being has not found a reason for life between the forty-ninth and fifty-second year then a crisis will be precipitated during the fifty-second year. During this time of crisis at low point 9, one may recall the ideals of one's youth (third house) and try to make them a reality now. In old age and with hindsight, we may be able to say, "The small things we find turn out to be the big ones we were seeking." The subconscious often shows the way out of this crisis of meaning, for example, through dreams.

53rd and 54th Years of Life *Building of*
LP 9 to 10th House Cusp *Spiritual Values*

In this last period before the passage of the age point over the MC, the human being has a last chance to concentrate on building the inner values through which he can give the rest of his life a deeper meaning. Those who miss this opportunity can look forward to an old age without meaning and comfort. In this mutable ninth house, these questions come to the forefront: "What does the world and mankind expect of me? Do I have responsibilities toward society?"

● Tenth House—Calling to Self-realization; Phase of Authority and Individuation

55th to 58th Year of Life *Peak, Fulfillment of*
House Cusp 10 to LP 10 *Life's Expectations*

The tenth house is the last house of worldly joys, so to speak. This sphere of life has to do with authority, power, and public position. One may become an authority figure for others, or gain real power over others, or be needed by the collective. At the same time, however, the private sphere becomes limited. When one is externally exposed, one may be internally isolated. This phase of experience should fulfill life expectations and therefore should corroborate the true qualities of the individual.

At this age, people are often called to public or communal duty. Relatively late success is found with people whose success planets are not strongly configurated with the MC. Apparent successes or careers which are based upon unsound dealings will be exposed. The tenth house on the life clock represents "the moment of truth." It is said that male menopause begins around age fifty-six.

58th Year of Life   *Isolation Crisis,*
LP 10 in the   *Resignation*
Cardinal Earth House

The experience of the tenth house, i.e., the responsibilities toward society that may cause a minimum of private life experience, often leads to an inner loneliness. The individual feels isolated and left alone although he is known publicly. He feels isolated behind glass walls. Outer success and honors are not taken quite so seriously any more; there is an increasing turn toward the inner self.

59th and 60th Years of Life   *Distancing from the*
LP 10 to 11th House Cusp   *Younger Generation*

Toward the end of the sixth decade, the individual is overtaken by the younger generation. The termination of the professional phase begins. One begins to feel that one is replaceable.

● Eleventh House—Freely Chosen Relationships, Friends, Isolation

61st to 64th Year of Life
House Cusp 11 to LP 11

Life's Harvest,
Age of Memoirs

The eleventh house brings a distinct limitation to human relationships. So-called "friends" who wanted to profit from one's success suddenly disappear. The aging individual pulls back toward a small and intimate circle of friends and acquaintances. The more carefully one chose friends in the fifth house (age twenty-four to thirty) the more surely one can rely now on true friends. This phase is also the time of harvesting a whole life's work, especially what was planted in the ninth house from forty-eight through fifty-four. Now, many people begin to write memoirs. At this time, the human being fashions for himself an idealistic picture of society— how it could be—and he tries to share these views in small circles with others. However, familiar faces begin to leave this planet, and the growing loneliness which accompanies these losses must eventually be confronted.

64th Year of Life
LP 11 in the Fixed Air House

Retreat Crisis,
Spiritual "Puberty"

In medical circles, sixty-four is often called the critical life-endangering year. Depression, panic, and fear of the emptiness of the future often come in connection with imminent retirement. All this may precipitate a serious health crisis. At low point 11, the human being needs to take inventory and separate the wheat from the chaff. The conscious living of such isolation can lead to contemplative-ness, calmness, and satisfaction; or, for those who have not prepared themselves earlier in life, to boredom, despair, and loneliness. Those who have been wasteful of their physical and spiritual energies in the past can quickly descend into senility at the passage of low point 11.

65th and 66th Years of Life   *Retirement Age,*
LP 11 to 12th House Cusp   *Beginning of*
                                          Aging Processes

This is the period when most working people actually leave their careers and begin retirement. It also brings a decrease in social life. There is a big increase in deaths (retirement shock) around sixty-five.

● Twelfth House—Phase of Introverson and Loneliness

67th to 70th Year of Life   *Life Completion,*
House Cusp 12 to LP 12   *Reduction in*
                                         Personal Striving

Now the cycle of life comes to fullness and completion. The human being withdraws from the outer world into himself. Often, he is isolated from society in a hospital or nursing home. The thoughtful and mentally active individual will become conscious of many things and will review all he can. He gives up personal striving, and the environment no longer challenges him. Only outstanding individuals are still capable of high achievements (political leaders, artists, scientists, etc.)

70th Year of Life
LP 12 in Mutable Water House

*Decline of Physical
Power, Health Crisis,
Isolation*

At seventy old age begins. Physical power lessens considerably. At the twelfth crisis point, the individual encounters the last great life challenge: he must find the way back to himself and become wise. "Wisdom is found above life as one sees past the transitory and knows about eternal, timeless truth." (Remplein) The true character of the individual becomes more focused and more recognizable than in earlier years. Those who were selfless, loving, just, and generous will now be even more so; the difficult, egoistical, hard, bitter, petty, suspicious, and argumentative individual will calcify along these lines.

71st and 72nd Years of Life
LP 12 to 1st House Cusp

*Finding New Life Style,
New Orientation*

Finding one's own personal style of life in old age is the test for the whole life. It reveals what the individual has made of himself or what he could have done. We now see if the human being has been able to reach personal maturity. The mentally balanced individual becomes wise; he shines with inner peace and kindness because he wants nothing for himself. He views the end calmly, as a necessary completion. He seeks to give spiritual meaning to life until the very end. Wisdom is the ideal goal of all human aspiration but reached only by few.

● The Ascendant

Age 72 *Phase of Rebirth*

At this age, the passage of the age point through the twelve houses and signs becomes complete. That does not necessarily mean the end of life. It can mean a renewed impulse for vitality coming from the AC, the point of birth. The years following, if things go well, are years that can be seen as encores, as extra gifts. These years are not of a unique nature but form a kind of repetition, a reliving of memories which are brought back into consciousness. Many experiences of younger years are only now fully understood, and problems or traumas of childhood (first and second houses) are clearer from this mature viewpoint. Lifelong experiences now have a new meaning.

Chapter 7

Age Point Progression Through the Signs of the Zodiac

Differentiated development through the signs—Sign changes—Quadruplicities (crosses) and triplicities (elements)—Age point and elements: fire, earth, air, and water—Passage from water to fire signs—Passage from fire to earth signs—Passage from earth to air signs—Passage from air to water signs—Age point in the crosses

● Differentiated Development Through the Signs

In each individual horoscope, the age point passes not only through the houses but also through the signs occupying the houses. The zodiac is fixed, and upon it we measure everything in astrology. If you look at your horoscope beginning with the ascendant, you see the signs in their natural order interfacing with the houses. With the help of the AP method, you can calculate when your development enters each of the twelve signs. (See Chapter 3, Part I for instructions.)

Due to the uneven sizes of the houses, there is also an uneven time passage of the AP through the individual signs. Passage through a sign can last from three to twelve years, depending upon house size. Although the succession of aspects stays the same and we can calculate them in advance, the rhythm of time is different from house to house. The reason for this is that the AP, measured against the zodiac, covers shorter distances in a smaller house and longer distances in a larger house. The rule is this: the age point passes over degrees of the zodiac in a small house more slowly than it does in a larger house.

Regardless of the size of the house, the AP always passes through each house in six years. This dynamic combination of sign and house results in an interesting variation in individual horoscopes—a differentiated rhythm of house and sign changes, as in figure 1.7.1.

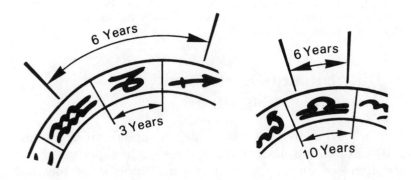

Figure 1.7.1. The AP always passes through a house in six years, but the amount of time it spends in each sign varies with the size of the house.

● Sign Changes

When the AP crosses into a new sign within a house, drastic changes in personal attitude (depending upon sign quality) can be observed. How pronounced the change will be depends upon different factors, such as the individual arrangement of the signs in the horoscope. The question—is the quality of the sign in harmony with the quality of the house?—becomes very important. If, for example, an angular house is occupied by a cardinal sign, the changes are not so obvious. However, if a sign change takes place in the middle of a house, as, for example, the change from Taurus (fixed) to Gemini (mutable) in the third house, the sign change will be felt quite clearly. Generally, it can be said that, with each change of a sign, a change of attitude is observed. It is not planned or willed; it happens subconsciously.

We must understand quadruplicities (crosses) and triplicities (elements) because they represent a basic classification of astrological thinking. With a thorough understanding of *elements* and *crosses,** the quality of the whole horoscope becomes clear in principle.

The sign qualities are established within us as predispositions. The change therefore comes from deep within and makes for a new attitude toward life. We have a new energy at our disposal that was not there before. The quality of this new energy, already within us in terms of potential, now comes intensely to the foreground, especially if planets occupy the "new" sign. Even if the sign is unoccupied, we become more conscious of its qualities through the movement of the AP and the obvious change in our basic attitudes

---

*Publisher's note: The American reader should note that throughout this chapter and the rest of the book, the quadruplicities are referred to as *crosses*, for this is the common term used in Europe. Triplicities are referred to as *elements*, a term already familiar to many American readers. The reader should be aware that the reference to "crosses" in the chart does not imply the grand cross aspect.

toward life. New interests abound. For example, at the sign change from Pisces to Aries, we may move from a feeling of insecurity to a sudden ability to prevail and succeed in life.

• Crosses and Elements

All signs in the zodiac belong to a cross and an element (see figure 1.7.2.), and also have a planetary ruler. When distinguishing the signs according to the four elements, we arrange them as follows:

> FIRE: Aries, Leo, Sagittarius
> EARTH: Taurus, Virgo, Capricorn
> AIR: Gemini, Libra, Aquarius
> WATER: Cancer, Scorpio, Pisces

The quality change of the AP from a sign in one triplicity into a sign in the next can be felt quite abruptly because the following sign is of a contrary polarity. Male (positive, active) signs are Aries, Gemini, Leo, Libra, Sagittarius, Aquarius, i.e., all fire and air signs. Female (negative, passive) signs are Taurus, Cancer, Virgo, Scorpio, Capricorn, Pisces, i.e., all earth and water signs.

The mode of expression change is measured according to the quality of the different signs. Each sign belongs to one of the crosses:

Cardinal signs are: Aries, Cancer, Libra, Capricorn
Fixed signs are: Taurus, Leo, Scorpio, Aquarius
Mutable signs are: Gemini, Virgo, Sagittarius, Pisces

We can substitute the keywords impulse, perseverance, and rhythm for cardinal, fixed, and mutable, respectively. These characteristics are enlarged by the qualities of the planets which rule each sign. Traditionally and empirically, Aries is the sign ruled by Mars, which means that the qualities of the planet Mars are most strongly expressed in the sign Aries. Of course, martian qualities prevail within the sign Aries even if Mars is not positioned there. The same holds true for all the other signs and their ruling planets.

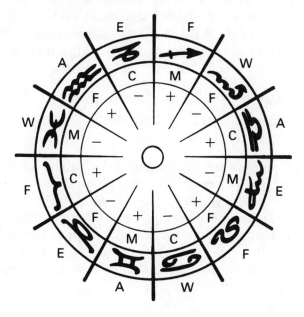

Elements		Crosses	
F	= Fire (+)	C	= Cardinal
E	= Earth (−)	F	= Fixed
A	= Air (+)	M	= Mutable
W	= Water (−)	+	= Active;
		−	= Passive

Elements = Triplicities   Crosses = Quadruplicites

Figure 1.7.2. The division of the twelve signs according to the four elements, the three crosses, and active/passive energy.

When we focus on the AP as it passes through the signs, it's important to recognize the background endowments of the crosses and elements. We can observe the qualities of a sign when, for example, we become more active when passing through a cardinal sign or more passive when a water sign is at hand. With a little experience we can differentiate between the qualities and adjust our life accordingly. We can, if we so choose, experience that specific sign quality if we are aware of the movement of the AP and change in accordance with that sign quality or activate that quality if it has been dormant.

● The Age Point and the Elements: Fire, Earth, Air, and Water

If we perceive the life path as a circle that ends where it also begins, we will experience changes in the way we think, feel, sense, and act whenever the AP moves from one sign to another. Our style or our temperament changes color. After a long period of optimism, for example, we may suddenly take on a dark outlook. Such "switches" don't happen by accident; they coincide in time with the change of signs marked by the AP.

● Passage from Water to Fire Signs

Pisces/Aries, Cancer/Leo, Scorpio/Sagittarius

When the AP changes from a water to a fire sign, for example, from Cancer into Leo, we can visualize the effect as pouring water onto a fire. The passive water is changed by the fire through a thermochemical process into steam. This is accompanied by loud hissing and new activity.

With the fire of Leo, this achievement will be impressive, or at least will want to be viewed as such. The AP passage from a water to a fire sign is an abrupt one because water seeks the form, the container, wherein it can adapt molecularly; where it can feel safely preserved. The fire offers no such comfortable place to the water. Water is changed by fire, or, to use the earlier image, it is forced into active performance.

A sign need not be occupied by a planet in order for it to make its qualities felt at the entrance of the AP. The sign Leo is always activity-oriented, even when no planet is present that could give an indication as to the focal point of the activity. All fire signs are.

When the AP is in a fire sign, we gain energy, generally speaking. The kind of activity and goal orientation depends upon the house in which the AP is located and upon the aspects the age point makes with the planets. With the AP in a fire sign we are not only generally more active and productive, depending upon the characteristic of the fire sign, but we are moving toward new goals, becoming more creative. Before the last spark dies away, a phoenix rises out of the ashes, the product of the fire. We find ourselves in a phase full of optimism with a good chance for self-realization.

• Passage from Fire to Earth Signs

Aries/Taurus, Leo/Virgo, Sagittarius/Capricorn

When the age point changes from fire to earth, the change is from an optimistic outlook to concrete realization. It is a stabilization phase. If adjustment and reorientation are not achieved, the effects are shock and a sudden loss of speed. We prepare for a landing after a long flight, so to speak. We are back on the level of reality, and both feet are planted on the ground. No fiery rocket propels us any longer. The keyword for the earth signs is not drive but planning. Long-term goals replace spontaneous projections. Each detail is critically thought through, carefully calculated, weighed, and often found wanting. Too critical an attitude in this phase can lead to depression: nothing seems to work. That is the negative side of the earth sign. Positively attuned, on the other hand, we can experience a step-by-step maturation of our long term plans whose details, redone a hundred times, finally stand up to any critical examination.

These traits are most characteristic of Virgo whose preoccupation with quality control allows nothing to be mentally slipshod. Patient planning, stabilization, and long-term effect are important keywords when the AP moves through an earth sign.

● Passage from Earth to Air Signs

Taurus/Gemini, Virgo/Libra, Capricorn/Aquarius

In the earth sign, planning is preceded by thought. Thinking is focused on long-term concrete goals. In an air sign, we are freed from material considerations and move into a purely mental atmosphere: our thinking has a theoretical orientation. Here, thinking no longer means planning but learning. We can more easily solve a theoretical problem, such as finding a scientific formula, then we can think through a plan which is tied to a specific project.

The passage of the age point through an air sign is always a good time for further learning, more education, or additonal professional training. Learning is now easy because we are tuned in intellectually. Learning can even become an end in itself. We become information "junkies" and want to know everything! Often, fate brings new contacts from which we can learn. Educational opportunities appear which were not available before.

We can become more flexible in our attitudes and better adjust to circumstances while the age point is moving through an air sign. This is especially so if we experienced rigidity while passing through an earth sign. In air, we can adjust our stubborn attitudes.

When we are able to perceive the meaning of the signs—e.g., learning and its connection to air signs, or the planning inherent in earth signs, we can then see how the signs are symbolic of phases of life. The age point, as it moves through the signs in the zodiac, becomes an indicator of how we can learn to integrate the sign values within us.

● Passage from Air to Water Signs

Gemini/Cancer, Libra/Scorpio, Aquarius/Pisces

The fourth passage of the age point within the elements is from air to water signs. We know that water embraces the emotional sphere. Here we explore the deeper spiritual dimensions. The change from air to water is not so abrupt as from water to fire, but we still change polarity from positive air to negative water.

At this change of signs it seems best to leave the mind out of the picture, in order to avoid a conflict with feelings. Strongly mind-oriented people (accentuation of air signs) can slide into a critical, depressive phase at this point. We must be aware of the fact that our thinking is now controlled and evaluated by our feelings. We know that feelings are not always objective. "I just have a feeling about it," often describes the way we evaluate a situation that we cannot control mentally. Because of a temporarily overwhelming emotion, we are unable to fathom it with the mind.

In this phase, we are sensitive to criticism. We will be moody and egocentric. During this phase we can also learn when it is difficult to be objective, to be subjective in a constructive way. By recognizing and reducing the introversion symbolized by the water signs, it is possible to present the "I" (the subject) openly to the "You" and have relationships without feeling so vulnerable.

Each sign passage can bring a healing shock in this sense, leading to a multilayered recognition of being and finally to self-knowledge.

● The Age Point and the Crosses: Cardinal, Fixed, and Mutable Signs

In our discussion of the AP passage through the elements, we have seen how we react differently to environmental conditions according to the characteristic of the elements. The elements always indicate the form and manner of our activities. The crosses, in contrast, refer to our deepest motivations. At sign changes, we react to the elements as well as to the crosses. This combination effects changes in the motivation dynamic, the basic outlook on life, the spiritual attitude and the relationship to the environment.

With the elements we were dealing with the number four—three signs in four elements. With the crosses we have a concept of trinity—four signs in three modes—the cardinal, fixed and mutable. These three qualities correspond to three basic energies. Impulse equals cardinal; perseverance equals fixed, and rhythm equals mutable in this case.

When the AP passes through a cardinal sign (Aries, Cancer, Libra, Capricorn), initiative for a new creative process is mobilized. A new path is created. The motion is forward; we feel energized and inspired and are goal-oriented in the application of our energies.

When the AP passes through a fixed sign (Taurus, Leo, Scorpio, Aquarius), we feel a tendency toward consolidation and perseverance. We resist any outside threat to what we have created and try to put everything in safe order.

In the mutable signs (Gemini, Virgo, Sagittarius, Pisces), discrimination within existing circumstances is awakened. We are willing to change direction and vacillate back and forth. We fluctuate between existing opportunities and short- and long-term goals.

When the AP has passed through these three forms of motion, a new impulse is manifested at the entrance into another cardinal sign. We gain new momentum for further creativity, build form and mass in the next fixed sign, and modify and change the design in the following mutable sign. These changes in impulse, perseverance and discrimination are broadly focused in self-expression and growth.

The motion of the AP through the crosses indicates when it is best to stay put (fixed), when we can change direction after careful evaluation (mutable), and when it is feasible to push forward again (cardinal).

Part II

*Life Phases and Cycles
in the Horoscope*

Chapter 1

Rhythms in Nature and Life

The rhythms around us—The sequence of developmental stages—Individual life rhythms—Life cycles in the horoscope

● The Rhythms Around Us

The essential rhythms that determine life on our planet are regulated by laws of nature. Every life begins with birth, embraces the course of life and ends with death. Through this life span and within the human being, a step-by-step biological and mental development unfolds that, in principle, has the same significance for all people while expressing itself in accord with individual differences. In all of nature, these laws of development can be observed; they produce a constant germinating, unfolding, maturing, and dying.

Understanding this developmental process gives us a comprehensive sense of time and allows for a practical application of the age progression method in order to capture the rhythmic unfolding of individual life. When we look over a broader span of time, our consciousness expands. The dimension of time helps us to a greater understanding of the present; we gain an overview of life.

Generally, we only live within the limits of the present moment or a chain of such moments which we experience almost unconnectedly; or we yearn for eternity and envision it as a static condition, in contrast to the continuous succession of life moments which know no standstill.

What is directly important and meaningful in the flow of life is the concept of "cycle." A cycle is the meaningful unfolding of vital processes from a beginning, through different phases of development, and onto fulfillment. The germination of a seed must occur in order for it to ripen into maturity. The same can be said with regard to the human being, the planet, and a whole solar system: the reason for all existence is to fulfill potential.

With this thought in mind, we can consciously accept fate. We can recognize that the purpose of all events in life balance and adjust the personality toward completion or perfection. Perfection here means to become an undivided whole being. Just as no individual exists separately but is part of a bigger whole, no cycle begins and ends unto itself. There are complex connections with other cycles, each with its own particular dimensions and characteristics. Just as a kernal of wheat meshes in its development with the seasons, human life needs to unfold in harmony with the laws of development.

The human being is part of a bigger whole: his individual life unfolds as and within a cosmic happening and is incorporated into the larger rhythms of our solar system and our planet. Everything that happens on our planet is subject to universal laws if it is to grow and endure.

We know the obvious rhythms of day and night, the changes of seasons, and the growth of the individual from childhood to youth, then maturity, and finally old age. Within a larger framework, the human being is also subject to cosmic time units, cycles, and epochs that correspond to planetary changes. The most profound global influence is the passage of the Aries Point from one zodiacal constellation into another. Many people discuss the passage from the Piscean into the Aquarian Age. A "world month" has come to an end, and a new one begins. Within all these cycles, life develops according to each individual life plan and in accordance with the rhythms of an individual's fate. These cycles carry life through its highs and lows like the waves of an ocean.

• Sequence of Developmental Stages

All of us are subject to the biological laws that are proper to our species. Clearly established steps represent developmental stages. No one can, for example, experience youth before childhood; no one can jump a level. This is a well-known fact and cannot be repudiated, and in addition to these biological and physical laws there are collective-psychological laws of development to which we are subject. These attract our attention as we study ourselves for the purpose of enlightenment.

Each phase of life has inherent psychological processes that are concurrent with specific problems and conflicts peculiar to that phase and no other. It is natural for a young man to strive for high athletic performance, but it is not expected of a sixty-year-old. If the old man were to concentrate obsessively on proving himself in such a fashion it would seem peculiar, not only because of his age but also because he should have left that psychological phase behind long ago.

The sequence of developmental stages in principle has always been the same, but there are certain psychological shifts and changes that meet the cultural and civilizational needs of man. In today's world, we live individual life rhythms that were not even possible fifty years ago. Through technology, we have freed ourselves from many natural laws. We can make night into day at will; we can change climate from one day to the next by taking a plane from north to south. There are many possibilities for moving away from natural rhythms and living by individually established ones.

● Individual Life Rhythms

Besides the physical and biological life phases, man is also affected by collective and personal psychological developmental forces. At the same time spiritual and mental energies (conscious or unconscious) push the individual forward on the life path. Age progression, applied to the horoscope, gives us information about that individualized motion, which in turn becomes a rhythmic pattern of life and development.

Man—since he possesses a mind—sometimes tries to avoid the natural sequence, to ignore it, or to jump over certain psychological phases of experience. These phases may be partly suppressed or simply ignored. Environmental factors—education, or sickness—may block development. In later life, we may find ourselves trying to make up for the accumulated lack and a developmental disruption ensues.

Sometimes there is a discrepancy between the individual's rhythms and the collective motions or challenges of the environment. This expresses itself through the clash of an inner need and an outer pressure. Sometimes the environment simply demands certain things that are not in harmony with the individual life. The result can easily express through social difficulties, psychological disturbances, neuroses, or even psychotic episodes to name only a few of the possibilities.

Some people, for example, miss the sexual experience of late puberty and try to make up for it at age forty or later. The drive toward sexual activity in the teens and twenties has the function of stimulating the awakening consciousness toward social integration. When one tries to make up for this missed phase between forty and fifty, it happens at a time when the integration of consciousness should have already passed its peak. Such experience must lead to difficulties when one pursues sexual experience with the blindness of a teenager.

In the life of every individual, crises take place at the transition from one age level to the next. The life phase between age thirty-five and fifty is an especially important time for everyone. In this period, questions must be answered that have never been asked before. For the first time, the transitory nature of life is recognized as an oppressive experience. Often marriage or professional problems appear. It is truly a mid-life crisis. With each transition into a new developmental cycle, insecurities and crises can be experienced. It is therefore important to know something about individual life cycles in order to live in harmony with them. We can even prepare for each level and then we can form ourselves into fully conscious and individuated human beings without great hindrance.

• Life Cycles in the Horoscope

The horoscope is based upon a 360 degree circle that can be divided in different ways. These divisions can be viewed in terms of time, as life phases that make up a whole life. Seen in such a way, the horoscope becomes a life clock, and different parts of the circle represent certain stages of life.

We can view the time phases individually, lifting each out of the whole; or we can understand them as developmental phases flowing into each other, which is the more realistic approach. The following rule of thumb must be observed:

When we divide the horoscope into time stages, the
years should not be judged rigidly, but should be
viewed as life periods with gradual transitions that
are in effect before and after the actual transition
moment.

The life phases are always in agreement with the basic
theme of the horoscope. A certain phase in time will be shaped
by the corresponding space (house) in which it occurs. As
discussed earlier, a six-year period corresponds to the psychological theme of each house; a phase of eighteen years
corresponds to the theme of a quadrant; twenty-four years to
one third of the horoscope; thirty-six years to one half; and
seventy-two years to the whole horoscope. After the seventy-
second year the cycle starts again.

We can also view the horoscope from another perspective.
By dividing the circle into two hemispheres (north and south),
we see the general developmental thrusts of extroversion and
introversion, of the conscious and the subconscious.

The number four has always been the symbol of form and
crystallization. It is represented in nature by the dice-shaped
salt crystal, the alchemical symbol of matter. By dividing the
circle into quadrants, we emphasize externally developmental
expressions of life: impulse, instinct, thinking, being. (For
further discussion, see *Man and His World*, page 54.)

The division by three is related to a special facet of the
personality: the number three symbolizes a creative, dynamic
process and the inner goal-orientation of a completed personality. The eye of God is symbolized by a trine.

The division by six corresponds to psychological and
sociological processes. The personality connects to the world,
and from this exchange come sensations, reactions, and
characteristics.

The division into twelve yields a chronology of life
development. The twelve houses represent our environment.

With the inclusion of the invert and low points in each of the twelve houses, we gain a further measure of the thirty-six parts that indicate the smaller rhythmic phases of life. In the following chapters, we will systematically cover the different divisions of the horoscope and the houses.

May we repeat once more that we use the Koch house system. Other house systems such as Placidus, Campanus, etc. do not bring satisfactory results to the age progression method.

Chapter 2

Division of the Horoscope into Different Life Phases

Division by two—First half of life: 0-36 years—Second half of life: 36-72 years—Left and right halves of the horoscope—Seasons and life phases

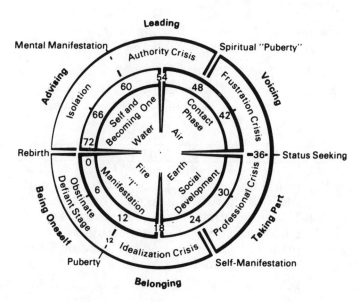

Figure 2.2.1. The division of the horoscope into life phases.

● Overview

I. Division by 2 and 4

Horizontal Line AC-DC
  Lower Half: 0 to 36 Years—Learning, Growing
  Upper Half: 36 to 72 Years—Affecting, Fading

Meridian Line IC—MC
  Left Half: 1 to 18 Years ⎰ Self-Experience and
                54 to 72 Years ⎱ Self-Manifestation
  Right Half: 18 to 54 Years—⎰ Relationship Experience,
                              ⎱ Attention to Environment

The Quadrants
  AC = 0; IC = 18; DC = 36; MC = 54; AC = 72 Years
  Developmental thrusts at the angles of the horoscope.

Division by 4: Formation
  1. "I"-Formation   3. Contact Phase
  2. Social Development   4. Self-Realization

II. Division by 3, 6, and 12

Division into 3: Personality Development
  1. Youth 2. Maturity 3. Old Age

Division by 6: Social Processes
  1. Being   3. Cooperating   5. Leading
  2. Participating 4. Voicing   6. Advising

Division by 12:

Six Phases of Manifestation	Six Phases of Crisis
Age 0 Birth	Age 6 Obstinate Phase
Age 12 Physical and Psychological Puberty	Age 18 Idealism Crisis
	Age 30 Professional Crisis
Age 24 Self-Manifestation	Age 42 Frustration Crisis
Age 36 Status-Seeking	Age 54 Authority Crisis
Age 48 Spiritual "Puberty"	Age 66 Isolation Crisis
Age 60 Mental Manifestation	
Age 72 Rebirth	

● Division by Two

First we divide the horoscope horizontally from the ascendant to the descendant. The lower half represents ages zero to thirty-six; the upper half thirty-six to seventy-two years of age.

● First Half of Life: 0-36 Years

Lower Half of Horoscope

The first half of life is formed by the need to develop from a single being to a fellow being. In the first thirty-six years (see figure 2.2.2.), we strive from the ascendant to the descendant, which means from the "I" to the "You." First we must become an "I" in this world and learn to be part of it in order to be accepted by the "You" and successfully participate and have a voice. Up to age thirty-six, we work to externalize what we received in terms of inherited and learned qualities. We aspire toward success and a "You," a partner in life. The

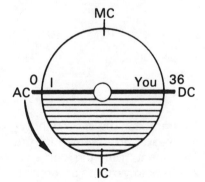

Figure 2.2.2. The movement from the ascendant to the descendant shows the first thirty-six years of life.

solution for problems is sought mainly outside the self, in the form of activities and creative urges. This primary urge is mostly subconscious since we are moving through the subconscious sphere of the horoscope. The whole development of the first half of life is directed toward self-experience and confrontation with the environment. We dream about great success in life and encounter the concomitant crises that are part of all growth.

● Second Half of Life: 36-72 Years

Upper Half of Horoscope

The second half of life begins with the fact that we have had some kind of success in life and still recognize that success, in the end, is not the only fulfilling goal in life. The age point moves now from the descendant, over the upper half of the horoscope, and back again to the ascendant. (See figure 2.2.3.)

Now, the psychological direction of development is reversed. We can observe at approximately age thirty-six that a

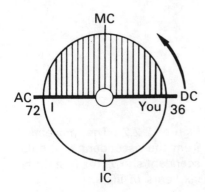

Figure 2.2.3. The second thirty-six years are shown in the movement from the descendant back toward the ascendant.

certain introversion occurs. The momentum and enthusiasm of the young years lessen. We become more deliberate and thoughtful as we move through the upper, conscious sphere of the horoscope. A quiet change in direction toward an expanded inner life takes place. We want to return again to ourselves, to be wholly ourselves, and finally to be satisfied with ourselves and the world. After the thirty-sixth year of life, with the AP crossing over the descendant, we step into full daylight and begin to live consciously in a spiritual/mental sense. The real individual self of the human being becomes effective, and can become fully integrated at the ascendant at age seventy-two.

This is, in a few words, the main theme of the second half of life; but there are also peak periods and crises that will be discussed in detail.

● Left and Right Halves of the Horoscope

We can also divide the horoscope through the meridian into left and right halves. The left side is introverted while the right is extroverted.

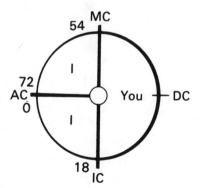

Figure 2.2.4. Two different periods of "I" development.

Then we can halve the left side once more (see figure 2.2.4) in order to differentiate between the beginning and end of life. Both are periods of "I"-development: the first quadrant from the ascendant to the IC (zero through eighteen years) serves the active I-formation; the last quadrant from the MC to the ascendant (fifty-four through seventy-two years) has again to do with the "I," but in a more spiritual sense. From within ourselves we go out into life, are formed and developed into individuals, and then return to ourselves with all the experiences of life we've gathered.

The long phase of extroversion, from age eighteen to fifty-four, from the IC to the MC, is almost exclusively dedicated to the environment and the mastering of life. We are interested in the "You," the world around us, the joys of external life. Our whole culture is geared to make us, from early childhood on, extroverted and world-successful individuals. Therefore, the second and third phases of life are accentuated in our consciousness, and this emphasis often leads to crises when the age point crosses the MC. Often, we do not know what to do with ourselves because, in today's world, we lack the concept for finding ways back to ourselves. This often leads to serious spiritual difficulties in the phase of old age.

Chapter 3

Division by Four

The seasons and life phases—Polarity and individuation processes—
Becoming whole—Finding the center—Developmental thrusts at the angles
and expansion zones—Phases of stabilization: the age point in the fixed
houses.

● The Seasons and Life Phases

In early cultures, the horoscope was already divided into
four life phases. The Egyptians compared life to the four
seasons: spring corresponded to childhood, summer to youth,
autumn to maturity, and winter to old age.

When we transfer this succession of concepts to our
horoscope, as in figure 2.3.1, we see the analogy in connection
with age progression.

The first eighteen years from the ascendant to the IC (first
quadrant) are identified with spring, which begins on March
21 with the entrance of the Sun into the sign Aries.

The second eighteen years begin at the IC on June 21,
when the Sun enters the sign Cancer. The second quadrant
starts here.

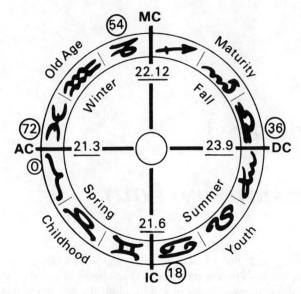

Figure 2.3.1. The seasons and the corresponding stages of life.

The third life-quarter begins at age thirty-six at the descendant, when the Sun enters the sign Libra on September 23. This is the beginning of fall in nature, and maturation within life.

The last quarter begins at the MC at age fifty-four, when the Sun enters Capricorn at the beginning of winter on December 22. This corresponds in our house system to finding ways back to ourselves, to meditation.

• Polarity and Individuation Processes

Our study of the angular cross (see figure 2.3.2) is of psycho-developmental importance because the tensions associated with the angles correspond to impulses toward individual growth. When the human being is born into the horoscope, he follows the course of house development but, at the same time, is continuously tied referentially to the grand cross. Two powerful impulses or thrusts force us to confront four different directions in our life and to develop accordingly. Those vital energy thrusts leave no other alternative but to grow in order to become what we are and want to be.

As you can see in figure 2.3.2, the horizontal line (the energy push from "I" to "You") symbolizes our instincts for contact; the vertical line (from the bottom to the top) symbolizes the instincts for growing towards individual selfhood. We are caught in these two motions and experience them as opposites in ourselves until we are able to integrate them.

On the one hand, we feel a strong urge toward individuation, a powerful wish to be a unique and original individual in contrast to others. On the other hand, we feel the urge to take our place in a larger whole, a collective. In order to survive, we almost always must limit our wishes and needs in compliance with the common good and the demands of the collective to which we belong. That is the polarity from the bottom to the top of the horoscope, from the IC to the MC.

The other directional thrust, from the "I" to the "You," demands that we develop from egoism to altruism. The path

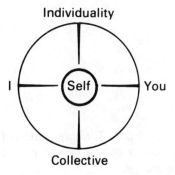

Figure 2.3.2. The angular cross.

from "I" to "You" demands that we open ourselves to others, the unknown, the "You," and engage in harmonious exchange. One is not compelled to give up the "I," but we know the need to compare ourselves with others. On this horizontal line, we are not better than others. We should not engage in competition, but strive for honest human exchange and relationships. What is important is the balance between dependence and personal freedom. The adaptability that is demanded here should always leave room for individuality and personal growth. The integration of these tensions occurs mostly over "the third way," the axis at right angles to any polarity. (This is discussed in detail in *Man and His World*.)

The angular cross consists of the angles "I-You" and "Collective Individuality." The process of individuation demands a constant balancing of the polarities from inside to outside as well as from below to above, from extroversion to introversion on all levels. A harmonious personality is always in the center of constantly changing inner and outer demands.

● Becoming Whole—Finding the Center

All energies flow together at the center of the grand cross. The essential integration of forces takes place at the center of the horoscope (figure 2.3.3). When we open ourselves to the movement toward that inner center, we live in our own center.

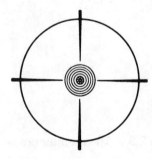

Figure 2.3.3. The integration of all forces at the center of the horoscope.

Through these unifying energies, we find the self. Here in the center, we overcome the tensions from above and below, left and right. The forces of time and space merge. Self-realization (individuation or wholeness) simply means finding one's own center, the true measure, the inner balance, or the well-rounded personality.

An essential part of being whole is turning toward others. From our center, unlimited spiritual energies flow. We give and receive them. We move forward on the path to wholeness by receiving love. Human wholeness is much more than the sum of its parts. It comes from the deepest center of being, from personal depth. Sometimes it lights up in us, and we feel totally one with it. Then it may disappear again, we fall out of the center, and find ourselves back within one of the polarities indicated in the horoscope. Then, we must again seek our own center and return to the path. Wholeness is not given to us permanently.

However, we can experience wholeness at any time when we are centered and open ourselves to others through love. Wholeness can not really be self-induced because it is subject to an overall evolutionary energy; but we can be "open" to striving for it by working on our spiritual-mental development.

We can reach for the center of our being by being open at any time during any stage of development. At the passage of the age point over the low points in each house, inner energies affect our development most strongly. They represent special opportunities for self-realization.

● Developmental Thrusts at the Angles and Expansion Zones

Next, let's observe the four angles and their zones of expansion (figure 2.3.4) in the horoscope, which start dyna-

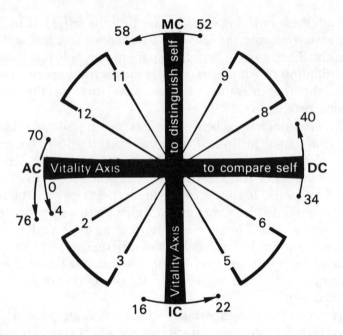

Figure 2.3.4. The cardinal and mutable houses set in motion a dynamic process of self-unfolding.

mic processes of renewal and self-unfolding. (For more discussion, see *Man and His World,* page 64.)

The previously described tensions focused on the angles of the horoscope (AC, IC, DC, MC). These angles are where life is transformed, where periods of reorientation trigger vital developmental processes. The years mentioned in Table 2.3.1 are not to be viewed as fixed points in time. Rather, renewal is already begun at the low point of the preceding house and fades away gradually.

Although the developmental thrusts in the expansion zones of the horoscope occur over a time span of about six years, the transits of the AP over the angles in the horoscope are especially strong. Shortly before the AP reaches each of the

Table 2.3.1. Phases of Becoming and Angular Tensions.

Phases of Becoming	Point of Maximum Intensity	External Processes	Internal Motivation
0- 4 years	AC: 0 year	Birth	"I"-Perseverance
16-22 years	IC: 18th year	Parental Separation	Seeking to Belong
34-40 years	DC: 36th year	Environmental Integration	Striving for Status
52-58 years	MC: 54th year	Authority Increase	Striving for Freedom
70-76 years	AC: 72nd year	Becoming One	Rebirth

four angles, we experience increased energy levels that can be connected with stress. The house cusps act like high mountains that we have to conquer. In the last stretch in particular every mountain climber finds special difficulty. With extreme self-application and often with his last bit of energy, he strives to reach a peak. That's how we experience each angle. If we find ourselves at these ages (18, 36, 54, 72) in a weak position, we can collapse just before the goal because the increased demands are not met by expanded energies. It is wise to conserve one's energies before that point in order not to be too exhausted.

Often long before the angle, people get caught up in hectic activity. They race, so to speak, up the mountain and arrive out of breath. No wonder they are often near a breakdown. One easily succumbs to the impulsiveness of the angular (cardinal) house cusp and overestimates one's own power.

The following developmental thrusts take place at the four angles.

At the AC the life impulse reaches its highest pitch, induces birth, and the human being appears on the scene. The urge for manifestation is so strong that "veils are torn" and the soul is transformed from an immaterial state into a physical form. The thrust continues far past the ascendant and allows the newly-born being to manifest itself in order to finally become an "I," a human being.

At the IC, at approximately age eighteen, two motions clash together: the "attachment to the ground" of the IC which seeks anchor in the roots, and the vertical bridge to freedom, to the MC, the point of individualization. There is a struggle between the rising urge for self-realization and the demands of the collective sphere. We want to be what we can only be when we reach the MC, a free individual, an authority, or a leading personality; but the need to belong still dominates. Individualization only appears as a goal or ideal.

At the DC, at approximately thirty-six years of age, we come upon another impulse toward expansion. We enter the upper sphere of the horoscope and suddenly become aware that circumstances do not agree with our goals. Much that was done with great conviction up to then suddenly seems senseless and wrong. Also, the image that we have had of ourselves and of other human beings often needs drastic correction during the expansion sphere at the seventh house cusp.

At the MC, at 54 years or so, another important crossroads appears. Often we have reached a certain status that we consider the highest point. We want to hold onto the social or mental position at all costs. Sometimes we want to climb further and are forced to recognize that our resources are not enough for such a journey. It is better then to honor the current responsibilities and secure the present holdings. Some people need an impulse from outside, a fateful happening, in order to realize and assert themselves because they may have leaned too much on someone else up to then.

At the AC, at about seventy-two years of age, we come back to the starting point and experience a new life impulse, a push for renewal. Those who can not accept that impulse will experience a crisis. Those who are tired of life and are without a will may be broken by the thrust of vital energies at the AC, but those who react joyfully and flexibly can experience a new blooming of life that will carry them past the ascendant.

● Phases of Stabilization: The Age Point in the Fixed Houses

In the eight houses which surround the two main axes (AC/DC and IC/MC), vital developmental processes take

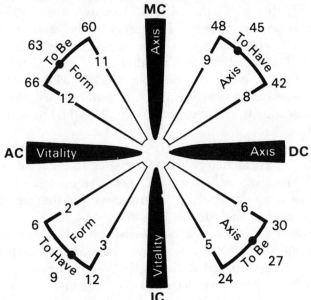

Figure 2.3.5. The fixed houses.

place. In the four fixed houses, all hard-won experiences are stabilized. Here again, the number four is a measure of form and matter: it is in the fixed houses (2, 5, 8, 11) that we find material conviction for our psychological conditions. Figure 2.3.5 shows the two fixed axes which are called *form axes,* and the angular or *vital axes.*

The four axes and their corresponding spaces make up the horoscope divided by eight, as used in ancient times. In the early development of astrology, the horoscope was anchored at the "four columns of heaven" (the fixed signs) and not as in modern times at the cardinal sign points (equinoxes and solstices). Figure 2.3.6 shows that this fact is still expressed in the assignment of rulerships of planets around a symmetrical axis which is polarized from Leo to Aquarius.

The Chinese I-Ching offers a counterpoint to this: the eight hexagrams are arranged in the circle around the signs Taurus and Scorpio. Both (astrology and I-Ching) developed in the epoch we call the "Age of Taurus," about 4000-2000 B.C. This was no accident. The terms "to be" and "to have" are primal terms against which man has always measured himself. They establish the foundations of our existence and create static conditions and role models which we must follow, whether we wish to or not. It is an old fact that we are only somebody if we have something: "He who has nothing is nothing."

These are concepts which determine our value systems and which have archetypal characteristics. In the fixed houses, we will not give in and we will not give up what we have gained or what we possess. We are convinced that we have to own something in order to be somebody.

In the fixed houses, we insist on a certain role, a recognized status. We orient ourselves almost exclusively toward well-established status symbols and believe we cannot live without them. We act out of total conviction and are unaware for a long while that there are other opportunities for living and developing. Our routine behavior creates fixed and

Figure 2.3.6. The ancients worked with a symmetrical axis based on the fixed signs of Leo and Aquarius. In this illustration you will note that the opposition between 0° Leo and 0° Aquarius forms a line which is bounded by the Sun/Moon on the one hand, and two phases of Saturn on the other.

static conditions in these fixed houses (2,5,8,11) which are very difficult to change or discard. They have a hold upon us from the collective unconscious and are to a certain extent super-ego functions. Only through our own self-realization and individuation can we gain the autonomous consciousness that allows us to choose and act freely.

Table 2.3.2. The Fixed Houses and Social Patterns.

HOUSE	MOTIVATIONS (ASPIRATIONS)	DEMONSTRA-TION	TYPICAL ANXIETIES	ARCHETYPES (CLASSIC ROLES)	MEASURE OF VALUE
2	Striving for Possessions, Securing, Defining	Territorial Behavior (marking)	Fear of Theft and Plagiarism	The Rich Man, Banker, Business-man, Estate-owner, "Capitalist"	Personal Territory, Bank Account
5	Striving for Power, Making Others Dependent, Radiating	Competitive Behavior (impressing)	Jealousy, Fear of Impotence	The King, Autocrat, Entrepreneur, Boss, "The Greatest"	The Vassals, Chivalric Code, Sphere of Privacy
8	Striving for Distinction, Ambition, Status	Demonstrating Righteousness, (impressing)	Fear of Law, Anxiety for Title and Status	The Aristocrat, General, Doctor, "Good Citizen"	Law & Order, Uniform, Status, Society
11	Striving for Learning, Recognition, Authority	Cultural and Educational Pretentiousness (marking)	Fear of Indiscretions and Isolation	The Wise Man, Oligarch, Teacher-Authority, Member of Secret Society	The Elite, Ideologies, "Knowledge is Power"

With the passage of the age point through the fixed houses we react automatically to some certain degree to well-established patterns of society. We may even believe we have a right to these values and think that our self-worth is dependent solely upon these role-functions. Table 2.3.2 shows the status symbols, motivations, and typical anxieties which give us the feeling that we are important in the world and part of it.

On the basis of these four roles or symbols of status—the owner, the entrepreneur, the representative, and the wise man—we are evaluated, arranged, and classified. We also evaluate our friends, family, and fellow human beings the same way. We are dependent upon public opinion and generally accepted rules and are vulnerable to manipulation. This role behavior is not unlike a corset: we must wear it until we realize that we can also live without it.

When the age point crosses over the low point in the fixed houses, we should try, at least temporarily, to take off the corset in order to reorient ourselves to the reality of life and grow through it. If we insist, nevertheless, on continuing the role we played so far, then the environment often questions, criticizes, and attacks us. In the fixed houses, there are often painful transformations, true psychological death and rebirth processes and crises of change. This is especially so if we stubbornly hold onto what has become, in the course of time, an empty, mechanical routine. When the "I" holds onto those lifeless roles, it cannot grow further, and life is imprisoned from within.

In the Second House (6-12 Years)

In this phase, we want to be "the owner"; we want to have something that belongs only to us, that nurtures our feeling of self-worth. It can be material or spiritual-mental possessions, but the more we possess, the more we are in the world.

In this life phase, the child tires to accumulate as much as possible in order to make an impression on others or to define its own territory which it will then defend against everyone.

At the low point of the second house (around age ten) the child must learn to understand that it cannot have everything it desires. It must learn that there are other people in its world and that it must share with them. If the child is not willing to learn that lesson, it is most often forced by the environment to give up something.

In the Fifth House (24-30 Years)

Here, we want to be "powerful" and do anything we want. We feel young and strong and believe that we own the world. This fact is not at all questioned. It is assumed, and everyone's respect is expected. We become "show-offs" in order to impress others and to express power and independence. We strive on behalf of our own enterprises and want to experience ourselves through what we do. When we are creative and able to achieve something through our own power, our self-worth increases. Sometimes we really feel "I am the greatest."

Until the low point (around age 28) in the fifth house, we feel strong and sure; only then do we become aware that we may not be as great as we thought. The lesson here, especially as the AP approaches the sixth house cusp, is to adapt to reality.

In the Eighth House (42-48 Years)

Here, we want to stabilize our position in society. We do everything we can to reach a goal, or if that has already been accomplished, to maintain it. When we have a solid position, we feel important and believe that it would not work without us. If our position, our image, or honor needs to be defended, we won't stop at anything.

In the eighth house we are respected—or at least need to be. We want to have some say in society, as an official, manager, or policeman, for example. We feel secure when we can administrate power in the name of the law or society. Here, the feeling of self-worth becomes dependent upon society, institutions, governmental agencies, titles, prestige positions, and uniforms. At the low point of the eighth house (approximately 46 years), we suffer from an anxiety of loss. We fear losing that which has functioned well so far and that to which we have given all our attention and energy. Nevertheless, we have to give up out-dated forms and functions to find the way to new sources of life.

In the Eleventh House (60-66 Years)

We want to establish and defend our own ideals, our mental integrity, our own originality. We seek out others with similar world views so that our attitudes are not doubted. Our feeling of self-worth increases through valued friends or through membership in an organization that is important to mankind—such as church, secret societies or alliances, a reform movement, etc.

In the eleventh house, we want to exercise our mental influence and be the authority in a field. That's why this is often the phase when memoirs are written: we want to show what we know and what wisdom we have won.

At the low point of the eleventh house (64 years), we are often no longer taken seriously, especially if our ideologies are not current with the spirit of the times. We have the feeling of not being needed any longer, that the world "turns without us." We feel alone and misunderstood and resigned. It is important in this life phase to exhibit fairness and true humanity and to be tolerant toward those of other views. Then we will always have friends—people to whom we are important and to whom we can give.

Chapter 4

The Four Life Phases—
Development of Form

The different levels in the four quadrants—"I"-formation (0-18)—Social development (18-36)—Conscious contact phase (36-54)—Self-fulfillment (54-72)—Three phases in each quadrant.

● The Different Levels in the Four Quadrants

The four quadrants of the horoscope correspond to four main periods in life, each eighteen years long. During the time span of each quadrant, we can observe a consistent orientation toward life. The four life phases can be divided as follows:

	Years	Houses
1. "I"-Formation	0-18	1st, 2nd, 3rd
2. Social Development	18-36	4th, 5th, 6th
3. Contact Phase	36-54	7th, 8th, 9th
4. Self-Fullfilment	54-72	10th, 11th, 12th

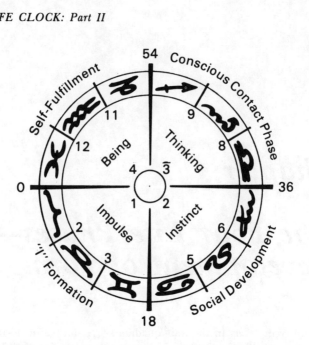

Figure 2.4.1. The four quadrants and how they relate to the developmental stages from childhood to maturity.

● "I" Formation

Ascendant: The first major thrust in life occurs at the cusp of the first house: birth. With birth, the hand on the life clock beings to move through the twelve houses.

In the first quadrant (or first three houses), the "I" receives its form (see figure 2.4.2.).The potential which is present at birth must be given expression and the opportunity to unfold. The newborn is dependent upon the environment. The child is unsure, insecure; it needs protection and help of all kinds. In the first quadrant, it develops personality, and impulsively and reflexively responds to opportunities. In this impulse quadrant, it concentrates on self-preservation and self-defense. The environment forms the child, who passively takes in everything that happens. Parents, educators, and siblings serve as examples. The pattern in the early home determines behavior in later life. Although the child wants to be himself, it will first be conditioned. This dual process dominates the first life quadrant. The instinct for self-preservation is strongly formed now. In the first life phase, we learn to assert ourselves, to make our claim to life. We react sensitively when we are not given attention, are neglected, or if our right to live is attacked. Such experiences are stamped deep into consciousness because this is the time when we have to build up the "I" and declare our right to life.

During this time when the environment acts upon us too intensely or wrongly or rejects or tortures us, then we construct and accumulate psychological defense mechanisms. These defensive patterns sets the tone for our responses later on in life when the same situation arises or wholeness is attacked.

The planetary positions in the first quadrant essentially determine the patterns that influence our later life and often cause psychological problems. The most important formation and imprinting take place in the first three houses and occasionally in the fourth house as well through the influence

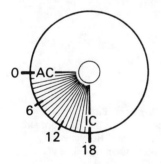

Impulse Quadrant: Fire
Unconscious "I" Perseverance
Unconscious "I" Realization
Education
Adaption to Outer Conditions

Figure 2.4.2. The first quadrant. Life phase: Age 0-18.

of education and home life. In the next chapter, we will discuss more important indications of all this.

● Social Development

Imum Coeli: The second significant impulse occurs at the cusp of the fourth house. Here, everything that's been learned during the first eighteen years of life is in opposition to what we want to be and become (MC). Here, self-realization and individuation begin. Separation from heritage and tradition, from the parental home is necessary. The young human being tries to find his own path toward self-education and looks for new anchors in relationships.

The second quadrant (figure 2.4.3) serves the social self. We are still in the unconscious sphere of the horoscope but are already on the You-side, and that is the reason why we turn toward the environment. An instinctive and therefore strongly egocentric urge for popularity, fame, or power comes to the foreground. Within this quadrant we find out that we are not alone in the world. Although we would like to believe that we

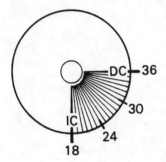

Instinct Quadrant: Earth
Unconscious Control of Environment
Unconscious "you" Relationship
Testing and Educating the Self

Figure 2.4.3. The second quadrant. Life phase: Age 18-36.

are the only ones in control, moving the world, we must learn to adjust to reality and relevant environmental conditions. The social position we hope for and the fight for survival demand our entire personality. We feel strongly drawn to the world, to life, and people. The attraction for the opposite sex is especially emphasized. Overall, all tendencies toward environmental identification are strongly marked.

In this period from the eighteenth to the thirty-sixth year, in this close encounter with the world and other human beings, we form and learn about our own reaction patterns and the reaction patterns of those with whom we are in close contact. Therefore we can deduce our capacity for love and social contact, our overall behavior toward the "You" from planets situated in this second quadrant.

Certain planetary positions make it clear that we expect happiness from the "You," from others, and we protest mightily when the "You" disappoints us. We insist on our preconceptions of a loved one and often suffer "for love's sake" because of those misconceptions. We make ourselves instinctively, emotionally, and existentially dependent upon the "You" and believe that this is love. During this period, inefficient behavior patterns are often corrected through fateful influences, disappointments, or personal failures.

● Conscious Contact Phase

Descendant: At the thirty-sixth year, we reach the middle of life ($72 \div 2 = 36$). The third major impulse of life takes place. Life's autumn begins. It is the true high point of life. We focus upon life's essence, calling the surrounding interactive environment and all its problems into conscious recognition and realization.

By crossing over the horizon, we enter the conscious sphere of the horoscope. Here there are no more excuses, illusions, or extenuating circumstances. Here, clear perceptions about the self and others are demanded; much appears in a new light. We stand on the horizon opposite the AC, the "I"-point, and gain new insights into ourselves through connection with the "You."

The third quadrant (figure 2.4.4) the thinking quadrant. In contrast to the instinct quadrant, we now consciously confront the environment. Although we find ourselves again in close relationship with others, we experience ourselves and others more clearly. In the thinking quadrant we react less instinctively to others while considering how we can best get along. By living more consciously in accordance with our inner selves we become more tolerant of others.

While the AP is moving from the DC to the MC we come closer to the main theme of the cardinal cross, the point of individuation and independence of the fully matured personality. Especially aware people notice this condition is at the low point of the seventh house; most confront the condition of the eighth house.

Since we are still living in constant contact with others in this quadrant, at times it can become too intense and burdensome. Problems can arise, especially if we have made the "I" and our self-worth too dependent upon environmental

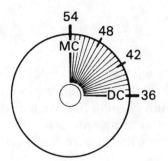

Thought Quadrant: Air
Conscious "you" Recognition
Conscious Adjustment and Life Focus
Self-Realization

Figure 2.4.4. The third quadrant. Life phase: Age 36-54.

acceptance. Identity crises or neuroses may take hold. If we have never learned to live without ties, without a focus on other people, we will miss the concept of emerging individual freedom; we cannot and will not let go of our ties and dependence; we refuse self-realization. At the same time, these responsibilities can be experienced as burdens because they hinder our individual development. If we stay a slave to existing conditons we are unable to reach personal freedom and suffer from a sense of meaninglessness in our present life situations.

If there are planetary concentrations in this sphere, the transit of the AP signifies the importance of clearing up the relationship between the "I" and "You." Each extreme should be balanced. We can find this balance only if we clearly recognize our position in this world. We must want to develop our life with meaning and evolve ever more human qualities.

● Self-Fulfillment

Medium Coeli: The fourth key impulse is released when the AP reaches the highest point, the MC. Here, the human being turns toward inner freedom and self-realization. In the fourth quadrant he should become aware of himself and his true destination.

At the MC, under certain circumstances, great worldly success and honors are received, yet at the same time a demand for separation from the outer world is felt. With the activation of the MC life turns away from the right half of the horoscope (outer world, "You"-direction) and toward a time of intensification and conscious "I" direction. That is why we have to be willing to cross the MC and move on, rather than remaining stationary at the peak. This turning point demands a readiness for inner transformation and, often, the acceptance of one's own limitations. Often we have to give up familiar things, leave traditions and routines behind, give up achievements, and take leave. Or, finally, we have to do what has not been done because of fear or inconvenience and meet whatever challenges have not been accepted (for example, self-reliance, responsibility, and solitude).

In the fourth quadrant (figure 2.4.5) we deal with the reality of being rather than the structure of pretensions. In this quadrant a distance is created between ourselves and the hectic activities of life; it leads us back to ourselves. Here we can deal with a conscious understanding of our own being. In this life phase, we should confront big life-questions and work consciously for self-identification, so that we may be free of the lures of the outer world of achievement.

The cultivation of a spiritual attitude toward life is very helpful here. We must try to seed the harvest of our experiences by passing on all the knowledge, experience, and awareness we have accumulated. Many who have the power to take responsibility for others can now help them and help prepare younger and talented individuals for the path. Life becomes meaningful again when we stand in the service of supra-personal goals, in community service which is oriented toward higher tasks. In the previous period we tended to measure all achievement against outer success; now we must take the human as sole measure. This demands a change in

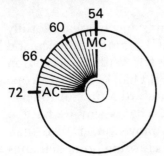

"Being" Quadrant: Water
Conscious "I" Realization
Conscious "I" Formation
Self-Awareness

Figure 2.4.5. The fourth quadrant. Life phase: Age 54-72.

life motivation, of which not every one is capable or for which all have not been prepared by fate's heavy blows.

Generally, in this life phase, we lose more and more interest in excessive activity and the many-sided experiences of the outer world; we prefer undisturbed distance so that we may live in contemplation of the self and the world. These dimensions increase the closer we come to the ascendant.

If the young human being was not given the correct spiritual tools through education or personal life experiences, increasing loneliness, spiritual-mental barrenness, senility, chronic and/or progressive illnesses can make life regressive. The general life expectancy has only expanded within the last one hundred and fifty years into the fourth quadrant, and our society, not liking to confront death, has not yet developed a vital concept for this age level. However, even in times when life expectancy was thirty, forty, or fifty years, there were human beings who reached an age of seventy or eighty, positive and creative to the end.

● Three Phases in Each Quadrant

The astrological conception is basically a combination of numbers three and four. Each of the quadrants contains three houses that correspond to the quadruplicities: cardinal, fixed, and mutable. This sequence repeats in each of the quadrants (figure 2.4.6).

In viewing the three houses of a quadrant in sequence, we encounter a new manifestation of the impulse activated at each angle. This impulse triggers a creative process that begins in the angular house as an idea or plan. In the following fixed house this impulse or idea is given form and existence. At the low point of the fixed house this form reaches its greatest density. The crystallization forces are strongest,

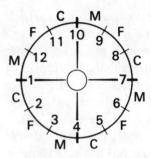

Figure 2.4.6. The crosses (or quadruplicities) as they repeat themselves throughout the horoscope.

and mostly the form no longer corresponds with the laws of life and development. Doubts arise about whether or not this form can satisfy further demands. That is why a new orientation is necessary at the low point and beyond. In moving toward the mutable house, we really need to change and expand what we have attained or begin something totally new.

These three-phase developmental rhythms unfold in each quadrant according to the qualities of the crosses and the age of the person. We can view each quadrant as a self-contained process, followed by another that has a new theme and again passes through all three stages.

This triple phase within each quadrant indicates that there are not only four but many cycles, that everything unfolds according to the same basic pattern but in context with other smaller and larger cycles. Each development begins at a zero point and reaches a maximum point; everyone grows from birth to death. To recognize and realize this law is especially important for the human being because, in contrast to animals, he can creatively influence his own life. The different observations of the age progression method should bring this basic law closer and more consciously to us.

Chapter 5

The Three-Part Division— Development of Personality

Three-part division of the horoscope—"I" development and maturation—The four elements—The three phases of personality development (Sun, Moon and Saturn periods)—Recovery needs—The first third of life—Transition to the second phase of life—The second third of life—Transition to the third phase of life—The last third of life—The Ascendant: focus of individual development—The influence of planets at the ascendant—Life phases and the three primary colors.

• Three-Part Division of the Horoscope

Dividing the circle (as we have done in Table 2.5.1) into three phases of sequential time development allows us to make a connection between the three personality planets (Moon, Sun, and Saturn), the three quadruplicities (cardinal, fixed, and mutable), and the three primary colors (red, yellow, and blue).

Table 2.5.1. Division of the Horoscope

Life Phase	Houses	Years	Ruling Planets	Physical Phase	Spiritual-Mental Phase	Color
1st Third of Life	1-4	0-24	☽	Growth	Awakening "I," Expansion, Personal Phase	Red
2nd Third of Life	5-8	24-48	☉	Effectiveness	Stabilizing the Environment, Contact, Fixation, Social Phase	Yellow
3rd Third of Life	9-12	48-72	♄	Crystallization	Separation, Freedom, Transcendence, Universal Phase	Blue

In dividing the horoscope into thirds with four houses each (figure 2.5.1), the first third contains the houses one through four (analogous to the signs Aries, Taurus, Gemini, and Cancer). We can observe from birth to age twenty-four there. In the second third, including houses five through eight (analogous to Leo, Virgo, Libra, and Scorpio), we see correspondences with ages twenty-four to forty-eight. The third phase, from age forty-eight to seventy-two, contains houses nine through twelve (analogous to Sagittarius, Capricorn, Aquarius, and Pisces).

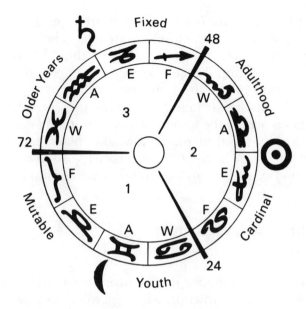

Figure 2.5.1. The three phases of life.

● "I"-Development and Maturation

The three phases in terms of maturity can be classified:

Phase 1: Maturation of the Personality (Youth)
Phase 2: Worldly-Social Maturation (Adulthood)
Phase 3: Mental/Spiritual Maturation (Older Years)

These three phases mainly serve the maturation process of the "I." Note the fact that each of the three phases begins with a fire house and ends with a water house. The first phase begins with the first house which corresponds with the sign Aries, the second phase with the fifth house, the natural house of Leo, and the third phase with the ninth house, corresponding to

Sagittarius. All three fire houses and fire signs are connected with the development of self-awareness. The fire element, which centers on personal identity, the "I," triggers a developmental impulse and introduces a new phase of self-manifestation in the fire houses.

In the first phase (age 0-24), personality formation of the "I" takes place. In the second phase, beginning at age twenty-four, worldly-social manifestation takes place, ending at age forty-eight, with integration into society. Afterwards, in the ninth house, mental and spiritual self-realization begins.

● The Four Elements

We again combine the numbers three and four when considering the horoscope with regard to the elements. In each third of the horoscope we find all four elements (fire, earth, air, and water). The age point passes through all four elements, and therefore we experience a continuing manifestation of "I" development.

In the fire house, the AP impulse ignites "I" manifestation. The earth house affects the concentration and integration of "I" substances; the air house develops the rational references of the "I"; the water house identifies instinctively with belonging, but also experiences the possible loss of the "I."

From the water houses we continue again into fire houses ("I" manifestation). The water houses (four, eight, and twelve) therefore contain a seed of change and transformation which insures a new orientation and a path for further development. During the life periods associated with the water houses we distill the quality of the preceding house group. It is always painful to move from one orientation to another. We must let go if further development is to be possible, and that is never quite accomplished without crisis.

● The Three Phases of Personality Development—Moon, Sun, and Saturn Periods

As already mentioned, the main theme of the three-phase analysis is the development of self-awareness, "I" manifestation, and personality unfolding on an ever higher spiral. It is the task of the human being to become conscious of his own "I" and to express this "I" consciously to its fullest potential. In the process, he meets a world full of people who have the same mission. We must learn step by step to see our self-realization as a common effort. A conscious and positive social integration is part of true personality unfolding. A thorough exploration of these life stages is of utmost importance. We can learn so much through this introspection and bring our inner attitude into harmony with natural laws. We must know that we cannot skip a developmental phase and that we may not forcibly hold onto any attained state for too long. We should always stay in motion and always adjust to new conditions. Only then will our development be harmonious and emerge without any greater interferences.

Of the three phases, the Moon rules youth; the Sun rules the blossoming or success phase; and Saturn rules maturity or old age, that last life phase in which all experiences are evaluated.

This distinction is very revealing when observing the individual phases of personality development. We should be aware that, at thirty-four, for example, one is a "Sun person." The Sun qualities are in effect and, therefore, the striving is focused outwardly; the main motivation is self-realization. That is why, in this mid-life phase, the human being is definitely oriented to success and logic, wishing to approach everything clearly and matter-of-factly, to establish his will as much as possible. If the Sun in his horoscope is poorly situated, he will have difficulties in this second life phase. If he happens to have a well-established Saturn he will be able to succeed in the next phase.

• Recovery Needs

In the Sun period it can happen that we try to make up for the time lost in the Moon phase. As is well known, this happens often in the last part of the Sun period, in the eighth house sphere. At this age, around forty-two (figure 2.5.2), we often experience a sudden breakdown of existing relationships. We may yearn for a love adventure because we were not "all there" at the beginning of the Sun period in the fifth house, or because the environment blocked or hindered us.

This compensatory reflex at the end of the Sun period (or end of the eighth house) is a kind of developmental panic. Often we are not successful in the manner we envisioned because demands and conditions have changed through time. We can still have beautiful and fulfilling experiences, but only if we are living something new and not just "catching up." This new way of loving may be something we had not previously envisioned. It is better, therefore, if we experience our new love more from an eighth house point of view as we call it, with the recognition that the body is no longer as

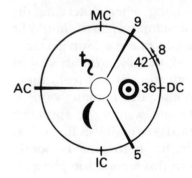

Figure 2.5.2. At the end of the Sun period, approximately age 42, a breakdown in relationships may occur.

young and pliable as that of a twenty-five-year-old. Human qualities are now more in the foreground.

Since personality development is a main theme of being and almost all problems and conflicts are somehow connected to it, we must go into further detail about these three phases in the horoscope. As we said earlier, the pertinent years are not fixed points in life: each phase changes slowly from one to the other.

● The First Third of Life

By observing people we can always again find that in the first third of life until age twenty-four (figure 2.5.2), the Moon qualities predominate. Experiences in this period are overtly lunar.

The Moon describes the childlike emotional "I." It is dependent like a child and cannot take responsibility for itself. A child lives in the safety and protection of the family. The family supports, maintains, advances, or hinders the child. One can observe the attitude in children and young people that someone must take care of them. The idea that they might be responsible for themselves generally does not occur to them.

By observing the Moon position in the individual horoscope, we can often draw conclusions about childhood

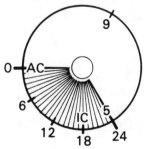

0-24 Years
Childhood and Youth
Personality Development
Houses 1 through 5
Moon Period
Mutable cross

Figure 2.5.3. The first third of life.

and the first part of life. The first four houses below the horizon describe childhood and youth. It is during the Moon phase that the human being grows up and, according to the quality of the individual Moon, reflects impressions and stores them in the emotional "I." The child is flexible, changeable, adaptable, and absorbs everything that happens. The planetary positions in the first few houses describe the stamp of early experiences, including trauma or other incisive experiences in childhood that affected the child's "I" formation either helpfully or harmfully. The reason for many difficult attitudes in the human being often originates in the difficulties encountered during the "I" building Moon phase.

With the help of the AP, we can see immediately when such experiences or influences took place. For example, if planets in the second house are in a difficult configuration, we can safely presume that the child had a decisive experience about seven years of age. If the Moon is in opposition to the Sun (figure 2.5.4) we are dealing with a father problem, which will be reflected in later behavior and which can be at the root of developmental disturbances. For the young human being, the Sun represents the father figure whose attitude toward life and toward himself is the model for the child's self-awareness.

If the parents, as key figures, do not disappoint the child, the "I" can develop with healthy self-assurance without damage. But if the feelings of trust and protection are

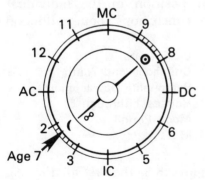

Figure 2.5.4. A Sun-Moon op-position from the second to the eighth houses may indicate childhood difficulties with the father.

disappointed in this Moon period (by parents or educators), then the child is left to his own resources. The Moon-"I" (or emotional body) expands and takes on a defensive position, thereby building up an overprotective "I." Later, in the Sun period, when the human being is developing self-awareness, he must recognize his overprotective shell and may even have to let go of it under difficult circumstances. The parents may also project their own wishes onto the child, which the child can not fulfill. The emergent human being has to free himself from these parental wishes at a certain point in his development in order to become himself.

• Transition to the Second Phase of Life

The Sun period begins with the twenty-fourth year, an age when the human being presses out into the world in order to gather experience and build his own sphere. During the earlier period, the Moon qualities were strongly developed, and now the Sun forces are expressed more and more. This natural urge toward an extroversion of the "I" corresponds

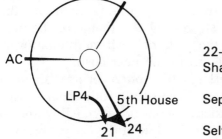

22-24 Years
Shadow Sphere LP4 to
    5th House Cusp
Separation from
    Parental Home
Self-Manifestation

Figure 2.5.5. The shadow sphere from low point 4 to the fifth house cusp.

with the cardinal principle and brings with it a turning away from the limiting factors of the Moon period and the parental home. This expansive energy allows the young human being to free himself from the psychological womb of the parental nest, to break away from conditioned emotional and intellectual attitudes, and to prepare for the establishment of his own personality.

This phase of separation very often begins around age eighteen when the AP enters the fourth house, and should be completed by the low point (about 21-½ years). Then the natural development of self-awareness can start harmoniously, and inner strength will be available to climb to the cusp of the fifth house. But if we are not able to detach from our family dependencies, we will have difficulties taking self-responsibility as the fifth house demands it.

To put it in more practical terms: the fourth house is concerned with the emotional ties we have toward our family, the security we can get from it, etc. But from the low point on, the quality of the fifth house starts pulling us out into the world. Though we still are in the fourth and occupied with family affairs, we eagerly begin looking for adventures, for self-experience. We try to create our own sphere of life.

Between the low point and the next cusp in every house we experience a dual field. Two different energies are at work: the one of the house we still are going through which wants us to fulfill the respective duties (in our example, the "family"); and the other suggesting the theme of the next house (in our example, the fifth or "self-manifestation"), thereby trying to heave us up to the next cusp.

Psychologically speaking, this often brings about a certain stress situation which may unleash individual "crisis-mechanisms," such as anxieties about not succeeding and so forth. We call these areas "the Shadow of the Cusp," because they feel like climbing up a steep mountain in its unpleasant shadow, without having yet the view from the top.

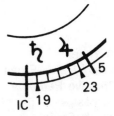

Figure 2.5.6. Saturn and Jupiter in the natal fourth house are activated by the AP at age 19 and 23 respectively.

With the help of the age point, we can judge how the individual will cope with the life phase just before the AP moves over the house cusp and how the separation will be accomplished. For example, if Saturn is positioned right after the fourth house cusp as in figure 2.5.6 (approximately age nineteen), then the Saturn placement may indicate that we are unable to make a separation at this time, that we are probably not yet ready to give up the security of familial belonging.

It is helpful to see what follows. In our example, Jupiter is also in the fourth house, but we reach this point only at age twenty-three, shortly before the cusp of the fifth house. We know that at this time the separation will be concluded harmoniously, because Jupiter strengthens our self-confidence and environmental conditions appear more supportive. For future development, it is of inestimable value to recognize these age point indications in order to know how best to negotiate life transitions.

● The Second Third of Life

The Sun rules development from age twenty-four (the cusp of the fifth house) until age forty-eight (ninth house cusp) as shown in figure 2.5.7. Sun energies come into the foreground with ever-increasing strength now. We are in full possession of our mental, spiritual and physical energies. What is generally referred to as a "personality" develops into a

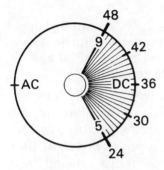

24-48 Years
Flowering Time—Freeing
    Creative Personal
    Forces
Worldly & Social
    Maturation
Houses 5 through 9
Sun Period
Cardinal Cross

Figure 2.5.7. The Sun rules the period of the AP passage from the fifth to the ninth house.

mature human being who is conscious of his own creative potential; someone who understands the purpose of his life and has a definitely developed life-program; someone who produces, as a result of his own labor; someone who has the courage to stand up for his actions if necessary. This is the period when we have the most success, whatever we understand that to be. The term "success," as it is understood today, is mainly connected with the Sun.

In this period, with the help of Sun energies, we are able to develop through our own energy, our own ideas, and our own will. It is the space in time that holds the greatest opportunities to lead a life as a creative individual. In this "You"-oriented period, the theme of relationship is always in the foreground and demands our definite corroboration that we, as integrated personalities, are productive in a new and unique way. We are producing something of value for society.

Life, in this Sun period, demands undivided attention from the human being. Everything that was painfully learned and gained blooms in this time of maturing. The meaning of the Sun years is fullness and openness to self-realization.

The Sun is symbolically represented as a circle with the fully aware personality as a point in the center. We only gain self-awareness when we experience our own identity in reality, in contact with the "You," with the world. That is why the signature of this period is conscious outward activity. The relationships and contact with the environment that we create on the strength of our personality control us fully during these years.

When we look at this life phase through the age point, we can recognize when we experience full self-realization. For example, if the Sun is positioned shortly after the seventh cusp (figure 2.5.8), we will try with every available power to secure a place in the world for ourselves at age thirty-six or so. We want to be important and indispensable to others. Everything we do is directed to finding recognition and appreciation from the "You," the partner.

With the Sun in the "You" sphere, we want to play an important role in our profession, in partnerships, and in society. Success is dependent upon the aspects the Sun receives. The transit of the AP to the Sun position triggers opportunities for self-realization. If we have not overcome the Moon period, then we have carried infantile behavior into the Sun period and cannot reach full maturity. We will be thrown back and forth by life and fate until we have reached and strengthened the center in ourselves, the Sun within, and evolved into peaceful beings who know who we are, what we want, and where we are going.

For example, with the Moon positioned in the sixth house carrying several tension aspects, we often find a certain

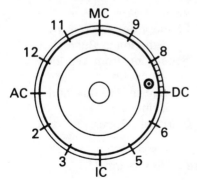

Figure 2.5.8. The natal seventh house Sun is activated by the AP around age 36.

psychological inability to deal with the existential challenges of life. We want to remain as children and refuse to take on self-responsibility; we usually find someone who looks after us. If the Sun happens to be in the eighth house we can look to the AP for an indication as to when these infantile and lunar needs are to be thrown off. Often it may take a considerable time to conclude a particular developmental phase.

● Transition to the Third Phase of Life

About forty-eight years of age, the Saturn period begins with a radical turnabout from the Sun phase. A switch from the extroverted, world-oriented Sun personality toward the spirit-oriented Saturn personality and its particular responsibilities occurs.

This change should already be happening at the low point of the eighth house (figure 2.5.9), about age forty-six, so that we may turn positively toward the ninth house cusp and be free from the value system of the outer world. Most often we are not prepared, because for twenty-four years we were formed and influenced by the strong Sun-like extroversion

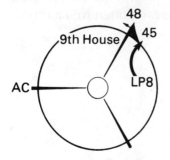

46-48 Years
Shadow Sphere LP8 to
    9th House Cusp
Separation from Worldly
    Ambition
Change in Attitude and
    Principles
Spiritual "Puberty"

Figure 2.5.9. The shadow sphere at low point 8.

and have had appropriate confirming successes. In such a case, the low point of the eighth house may only be an uncomfortable period, when nothing much will turn out right—a time we want to forget as soon as possible after it is over.

In such a case, it often happens that shortly before or after the ninth house cusp we suffer a heavy blow that shakes us up mentally. Therefore we must approach the low point of the ninth house (age forty-two) very gently and consciously, extracting the optimum genuine inner enlightenment in order to realize the fruits of our future. A change in personality is almost a forced necessity. By age forty-eight, we should begin to clearly reorient our life on ethical grounds. If we do this, the mind can become independent of the physical changes that take place during the aging process, and it can turn toward higher challenges.

Saturn can be experienced spiritually and become a genuine source of wisdom, being the summation of all preceding experiences, of two thirds of life. This stored inner capital can be expanded and made available to other people who are younger. We can advise them; we can take on tasks and responsibilities for them.

● The Last Third of Life

While the other two life periods were egocentrically involved and forward-moving, now the energies move back to the point of origin, the ascendant (figure 2.5.10). In this process of retreat and natural scaling down, certain discrepancies exist because of two forces: Saturnian crystallization, ie., the aging process, and the mental maturation process. Saturn can move in two directions. For people who live along materialistic dimensions and have always been physically fearful, perhaps even overly anxious, only the purely physical

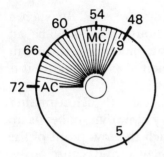

48-72 Years
Older Years, Mental Maturity
Houses 9 through 12
Saturn Period
Fixed Cross

Figure 2.5.10. The return to the point of origin; the journey from the ninth house to the ascendant.

is experienced. On the other hand, life experiences can solidify into mental clarity and wisdom.

What is important now is the level of growth that has been reached. Have we been able to comprehend the purpose of life at the turning point (age forty-eight), and have we adjusted our lives toward ethical and suprapersonal goals? Or have we been unable to adjust to reality, to the aging process, and as well to other changes in outer conditions? In the latter case unfortunately, Saturn is often only focused in the body. The decline of physical prowess becomes the main problem for many people. Anxiety over the body and its health can so dominate the consciousness that there is a constant preoccupation with the physical. The world and all that happens are seen only in terms of the physical condition and its context.

If we are successful in redirecting our lives and in giving new meaning to them, we can discover new life sources and, thus, new life styles. If we fail, the crystallizing energies of Saturn become stronger: feelings of depression, lack of meaning and direction, or even senility will win the upperhand and undermine all joy in living.

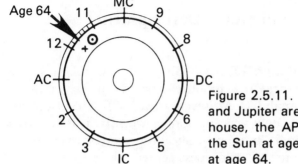

Figure 2.5.11. If the natal Sun and Jupiter are in the eleventh house, the AP would activate the Sun at age 61 and Jupiter at age 64.

We can see the influence of Saturn clearly in older people. Those who stay mentally awake and active also generally maintain their bodies without much effort. They are healthy and relatively young. But to guarantee this development, preparations must be started much earlier, i.e., in the first quadrant (or third) of life. It is not unnatural for adolescents to be intensely interested in spiritual matters, even though they will not pursue spiritual development at the same depth as someone in the third phase. The seed that is planted in the first quadrant will bear fruit later in life.

For example, if we have the Sun in the eleventh house (figure 2.5.11), at age sixty-one, as a result of the movement of the AP, we'll receive an infusion of self-confidence. If Jupiter follows nearby, then at age sixty-four there will be especially positive opportunities for consciously experiencing our lives' work; perhaps we write an autobiography or find a receptive audience for our thoughts. In this period for sure, there is a change of interests, of overall viewpoints, of basic attitudes, because life now responds to a different law than it has previously. The closer the AP gets to the ascendant, the stronger its magnetism will be felt, because in our total developmental scheme the AC represents the goal. (This is also true for interpretation of the basic horoscope analysis.)

● The Ascendant:
Focus of Individual Development

In the evolution of personality, the ascendant has a special significance. It symbolizes the "I" point in astropsychological analysis. At seventy-two self-perception becomes acute in a new way; no longer worldly, it is spiritual and suprapersonal. By now we should perceive ourselves the way we really are at our deepest center.

Figure 2.5.12 shows how the ascendant is both the beginning and end of life. Here the wheel of the houses closes; death and life lie closely together. At the ascendant, we come in from a void and enter life or we go again back to a void. That is why the ascendant at this age phase serves a double purpose: either we react positively to the renewed impulse to manifestation and feel revived, or we return to the void from which we came. At this "zero-sphere," the human being comes in touch with transcendental dimensions, which allow, if he is so inclined, a spiritual rebirth. We are assigned to two worlds: the visible material world and the invisible spiritual world. We become conscious of this through the crises at the ascendant which demand a clear inner attitude.

At age seventy-two, after passage of the AP over the ascendant, the mutable qualities of the first third of life

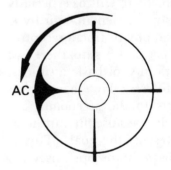

Figure 2.5.12. Our life starts at the AC and we complete the cycle by going back to the AC in order to begin anew.

become activated again. We are able to adjust more easily to changes in life because we leave the fixed cross and its holding patterns behind. We often go forth like newborn children.

Our journey through the wheel of houses began at the ascendant and ends at the same place. We can view our life again with distance and a different perception. We ask ourselves, "What did I want to accomplish in life? What should be brought to the foreground? Where did this long journey around the wheel of life lead me? What was and is the purpose, the meaning of my being?" We now can solve such questions; the answers will be unveiled by the sign at the ascendant to which we have returned.

Through further self-examination, we can recognize what we gained in the first phase through a consideration of the Moon's natal position. Through the Sun, we recognize how actively we were involved, how everyday problems presented themselves, and how we mastered them. At the ascendant, we finally recognize what we have made of life.

We should regard the ascendant in this light especially as it relates to the technique of age progression. It is much more important to see the ascendant as a goal direction, the meaning of our lives, rather than the attributes of the outer personality or physical appearance as is the custom in traditional astrology. The goal direction comes from the mental or psychological qualities of the signs. The "seed thought" of each sign describes our goal direction, what attitude and what qualities we should develop in ourselves.

The function of the ascendant as a guide to our correct attitude and an indication of the future is highly meaningful for us and helpful throughout life. So many people are in the dark and have no idea where they are going! They move in the wrong direction for long periods of time, often losing sight of their orientation or even their life goal. They know nothing about the compass-like influence of their ascendants and the possibilities for inner guidance they afford us.

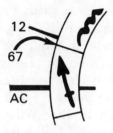

Figure 2.5.13. The AP reaches the sign on the ascendant at age 67.

When we reach the ascendant at age seventy-two, we have often entered the ascendant's sign some years before. Figure 2.5.13 shows a sample indicating that the AP entered the ascendant sign of Sagittarius at age 67. When this happens to an individual, he should begin to explore the inner qualities of the sign as well as its spiritual and psychological dimensions. We will find it relatively easy to identify ourselves with these qualities at this age. The ascending sign has become part of our inner self. Many people react to their ascending sign much sooner in life especially if planets are positioned there. Some, in later years, even lose their Sun characteristics completely!

● The Influence of Planets at the Ascendant

Planets at the ascendant have an especially strong effect. We can even go so far as to say that only an ascendant occupied by planets will be effective through the entire life.

When energy-laden planets such as Mars, Uranus, or Pluto are situated just before the ascendant (figure 2.5.14), prenatal traumatic influences can be inferred. During pregnancy, strong reactions may have been transferred from mother to child. Perhaps the mother had an accident or was

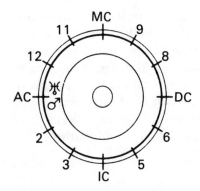

Figure 2.5.14. Mars and Uranus at the ascendant may indicate turbulent prenatal influences.

under strong psychological pressures. If Mars or Saturn is exactly on the ascendant, this often indicates difficult circumstances accompanying birth, such as a forceps delivery or a Caesarean section, or even acute danger to life during birth. Quiet planets such as Mercury or Jupiter before, on, or after the ascendant rarely affect the birth one way or another.

Difficulties after birth can be seen when planets are situated directly after the ascendant. We are referring, for example, to a difficult Neptune on the ascendant (figure 2.5.15) where a weakened baby may need to be put into an iron lung right after birth. Neptune as the planet of "diffusion," and placed on the ascendant, may have an influence that regresses into the void from which we came. Such children often are very delicate, "transcendental," have little will to live, and for an extended period of time long for a return to infinity.

Figure 2.5.15. Neptune conjunct the ascendant can indicate physical difficulties following birth.

Human beings with a strongly occupied twelfth house, especially the latter part of the twelfth, often have a contradictory nature. On the one hand, they tend to withdraw to the inner world; while on the other, they feel a longing to partake in the outer world. This is typical for the "shadow of the AC," where the duality of the two bordering houses (the twelfth and the first) present the simultaneous experience of contradicting energies—withdrawal and manifestation.

● Life Phases and the Three Primary Colors

Some revealing results can be gained from color psychology by projecting the primary colors red, yellow, and blue onto the horoscope wheel (figure 2.5.16). The primary colors correspond with three different psychological qualities and approaches in the individual life.

> Red—the manifestation or action color
> Yellow—the contact, motion color
> Blue—the retreat, separation, introversion color

We could call the Moon period "the red period" since red is the color of activity. In the first third of life, the human being tries actively to establish himself in life, to grow roots, and find a way to succeed.

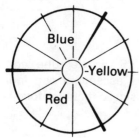

Figure 2.5.16. The three primary colors and their relation to the three quadrants in the horoscope.

The Sun period parallels the yellow phase when the human being lives mainly in the relationship to the environment, seeking contacts and fulfillment. In this phase, the community is most important.

The Saturn period begins around age forty-eight, when the AP reaches the ninth house cusp, the Sagittarian house. Here, the transformation to the blue phase occurs. Blue as the color of retreat expresses the opposite of red. Red manifests through action, blue through retreat or passivity. It is the quietest color. If we sit quietly at the window and watch life on the street, it means we are not actively involved anymore. In our "blue phase," the urge to take action decreases; the color blue symbolizes tranquility and purified energies.

Chapter 6

Division by Six—
Social Processes

Phase 1: being oneself (0-12 years)—Phase 2: belonging (12-24 years)—Phase 3: taking part (24-36 years)—Phase 4: voicing (36-48 years)—Phase 5: leading (49-60 years)—Phase 6: advising (60-72 years)—Turning points at the twelve house cusps—The six manifestation impulses—The six phases of crisis.

● Division by Six

Present-day psychology does not acknowledge regular rhythmic classifications that correspond to human development. It recognizes shorter and longer phases, especially in childhood, that are individually named and described. It is always pointed out, however, that each phase varies with the individual, that any phase can be shortened or lengthened or can even overlap with another for prolonged periods. A more exact individual life plan has not as yet been recognized.

In contrast, in the horoscope we approach the different developmental phases from a different point of view. We have

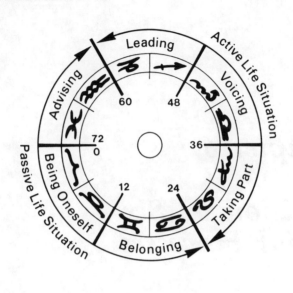

Figure 2.6.1. The six stages in the horoscope.

the means to recognize individual phases that may be prolonged, delayed, or overlapped. The following division by six is especially informative when evaluating psychological processes.

When we subdivide the three phases in the horoscope even further, we have six life phases of twelve years duration each. Each phase encompasses two houses. These pairs are comprised first of an active-masculine phase and then a passive-feminine phase.

● Phase 1: Age 0-12—Being Oneself

Houses one and two support "I" expression and "I" formation (figure 2.6.2). In the first, a masculine house, we

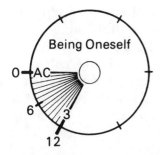

Figure 2.6.2. The first phase supports being: the expression and formation of the "I."

first experience the "I" through biological and psychological processes. Increasing demands for adjustment from the environment (parents, siblings, etc.) produce a crisis of the "absolute I" (an obstinate and defiant phase). This crisis leads to the second house, or a feminine phase, and to social defensiveness. Establishing "space," taking possession (children building tents, tree houses), bartering with possessions, are all essential processes in the development of a social personality.

• Phase 2: Age 12-24—Belonging

In houses three and four we want to take part (figure 2.6.3). The social personality expresses itself. We do not want to be alone, or we cannot be; we are dependent upon the

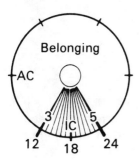

Figure 2.6.3. Concern for the development of social and familial ties occurs in phase two.

family; we want to be safe within the collective. We adjust to society by thinking along with it in the third house, and feeling along with it in the fourth. In the third house we actively take on the thought patterns of the collective (communicative and ideal-building phase), and in the feminine fourth house we adjust emotionally to the collective or the family. The selection of an appropriate collective or group leads to identification with a majority or minority. This decision can be significant for the whole life.

● Phase 3: Age 24-36—Taking Part

The activities of the fifth and sixth houses symbolize our attempts to become part of the world, to find our place, to make our mark (figure 2.6.4). The emphasis in both houses is on making and doing. In the fifth house, an active one, we try to establish the personality; we want to make an impression in order to have influence in the world (impress behavior, "vibes"). In the sixth, a passive house, we learn our limitations. Here, the "You" confronts us with concrete demands for performance and productivity. A second social crisis begins at age twenty-eight and demands from us existential or concrete, economic trial and proof. If responsibility for one's own life is not accepted and one continues to

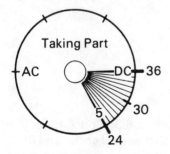

Figure 2.6.4. Phase three indicates the attempts made to become part of the world.

be a burden on others, social isolation or material difficulties may develop. This crisis in present times is especially emphasized among suburban married women trying to return to work.

● Phase 4: Age 36-48—Voicing

After crossing the descendant we are above the horizon in the conscious sphere of the horoscope (figure 2.6.5); here, thinking is more important than doing. Verbal participation is decisive for self-realization.

In the active seventh house we want to offer our concepts to the "You," to have a dialogue. Through contracts and agreements we try to establish a legal basis that serves the "You" and us equally. In the eighth house, we must find out how the environment reacts to our efforts to have our say in the world. We are being weighed, classified, even judged depending on our behavior and integration in the social structure. The sudden and increasing need for freedom in the face of approaching age sometimes leads to grotesque attempts to get rid of social pressures.

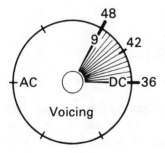

Figure 2.6.5. Conscious contact is made with the "you" in phase four.

Figure 2.6.6. Greater individuation accompanies phase five.

● Phase 5: Age 48-60—Leading

This phase (figure 2.6.6) supports increased individuation. After the phase of verbal participation, we try to actively integrate ourselves and understand the world through the ninth house. We establish a world view and become an authority on a given subject. Thus, in the tenth house, we may be called upon by the public to take on a responsible task or leading role. Burdensome responsibility, mainly during the tenth house phase, may lead to diminished pleasure in success (management stress). Toward the end of the tenth house phase, resignation may get the upper hand.

● Phase 6: Age 60-72—Advising

In this phase (figure 2.6.7), we become aware that our interest in the environment is waning and we are not as active as before. In the eleventh house phase, it is important to stay

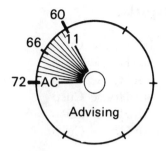

Figure 2.6.7. Interest in the environment is withdrawn during phase six.

mentally active in order to be in demand. By taking mental inventory we notice that, although outer activity is no longer required, our knowledge is needed that much more. The increasing confrontation with death can lead to a developmental panic. Reactions such as falling in love, being stubborn, etc., are called "childish" and "senile" by the environment. In the twelfth or passive house, we have to learn to be satisfied with ourselves and to find inner peace. We no longer pursue people to give them advice; we are simply there when needed.

● Turning Points at the Twelve House Cusps

The age point, when passing through the twelve houses, activates a developmental stage every six years. It therefore follows that, at the house cusp a more or less decisive turning point takes place. We can classify the houses according to alternating rhythms of active and passive impulses. At the twelve cusps, six manifestation impulses and six crisis points alternately occur either shortly before or shortly after the actual point of contact.

● The Six Manifestation Impulses

1. Birth	1st House Cusp
2. Physical Puberty	3rd House Cusp
3. Self-Manifestation	5th House Cusp
4. Status Seeking	7th House Cusp
5. Spiritual "Puberty"	9th House Cusp
6. Spiritual Manifestation	11th House Cusp

The manifestation impulses occur at the beginning of the active houses (figure 2.6.8). At the first house cusp, birth takes place; at the third (age twelve), puberty begins; at the fifth (age twenty-four), the phase of self-manifestation begins. Here, strong impulses for proving the self are triggered. At the cusp of the ninth house, age forty-eight, a kind of spiritual "puberty" begins, which is in contrast to the physical/emotional puberty that takes place at age twelve.

At age sixty, at the eleventh house cusp, a spiritual manifestation is experienced which is in contrast to the worldly self-manifestation of the fifth house phase. Here, creative impulses that were dreamed of at twenty-four are finally realized. The creative individual will use these later years to reap the mental or cultural-social harvest of experience and reflection and offer these back to society.

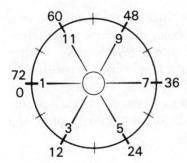

Figure 2.6.8. The active houses

● The Six Crisis Phases

1. Obstinate Phase	2nd House Cusp
2. Crisis of Ideals	4th House Cusp
3. Career Crisis	6th House Cusp
4. Frustration Phase	8th House Cusp
5. Authority Crisis	10th House Cusp
6. Isolation	12th House Cusp

In between the six active houses there are six passive crisis phases (figure 2.6.9). The first crisis phase (about age six) corresponds to the classic obstinate phase. About age eighteen, the young human being reaches a crisis of ideals. He must recognize that the world is stronger than his ideals and not likely to be changed.

With the career crisis at age thirty, we must recognize that we cannot do as we want. We have to adjust in order to survive. We should be able to be responsible for ourselves and to do our share for society joyfully.

About age forty-two the frustration phase begins. Here we find that the drive for status in the world has fallen short of expectation. Or if we have been successful, we become suddenly aware that external successes may not make us happy. In reality we seek love, warmth, and understanding, and we now tend to make up for suppressed and unfulfilled desires from earlier years.

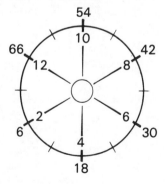

Figure 2.6.9. The passive houses.

At age fifty-four, we encounter an authority crisis that reveals how competent we really are. Here we must clearly understand our task and accept our limitations. Our authority may be rejected or corrected. We can fall from a height if we have not built a solid base.

The old-age phase (sixty-six years) can be termed an isolation phase. The emphasis is upon accepting loneliness while maintaining self-satisfaction. If this is not possible, the dissatisfaction is often expressed in some form of illness or senility.

Chapter 7

Age Progression in the Horoscope of Jimmy Carter

The age progression with age point data—The life of Jimmy Carter—
Difficult childhood (age 2-13)—Years in the navy (age 18-29)—Economic
build-up and times of crisis (age 29-38)—Political struggle (age 38-42)—
Inner changes and religious experience (age 42-46)—Political ascent (age 46-
56).

● Life Developments in the
Horoscope of Jimmy Carter

This chapter is presented to give you an example of how
the age point works in a horoscope. Table 2.7.1. shows you a
computer calculated printout showing key periods of activity
and stress. These major activity periods have been added to
Carter's natal horoscope in Figure 2.7.1, so you can easily see
how the age point can be used. The rest of the chapter is a
discussion of the specifics of Carter's life as it relates to the age
point data. Carter's political and personal information is
taken from his autobiography, *Why Not the Best.*

Table 2.7.1. Age Point Dates in Jimmy Carter's Life

The following table is an Astrodate-Computer calculated age progression. Dates marked with a bullet (●) are referred to in the text.

***	Age 16	***
1 Nov	1940	OPP PLUT
7 Nov	1940	SXT LUNA
31 Dec	1940	SSX JUPI
13 Oct	1941	SXT URAN
1 Feb	1942	QCX NODE
18 Mar	1942	TRI MERC
28 Apr	1942	QCX NEPT
6 Aug	1942	QCX VENU

***	Age 18	***
1 Oct	1942	HC 4
2 Feb	1943	SSX G.C.
8 Feb	1943	SSX MARS
16 Dec	1943	IN Aqu
8 May	1944	SQR SATU

***	Age 20	***
15 Jan	1945	IP 4
15 Aug	1945	TRI SOL
● 17 Jun	1946	LP 4

***	Age 22	***
3 Oct	1946	QCX PLUT
10 Oct	1946	SQR LUNA
10 Dec	1946	SXT JUPI
5 Nov	1947	SSX URAN
12 Mar	1948	OPP NODE
3 May	1948	QCX MERC
18 Jun	1948	OPP NEPT

***	Age 24	***
1 Oct	1948	HC 5
12 Oct	1948	OPP VENU

● 21 Apr	1949	CON MARS
21 Feb	1950	IN Pis
14 Jul	1950	TRI SATU

***	Age 26	***
16 Jan	1951	IP 5
14 Oct	1951	QCX SOL
16 Jun	1952	LP 5

***	Age 28	***
24 Nov	1952	TRI PLUT
1 Dec	1952	TRI LUNA
31 Jan	1953	SQR JUPI
● 21 Dec	1953	CON URAN
26 Apr	1954	QCX NODE
17 Jun	1954	OPP MERC
2 Aug	1954	QCX NEPT

***	Age 30	***
1 Oct	1954	HC 6
23 Nov	1954	QCX VENU
26 May	1955	SQR G.C.
1 Jun	1955	SSX MARS
31 Mar	1956	IN Ari
● 19 Aug	1956	QCX SATU

***	Age 32	***
15 Jan	1957	IP 6
15 Nov	1957	OPP SOL
17 Jun	1958	LP 6

***	Age 34	***
25 Dec	1958	SQR PLUT
31 Dec	1958	QCX LUNA

Table 2.7.1. Continued

29	Feb	1959	TRI	JUPI			
18	Jan	1960	SSX	URAN			
21	May	1960	TRI	NODE			
11	Jul	1960	QCX	MERC			
26	Aug	1960	TRI	NEPT			

8 Apr	1971	SSX	PLUT

```
29 Feb 1959 TRI JUPI        •  8 Apr 1971 SSX PLUT
18 Jan 1960 SSX URAN          15 Apr 1971 QCX LUNA
21 May 1960 TRI NODE          14 Jun 1971 OPP JUPI
11 Jul 1960 QCX MERC           5 May 1972 SQR URAN
26 Aug 1960 TRI NEPT           7 Sep 1972 SXT NODE

***      Age 36      ***     ***      Age 48      ***

 1 Oct 1960 HC   7             1 Oct 1972 HC   9
18 Dec 1960 TRI VENU          26 Oct 1972 SQR MERC
24 Jun 1961 TRI G.C.           5 Dec 1972 SXT NEPT
30 Jun 1961 SXT MARS          15 Mar 1973 SXT VENU
 5 May 1962 IN  Tau           26 Aug 1973 OPP G.C.
•26 Sep 1962 OPP SATU         31 Aug 1973 TRI MARS
***      Age 38      ***      28 May 1974 IN  Can
                            • 1 Oct 1974 TRI SATU
16 Jan 1963 IP   7
 1 Jan 1964 QCX SOL          ***      Age 50      ***
16 Jun 1964 LP   7
                             16 Jan 1975 IP   9
***      Age 40      ***      8 Nov 1975 SQR SOL
                             16 Jun 1976 LP   9
16 Feb 1965 SXT PLUT
23 Feb 1965 OPP LUNA         ***      Age 52      ***
25 Apr 1965 QCX JUPI
19 Mar 1966 SXT URAN        • 1 Nov 1976 CON PLUT
24 Jul 1966 SQR NODE          7 Nov 1976 TRI LUNA
15 Sep 1966 TRI MERC         30 Dec 1976 QCX JUPI
                             13 Oct 1977 TRI URAN
***      Age 42      ***     31 Jan 1978 SSX NODE
                             18 Mar 1978 SXT MERC
 1 Oct 1966 HC   8           27 Apr 1978 SSX NEPT
•31 Oct 1966 SQR NEPT         6 Aug 1978 SSX VENU
22 Feb 1967 SQR VENU
27 Aug 1967 QCX G.C.         ***      Age 54      ***
 1 Sep 1967 SQR MARS
 4 Jul 1968 IN  Gem           1 Oct 1978 HC  10
                              2 Feb 1979 QCX G.C.
***      Age 44      ***    • 8 Feb 1979 QCX MARS
                             15 Dec 1979 IN  Leo
23 Nov 1968 QCX SATU        • 8 May 1980 SQR SATU
15 Jan 1969 IP   8
•24 Feb 1970 TRI SOL         ***      Age 56      ***
17 Jun 1970 LP   8
                             15 Jan 1981 IP  10
***      Age 46      ***     15 Aug 1981 SXT SOL
```

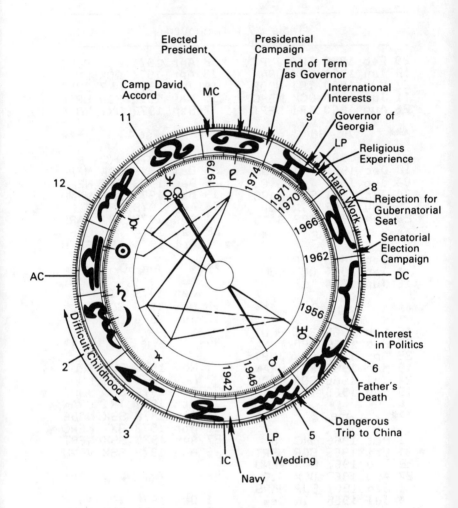

Figure 2.7.1. Jimmy Carter's horoscope. He was born on October 1, 1924 at 6:42 AM CST in Plains, Georgia. Data is courtesy of the Carter family; Koch Houses are used in this chart. Dates on the inner wheel correspond to events listed on the outer circle.

Age 2-13 (1925-1938)
Difficult Childhood
AP in 1st and 2nd Houses:
Scorpio and Sagittarius
AP Contacts with Saturn, Moon, Jupiter

When we study Carter's horoscope, we find two personal planets in the first quadrant—Saturn and the Moon. This indicates an important molding of the personality took place in childhood. Harsh physical discipline was demanded of him which in turn was helpful to him in later years.

Jimmy was the oldest of four children. His father was a farmer. The family lived in a rural setting, far from any comforts. There were outhouses for toilet facilities. Water came manually from a well. Young Jimmy had to rise at 4 AM and work on the farm. The conditions of his childhood were hard and primitive. He himself writes that he lived and worked as if he had been born in the Middle Ages.

In those days, the AP crossed Saturn and the Moon. Saturn in Scorpio is often assigned such hardships. How the hardships are handled is what matters. The AP transit of the Moon indicates that these living conditions influenced the Moon "I" deeply and gave rise to an attitude of renunciation of anything that made life easy. This time also formed his character. It made him tough and determined to reach his goals despite all odds.

After the AP passage of the Moon, at approximately eleven years of age, the AP reached Jupiter in Sagittarius. This AP contact enabled Jimmy to overcome his hard childhood, to keep his faith and joy in life, and even to translate his experiences into a life philosophy. The basis for his ethics is grounded here. According to indications from his family, it was at this age that he spoke of his wish to become president for the first time (quincunx Pluto).

Age 18-29 (1942-1953)
Navy Years
AP in 4th and 5th Houses:
Aquarius and Pisces
AP Contacts with Mars and Uranus

At age eighteen, Carter entered the Naval Academy at Annapolis. He was the first in his family who went to college.

In July of 1946, exactly at low point 4, he married Rosalynn. She bore him three sons (1947, 1950, 1951:AP passage through the fifth house).

These years were spent on board an atomic submarine under the command of Admiral Rickover, who made a deep and lasting impression on Carter.

When the AP crossed the fifth house cusp several things happened at once. He passed his examination as a navy officer in December, 1948, and moved with his wife and son Jack to New London, Connecticut. Two days later he had to leave them to take part in dangerous maneuvers in the Pacific near China. In 1953 his father died, exactly at the transit of the AP over Uranus; Carter's life changed suddenly.

Age 29-38 (1953-1962)
Economic Build-Up and Times of Crisis
AP in the 6th and 7th Houses: Aries
AP Opposition to Sun

After the death of his father, Carter decided to return home. He left the Navy and returned to Plains with his wife Rosalynn. He fought with her because she did not want to go back to Georgia. Carter wanted to use the farm in order to make his living. In the beginning, business was not very good; there was a drought, and he could not get credit from the bank. This is often a sixth house lesson: we learn our limitations and some humility and then carry on.

In 1956, Carter discovered politics. His age point reached the cardinal sign Aries, which awakens personal courage and political ambitions. As the first sign of the zodiac, it often indicates a new cycle. The personal energies are activated; Carter was able to express himself and his ideas. By this time, he held several offices already, but they had little political significance.

When the AP approached a quincunx to Saturn, he was called to fill a position on the School Board. From then on, he concerned himself with questions of educational politics. He developed a reorganization program, but his proposal was not accepted. The unaspected Saturn gave him some difficulties: mostly physical insecurity and an unclear sense of reality. Carter wanted to accomplish too much too soon and first had to learn to adapt his ideas to existing circumstances. He writes that he learned a lot during this period (the will-building and learning quincunx aspect to Saturn).

In November 1957, the AP reached the opposition to his twelfth house Sun, whose single aspect natally is a square to Pluto. This always indicates difficult conditions for successful self-realization. Carter found himself in difficult situations over and over again. He felt called upon to uncover political misrepresentations, which brought him enemies and even lawsuits. He committed himself totally to the task and writes, "...I worked day and night in order to gather evidence. My opponent and his friends also worked feverishly. The fight took place on two fronts which were totally independent of each other."

Age 38-42 (1962-1966)
Political Struggle
AP in 7th and 8th Houses:
Taurus and Gemini
AP Opposition Saturn and Moon

For the whole time that the AP passed through the sign Aries, Jimmy Carter fought for political attention. He aspired to a seat in the State Senate of Georgia, and in 1962 he won after a heavy election fight. The AP moved into Taurus and reached the opposition to Saturn in the same year. Again it was the unaspected Saturn that almost lost the victory: his opponent threatened to contest the election results. Carter prepared for a renewed fight, but the threat was withdrawn, and Carter was finally the uncontested victor. When the legislative period ended in spring 1966 he entered the race for governor.

Before the AP reached the eighth house cusp he began with the help of his family to mount a hectic election campaign. He had no support. He was so unknown in Georgia, that several journalists called him "Jimmy Who?" This is typical of a Sun in the twelfth house, "the man who came from nowhere."

By election time in November 1966, the AP had reached the cusp of the eighth house and was square Neptune and the Node. This aspect in opposition to Mars on the 11/5 axis* indicates in the natal chart a relationship problem. Carter lost the election; he was rejected. He writes, "This experience was extremely disappointing. I was deeply in debt and had lost twenty pounds."

In addition to the Mars-Neptune opposition in the natal horoscope, the Node-Venus conjunction indicates far-reaching social plans but also a miscalculation of existing relationship possibilities. The age point square to these planets from the eighth house brought about the need for an inner transformation. As long as he was only striving for the realization of his political ideals on a worldly level, he was unable to succeed.

---

*The relationship axis is discussed in *Man and His World*, p. 80-83.

Age 42-46 (1966-1970)
Inner Change and Religious Experience
AP at 8th House Cusp to Low Point:
Taurus, Gemini
AP Opposition Jupiter

After losing the first election, Carter received spiritual support from his sister Ruth, which had a transformative and renewing effect on him. Carter describes it as being reborn. He gave more and more of his energies to needy people. Carter had to experience rejection in order to live through the changes characteristic of the eighth house. Enlightenment came after the low point at age forty-six, and he was ready to become governor.

In his autobiography, he describes this period, "My life in the church community gained a new meaning and each year together with fellow Christians I went on missions to other states or to special areas of Georgia." Deep religious experiences were repeated again and again. On a mission to Mexico he "experienced the reality of God in a way as never before."

He took his political tasks and responsibilities very seriously at this time. Carter describes this period in this way, "From 1966 to 1970 I worked with more concentration and intensity than ever before. I tried to gain knowledge on as many subjects as possible, to build the seed business into a profitable and stable firm and to carefully work out a political strategy in order to win the 1970 election for governor."

Age 46-56 (1970-1980)
Political Ascent
AP in 8th, 9th, and 10th Houses:
Gemini, Cancer, Leo
AP Conjunction Pluto

In 1970, at age forty-six, after low point 8, Carter tried again for the governorship, and this time he won the election campaign (January, 1971). The age point was exactly semi-sextile to Pluto.

As the AP neared the ninth house cusp Carter reorganized the whole administration and bureaucracy of the state of Georgia and fought against race discrimination. Many influential people were against him, and he had to swallow much criticism. Many found him too stiff and dogmatic in his goals (a typical situation before a house cusp, similar to the phase before the eighth house cusp).

In 1974, when the AP was trine Saturn, the governorship came to an end. He prepared for the national election campaign for president, "Our strategy was simple, to give it everything all over the country. After leaving the governor's seat, I visited in the first few months more than half of all the states, some of them several times. Each visit was thoroughly prepared...." It was typical of his unaspected Saturn that Carter led his campaign alone, without prestige or support from big-interest groups. Outside Georgia, he was almost unknown. During the trine from the AP to Saturn, he was able to convert the poor conditions for a presidential election into positive ones.

In 1976, Carter won the race against Gerald Ford and became president. The AP was exactly conjunct Pluto. Pluto always symbolizes power of some kind. In Carter's horoscope, Pluto is the most elevated planet, situated shortly after the low point of the ninth house. It is characteristic that he became president when the AP crossed Pluto, that he gained power which, according to the theme of the ninth house, he could use only for the benefit of others. This also suggests that his motives for becoming president were humanitarian and religious ones. With the exception of Kennedy, no one in American politics since Lincoln had spoken about religious issues! Only a man with intense idealistic powers, as indicated by the opposition between Mars and Neptune/Venus/Node, could dare to introduce religious thinking into politics. In Carter's case, the stubbornness of this aspect works positively, although there is always a tendency toward exaggeration. The President of the United States has enough checks and balances, however, to keep his extremist tendencies from succeeding.

Carter's preoccupation with human rights has kept the issue in the news. In the spring of 1979, when the AP was in quincunx to Mars, he was able to negotiate a peace treaty between Israel's Begin and Egypt's Sadat. That surely was a high point in his political career. To be a mediator and peacemaker for two hostile parties is a true Libra function and also the greatest victory!

Carter's age point reached another change of sign (Leo) at the end of 1979 and then, in May 1980, a square to Saturn. On May 8th, he attempted to free the hostages in Iran and failed. That hurt his image and popularity greatly. He lost many supporters and continued to lose the trust of the people.

During the summer of 1980, he was still under the Saturn square. The influence of a past aspect can last until a new aspect comes into play. He postponed many decisions, and the impression of unsureness emerged. This is a typical expression of Saturn, especially if there are no connections to other planets. Saturn, symbol of the principle of limitations, was involved in this painful rejection. He lost the presidential election to Ronald Reagan in the fall of 1980, even though the age point formed no aspects.

Appendix

The Huber Method: An Introduction to Astrological Psychology

Drawing the chart—The four levels of man—Basic functions of the planets—Planets in signs—Planets in houses—Strong and weak planetary positions—Aspects—Aspect configurations on structures of consciousness —Sign and house correspondences.

• Drawing the Chart

The aspect structure is of the greatest importance in the astrological-psychological analysis of the horoscope. It represents a picture of the consciousness of a human being. Deep life motivations, unconscious tendencies, and inner life goals are visible in the aspect structure, especially within the spatial and timed positions that become obvious when a house system is used. For this reason, we draw the horoscope differently than most astrologers do. We want to see the aspect structures as clearly as possible. Using this kind of a wheel enables us to

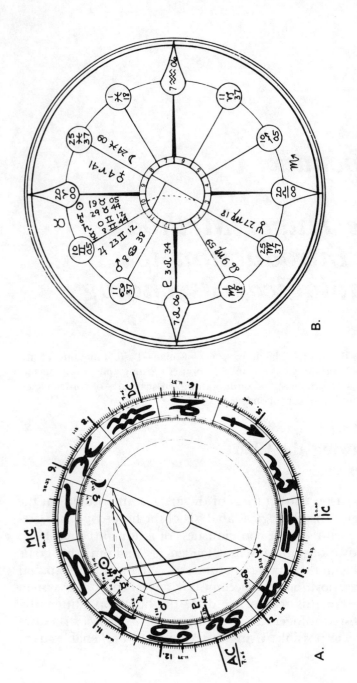

Figure 1. a) The chart showing the houses drawn in according to size, with aspects clearly visible. b) The traditional chart blank with predrawn houses. Both charts were calculated for a birth time of 11:30 AM, May 10, 1942 in Zurich, Switzerland.

see individual problems within a few hours, while it would take a testing psychologist many more hours of work.

Most Americans use a chart form with equal house sections. We feel that this doesn't show the aspect relationship as clearly as the one we like to use. Our charts are drawn using a 360° basis—which means the size of each house will vary according to the number of degrees in the house, giving a graphic image of the aspect picture. Figure 1 shows the difference between a chart calculated using our chart blank in contrast to the form where the houses are already set up.

The horoscope that is calculated to the exact time and location of birth is the basis of any astrological analysis. Those who are not yet familiar with horoscope calculation can either learn the technique from a textbook, or by taking a class. Many curious students order computer-calculated charts from the various chart services known to bookstores and advertised widely in astrological publications.

● The Four Levels of Man

In astrological psychology we basically distinguish between four layers in the horoscope. These layers are arranged around an inner core, from inside to outside as shown in figure 2.

1. The Aspect Picture = Consciousness Structure
2. The Planets = Vehicles of Life or Vital Functions
3. The Signs = Predispositions
4. The Houses = Behavior

These four levels, together with the inner circle, symbolize the whole human being. They must always be analyzed in relation to each other.

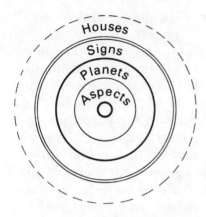

Figure 2. The four layers of the horoscope.

Newspaper astrology only focuses upon one astrological element, the position of the Sun in relation to the zodiac. A very one-sided picture of man emerges since the nine other planets, the twelve houses, and any number of aspects are totally ignored. People with the same Sun sign don't share the same destiny. The similarities that do exist are indirect and consist of a more or less basic collective attitude and motivation toward life. Each human being has his own horoscope in which all the planets appear. The Sun is only one factor. Also, the horizon line of the birthplace (rotation of the earth) changes constantly, so that the ascendant changes as well. (The ascendant is the sign rising on the eastern horizon at the moment of birth at the place of birth).

● Basic Function of the Ten Planets

The ten planets (actually eight planets plus the Sun and Moon) represent certain life functions and character traits which are present in all human beings. Each is a potential life

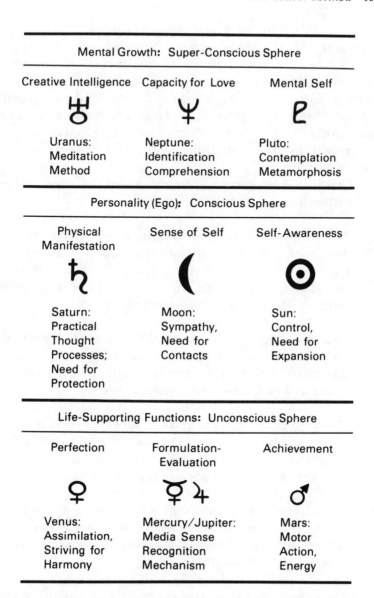

Figure 3. Planetary keywords for the various factors that encompass a personality.

force we can use in life. Figure 3 gives us some keywords, but none of the planets can be categorized definitively or finalized with one term because they appear in different combinations and connections. A planet is a symbol and can only be analyzed correctly within the context of the total astrological picture. One of the ten basic functions in the human being can hardly be put into action meaningfully if it is not understood in its connection with other elements in the horoscope.

Consider these essential definitions of the ten faculties within the human being.

⊙ *The Sun* represents the mentality of the human being, that is, the quality and condition of self-awareness. It represents the vital energies and has a directing function in relationship to the planets. Its most important function is the willful direction of energy.

☽ *The Moon* shows the emotional nature of man, his wish for contacts on all levels, and his need for tenderness and understanding. As the reflecting principle, its central function is sensitive adaptation to life.

☿ *Mercury* enables us to assimilate our experiences mentally. It symbolizes our need for learning, gathering information and knowledge, and translates everything into words and concepts (communication).

♀ *Venus,* as the aesthetic principle, always seeks balance and harmony in order to reach a condition of perfection. It is an introverted tool of selection in any assimilation process, the female libido.

♂ *Mars* expresses productive energy, the ability to convert energy into performance and work. Mars symbolizes extroverted involvement and motion, the masculine libido.

♃ *Jupiter* symbolizes the sense function with which we perceive the world: sensuous joy, value consciousness, capacity for judgement, perspective, and fairness.

♄ *Saturn* corresponds to the physical, the sense of form, the need for order and demarcation that secure and protect life but also may make it more difficult. Saturn's symbolism suggests security and the wish for peace and comfort as well as maintenance of the status quo.

The three recently discovered planets, Uranus, Neptune and Pluto, represent the higher spiritual abilities of man.

♅ *Uranus* is creative intelligence, seeking new horizons in everything; the spirit of research and discovery; gaining security through technical or spiritual systems.

♆ *Neptune* is universal love, our highest love ideal; the ability to identify idealism; the will to help; social involvement.

♇ *Pluto* symbolizes the higher self, the spiritual will, the essential motivational forces which can transform the persona (in the Jungian sense). Metamorphosis of personality.

• Planets in Signs

A planet never stands alone in the horoscope; it is always placed in a certain sign and house and, at the same time, usually in angular relationships (aspects) with other planets. The basic quality of a planet is modified by its position in a certain sign. It gains a specific coloration. For example, Jupiter in the sign Libra symbolizes awareness focused upon the "You." This awareness is stimulated by the "You," because Libra is a "You" sign. If Jupiter is in Aries, an "I" sign, our awareness is focused through the "I," and we perceive what we would like to see. We perceive what is beneficial for ourselves, what would be helpful to the self, and what would support, promote, and verify self-awareness or self-confidence.

The signs represent nature and the laws of nature, and therefore they represent all the structures that we have inherited genetically. From the position of the planets in certain signs we can see what is called *predisposition* (or heredity) in psychology.

• Planets in Houses

Each planet occupies not only a certain sign, but also one of the twelve houses of the horoscope. The twelve houses represent specific life arenas. They are fields of activity in which we can experience and be active. They indicate the whole range of life possibilities. Since the houses represent the sensitizing mechanism into which we are born, we can read the effects of environment and education in childhood and youth from them.

If Jupiter, as mentioned earlier, is in the sign Aries (see figure 4), it helps us to perceive those things that serve the development of the "I"; if Jupiter is additionally in the third house, which has to do with collective thinking, then the environment will support one's own learning. We will receive from the collective that which will help us along in our development and through which we will be able to expand

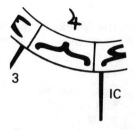

Figure 4. The placement of a planet in a sign and house gives us an opportunity to see the coloration of the personality. Here Jupiter is placed in Aries in the third house.

our knowledge with relative ease. Houses are essential for the analysis of how a human being will be able to develop in life. Through the position of the planets in the houses, we know if specific abilities, as characterized by the planets, will develop or remain latent.

● Strong and Weak Planetary Positions

Next we have to consider how the signs and, more so the houses, are arranged so that we will know if a planet can express itself outwardly or if there are obstacles. This depends on the planet's position: is it strongly or weakly situated in the sign, at a cusp, or at the low point of a house?

When we want to determine how powerful a planet is we must keep these factors in mind. A planet is always in a sign of the zodiac; in a house; in connection with other planets (specific aspects).

A planet can be either strongly or weakly positioned in each sign and in each house. In both reference systems, there are different positions of strength. This is a relatively new assertion, resulting from empirical research in daily counseling practice. Figure 5 shows how this works.

*See *Man and His World,* pages 95-103.

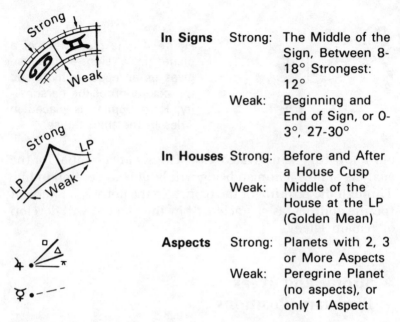

In Signs	Strong:	The Middle of the Sign, Between 8-18° Strongest: 12°
	Weak:	Beginning and End of Sign, or 0-3°, 27-30°
In Houses	Strong:	Before and After a House Cusp
	Weak:	Middle of the House at the LP (Golden Mean)
Aspects	Strong:	Planets with 2, 3 or More Aspects
	Weak:	Peregrine Planet (no aspects), or only 1 Aspect

Figure 5. The strength and weakness of certain signs, houses and aspects.

These three factors must be weighed against each other. The position of relative strength or weakness of a planet in a house essentially determines the person's ability to cope with life.

● Aspects

Next in importance to the sign and house positions of a planet are the aspects and their modifying relationship with other planetary forces. It is clear that if Venus, for example, is connected to Jupiter, aesthetic grows into sensuous joy. If Venus is affected by a Saturn aspect, the lightness of Venus is reduced. This manifests either as a seriousness toward life, a sense of responsibility, depth, or an attitude which rejects all life joys through moralization. It depends on the kind of aspect. The aspects of the AP will be discussed in Volume II.

In the astrological-psychological analysis of the horoscope and the AP, we only use the seven classical aspects originally used by Ptolemy. These are the multiples of 30° and include 60°, 90°, 120°, 150°, 180° and, of course, the conjunction or 0°. Other schools of thought use 45° and 135° aspects, but they are not used here as we feel they leave holes in the aspect structure. By not drawing in these aspects they become visible holes.

0° Conjunction (Orange) ♂
Seed, talent, chain of components, inner tensions (mostly subconscious)

90° Square (Red) ☐
Tension-release, power, production, friction, tendency toward stress or aggression

180° Opposition (Red) ♂
Energy blockage, pressure, rigidity, tendency toward repression (displacement and compensation through other aspects)

30° Semi-Sextile (Green) ⊻
"Small Ideas," informative (recognizing, mediating), objectivity, lack of interest

150° Quincunx (Green) ⊼
"Big Ideas," will-strengthening, challenge, yearning, tendency toward projection

60° Sextile (Blue) ✶
Growth, assimilation, striving for harmony, fear of conflict, tendency toward compromise

120° Trine (Blue) △
Fullness, blossoming (also compulsion toward perfectionism), sensual joy, tendency toward indulgence or addiction

---

In order to absorb the aspect structure with our senses, we draw the different aspects in four colors, as derived from color psychology:

0°	Orange	— intensive contact, direct, binding
90 & 180°	Red	— active, tense, action/efficiency-oriented
60 & 120°	Blue	— restful, relaxed, harmony-oriented
30 & 150°	Green	— flexible, informative, seeking, undecided

● Aspect Configuration or Structures of Consciousness

The arrangement of the whole aspect-configuration within the horoscope, its dynamic direction, coherence and coloration are the first steps to consider when delineating a chart using astrological psychology.

The planets with all their aspects result in a portrait of the individual consciousness of a human being (see figure 6).

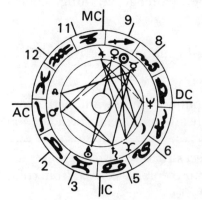

Figure 6. When the aspects are drawn in the natal chart it becomes easy to see the portrait of the individual.

This aspect picture represents an individual's central motivation and the structure of consciousness. It shows the human being as a whole at the deepest levels of being. The aspect structure can be absorbed in one glance. To the trained eye, it reveals the coloration, arrangement, structure, and the problems of a human being's individuation. It can be viewed as an inner blueprint, an energy pattern, in response to which consciousness moves and acts.

So viewed, the aspect picture is a dynamic lineal structure, a living, pulsating whole, moving according to life motivations. Motivation causes force, and this force most often manifests as energy in motion toward a certain goal. Coming from within, the focus is upon developing certain life qualities that aid in self-realization. We can deduce the inner concentration of motivational forces from the aspect configuration. For example, if the aspect structure is concentrated in the thinking quadrant, the human being will concentrate mainly on the theoretical, philosophical knowledge of the world and society.

A short definition of the meaning of certain color combinations will be helpful in analysis. These color combinations are easily discernable when you draw in the aspects using the color codes previously outlined in this section.

Red and Blue = ambivalence, thinking in terms of black or white, creative contradiction, overcompensation, swinging back and forth, striving for diplomacy and harmony.

Red and Green = restlessness, the spirit of contradiction, the tendency to exploit, thinking about productivity without attaining goals, loss of energy, wanting to get the most out of a situation.

Blue and Green =   tendency toward flight (evasive aspects), undefined unstable attitudes, roving fantasy, not oriented toward achievement, able to understand experiences.

Red-Green-Blue =   conditioned growth, strong developmental possibilities through continuous crisis which has three phases: conflict, striving for solution, harmonizing.

• Sign and House Correspondence

Another tool of astrological psychology is the correspondence between sign and house: to what degree the function of the house and the quality of the sign help or hinder each other. This method, like age progression, is new and revolutionary in astrology. It evolved through daily counseling practice along with the latest findings in psychology.

We begin with the assumption that there are always two forces opposed to each other—predisposition and education. Comparing planetary positions in signs and houses shows if there is harmony or conflict between predisposition and education. This is an important analytical tool since most problems develop because of the divergence between inner needs and outer pressures, i.e., between sign and house. We have developed a method of counting which expresses this divergence in numbers (12) and which allows for a differentiated analysis.

Right now, it is enough to determine the harmony or divergence between sign and house in their quadruplicities and triplicities (see **AP** through the Signs, page 91). For example, if a fixed sign falls in a mutable house, it becomes clear that the environment is trying to change certain characteristics, to make the person something other than he is. If a cardinal sign falls in a cardinal house, the development of life forces is supported, or at least not suppressed.

In the earlier example Jupiter in the third house—the environment affords the opportunity to learn and study, and through this, a certain behavior is developed. Such behavior, a product of education and environment, becomes activated when the age point moves through the house. When the AP moves through a house whose qualities played a constructive role in our upbringing, we know how to behave. We may react in a constructive manner when corresponding challenges or opportunities come our way. We may have also taken on negative behavior patterns. Then, we react to demands with anxiety and negativity. We might feel constantly under pressure, unable to free ourselves from restrictions. In time, this could cause psychological problems. The signs and houses interrelate and help us diagnose the potential for such types of life response.

Recommended Reading List

Addey, John M. *Harmonics in Astrology*. London: Fowler, 1976.

Bailey, Alice. *Esoteric Astrology*. New York: Lucis Publishing, 1951.

Carter, Jimmy. *Why Not the Best?* Nashville, TN: Broadman Press, 1975.

Huber, Bruno and Louise. *Man and His World*. York Beach, ME: Samuel Weiser, 1978. Now published under the title *The Astrological Houses*.

Jaffe, A. and C. G. Jung. *Memories, Dreams, & Reflections*. New York: Random House, 1961.

Krishnamurti, Jiddu. *Freedom from the Known*. Ojai: Krishnamurti Foundation, 1969.

Ruperti, Alexander. *Cycles of Becoming*. Reno, NV: CRS Publications, 1978.

Index

LIFECLOCK

Volume 2
Life Clock: Practical Techniques for Counseling Age Progression in the Horoscope

Bruno and Louise Huber

Translated by Transcript, Ltd.

SAMUEL WEISER, INC.

York Beach, Maine

Dedication

"Die Zeit vergeht, und die Weisheit bleibt.
Sie wechselt ihre Formen und Riten, aber sie beruht
zu allen Zeiten auf demselben Fundament: auf
die Einordnung des Menschen in die Natur, in
den kosmischen Rhythmus."

Hermann Hesse

*Time moves on, but Wisdom remains. She varies
her forms and rites, yet rests in every period
on one and the same foundation: the incorporation
of Mankind in Nature, in the rhythm of the Cosmos.*

Contents

Symbols of the planets

Sun	☉		♂		Mars
Moon	☽		♃		Jupiter
Saturn	♄		♅	(⛢)	Uranus
Mercury	☿		♆		Neptune
Venus	♀		♇	(♇)	Pluto
Dragon's Head	☊				

Symbols of the Signs

Aries	♈		♎	Libra
Taurus	♉		♏	Scorpio
Gemini	♊		♐	Sagittarius
Cancer	♋		♑	Capricorn
Leo	♌		♒	Aquarius
Virgo	♍		♓	Pisces

Abbreviations

AC = Ascendant   AP = Age Point

IC = Imum Coeli   HC = House Cusp

DC = Descendant   LP = Low Point

MC = Medium Coeli   IP = Invert Point

Synonyms: Age Progression, Hand on the Life Clock, Age Point (AP)

Acknowledgments

To all the friends who devote themselves so unreservedly to our Work and are always there when needed, we should like to express our warmest thanks. Our gratitude is also due to our colleagues for their active help in the preparation of this book.

Mirjam Bertsch
Daniel Cuny
Marianne Egli
Dr. Maja Hodler
Michael-A. Huber
Margrit Huser-Schwaninger
Rita Keller
Johanna Kohler
John Portmann
Jak Riger
Lilian Schatz
Max Senn
Werner Stephan
Irene Wieser
Lydia Wittlin

And we should also like to thank for their patience all those who have waited so long for this book to appear.

Note to the Reader

In the last few years much new knowledge has been won in regard to the application of the Age Progression method, and we can now take a look at it in this second volume. In Volume 1 we presented full details of the structure, mode of action, and technique of Age Progression, as well as the phases and cycles in life and in the horoscope. In Volume 2 we can concentrate on how all these rules work in practice. In order to bring the dry bones of the subject to life, we include interesting case histories, and present a new way of looking at aspects which you will find useful when reading your own horoscope. Considerable attention is devoted to the meanings of the planets, and this has been done quite deliberately so that you can work out what is likely to happen when the Age Point transits a planetary position. This will enable you to obtain the greatest possible help from Age Progressions, both in daily life and in your astrological studies. Above all you will be persuaded of the correctness of the method. It has been very satisfying to hear—from many in the astrological fraternity and from lay people alike—how well the Age Point corresponds to life. And you have only to read the biography of C.G. Jung as given in this book to reach the same conclusion.

There is still much to add on the subject of Age Progression as a new science of biological cycles. The present volume is by no means a full statement of everything known about it and a third volume entitled *The Spiritual Meaning of the Age Point* has just been published in German.

Bruno and Louise Huber

Part I

*How to Apply
the Age Point Method*

Chapter 1

Overview of Volume One

Introduction—Comparable methods—The technique—Retrospect—Spatial rhythms, temporal rhythms, life rhythms—Temporal dimension in the horoscope—Life cycles—Time sectors—Experiences matter more than events—Points the AP helps to clarify.

• Introduction

The first volume in this series has been widely acclaimed. Time and again it was confirmed that with the aid of the new Age Progression Method, exceptionally accurate and interesting statements could be made. Time and again this method has "hit the nail on the head" in greater or lesser ways and, what is more, it has shown itself capable of revealing underlying strands of meaning running through life. It is very easy to use. After a little practice, anyone can tell from one glance at his horoscope just where he is in life and the reason for his current situation. A quick survey can be made of the whole life, without resort to complicated calculations.

Bruno Huber, the well-known astrologer and psychologist based in Switzerland, has developed and proved the Age Progression method in his long-established teaching and consulting work. It has been employed with success since 1973 by many students of astrological psychology (including physicians, psychologists, social workers and educators). Mankind has always been fascinated by the topic of life cycles and the "Ages of Man," but until now no one has succeeded in presenting a simple yet exact method applicable to the individual horoscope and open to use by anybody.

Comparable methods

In a bygone century a method already existed employing, not the six-year rhythm of Age Progression, but one of five years per house. A French clergyman, *Pater Yves*, described in 1654 in his book *Nova Methodus*, a sixty-year cycle through the Placidus Houses. In our own century, the German astrologer *A. Frank Glahn* of Hamburg experimented (rather fruitlessly it would seem) with a life cycle of one hundred years read clockwise on the chart, that is to say against the normal run of the houses. Since 1956 the Munich astrologer *Wolfgang Döbereiner* has been teaching a similar system, though instead of one hundred years, he has adopted a life-span of eighty-four years—again taken clockwise round the chart. In 1932, *C.C. Schneider* published in an astrological magazine an article on the life cycle, proposing that this moved in seventy-two years by six-year stages through the areas of the horoscope. However, he made no specific assertions. *Wilhelmine* and *Arnold Keyserling* of Vienna have developed a method that comes closest to Age Progression. They move in a seven-year rhythm from house to house and stress that, with changes of sign and transits of planetary positions, there occur noticeable changes in the native's comportment.

The Age Progression method as proposed here describes our life through the twelve houses in a six-year rhythm (calculated according to the Koch House System). During the course of our life we travel through our own horoscope and experience the characteristic effects of the planets, signs and houses at times which may be precisely determined. Using an appropriate method, we can therefore make differentiated statements in such matters as how the personality will unfold, the significance of changes and crises in consciousness for spiritual growth, which hindrances to the individuation process have to be overcome, and much more. Our intention is to concentrate on the basic psychological situation and on the individual plan of development in man, not on future events. This is one essential difference between the more usual methods of progression and our method.

Traditional methods

In the traditional methods of prognosis, practically exclusive use is made of *planetary transits* in order to determine coming influences. The positions of the planets at some given point in time are determined and so are the aspects they throw from these new positions to the planets in the natal chart. Inferences are then made concerning the good or bad luck to be expected in the near future. Generally speaking, however, it is impossible to integrate these frequently conflicting aspects. And it is even harder, if Age Progression is not used, to ascertain which of the transits are important for the individual concerned and which are not. When other methods of progression are employed as well—*axial directions* or *progressed planets*—the upshot of hours of careful study of the horoscope can be much confusion but little benefit. Mixing methods makes it difficult to evaluate the situation as a whole.

In contrast to the above, the Age Progression Method relies on a single element: the Age Point. This method makes use of a time mechanism present in the horoscope itself. As the hand swings round on the "clock of life," the planetary positions, signs, and houses light up one after another, and show the leading influences at every stage.

The technique

The technique is a simple one and can be grasped immediately. Life starts at the Ascendant. The hand on the life-clock begins moving counterclockwise, that is to say it follows the sequence of the houses from one to twelve. Commencing with the AC as zero, we

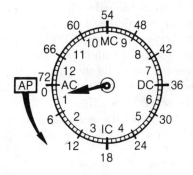

Figure 1.1.1. The path of the Age Point through the houses.

proceed through all twelve houses as shown in figure 1.1.1. At the cusp of the second house we are six years old, at the third cusp we are twelve, at the fourth cusp or IC we are eighteen, and so on, regardless of how big or small a particular house may be. At the age of seventy-two we have returned to the Ascendant; at seventy-eight we are back at cusp two, etc. To obtain the annual movement merely count the number of degrees in the relevant house and divide by six.[1]

Koch Houses

There are various house systems in astrology. Therefore before you start using Age Progression you should make sure which house system is employed in your chart. Those most often favored today are those of Dr. Koch, Placidus, Campanus and the Equal House system. We have chosen Dr. Walter Koch's Birth-place Houses because these are the only ones which give correct results with Age Progression. The house division, already described in Vol. 1, is much the same as in other systems, the main difference being the placements of the intermediate cusps. These placements are, however, crucial.

Retrospect

The discovery of the Age Point some twenty years ago, at the Institute for Psychosynthesis run by Professor Roberto Assagioli in Florence, happened almost by chance. During a very intensive piece of research (in which house systems were compared, the Low Point identified, etc.) Bruno Huber examined many individual natal charts. One day he noticed a remarkable number of changes of occupation in certain of the natives. Although the reasons for such intended or effected changes differed widely, they did have one thing in common: roughly in the middle of the sixth house in each map lay the dividing line between two signs. Without reference for the moment to the tenth house (of public position) it became obvious that in the sixth house (of work and the struggle for existence) there was a regular change of sign as, for example, from Libra in the first half to Scorpio in the second. (See figure 1.1.2.) What is more, all those concerned were in their thirties and had reached the half-way stage in their lives. So here was a double halving (a halving of the

---

[1]For further information, see pages 37-41 of *Life Clock*, Volume 1, Samuel Weiser, York Beach, ME, 1982.

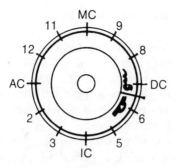

Figure 1.1.2. The Age Point is significant when the signs change mid-house, indicating important stages of life.

house corresponding to the halving of the life); plainly some time mechanism was in operation. This was where work on the problem really started. What was required was to find the mathematical quantity (the time unit) that might be underlying the mechanism. An extensive series of calculations led to the conclusion that, when the sixth house was divided into seventy-two parts corresponding to a presumed life-span of seventy-two years, any border separating two signs in the sixth house always coincided with the age at which the native changed his occupation or at least seriously considered doing so.

Bruno Huber was able to confirm this important discovery by testing it in situations not directly related to the occupation: for example, familial changes intimated in the fourth house, change of dwelling and emigration in houses three and nine, changes in relative prosperity in houses two and eight. He found invariably that where there was some alteration in the course of a life, a shift in sign occurred in the corresponding house, not at any old time but at the very time, measured on the seventy-two year scale, when the said alteration occurred. He dubbed this *exact* place in the house the *Age Point*.

In keeping with the law of analogy enshrined in the well-known esoteric dictum "as above so below" a further discovery was made. The time-scale of seventy-two years could be employed not only in the *micro* single house but also in the *macro* whole horoscope as a standard of measurement. Hence there is a bigger Age Point moving over the entire circle of the horoscope in seventy-two years, which divided by twelve gives a stay of six years in each house (further information on the cosmic number 72 can be found in Vol. 1, p. 30 ff).

The results of countless case studies where this mechanism was recognized were breath-taking, and it was found that in addition to the cross-overs between the signs, the transits of the Age Point over the house cusps, Low Points and planets were also relevant. Other aspects (oppositions, trines, etc.) between the Age Point and the planets were significant too. Therefore the Age Point is comparable to the hand of a clock. It sets out from the cusp of the first house (on the Ascendant) and during a period of seventy-two years makes constantly new aspects with all the prominent points in the horoscope.

House rhythm, time rhythm, life rhythm

In interpreting the horoscope we are accustomed to thinking in terms of the houses. A Moon posited on the left-hand side of the chart in the fourth quadrant is regarded as introverted and definitely different from a Moon on the right-hand, extrovert side. Or, we take it for granted that a person with aspects mainly formed in the lower half of the horoscope is less aware of his motivations than is someone whose planets are concentrated in the upper half. Furthermore, the houses represent spatial regions for us: twelve different spheres of existence with their own themes and no ranking among themselves. When, to stay with our given example, we are studying "change of occupation" we interrogate the sixth house and, if necessary, the tenth (with its theme of the career). We are hardly likely to look for information on occupational possibilities in the twelfth house of retirement and cosmic attachment. Obviously this type of approach is space-oriented, it is concerned with rhythm in space. Until now, the time dimension has been introduced in the horoscope solely through transits and progressions. These work in a more or less complicated manner with elements lying outside the horoscope which project their influence into it. How different, however, is the six-year rhythm of the Age Point—a time mechanism inherent in the horoscope which, like the planets, aspects, signs and houses, forms a natural part of it and is an essential component in interpretation!

The time dimension in the horoscope

In everyday life we frequently encounter time as a negative factor. We find that we do things at the wrong time, that on the whole we have too little time, that we grow old too soon. Time then is a fact of life of which we become conscious only when it obtrudes itself on us unpleasantly.

We are much less aware that time is constantly in motion, ceaselessly flowing out of the past into the future, and that the present in the midst of these is not an isolated unit. Admittedly we experience the present at every moment, but we are also able to enhance each moment with memories of the past and with anticipations of the future, and to perceive it in its spatial, geographical dimension; to get to know it in fact as a "total association." It is all the more important therefore to break out of our space-orientated here-and-now way of looking at things and to get the feel of the flow of time.

Time does not start, it does not stop, and because of its sheer continuity is hard to grasp. All we can do is to seize on a few present moments as they pass along its endless conveyor belt and to store them in our memories. But time is more than this. There is a vital dimension in it, symbolized in the horoscope by the circular path turning back into itself; there is a *Significance* deeper than the stringing together of isolated time points. Time tends to develop!

If only we could succeed in taking hold of all the developmental possibilities brought to us by time in its perpetual flow and could incorporate them in the spatial dimension of our experience, we should loose ourselves from the "tyranny of the moment." We should shake free from inflexible determinism to take advantage of ever newly available possibilities. Having become actively aware of all the dimensions enfolded in the present, we should have the power to change our futures.

This spatial view of time gives us the opportunity to use Age Progression creatively and to see human freedom and fate in more holistic terms. External and internal events can be integrated with the (multi-relational) totality of life, and assimilation be deeper and more aware. What is more, the planetary constellations highlighted one after another by the moving Age Point can be seen in their bearing on past and present as well as on the future. In other words, they become sign-posts along the road to self-determination.

Thus the horoscope, when studied in its tempero-spatial connections, enables us to grasp fate and character in the aggregate. By getting to know the causality of our Karma we can better perform our Dharma, and so evolve in a productive way.[2]

Admittedly, the complexity of our own make-up binds us to a great extent, and this is reflected in the determinism in our personal horoscopes. A plant which grows from a daisy seed will never turn into a poppy. Nevertheless, a frank acceptance of the way in which life has to develop does not exclude gradual change. Change comes, and it is mutation, it is growth, it is the attainment of new life-forms and qualities.

A preset consciousness and the hand of fate fashion each moment of life and decide whether and how change will occur in the course of time. Hours, days and years are taken in prospect, and the future is moulded in the now. When consciously assimilated, the past may enter into this process in the form of experience, and show us how the linear chain of life's moments joins up into whole sections of life and becomes part of the full circle of the horoscope.

Life cycles

The development of men and women tends to follow a basic pattern. In infancy and youth we are all linked by common principles of development and go through the same phases. Yet, equally, each of our lives has its own unique character and pursues its own special way.

Life is like a journey whose starting point is birth and whose end point is death. No one can avoid making the trip, but there are many cultural, social and individual detours on the way. The time-scale can be extended or compressed within certain limits, and in extreme cases the journey can come to a complete halt.

The process of develoment is no easy, unbroken, even flow. There are various times, good and bad, with happy and not so happy hours. Each of us has some notion of periods within the life cycle. These periods can be found in the horoscope itself. The Age Progression method divides the house system into twelve large time

---

[2]Karma and Dharma are two Sanskrit words which have acquired a technical sense in Indian philosophy. Here it would be safe to render Karma as circumstances, and Dharma as duty, though more strictly speaking the first means action and the second means law. *Tr.*

sectors and the individual houses into three smaller time sectors (see Vol. 1, pp. 66-67). This provides us with thirty-six different time qualities; for each of these sections has a quite specific character and is distinct from the one which precedes it and from the one which follows. The concept of time takes many forms. We have only to think of the seasons: spring is a time of awakening when everything is in bloom; winter is a time of death, and also of rebirth, standing as it does at the beginning of a new cycle. Then there are the times of day: daybreak, noon, twilight and the dark still night—and each has its special, recurring, atmospheric and psychological features. Even the ancients have left us representations of the connection between the seasons and the phases of the human life cycle. The Greeks early on divided the horoscope into the four seasons.

Time sectors

When we talk of time sectors we are implying that the course of life has a definite structure and that it follows certain guidelines. Life's development can be regarded as a series of identifiable time factors, corresponding to the themes of the twelve astrological houses. A time sector is a relatively stable part of the whole life cycle, just as a house is of the entire house system, but a significant change does occur in each sector and house.

No time sector is better or more important than another: each contributes something to the character of the life cycle of which it is an organic part. Each contains in miniature the past and the future in combination. And the series of sectors is a macro-structure of the entire life cycle, a framework for the processes of development in everyday life.

Experiences matter more than events

From what has already been said, it will be clear not only that the Age Point is a very important time factor in the horoscope, but also that its significance in the various houses can sharpen our understanding. It enables us to enter into the inner meaning of an individual's progress through life. And in doing so we quickly discover that what is of paramount importance are not the isolated events but the experiences to which they give rise.

The distinction is a crucial one. Some methods of progression confine attention to certain outstanding incidents. The concern of the Age Point Method is with a person's experience, those psychic events which have a transforming effect. An extremely dramatic episode can be played out and leave little impression behind it and, on the other hand, a profound, spiritual experience may take place over many months, without a corresponding chord being struck in the external world. But in any case, between these extremes, there are events in every human life which are accompanied by intense inner experiences.

In general, only by consciously recognizing the process can we see what sense they make in life's wider context. And then it is not merely the psychic happenings that count, but what we have learned from them. In other words, the consequences of external events have to be faced; we have to come to grips with each suddenly activated psychic constellation, or, to put it yet another way, we look for the whys and wherefores and then recognize the inner forces applied by the individual constitution to a specific situation.

Right here the Age Point can help us to graduate from general character reading to true insight into experience and behavior; and this it does as its position in sign and house activates aspects to given planets.

● Points the Age Point Helps Us to Clarify

It is instructive to study the effect on our lives as the gound-themes of the individual houses come into focus. We can make a better assessment of the influences of transits and progressions.

1. We come to realize how one-sided our view of the universe has been—the extent to which we tend to choose to do (or to accept) only those things immediately interesting to us, and to ignore other things.

2. With one glance at our charts we can identify the area, sign or house that currently concerns us, our present problems, and our chances of solving them.

   a) As soon as the AP approaches a planetary position, we notice an intensification of development on which we can focus beforehand (according to the nature of the planet in question).

b) When the Age Point transits a house cusp or one of the two sensitive points (the Invert Point and the Low Point), it signals heightened readiness for action if the house cusp is involved, long-term planning if the Invert Point is involved, and a pause to take fresh bearings if the Low Point is involved.

c) When the Age Point crosses from one zodiac sign into another, there is a change in our temperament, in our attitude, and in the type and method of our performance, corresponding to the nature of the new sign. Since it is possible to calculate the sign our Age Point will occupy at any given period in our lives, we can allow for it in advance.

3. The Age Point can be used to give us an overview of past, present and future. It can show us which actions and attitudes in the past have brought about our present situation, and can give us a lead on what to do in order to overcome difficulties and to encourage the growth of what is only weakly developed.

4. We can uncover traumatic events in our childhood which have left their imprint on our lives, and can identify those faults in our characters which have been caused by them. This enables us to take steps to try and correct the faults.

These are a few of the possibilities and advantages offered to us by employment of the Age Point. We shall now take a look into this material in greater depth and, by giving different case notes in the second part of this book, shall endeavor to show how it may be used in practice.

Chapter 2

Rules of Interpretation

High and Low Points in Age Progression—The duration of the High and Low Points—Three phases in each house—The three Quadruplicities operative in each house—Life's episodes—Structural changes—Advance influence of the cusps—Angular, Succedent and Cadent cusps—Advance influence of the planets upon sign entry—Signs without Low Points—Signs with two house cusps—Intercepted signs—Passage of AP through empty houses—Aspect holes—Distance Halving: turning points—Change of configurations—The significance of secondary aspecting in configurational change—Passage of AP through heavily tenanted houses—Stellium—Cycles involving transits and progressions—Joint action of transits and AP—Transit-AP relationships—Cycles in tandem with transiting and progressed planets—The AP and slow transits.

We have already presented Rules for Application of the Age Point, important rules of analysis in some detail. We now wish to enter into these rules more fully. (See *Life Clock*, Vol. 1, pp. 53-64.)

- ## Rule 1: High and Low Points in Age Progression

Each house is divided into three regions by the intensity curve; there are entered via the house cusp, the Invert Point and the Low Point. This creates a cyclic rhythm of the Age Point with natural crests and troughs (see also Vol. 1, p. 49). We experience the high

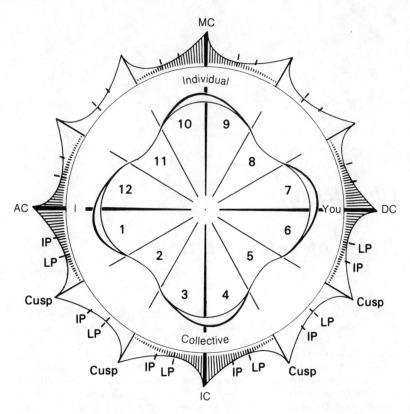

Figure 1.2.1. The intensity curve.

points at the house cusps (HC), the low points at the appropriately named Low Points (LP = golden mean) of houses.[1] See figure 1.2.1. It is of course important to know the time durations of the high and low points.

The high points last from the house cusps to the Invert Point (IP). The Age Point traverses this stretch within 2 years, 3 months and 15 days. From the house cusp to the Low Point the time taken is 3 years, 8 months and 15 days, or almost 4 years. Experience teaches that the Low Point starts to take effect as much as 8 months before

---

[1]See Bruno and Louise Huber, *The Astrological Houses*, Samuel Weiser, York Beach, ME, 1984. First published under the title of *Man and His World*, 1978.

exact transit by the Age Point, and so we speak of a "Low-Point Year." The space of time from the Low Point to the next cusp is therefore barely 2 years, 3 months and 15 days.

Taken together, these phases give six years for each house. The two extreme regions (the cusp and the Low Point) plainly differ from one another in qualities: the first is a phase of construction and action, the second is a phase of retrenchment and rest. The transit of the Age Point over the LP positions brings times of introspection, of turning inwards, whereas transits over cusps motivate us to summon all our powers to achieve external goals—though in different ways according to the natures of the crosses: cardinal, fixed and mutable.

• Rule 2: Phases in Each House

Accordingly in each house we find three different phases (see figure 1.2.2), in which the high and low points stand out most clearly. This tripartite division provides us with information on smaller life cycles. As is well-known, the three quadruplicities are essential to an understanding in astrology of basic human motivation. The principle of cardinality motivates us to exert our will power to become an achiever, the principle of fixity craves for security in order to conserve what has been produced, and the principle of mutability is always looking for something new with a view to abandoning static conditions and recommending develop-

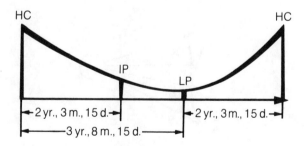

Figure 1.2.2. The house broken into Invert Point and Low Point periods.

ment (see also Vol. 1, pp. 100 and 143-44). In accordance with the analogy "That which is above is as that which is below" we shall apply the same division to the individual houses.

The Quadruplicities in each house

If we superimpose the quadruplicities on the three regions in each house, a picture emerges such as we see in figure 1.2.3. The region following the cusp corresponds to the cardinal quality. Here we find it relatively easy to devote our energies to external matters. At the Invert Point we reach the Fixed region of the house and encounter a braking effect, and at the Low Point (LP) our energies tend to touch zero as far as our outer life is concerned; they are still present but are turned inwards.

After this the curve turns upwards, and we find ourselves in the mutable region of the house, which usually requires some form of adjustment or reorientation on our part. The cuspal influence which accords so well with the cardinal quality, is experienced most intensely in the cardinal houses (one, four, seven and ten). The Low Point experience corresponds to that of the Fixed Cross, and so stagnation and the introversion of energy are most clearly traceable in the four fixed houses (two, five, eight and eleven). Finally, the theme of mutability is expressed most strongly at the Low Points of the mutable houses (three, six, nine and twelve).

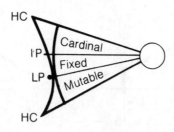

Figure 1.2.3. Each house has a cardinal, fixed, and mutable quality contained within it.

Life's episodes

During the course of our lives we experience these episodes in an invariable rhythm. An impulse to engage in fresh undertakings is always present at the house cusps; active achievement is the order of the day. When we concentrate on our aims, greater success can be achieved than at other times. For two years we are fairly successful. At the Invert Point our energies are brought to the right pitch and goals towards which we have been working can now be reached. As we aproach the Low Point, our activities begin to die away. At the end of the phase of movement, not quite four years after the axial impulse, our energies come to a state of repose at the Low Point. In comparison with the previous period, we often have a feeling of failure. It is a time for taking stock. Furthermore, the Low Points signal a reorientation or a development crisis, all according to the way we react to them. More will be said about this in the chapter on "Low Point Experiences in the Crosses as Doors to the Inner Self," in Vol. 3. Here we would merely observe that whoever deals properly with the Low Points and learns the message coming from within, will find life easier at the next house cusp. Neglect to turn inwards and a lack of insight into how life is motivated will give a harder climb to the following cusp.

Structural changes

Looking at it another way, this three-phase develoment process brings about a progressive change in our behavior structure. At the commencement of a stage of development or a new cycle, which generally means at the cusp of a house, we have plenty of energy and potential available to us, but a proportionately limited structure. Our behavioral repertoire is small as yet, and our adaptability is narrow in scope—we expend a large amoung of energy on our personal concerns. Nevertheless, as time goes on and we approach the Invert Point, our behavior becomes more structured and includes an increasing number of components, making possible an increasingly differentiated approach to the business of life. In the fixed phase of the house, all the components and capacities are integrated into a complex arrangement. The structure becomes more stable, and functions for a period in the fixed region, but then slowly disintegrates until it finally falls apart at the Low Point to give way to some new form.

● Rule 3: Advance Influence of the Cusps

A further rule of interpretation of the AP is the following:

It is not only the exact moment when an axis is transited that is important, but also the build-up time, especially the phase before the cusp.

This pre-cuspal phase is usually a stressful time, especially in the short section before the poles of the main AC/DC and IC/MC axes. Here we enter the wake of the cardinal impulse so suddenly that we tend to be taken by surprise, and the trim craft on which we were peacefully sailing through life takes a battering in the turbulent eddies.

Prior to reaching the cardinal cusps (1, 4, 7, 10) shown in figure 1.2.4, we usually can not respond fully to the new type of energy since, in general, we have a passive, waiting attitude and are less inclined to strenuous activity. The reason being that a cardinal axis is always preceded by a mutable house, concerned not so much with doing as with understanding and reflection. Suddenly the action-oriented main axis begins to work in a way that is out of keeping with the more contemplative mutable house. This creates oppositions which we must overcome in spite of an inner reluctance.

The periods before a cardinal cusp are fraught with difficulty. In extreme cases, we may collapse under the burden of duties.

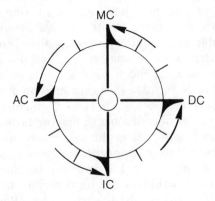

Figure 1.2.4. Cardinal, or angular, cusps.

Frequently there are warning signals in the form of stress symptoms and mild exhaustion. We are plagued by doubts and think, "I can't go on, everythng is getting on top of me." There is a desire to resign, to let everything drop and to cease to bother with anything. However, this is not possible, since so many obligations or self-chosen tasks need our attention. We have to summon up our last reserves of strength in order (like the mountaineer) to reach the top. This demands great exertion with accompanying anxiety states, tensions or a sense of cramping; and yet there is no giving up, no way back—only forward.

Succedent and cadent cusps

Similar considerations apply to the other house cusps, although to a lesser degree. The cross to which a house belongs is always decisive. Before the *fixed* axes of the succedent houses (2, 5, 8, 11), life usually becomes less hectic, but also more stereotyped and unadventurous. Whatever the case, the thrusting cardinal energy is on the wane; in the fixed houses we have to create a fixed form.

Before the *mutable* axes of the cadent houses (3, 6, 9, 12) we are still in fixed houses; usually we seem to be incapable of fitting in to new or changed circumstances. Often our attitude needs to undergo a radical change.

While on the subject of transiting the axes, we should mention that as each cusp is approached, special care ought to be taken to find out how to handle the inflow of new energies and to master the increased demands.

● **Rule 4: Advance Influences of the Planets upon Sign Entry**

Another rule of interpretation for the correct employment of Age Progression is the following:

> *The qualities or problems associated with a certain planet do not remain in abeyance until the planet is transited by the AP, but come into play as soon as the AP enters the sign in which the said planet is posited.*

Frequent are the passages into new signs which evoke clear and important changes and, in many instances, the latter are attributable

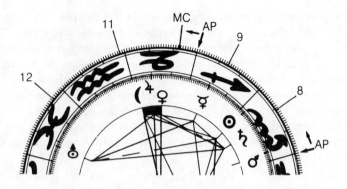

Figure 1.2.5. Planets in the tenth house will begin to act as soon as the Age Point enters the sign of Capricorn in this chart.

to direct planetary contact. It is as if the planets within a sign make their influences felt as soon as the sign is entered. (See figure 1.2.5.) A good analogy is coming into a room already occupied by a number of people. As soon as we walk inside the door we become aware of those present and take in everybody at a glance; we then proceed to greet them individually. The same thing happens when the Age Point enters a sign in which important planets are located. We immediately sense that we have encountered something essential to our development. We do not know just what this is or what it has to teach us, however, as it is only as the AP makes conjunction with the planets that we learn the details.

● Rule 5: Signs Without Low Points

It happens from time to time that a sign is so placed in the house system that there is no Low Point in it. Instead, we generally find a house cusp in the middle of the said sign. Therefore throughout the native's life the sign in question is *axially active* and is correspondingly conducive to success during the passage of the Age Point through it. The curve of success usually rises sharply as the sign is entered and normally remains on a high level for several years. When we find transits through axis-active signs in our charts, we may permit ourselves to take a few risks during this period, as they are fairly certain to prove profitable. Our activities tend to be

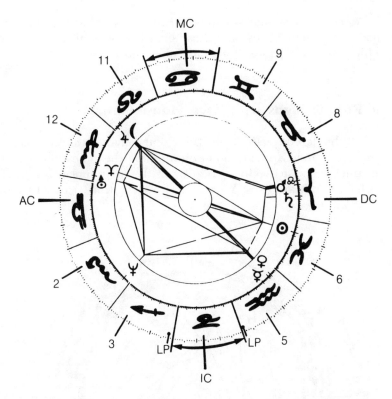

Figure 1.2.6. An example chart indicating a Low Point free period in life because of the placement of the signs Cancer and Capricorn in the tenth and fourth houses.

rewarded, according to the nature of the house, more generously than usual. For instance, with the AP in the fourth house there is success in collective matters, in the tenth house we achieve public recognition, in the seventh house our partnerships flourish, and so on. Our example will make this clearer.

In figure 1.2.6, Capricorn and Cancer are both axis-active and also "Low-Point free." In the third house, just after the Low Point at 28° Sagittarius), the AP enters Capricorn, and the IC (at 12°55′) is near the strongest point in the sign.[2] The transit through Capricorn lasts until shortly before the Low Point of the fourth house at about

---

[2]See *The Astrological Houses* for instructions if you don't understand this.

1° Aquarius. A similar situation occurs in Cancer at the opposite side of the chart. Thus only those signs can be termed axis-active which enclose no Low Points at either end.

● Rule 6: Signs with Two House Cusps

If the sign traversed by the Age Point contains two house cusps (as Cancer and Capricorn do in figure 1.2.7), the indications are for an intense and active life-period when the environment brings its influence to bear on us. We may feel overburdened, easily tired or

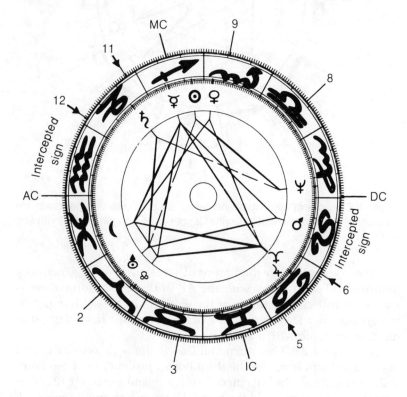

Figure 1.2.7. Cancer and Capricorn both contain two house cusps in this chart, indicating an intense and active period when transited by the Age Point.

even exploited, since it is hard for us to avoid the claims made on us by the world around. Whatever we take in hand we have to keep working on. The period is full of incident according to the sign, house, or planet concerned and is certainly not a restful one. We may feel that no one is showing us any consideration; everybody seems to believe that we have inexhaustible reserves of energy. Now between the house cusps there is a Low Point signalling recuperation, repair and reorientation, but the claims of the outside world run counter to our needs in this respect: we long for rest, yet are compelled to exert ourselves. In houses like this it is not easy to take proper advantage of the Low Point and often the native is assailed by great weariness. One should adopt a very positive attitude during such periods and should avoid stirring up any unnecessary inner resistance. We shall be helped in our own development if we can work closely with those around us and profit by the stimulus they offer.

• Rule 7: Intercepted Signs

If there are signs with two cusps in them in a chart, there will also be two cuspless signs in it, the one facing the other (see figure 1.2.7). They are known as intercepted signs. The period represented by the progression of the Age Point through these signs is frequently experienced as a resting phase succeeding a particularly hectic period. Resistance to the impulse to take things easy will give us the feeling that we are "running on the spot" and failing to make progress. Our mood can become one of deep dissatisfaction, robbing life of its pleasures and often impairing our health. We become introverted at such times, much as we do when experiencing Low Points. If we picture the Age Point as a locomotive running along a track, we can see that intercepted signs are like sections of track without "points." Therefore the energies cannot be switched to a line running clear out into the outside world, so to speak, but loop further into the inner life via the Low Point. Our impulses cannot escape without a great deal of trouble and we tend to be misunderstood, ignored or unsuccessful. However, if we employ this period to recruit our energies or to reorientate our thinking, we may learn to understand ourselves better—our inner motivation and approach to life.

• Rule 8: Passages of the AP Through an Empty Space

In many charts there are empty spaces unoccupied by planets. (See figure 1.2.8.) As long ago as 1940, the so-called "minor aspect configurations" started to become increasingly frequent. In the forties we were still finding the green quincunx aspects of 150°, but oppositions had disappeared. Between 1982 and 1985, especially in the autumn and winter months, the aspects will be so small that the sextile will be the largest of them. When the planets are bunched, the correspondingly large empty space in the chart creates a sense of uncertainty, or even of helplessness, in the native. The empty space nearly always creates anxiety over the contents of the unoccupied signs and houses. Its vacuum tends to suck in those things that are

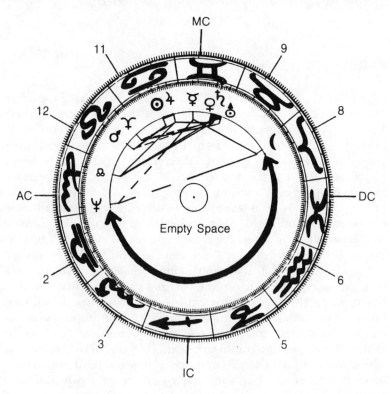

Figure 1.2.8. Passage of the Age Point through empty space in the chart.

deficient or strange automatically and, at times, threateningly. One the one hand, there is an increased capacity for finding out and integrating those things that are lacking, while on the other hand there is an unhappy sense of being at the mercy of external influences. The empty spaces are unprotected and allow the entry of all sorts of influences, in fact, especially when the Age Point is moving through them.

If, for example, the aspects are clustered in the upper, "consciousness" part of the horoscope, there are no transits of planets to affect the native until middle life—his forty-third year in figure 1.2.8. Most people seem to come awake only when the AP makes contact with a planet for the first time. They themselves say that until then they have "been asleep." Life has just been lived or, to express it more accurately, has been lived from indefinable motives. Often no outstanding events have marked childhood, and those that have been in any way memorable have been linked with oppositions between the AP and the planets in the upper hemisphere of the chart. Nevertheless, life begins to be lived consciously only when the AP enters the aspect configuration.

Should the planetary cluster be in the lower hemisphere, the AP will exit from it as it enters the upper hemisphere. If the last planet in the aspect configuration stands at the DC, for instance, the significant event will occur at the age of thirty-six. In this case, the Age Point has already transited all the planets during its passage through the first quadrants. The individuals concerned usually undergo many experiences in their early years. Life has been lived very intensely by them, usually in the context of the family or of the profession or of the struggle for existence. When they leave the configuration behind them, they have a more peaceful time in front of them, and they are able to enjoy the fruit of their labors. The empty space does not mean that nothing more will happen; it means that what has already been gained may be improved at leisure, whether the acquisitions in question are inner or outer values. Further information on this point will be found on page 71 in the chapter on the AP Cycle in the Four Quadrants.

● **Rule 9: Aspect gaps**

Nearly all aspect structures exhibit bigger or smaller gaps, and these have to be taken into consideration. This may be a matter of two planets out of aspect, or of gaps between two aspect configurations. Even when the latter are superimposed or indirectly connected, we react more or less sensitively at the Age Point transits the aspect holes.

Distance halving: turning points

On reaching the midpoint of a gap between two planets or two aspect configurations, we find ourselves at the so-called turning point of the different force-effects. We are leaving the sphere of influence of the first planet (or aspect configuration) and are entering that of the second. Understandably, a change of this sort will be reflected in the life. Where two distinct aspect configurations are involved, there may be a striking change in the native's destiny. Perhaps an example will make this clearer (see figure 1.2.9).

In the aspect picture of this individual, we find in the YOU sphere a gap between Venus and Jupiter. The native reaches the turning point just before the DC when about thirty-five years old. Six different relationships of the Age Point have to be studied in combination for a true appreciation of the significance of its position here. These are:

1. Occupation of the open YOU sphere;
2. Proximity to the sign-change from Sagittarius to Capricorn;
3. Effect of the shadow of the angular seventh cusp;
4. Departure from the unconscious hemisphere and from the lower aspect configuration;
5. Entry into the upper, conscious hemisphere of the horoscope;
6. Position at the turning point between Venus and Jupiter.

Example Analysis

The gaps in the aspect configuration in figure 1.2.9 coincide with the sixth and seventh houses. It coincide with the YOU sphere, which extends here right into the center. Generally speaking, and especially during the period represented by the transit of the Age Point, encounters, contacts and relationships affect people with aspect gaps in this position very intensely. They find it hard to avoid

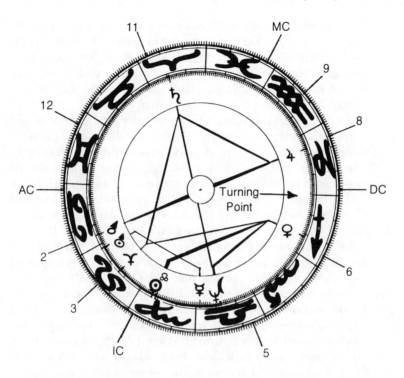

Figure 1.2.9. Turning points in the "you" sphere at age thirty-five.

them or to guard themselves from any adverse effects. An over-exposed YOU-sphere can signify a close-knit relationship with one's opposite number and much uncertainty and vulnerability in respect of everyone else. Since there is a permanent breach on the YOU-ward side of the native's defenses, he feels endangered by all those with whom he has any dealings. He may see he needs someone to help him keep the rest of the world at bay. Maybe he will look for some strong and capable woman to take him under her protection, preferring to accept her discipline than to fend for himself. If not, he will need to gain mental toughness through spiritual development. Ordinary defense mechanisms are of little use, even though his Mars/Jupiter opposition might suggest that he could resort to attack as the best form of defense—it is better for him to try to understand the fundamental lessons of the aspect gap in his chart.

Since the problem is one of relationships, this man will have to learn to overcome his nervousness and to approach others in an open-hearted way. This he can do only from his center, where love itself protects him and saves him from being so easily hurt. He should cultivate inner strength and independence (Capricorn/ Sagittarius) and harmlessness at the Center (or soul).

The *sign-change* is between the mutable fire sign Sagittarus and the cardinal earth sign Capricorn. These individualistic signs have to do with maturation of the personality—mainly in connection with the partner in this particular case. Sagittarius is embedded in the unconscious region and therefore the striving after a more aware spiritual autonomy is as yet ill-defined, and sentimental values and collective thought-patterns are the order of the day (Venus square the conjunction of the Sun and Dragon's head near the IC).

Thus in Sagittarius the native has an opportunity to think for himself, to develop a personal point of view and to wean himself from dependence on the group and their way of thinking. In Capricorn he has the chance to put his new-won autonomy to the proof, and to take responsibility for his own words and actions without advice from the community and without referring everything to his partner for her approval. Potentially, he has a chance of learning to look after himself, without relying so much on her, especially if he can find repose at the center of his being. In any event, an intense learning phase is marked by the passage of the AP through the empty space in the chart and by its transit of the *turning point*, an awakening process where intimate personal relationships are concerned. Something stirs in his soul that urges the native to try and see the world through his own eyes instead of through the eyes of his partner. But, remember, the YOU-side of his chart is very much at her mercy, and she is already in charge of him. She will probably react vigorously to turn him back to herself and to tighten the bonds that bind him to her, perhaps becoming less supportive for a while until he gives in to her demands. He may, indeed, long to "get away from it all" in order to gain inner strength. It is in fact a period in which he could be thrown back on his own resources and has the opportunity to learn self-reliance (provided he is not prevented from doing so by a managing wife).

In our sample horoscope, the native is entering the shadow of the DC and will shortly be moving on into the seventh house (the house of partnerships), and further tasks and lessons are being set that are indispensable to the individuation process. The signs in the YOU-sphere are individualistic and frequently cause conflict between the desire for recognition and its real reason. We may conclude from the Sun and Dragon's Head being conjunct near the IC that an unthinking acceptance of collective norms is now yielding to a conscious adaptation to the native's fellows. Not until the AP reaches Capricorn, however, will this begin to affect the partnership. When Capricorn is entered, Jupiter (on cusp 8) is also activated, indicating that a better balance will be achieved in regard to possession and rigid behavior within the relationships. With expansion of consciousness should come a cheerful assumption of enhanced personal responsibility: the Virgo Sun on the IC indicates a motivation to social work, and Saturn in the region of consciousness gives necessary strength and tenacity of purpose.

• Rule 10: Change of Configurations

In figure 1.2.10 on page 32 we see two separate aspect configurations. The bigger aspect configuration consists of a Sun/Mercury/Dragon's Head conjunction in opposition to Neptune with its attendant aspects to Pluto and the Moon. The other is a "near structure" formed between Uranus, a Jupiter/Venus conjunction, and Mars. It overlaps the main figure, but does not form part of it.

The distances between the tips of the intersecting arms of the two configurations are halved like this: the degrees between the two limiting planets (i.e., the planets at the tips of the two intersecting arms in each case) are counted and divided by two. The midpoint between the two planets is called the turning point. In figure 1.2.10 we find six turning points, and these have been marked by arrows. They enable us to date the ages when the native's life branches out in new directions.

Before anything else, we have to understand what the individual aspect configurations signify. The essential meaning of there being *separate* configurations is that we have to consider two (and in other charts sometimes even more) distinct functions, as revealed by the planets distributed in them. In figure 1.2.10, the linear configuration refers mainly to the sexual desires of the native—thanks to the presence of the libido planets Mars and Venus—but the involvement of houses two, ten and five tells us about his attitude toward economic and professional interests as well.

In the second configuration, the placement in the house system and the planets Neptune, Pluto and the Moon forming the base of the aspect pattern, point to idealistic aims and motivations. What is more, the three leading planets (Sun, Moon and Saturn) are implicated. This has to do with self-realization and with the realization of ideal images of the future. As the Dragon's Head (the Moon's north node) is placed in the eleventh house, aims are fulfilled, especially through friendships, congenial companionship and humanitarian undertakings.

At the *turning points* life is often radically altered, as one constellation and its functions takes over from another. The Age

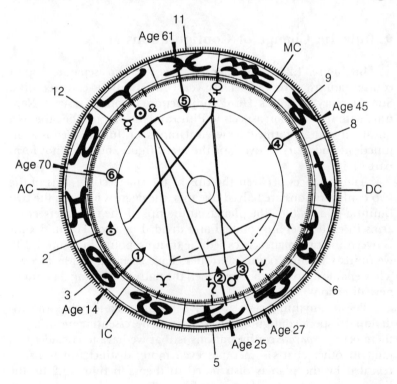

Figure 1.2.10. A linear structure configuration.

Point is our clue here. In the present example the native is male. At his *first turning point* (between Uranus and Pluto), when he was fourteen years old, he doted on a young woman older than himself and left home for her. A contributory factor was that, at the transit over Uranus when he was six, his father had run off with another woman and had left him with his mother.

When the AP entered Leo, just before reaching the IC, he returned home to train as a technical draftsman, and graduated when it crossed into Virgo some time during his twenty-third year. Virgo is very compatible with the start of professional life, and because he was conscientious (Saturn being in Virgo on cusp 5) his efforts were crowned with success. When the *second turning point* arrived in his twenty-fifth year, he started his own family and became the father of a son as Mars was being transited. At the *third turning point* when he was twenty-seven, his life changed once more. He obtained an overseas post and went to South Africa for three years. There he was disturbed by the plight of the oppressed Blacks but felt powerless to offer any solution to the problems. However the foundation had been laid for engaging in a more idealistic type of work (Axis 5/11 in the second configuration.).

The next great change may be expected at the age of forty-five when the *fourth turning point* is reached. Since this will occur in the eighth house and in Capricorn, he should then be ready to accept the responsibility for a bigger assignment. An Aries Sun in the eleventh house always needs some ideal, for which it prepares the way and with which it fully identifies. The Sun here is in an intercepted sign and is also close to the Low Point, so that apparently this individual will not be able to realize his true goal in life until the age represented by the *fifth turning point*. An intercepted Low-Point Sun invariably takes longer on the road to self-realization than does a Sun on a house cusp.

The significance of secondary aspecting in configurational changes

It is not only the turning points which are the springs of action, but also the change in aspecting from one configuration to another. Figure 1.2.11 on page 34 shows two aspect configurations. The smaller configuration, through which the AP aspects since 1979 run, tends to make the native hyper-sensitive and intent on making harmonious contacts due to the influence of Venus, Neptune, the

Moon and the Moon's node. With Venus on the AC, the reactions can be frankly opportunist, so that the appearance of being a lovable person can be kept up.

From January 3, 1982, the AP aspects have left this configuration to enter the larger one. The last aspect to a planet in the smaller configuration was the trine to Neptune on January 22, 1981; also signalling a "Low-Point year" in the ninth house (Low Point on December 17, 1981).

Since the beginning of the transit of the secondary aspects through the "soft" configuration, starting with the trine to Venus on June 25, 1979, Kohl was thrown on the defensive: Strauss won the

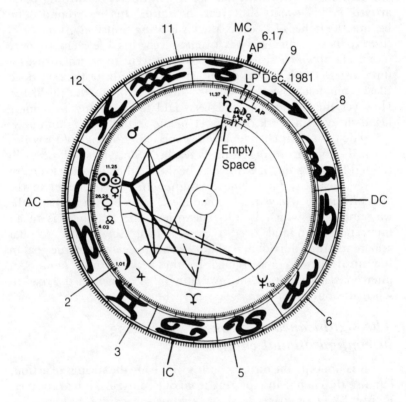

Figure 1.2.11. The horoscope of Helmut Kohl, born on April 3, 1930, at 06.30h, in Ludwigshafen, W. Germany. He became Chancellor of West Germany in 1982.

battle for selection as candidate for Chancellor, giving Kohl time to forge his plans during his "Low-Point year" of electoral defeat.

Subsequently, when the final aspect in the soft configuration was reached (a trine to the Moon's node) he became active again, and organized insidious agitation against the Government (from January 1982).

The main configuration in Helmut Kohl's chart is governed chiefly by the Ego-planets Saturn and the Sun. He gained the ability, thanks to the planets, to the prominence of the cardinal signs and to the T-cross anchored on the main axes, to engage in a compensatory power struggle with extraordinary energy. The AP aspects began to relate to this configuration from January 3, 1982, and when the native was chosen as West German Chancellor, the AP had reached the "minor golden mean" of the vacant space between the configurations. It is hardly surprising that Helmut Kohl became Chancellor, since this new configuration, which is now "ignited" by the AP, gives him an altogether different look. He can assert himself much more forcefully and successfully as Chancellor. The first aspect in this group (a square to Uranus), occurred at the end of May 1984 and at the beginning of June he finally reached his Saturn.[3] Herr Kohl could not have had better timing for a take-over of power.

• Rule 11: Passage of the AP Through Heavily Tenanted Houses

As we follow the course of the Age Point through the chart, houses heavily tenanted by planets are exceptionally significant for interpretation. In figure 1.2.12 on page 36 we see a bunching of planets in the eighth house. Obviously the center of gravity of the horoscope lies here.

Where there is a close-packed grouping of planets, it may be taken for granted that even in his youth the native will consciously experience the simple, physical facets of the area of life (and house) concerned, and that in middle age he will be well acquainted with its theme and concentrate more and more on its spiritual aspects, especially when the "immaterial" planets Neptune, Pluto, and Uranus come to play an important part. In this chart, Uranus and

---

[3] The German edition was published in 1983, so these dates are now in the past. *Tr.*

Pluto form to some extent the framework of the great conjunction in the eighth house.

In order to interpret the passage of the Age Point correctly, we must first be clear about this heavy tenanting of the house and, simultaneously, of Leo. We already know that the eighth house has to do with social structure and with the tendency to protect possessions, status, position and indeed anything owned which could be lost.

Now Leo is a fixed sign, and therefore the struggle for security is partly devoted to the individual's ego, his image, and his intimate sphere. From a psychological point of view, the planetary bunching in Leo in the house of dying and becoming demands the transformation of selfish ambitions into a recognition of the claims of YOU, *i.e.*, of other people and of objective reality. Self-glorification (Leo) is unacceptable to the rest of humanity and has to

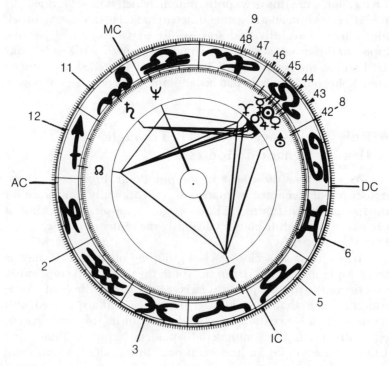

Figure 1.2.12. The Age Point passage through a heavily tenanted house means a really significant period in life.

be alchemized in the athanor of the eighth house. Pluto, the planet of transmutation, at the Low Point of house eight demands sublimation of the will to higher, spiritual motives.

With the transit of the Age Point through the eighth house between the forty-second and forty-eighth birthdays, the native will be moved to take a hard look at the established structures, the well-worn systems and the crystallized forms both of the eighth house and of Leo; that is to say both at his own set ways and at those of the community. He will have to decide whether the traditional ways and achievements of the past are still viable and worthy of support, or are a hindrance to further growth and in need of being discarded. Personal desires will have to take second place to the welfare of others, and the individual will have to learn to strike a proper balance between his own aspirations and the justifiable claims of society. There lies the significance of this constellation.

A concentration of planets in one house shows that considerable experience will be gained during life in regard to the matters ruled by the house in question. With the eighth house there is a great readiness to make changes, and changes are regarded as a normal part of life. The sign Leo inclines the native to find his own limits, to mark them out, and then to overstep them! It is a fixed sign in a fixed house, so that development will always go hand in hand with crises and the fight to maintain self-control. The heavily tenanted eighth house provides the equipment for this. Uranus stands on the house cusp and points to a scientific interest in discovering and testing the limits of endurance of self and of others, and in effecting structural and other changes.

An aspect gap exists between Uranus and the Jupiter/Venus conjunction. It is transited in the forty-third year and marks a turning point in life. The native will have to experiment less with his own and other people's resources in the interests of sensible and responsible utilization of his acquired capabilities. Jupiter and Venus come into play and, with their responsiveness to whatever is genuinely true and harmonious, emphasize all constructive aspects. Next to them are found the Sun, Mars, Mercury and Pluto, strewn as it were like seeds of undreamed-of powers now ready to sprout and blossom. The Sun and Mars are experienced as strength, as a compressed ball of energy, mobilizing the internal and external forces and bursting the bounds of the ego. The native will have to emerge from his shell and show who he is, what he can do, and what he has learned in life. The mask so readily assumed by the "Lion" has to be put away so that the true expression of his inner forces may be seen.

During the period represented by the eighth house, this individual will have a golden opportunity to step out of the wings of self, to walk onto the center of the world's stage and to "give it everything he's got." Whether this will turn out more to his own benefit or to the benefit of others will be decided at the transit over Pluto, which as the outermost member of the great conjunction acts as a guardian. In other words, at the age of forty-six, the personal ideal can be reached with the help of Pluto, and the motive-shifting can be completed. It will now be seen whether the native will identify with a nobler goal in life or will abandon his ideals in favor of material ends and of personal aggrandizement.

• Rule 12: Cycles in Tandem with Transiting and Progressed Planets

In this chapter we want to discuss the interplay between the traditional astrological progressions and the Age Point cycle. The way to use the traditional methods is fully explained in various astrological treatises, which it should be quite easy for the reader to acquire, but reference should also be made to the section on "Differences between Age Progression and Other Progression Methods," pp. 10 ff. in *Life Clock*, Vol. 1.

Planetary transits

For transits, the current positions of the planets are taken; their coordinates are looked up in the ephemeris for the time in question and their aspects to the planets in the natal chart are calculated. Long experience has shown that, in this connnection, the slow-moving planets Saturn, Uranus, Neptune and Pluto have a more noticeable effect than the quick-moving planets Mercury, Venus, Mars and Jupiter. Transiting planets either transit their own places in the natal chart or make aspects to the other planets. We have found that as far as Age Progression is concerned the only transits which are effective are those which happen to be in agreement with the theme of the Age Point. Actually, there are two types of agreement: one where the theme of the transit is the same as that of the Age Point, and one where the theme is related.

Identity of theme

This means that the same planet or the same house is concerned in the transit and in the movement of the Age Point. Three possibilities can be distinguished here, as explained by the following examples:

Example A

Let us assume that, in a natal chart, the Age Point has reached the place of the Moon. At this time, which may last for from three to four months, the emotional pole of the native is sensitized and consciously experienced. All transits or progressions affecting the Moon during the said period are felt particularly clearly, since they are in tune with the stimulation of the Moon by the Age Point. Now, while the Age Point is in conjunction with the natal Moon, the transiting Moon (which makes a complete circuit of the zodiac in 28-29 days) crosses the Sun two or three times. From what we have seen, the person concerned is easily irritated on such days, and is apt to lose his temper. There is nothing very significant about this, except that is does enable us to recognize the connection between the AP and the transiting planets. With the quick-moving Moon, transits are more frequent than with any other planet, and so we can observe them more often. Usually a person may not react to such fleeting transits; but when these are supported by an Age Point conjunction with the Moon the entire feeling nature is often thrown into turmoil. There is more on this topic in the chapter on the AP aspects to the ten planets.

Another example would be when the Age Point makes an aspect to Saturn, and transiting Saturn simultaneously crosses the Ascendant or some other strongly emphasized place in the chart. The effect of Saturn on the Ascendant is intensified due to the stimulus of its Age Point aspect.

Example B

Somewhat different is the case when the Age Point and a transiting planet simultaneously aspect one another and a third planet in the natal horoscope. If, for instance, transiting Jupiter makes a square aspect to the Age Point, nothing much happens; but if both Jupiter and the Age Point jointly aspect a third element, the effect is felt. *General Rule:* Only a triangular relationship between the transiting planet, the AP and the radical planet will have any detectable effect on the native. Linear relationships do not seem to work.

Example C

A further possibility for theme identity is when the Age Point is in the same house and in the same sign as a transiting planet. Say the Age Point is in the sixth house in the vicinity of the Low Point, and transiting Jupiter is on the cusp of the sixth house and aspecting a planet in another house at the Low Point. Transiting Jupiter will be strongly felt and we shall also experience the contrast between Low Point and cusp.

Theme identity might also be illustrated when, for example, transiting Uranus passes over the radical Sun as well as the Age Point. A feeling of unrest is experienced, but not more so than when only the Age Point passes over the Sun. It is the same phenomenon that one has observed when the Sun and the Ascendant occupy the same sign: the intensity of the sign's effect is not doubled but on the contrary, weakened. In the case where Uranus transits the Sun, Uranus can, however, serve as a timer when there is a time interval between the conjunctions of the AP and of transiting Uranus to the Sun. We do not perceive the conclusive action of the AP/Sun conjunction until the moment when Uranus passes over it—and this can occur one or two months earlier or later.

Relatedness of theme

This occurs either when the transit is in the same house as the one currently occupied by the Age Point, or when it makes aspects with planets also aspected by the Age Point. The following examples should help to elucidate this:

Example A

If, say, transiting Saturn reaches the place of Mars in the radix in a house which is also occupied by the Age Point, then its effect will be definitely felt. However, if the Age Point is not present in the house in question, the transit will pass without trace. Here is the reason why so many predictions made from planetary transits fail to materialize. Experience goes to show that the slow-moving planets have a more pronounced effect on our development when they are able to make common cause with the house theme as activated by the Age Point. Therefore, the Age Point enables us to get our bearings both as to the sphere in life and as to the age level of the person concerned, whenever we are studying his situation with the help of transits.

Example B

Relatedness of theme also occurs among the planets themselves. In figure 1.3.4 on page 55, the planets have been arranged in three columns according to the Huber Method. Column one contains the female planets, Venus, Saturn and Uranus. Column three contains the male planets, Mars, the Sun and Pluto. And colume two contains the neuter planets, Mercury, Jupiter, the Moon and Neptune. So if the Age Point is conjunct the Sun at the same time as transiting Pluto makes an aspect with Mars, the native's self-awareness will be challenged and activated. All three male planets have a common theme: self-assertion, decisiveness, self-control, etc. Should the conjunction of the Age Point and the Moon coincide with an aspect from transiting Neptune to Jupiter, the capacity for love and affection will be increased not only by the AP aspect itself but also by the theme-related transit.

Progressed planets

By these we understand the planetary positions on the days after birth as given in the ephemeris. Their motions are interpreted by the rule: "A day for a year." The aspects made to each radical place during these "day-years" are then studied.

Interest centers mainly on the quick-moving planets—the Sun, Moon, Mercury, Venus, Mars and Jupiter—and how their influence is strengthened by Age Point aspects to radical positions. The Moon's directions are especially liable to stir up emotional conditions when the Age Point happens to be aspecting the Moon.

Table 1. List of Planetary Correspondences with the Age Point

Age	AP Cycles in Relation to Planets
Age 6	AP at cusp 2, tr. Jupiter in opposition to radical Jupiter.
Age 12	AP at cusp 3, first return of Jupiter to its radical position.
Age 18	AP at cusp 4 (IC), tr. Jupiter in opposition to radical Jupiter.
Age 22	AP at Low Point of 4th House; tr. Saturn square radical Saturn.
Age 24	AP cusp 5; second return of Jupiter to its own place in the radix.
Age 28	AP at Low Point of 5th house; tr. Uranus trine radical Uranus, tr. Neptune sextile radical Neptune.
Age 29½	AP coming up to cusp 6; tr. Saturn conjunct radical Saturn.
Age 30	AP at cusp 6; tr. Jupiter in opposition to radical Jupiter.
Age 36	AP at cusp 7; third return of Jupiter to its radical place.
Age 38	AP at IP in house 7; the Dragon's Head reaches its own place in the radix for the second time.
Age 42	AP at cusp 8; tr. Uranus in opposition to radical Uranus; tr. Jupiter in opposition to radical Jupiter; tr. Neptune square radical Neptune.
Age 48	AP at cusp 9; fourth return of Jupiter to its own place.
Age 52	AP at Low Point in house 9; tr. Saturn square radical Saturn.
Age 55	AP separating from MC; the progressed Moon reaches its own place in the radix for the second time; tr. Uranus trine radical Uranus, tr. Neptune trine radical Neptune.
Age 56	AP at IP of 10th house; Dragon's Head reaches its radical place for the third time.
Age 60	AP at cusp 11; tr. Jupiter conjunct radical Jupiter (for the 5th time).
Age 72	AP at the Ascendant; tr. Jupiter conjunct radical Jupiter (for 6th time).

Table 1: Continued.

Age	AP Cycles in Relation to Planets
Age 82	AP at Low Point of 2nd house; progressed Moon conjunct radical Moon; tr. Saturn square radical Saturn.
Age 83-84	AP approaching cusp 3; tr. Uranus conjunct radical Uranus; tr. Jupiter conjunct radical Jupiter, tr. Neptune in opposition to radical Neptune.

AP cycles in relation to transits and progressed planets

On considering the transits and progressions of planets, we observe an interesting relationship to Age Progression. The stages of life as defined by Age Progression receive surprising confirmation from transits and secondary directions. Transits taken out of context can create a false impression. The interconnections between the orbits of all the planets in the solar system and the bearing of these on the various stages of life are described by Alexander Ruperti in his book *Cycles of Becoming.*[4]

Since we are dealing here with the concerted action of many elements, we shall review them chronologically as shown in Table 1. We shall designate the planetary positions in the natal horoscope as "radix" or radical positions. The only progressions we have included are those of the Moon.

In figure 1.2.13 on page 44, the correspondence of the transit cycles of the slow-moving planets and of the Dragon's Head with the Age Point is shown. In constructing this diagram, we used the average values of all respective revolutions of the planets in our own century, because the main intention is to offer something which can be usefully employed for persons alive today. If a study is being made of famous individuals of past centuries, allowance will have to be made for deviations in timing.

In the case of Pluto, the deviations are considerable in our own century also: its speed has doubled since 1900. Therefore we have drawn the topmost line in three variants, showing its real

[4]Alexander Ruperti, *Cycles of Becoming*, CRCS Publications, Reno, NV, 1978.

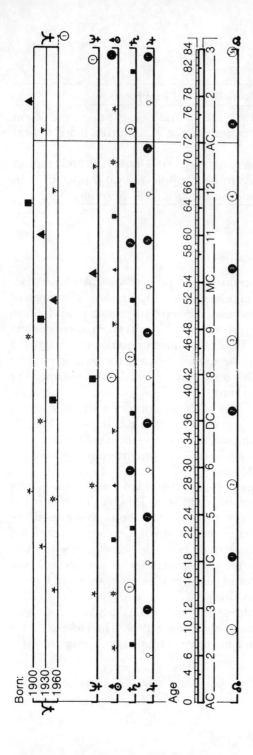

Figure 1.2.13. Correspondence of the transit of the slow-moving planets and Dragon's Head with the Age Point. At the bottom of the chart the years are indicated, with special prominence given to cuspal Age Points (6, 12, 18, 24, etc.) and Low Points (4, 10, 16, 22, etc.). The actual houses are given underneath. The upper lines display the transits of the slow-moving planets on the same time-scale. The prolonged transits of these planets to their radical places are shown. Where the more recently discovered planets are concerned, all the aspects in the thirty-degree series are listed. With Saturn, for the sake of clarity, we have confined ourselves to four positions: the ascending square/opposition, and descending square/conjunction. With Jupiter and the Dragon's Head, only the opposition and the conjunction are given. The numbers in the symbols representing the latter mean "revolutions." Thus, 1 = first revolution, 2 = second revolution, and so on.

● Conjunction   ⚹ Semisextile   ⚹ Sextile   ■ Square   ▲ Trine   ⚹ Quincunx   ○ Opposition movements (not the averages) for people born in 1900, 1930 and 1960. In neighboring years the pattern is similar. The considerable differences for those born earlier or later are evident; the distances between the aspects become shorter and shorter (e.g., lines 1 and 3 in figure 1.2.13).

Several interesting patterns emerge on closer inspection, such as, for example, the almost exact coincidence of Jupiter's returns to its own place (in 11.96 years) with the passage of the AP over alternate house cusps.

As compared with this, the rhythm of Uranus and Neptune takes the form of an octave of seven intervals, and this overlaps the AP and Jupiter only at the ages of 42 and 84. Thus Neptune's ascending square, the first opposition of Uranus and the fourth opposition of Jupiter to their own places, all occur in the forty-second year of life just before the Age Point transits cusp eight.

The other planets do not follow either the six-year or the seven-year rhythm, but help to highlight important stations of the Age Point. Thus Saturn's first descending square occurs shortly after the passage of the AP through LP 4 (separation from the parents), etc. We shall have to leave it to the reader to find further interesting "meshing points" (there are many more!).

Chapter 3

Age Point Aspects

AP activity and its evaluation—Rules governing aspect activity—Rules for finding the AP aspects—List giving sequence of aspects—Duration of the AP aspect activity—The natures of the planets—Feminine, masculine and neutral planets—Hard and soft planets—Aspects by color—Triggering a configuration—Planets void of course—The comprehensive approach—Aspect interpretation in three stages—Planetary tables—The aspect cycles of the AP—Primary aspects of the AP—Conjunctions—Oppositions—Beginning of the full cycle—The two semi-cycles—Five intermediate stages—First semi-cycle—Second semi-cycle—General rules for the sequence of the aspects—Primary aspects in childhood—Hints on interpretation—Beginning of the AP cycle in the four quadrants—Three kinds of aspect—Red aspects: conjunction, opposition and square—Blue aspects: sextile and trine—Green aspects: semisextile and quincunx—Three development stages in the quincunx aspect.

• AP Activity and Its Evaluation

In Age Progression we use only the seven classical aspects (see figure 1.3.1 on page 48), by which is meant all aspects of thirty degrees or multiples thereof, including of course the zero degree, (0°, 30°, 60°, 90°, 120°, 150°, 180°); the conjunction (0°) and the opposition (180°) being the most powerful—for which reason they are termed the primary aspects. All other angular relationships, such as the semi-square, sesqui-square, quintile etc. are not considered. Nor is any notice taken of the ill-conceived division into good and

Semisextile 30° Quincunx 150°

Sextile 60° Trine 120°

Square 90° Opposition 180°

Conjunction 0°

Figure 1.3.1. The seven principal aspects in a horoscope. When we use colors to indicate aspects, we draw them in as follows: green for the semisextile and quincunx, blue for sextiles and trines, red for squares and oppositions, and orange for conjunctions.

bad aspects, which unfortunately is still made at times, even today. The evasive reformulation of "bad" and "difficult" or "hard" and of "good" and "easy" or "soft," had been rejected also. Such terms as good and bad are inapplicable to the Age Point, too, because this evaluation a) is useless from a psychological point of view; b) is not applicable to the individual in his developmental phases; c) does not take into account that in Age Progression the aspects work differently from the way they work in classical astrology; d) ignores the concern with inner experiences rather than with outer events.

In astrological psychology we are interested in the development of the inner person and not with what is going to happen next (or with good luck and bad luck). The method of interpretation and, indeed, the effect of the aspects, both differ from what we would expect in the traditional modes of prognosis. What is more, Age Progression deals with an internal clock, timing mental and spiritual processes—not happenings in the physical world, although there is of course a functional relationship between the inner and the outer. "Why and wherefore" is more important than "what" in Age Point aspects because the crux of the matter is self-knowledge.

Since the Age Point position is the focus of our present consciousness (see Vol. 1, p. 46), the way the aspects operate depends very largely on our conscious attitudes. How we react to the stimulus provided by the AP and its aspects is the decisive factor: everything depends on whether we are prepared to come to grips with what the inner selectivity draws (so to speak) into our orbit from outside, or whether we are more inclined to shirk the challenge.

Finally, it is we ourselves who decide if an AP aspect has a positive or negative effect on us. Often we find that the so-called good or easy aspects create more problems than do the bad or hard ones. The latter can have an extraordinarily helpful effect on our psychic development.

Rules governing aspect activity

Another essential difference from traditional methods of prediction is that in Age Progression the only events indicated by aspects are those having some subjective content; events, in other words, making a deep and lasting impression on the mind. Such impressions are made when the archetype corresponding to the currently aspecting planet is activated in our psyche, and our own creative power provokes or selects (as the case may be) the experience necessary to our development. The Age Point represents the everpresent consciousness, which moves through time "zipping together" the inner and the outer life at each moment.

For astrology, each planet represents one of the ten basic properties of mankind. In the course of life, these are stimulated, made active, and brought into consciousness by the Age Point aspecting the planets in the horoscope and we become acutely aware of the planetary qualities. If we are sensible, we will come to terms with it and will learn how to make best use of the tools or weapons with which we are furnished at that time. Nevertheless, the matter is a personal one and it is difficult, if not impossible, to lay down rules for the influence of the aspects.

It is advisable to ask oneself, "Is the experience which I am trying to associate with the Age Point one which has been significant for me, causing me considerable concern and presenting me with a challenge, or is it one I have been able to live through without problem?" Quite often we undergo sensational experiences which leave no trace behind them; others of apparently no significance may almost swamp us in their wake. It is our subjective evaluation of them which matters: everything depends on what they mean to us. The fact that a person nearly always places a subjective construction on whatever happens to him is a psychological truism. Accordingly, only those experiences stamp themselves on the mind which touch our inner being; they, only, are registered by the Age Point, and the latter fails to respond to what is purely objective. Perhaps the following examples will help to put these ideas into perspective.

When a mother dies after several years of illness, one would imagine that the exact time of her death would be revealed by the Age Point. Yet this is not inevitable. Say that, owing to the terminal nature of the disease, the native had become resigned to the loss of his parent several years before it happened; it is this psychological event and not the death itself which is signposted. Again, in cases of separation and divorce, events will often cast their shadows before, even though the partners may stay together for several years longer. And the reverse can also be true if a decision is forced upon the native. Therefore, the exact date when the decree is made final is not so relevant. Many a time we fail to notice the commencement of a new cycle or process of inner changes; we do not see how our attitudes and reactions are being subtly remodelled. Then sudden external circumstances may reveal that something has taken place within us that we may have consciously or unconsciously refused to face in the past. Hence there is little sense in compiling a list of events with which to test the Age Progression method, unless those events have been deeply experienced. The Age Point indicates solely those things that have changed us.

Rules for finding the AP aspects

As we know, astrological aspects are specific angular distances between individual planets. Frequently in a chart we find two or more planets so close together that we can say they are in conjunction (0°). When the Age Point reaches the radical position of a planet, this too is regarded as a conjunction. We then refer to the AP transiting a planet. If the AP confronts the planet across the chart, at a distance of 180° measured round the 360° zodiac, then it is in *opposition*. They are the two most important, or *primary*, aspects as far as the Age Point is concened. However, five further aspects are formed between the extremes of conjunction and opposition: 30° (semisextile), 60° (sextile), 90° (square), 120° (trine) and 150° (quincunx). These are the seven classical aspects already mentioned by Ptolemy.

Example

For aspect-finding practice, we shall look at the 1983 position of the Age Point in figure 1.3.2. on page 52. In this year the native is forty-one years old. The AP has reached 25° Aquarius and makes a semisextile with the Moon (at 24°09′ Pisces) and shortly afterwards a quincunx with Neptune (at 28°18′ Virgo). When he attains the age of forty-eight, the AP is on the ninth cusp and comes into conjunction with the Moon and, almost simultaneously, into opposition to Neptune.

For beginners, an aspect-finder may prove useful. With its zero marker placed over the Age Point, the aspects can be read directly. Naturally, the appropriate orb is allowed for the AP and for the planet concerned. Advanced students can easily recognize the aspects without any aids however.

In temperate zones, the transit of a sign by the Age Point can take anything between three and twelve years, and the rapidity of aspect formation with each planet varies accordingly.

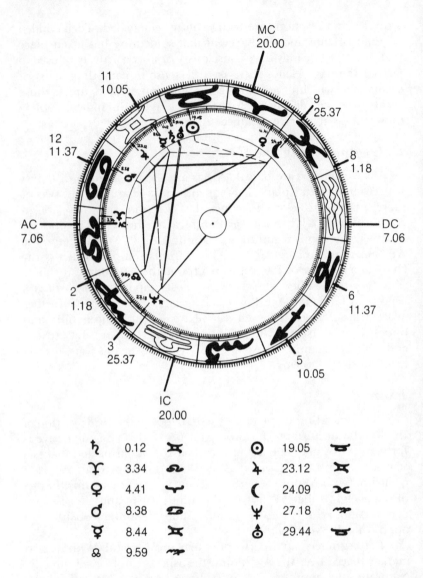

Figure 1.3.2. Example chart calculated for May 10, 1942, Zurich, Switzerland. The planets are arranged according to *degree number* (irrespective of sign) below the chart. The Age Point always follows the same order of the planets in making the various aspects, and aspects them (potentially) once per sign.

The natal chart really reveals an individual pattern of response linked with time, a pattern that remains the same throughout the native's life. As already mentioned, however, the time spent by the AP in the various signs can differ considerably. Hence in a large house (embracing more than a sign) the aspects may follow one another quickly (many experiences). For example, during the six-year transit of a house all the planets can be aspected twice (making 20 or more aspects in 6 years when a house covers more than 60°).

By way of contrast, in a small house the AP "creeps" over the degrees of the zodiac contained in it. So perhaps no more than three, four or five aspects are formed within 6 years. Nevertheless the poverty of aspects is compensated by the intensity of experience (see also Vol. 1, p. 62).

This phenomenon evokes different responses in people of different types. For instance, someone with a more static personality (with strong occupation of fixed signs and/or houses; several squares) can be "overrun" by the activity going on in a big house. A flood of sensations, together with unsettled feelings, inhibitions, and anxiety in the face of responsibility can result. A dynamic personality (with emphasis on cardinal and mutable signs and/or houses; aspects of the triangular or linear type) may find time hanging heavy on his hands during a slow period, *i.e.* in small houses. Restriction or paralysis, lack of success, lack of drive, and introspective or depressive phases may frequently be explained by this phenomenon, especially when such reactions are atypical.

Duration of the AP aspect activity

In analyzing the Age Point aspects, care must be taken that the so-called *time orb* is observed (see Vol. 1, p. 57). It goes without saying that this can be expressed in degrees, according to the house size. However, since in the Age Point we are dealing with temporal measurement, it is expedient to express the extent of the activity in terms of time. The duration of an aspect is longest in the case of conjunctions and oppositions—the main AP aspects, and the effective influence (the time orb) is often in the region of a year. When the Age Point comes into conjunction or opposition with an ego-planet (Sun, Moon, Saturn) or occupies some other significant place in the aspect structure (a center of tension, or a stellium), the following points should receive due consideration:

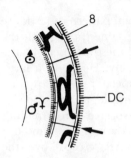

Figure 1.3.3. An example of planet activity upon entering a sign.

1. The aspect activity begins with a conjunction and an opposition upon entry of the sign, in which one or more planets stand, regardless of whether the first degrees of the sign are before or behind a cusp. (See figure 1.3.3.)

2. The activity becomes more intense as the planet is approached and quite often reaches its high point on the very day the aspect is exact.

3. A clear cessation of the effect is observed—if not immediately, then within two or three months following the transit. In other types of aspect the orb is naturally smaller. On average, 1° before and after the exact aspect is the orb in a 30° house. If the house is small, the orb is smaller too—sometimes only ½ degree; if the house is large, the orb before and after the aspect place can be anything up to 2°.

● The Nature of the Planets

Generally speaking, in the aspects there is a reciprocal action between the different planetary principles. In judging the aspects, attention should be paid (both in radix and Age Progression) to the natures of the planets involved; so it will be useful, at this stage, to discuss one or two planetary categories:

Feminine, masculine and neutral planets

From this division it is easy to determine whether the qualities of planets are in tune or not. Take a look at figure 1.3.4 and

Spiritual Growth: Super-Conscious Sphere

Creative Intelligence	Love Ideals	Spiritual Self
♅	♆	♇
Uranus: Meditation; Method or System	Neptune: Identification; Understanding; Empathy	Pluto: Contemplation; Metamorphosis; Growth

Personality (Ego): Conscious Sphere

Physical Manifestation	Feeling of Identity	Self-Awareness
♄	☽	☉
Saturn: Practical Thinking; Need for Protection	Moon: Sympathy; Need for Contacts	Sun: Will; Need for Expansion

Life-Supporting Functions: Subconscious Sphere

Perfection	Formulation/ Evaluation	Achievement/ Efficiency
♀	☿ ♃	♂
Venus: Assimilation; Longing for Harmony	Mercury/Jupiter: Media Sense; Learning Capacity	Mars: Motor Action; Energy

Figure 1.3.4. The nature of the planets.

you will find three columns showing which planets have related qualities and which have not. The planets on the left side, that is to say Venus, Saturn and Uranus, we shall treat as feminine; Mars, Sun and Pluto on the right side, we shall treat as masculine; Mercury, Jupiter, the Moon and Neptune are counted as neutral. Planets in the same column are related in quality and motivation and supplement or support one another, even though they can differ considerably in their reactions and functions. Planets taken from different columns contradict one another when in aspect, causing problems and tensions.

Hard and soft planets

A further distinction has to be made in reading the aspects, and that is between soft (sensitive) and hard (purposive) planets. From this it is possible to tell whether certain planets harmonize in their basic qualities or not. The *soft, sensitive planets* are the Moon, Mercury, Venus and Neptune, and to some extent Saturn (depending on sign and house potential). The *hard, purposive planets* are the Sun, Mars, Saturn, Uranus and Pluto, and to some extent Jupiter.

Effect of the AP aspects on sensitive planets

Sensitive planets team up well with blue and green aspects since their natures are similar to the latter. But these planets often begin to make their presence felt for the first time under the influence of red aspects, because the latter activate the planets more vigorously. Frequently, however, such aspects behave as irritants, and cause exaggerated behavior and hypersensitivity. What is significant, of course, is whether the native develops in keeping with the Age Point, or raises resistance to inner or outer change—which might change the effect accordingly.

Effect of the AP aspects on purposive planets

Purposive planets react exceptionally strongly to red aspects because the natures of planets and aspects are similarly forceful. The planets' energies are activated and changes are produced in the outside world. Green and blue aspects, on the other hand, act as irritants on hard planets; they often make the native uneasy and indecisive. Many people fail to react to them at all.

● Aspects by Color

We have color-coded the aspects in order to make classification possible. The colors orange, red, blue and green have been adopted from a color-psychology scheme as follows:

Conjunction—Orange—Power
Compressed, creative force is expressed by this color. Note, however, that according to the qualities of the planets a conjunction can also be "red" or "blue." The deciding factor is whether hard or soft planets are involved.

Opposition and square—Red—Energy
This color has been chosen because it corresponds to the energy and its realization as found in these aspects. These are the aspects of Action.

Trine and sextile—Blue—Matter
These are the aspects which have a peaceful, relaxing quality. They are the aspects of Matter, or rather of Feeling.

Quincunx and semisextile—Green—Consciousness
These are seeking, informational, often undecided, too; they are the aspects of thought and perception.

We shall study the aspect colors in more detail later, but at this point would like to introduce the reader to a further rule to be used in judging the Age Point aspects: first of all determine the type of aspect(s)—red, blue or green—made by the planet in the radix. For example, when the relationships are only *green-blue*, then the reaction to red AP aspects is very strong. The expansion of consciousness receives a big impetus with the input of a force that was not previously there.

The same sort of thing happens when a planet has only *green-red* aspects. If it receives a blue aspect from the AP, the capacity for relaxation and enjoyment is improved, which is all to the good in this tense type of aspect formation.

Finally, if the planet's aspects in the radix are *red-blue* and it receives a green aspect from the AP, the ambivalence inherent in the polarization into energy and feeling (red and blue) can be handled with greater awareness. The prevailing either-or attitude is toned

down and the individual becomes more tolerant and wiser, because
he can perceive the intermediate shades.

● Triggering a Configuration

The next important rule for a psychological elucidation of the
aspects is never to confine attention to single aspects but to consider
the total configuration at all times. On comparatively few occasions
do we have to do with individual planets or aspects where the Age
Point is involved. Usually the Age Point triggers a whole aspect
figure. Therefore we should determine which planets in a configuration are touched in rapid succcession. Only in this way can we
obtain an accurate idea of which tasks still await accomplishment
and of which problems can now be solved.

● Planets Void of Course

The Age Point will often cross a planet that is aspect-free; this is
full of importance, because hidden or latent qualities are then
brought into the open. The period is one of experimentation and of
gathering experience. Each Age Point aspect represents a fresh
opportunity to experience something new through the planet in
question, to observe the non-integrated factor in one's reactions and
improve one's self-knowledge step by step. A conscientious observation of oneself is imperative. A transit of the Age Point can be an
enriching experience or, on the other hand, a source of vexation.
Our friends may find it difficult to understand why we suddenly do
something entirely out of character.

● The Comprehensive Approach

In astrological psychology we are well aware that in order to
comprehend the native, we have to study his horoscope as a whole.
Excessive concentration on details will lead to error, as experience
has shown; alas, the pitfall is often hard to avoid! It can hardly be
emphasized enough that we gain most help for our development
from the Age Progression Method when we keep the total aspect

picture in view—which should not be too onerous a task if the mode of representation used in this book is adopted. Observe how the aspect configuration is neatly delineated in the chart in red, blue and green. From this it is easy to pick out various geometrical figures: big, all-embracing triangles, small triangles, quadrilaterals and straight lines.

● Aspect Interpretation in Three Stages

As we have seen, a number of different factors have to be taken into account in judging the aspects. The best course is to proceed as follows:

1. First determine the house in which the Age Point is currently placed. For a differential diagnosis of the possibilities, note whether the AP is in the beginning, middle or end of the house (see The Age Point and the Intensity Curve, Vol 1, p. 49).

2. Next identify the sign involved and, once again, note whether the AP is situated in its beginning, middle, or end.

3. Finally see whether any of the planets in the house are being approached closely by the Age Point, calculate when the conjunction is exact, and find out what other aspects to individual planets or to the whole aspect configuration are being made.

When we have learned to combine these three elements satisfactorily, we shall be in a position to assess the effects of the aspects with accuracy.

The sequence of the different Age Point aspects can be seen as a temporally ordered whole when it is considered from the standpoint of a history of development. In seventy-two years each planet goes through one entire aspect cycle of the Age Point. This cycle consists of two half-cycles (one ascending and the other descending), of thirty-six years each. Only the seven main aspects are used, and successive aspects represent successive stages in the native's development (see figure 1.3.1 on page 48). The following rules have to be observed:

1. In order to trace the development of the capability indicated by a given planet in a given position (house, sign, aspect), the Age Point aspects must be seen not in isolation but as stations along a cyclic

track through the whole chart—and, by extension, through the whole life.

2. An aspect cycle begins with the *first primary contact* of a planet (conjunction or opposition). During a half-cycle, the Age Point runs in thirty-six years to the opposite place in the chart; taking a further thirty-six years during the second half-cycle to return to its starting position. But in seventy-two years we experience only *one* half-cycle as a unit. The other is divided into two widely separated time periods by the beginning-cum-end of life (the AC).

3. The self-contained half-cycle invariably starts in the first half of life, with either a conjunction or an opposition with or to the planet concerned, all depending on the sector of the chart in which the planet stands. With planets below the horizon we begin with the conjunction (ascending cycle), with planets above the horizon we begin with the opposition (descending cycle).

4. *Sign aspects*. In every sign, the AP makes an aspect of one sort or another with the various planets. When, for example, a planet is 18° Scorpio, the aspects always fall due at the eighteenth degree of each sign. When a planet is 5° Sagittarius, we have to inspect the aspects made at the fifth degrees of each sign as the AP travels through the zodiac.

5. *House aspects*. The Age Point activates the planets not only in the signs but also in the houses. As it transits the cusps or Low Points of the several houses, it triggers planets on cusps or Low Points in the radix. Once again, the dynamics of development are in seven stages, and understanding should be gained through introspection. Such aspects produce no spectacular effects, but do have a subliminal action that is valuable for our spiritual development.

● Primary Aspects of the Age Point

Figure 1.3.5 shows that the aspect cycle commences either with a conjunction or an opposition to some radical planet. Therefore these two aspects are the most important of those made by the Age Point. They are known as the primary aspects and usually elicit unequivocal, powerful effects which boost our development. Being formative factors of the first rank, they mould our characters—but in such a way as to cause traumas and complexes if the planet in question is poorly placed.

Aspects preceding the start of the aspect cycle are preparatory; so to speak setting the scene. The actual performance does not open until direct contact is made with a planet, and the particular branch of drama to which it belongs is decided by whether the ascending or the descending half-cycle is being entered. In practice we can distinguish the following effects:

a) *Active effect* (Conjunction): This occurs in all conjunctions where planets are situated in the lower part of the chart. Say a planet stands at the third cusp, the cycle will then commence in the twelfth year of life and will reach the opposition thirty-six years later when the native is forty-eight, after the first half-cycle has been completed. During this period the specific influence of the planet is stimulated until it reaches consciousness.

b) *Passive effect* (Opposition): This is produced when the aspect cycle starts with an opposition, *i.e.*, when the planets occupy the third and fourth quadrants. During the passage of the AP through the empty lower houses the native is mainly subject to the influence of his environment; a state of affairs over which he has little control. He is quite likely to repress some of the contents of his mind, even to the extent of amnesia: events and experiences being often forgotten unless they have been impressed on the native for some reson or other by parents or educators, especially when they occurred early in life. The conjucntion and opposition of the Age Point will now be examined in greater detail.

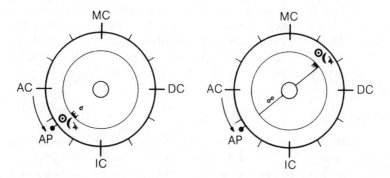

Figure 1.3.5. The primary Age Point aspects are the conjunction and opposition.

Conjunction of the AP

Whenever the Age Point makes a conjunction with a planet, the latter's basic influence emerges into full consciousness. The planet is experienced quite intensively and at close range. It gives us no peace; we have to keep paying it attention to find out what it means for us. The best approach is one of positive, even welcoming, acceptance. Putting the matter a little quaintly, we might say that the planet conjunct the AP lies right under our nose, and there is no possibility of stepping back to see how wide and deep its influence goes—no way either of taking the bearings of the attendant problems, because we are too much involved in them. At such times the unknown is liable to fill us with dread. The more we attempt to avoid a confrontation (either through fear or ignorance) with the principle represented by the planet in question, the more we are likely to be confronted with it by fate—perhaps in a drastic fashion. It depends on the planets and their aspects in the birth chart whether it is in youth or in adulthood that conjunction aspect cycles start. As for the planets in the upper part of the chart, something is learned about their effects when the AP makes an opposition with them, long before it reaches their conjunction. Coping with them at the time of conjunction is therefore so much easier.

At all events, it is the significance of a conjunction that we identify ourselves with the life-force concerned and note in actual experience what the planet does in us, what qualities it promotes, and which functions it performs in our lives. During the conjunction, which lasts for several months, we learn most about the planet. Therefore we should take advantage of the opportunity and undertake a conscious exploration of its relationships. By so doing we shall learn more, more quickly, and shall move on to maturity. Five additional aspects lead up to the opposition, which marks the end of assimilation and development and indicates the time when we can take stock of what the learning process has had to teach and of where it has led us.

Opposition of the AP

Matters are different where the opposition is concerned. Not only is it true that when a conjunction has preceded the opposition we do not have the same situation as when AP contact is being made for the first time, but also, in either case, we now find ourselves at some distance from the planet as we ride along with the Age Point; hence we are unable to identify with the planet fully. On the credit side, everything to do with it is spread out before us as in a panorama: its other aspects, its position in house and sign, and its neighboring planets. We are able to see its interconnection with the rest of our environment and to gain insight into the psychological and spiritual background. A disadvantage is that the opposition can easily throw us into a passive, defensive position. Over against us, on the opposite side, so many things are happening out of reach of our direct control. Nevertheless, the resultant tension does have a considerable teaching effect: we start to see how various factors in our lives hang together, and we understand the meaning and purpose of the learning process—which is worth a great deal! Consciousness is expanded and so is self-assurance. If the aspect cycle commenced with a conjunction and the AP has already transited the planet, everything the planet has to offer is now available to the conscious mind. With the opposition we reach what might be called a peak, and what we require are maturity, responsibility and deliberation. Before us lies the *phase of realization*, which opens the way to greater freedom.

• Beginning of the Whole Cycle

As already mentioned, the AP moves once around the entire chart in seventy-two years, aspecting each planet as it goes. Depending on house position, the AP can come into contact with a planet very early in life (if the first quadrant is occupied), or perhaps not until the native is middle aged. Whatever the case, the technical rules remain the same, but for the purposes of psychological interpretation, due regard must be paid to the age of the native when the planetary organ (capacity) begins to develop. There are certain relevant questions:

1. Is the planet above or below the horizon in the radix? If below, the causes for the subsequent development of the capacity are unconscious; if above, they are conscious.

2. In which quadrant is the planet? In other words, at what age does the aspect cycle commence? We shall have more to say about this later.

3. In which half-cycle do we currently find ourselves? If in the ascending, we are fully occupied developing the planetary quality, but if descending, we can put it to good use in our life.

The two half-cycles

The full tour of the chart is divided into two parts. The first runs from conjunction to opposition and lasts thirty-six years; the other returns from opposition to conjunction and also lasts thirty-six years. Figure 1.3.6 shows how we start with the conjunction of the AP with a planet and make five other aspects before reaching

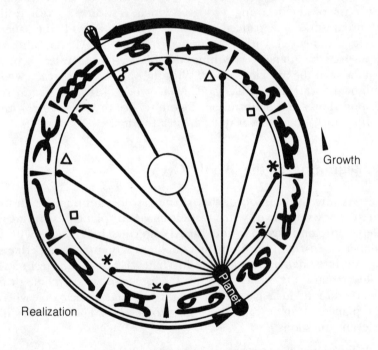

Figure 1.3.6. The Age Point aspect cycles. We have called the ascending AP *growth* and the descending AP cycle *realization.* The ascending cycle starts when the AP is conjunct the planet concerned, wherever the latter may be in the chart; the descending cycle starts with the opposition, *i.e.*, when the AP faces the planet across the chart. The individual stages are the seven classical aspects (each separated by 30° from its neighbor), marked by their respective symbols.

their opposition. This is a process of mental growth and provides an opportunity for learning and gaining competence in some special ability. After opposition, the road back to conjunction is characterized by a process of practical application, and realization.

The time has now come to speak in more detail of the *secondary aspects*, which make five stages between the two *primary aspects* in each half-cycle. There are five of these.

The five intermediate stages

These five intermediate stages, or secondary aspects, are the semisextile, sextile, square, trine and quincunx—taken either in this or in the reverse order for either of the half-cycles concerned. The interpretation of these aspects depends on whether the half-cycle is ascending or descending. For example, we can say that a square in the ascending half-cycle strongly stimulates the desire to reach a goal, whereas in the descending half-cycle it stimulates the urge to make good and active use of what had already been acquired.

The following cycle of aspects is presented so that the principle we shall now discuss can be well understood.

First Half-cycle
(the ascending one in this instance)

Conjunction of the AP (0° angle): Let us suppose, for the sake of simplicity, that a certain planet is standing on the Ascendant. (See figure 1.3.7.) Here the AP conjunction is present at birth, and the given influence begins to unfold right away. There can be no question of a conscious perception of such subtle qualities in infancy; planets on the Ascendant frequently point to a traumatic birth (see also page 117).

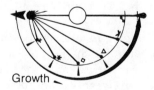

Figure 1.3.7. An ascending half-cycle.

Semisextile of the AP (30° angle): Some six years later (the exact time depends on the size of the house) there is a semisextile to the planet. In our example, this happens at a very early age, but perhaps even at this age the native had a dim inkling of the nature of the planetary influence on him or her. There is a certain amount of repetition, usually as the native becomes aware of the more obvious consequences of the conjunction. Basically, the semisextile is a mercurial aspect, relating to the field of information. Circumstances come into our lives which compel us to cope with each of the planetary influences. Many a time we learn by our mistakes.

Sextile of the AP (60° angle): Some six years later again, when the native is twelve years old, he or she enjoys the feeling of having come to terms with the planetary influence concerned; having had the first taste of success in overcoming certain problems connected with it. A hope arises in the mind that the individual's objectives have already been gained.

Square of the AP (90° angle): But then, six years further on, at the age of eighteen, the square produces a crisis. Everything seemed to be nice and safe during the sextile period, but now comes the "crunch" when the native must prove his or her command of the situation. Wrong judgments, absurd behavior and illusions will often arise from the conscious mind in response to external stimuli. It turns out that the planetary influence has not yet been fully understood, and the more rashly the native jumped to conclusions during the sextile period, the heavier is the reckoning now. More intensive work is required to elucidate the qualities symbolized by the planet. But since a fresh surge of energy accompanies this Martian aspect, the native will be able to set to work with a will. The square is the most important aspect next to the conjunction and the opposition, because it represents the midpoint, and therefore the crisis point, between the two main aspects.

Trine of the AP (120° angle): In another six years the AP reaches the trine to that planet with which the cycle began. The planetary capacities have ripened slowly and are now in full bloom. Everything comes relatively easy and there are a few genuine triumphs. Subjectively, a sense of optimism infuses the native when applying the resources of the trined planet. Smugness and pride are the danger, and the native may think there is no need to do anything more; yet, much more is on offer, even from the point of view of worldly achievement, than has so far been suspected.

Quincunx of the AP (150° angle): At the age of thirty or thereabouts the effect of the quincunx is felt, encouraging new and (this time) spiritual aims. An unknown world, stretching out in a spiritual dimension, can suddenly break in and change the life. Here is the start of a wider program of perception and learning, often linked with decisions of crucial importance. The abilities are applied to fresh goals in life. The quincunx has deep significance in Age Progression: it plays the most direct part in building consciousness, with the Age Point representing as it does the focus of the native's consciousness in time and space. When we come to describe the green aspects we shall have more to say on this.

Opposition of the AP (180° angle): The opposition is reached just thirty-six years after the conjunction. There are two possibilities here. If the native has failed to cultivate the abilities represented by the planet, the opposition may herald collapse, presaged by a certain feeling of helplessness during the quincunx aspect. If, however, the proper adjustment has been made at the time of the quincunx, concrete opportunities of which the native has not yet dreamed will open up at the opposition. The opposition can create extraordinarily favorable situations, since we have swung out to the greatest possible distance from the planet in question and can look at it in all its bearings.

The Second Half-cycle
(*descending in this case*)

Now comes the second half-cycle of thirty-six years, covering the same aspects (in reverse order) back to conjunction. (See figure 1.3.8.) Just as the first thirty-six years relate to growth so do the second thirty-six years relate to the realization of what has been developed. The faculties can now be put to good use in the outside world. Disintegration will occur only if the opposition has not been mastered and the native has remained immature and infantile.

Once more a part is played by the five intermediate aspects in making practical applications easier for the native to handle. Naturally, these aspects do not have quite the same significance they

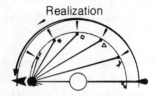

Figure 1.3.8. A descending half-cycle.

had in the first period, inasmuch as stages of manifestation are not the same as stages of growth.

The ascending and descending movement may be compared to the life of a plant, which begins with a seed buried in the earth. We could say that the seedling breaks the surface at the semi-sextile and sprouts up until it reaches its first flowering at the sextile. The blossoms are beautiful but have to give way to the start of fruiting, corresponding to the square aspect. At the trine the fruit are fully ripe, and at the quincunx we find out whether they are sound or rotten. Come opposition the fruit are picked, and during the second half-cycle they are enjoyed and digested. What is more, in the first phase the plant grows toward the sky into a spiritual dimension, while in the second phase its forces return to the soil. In the negative sense there is a process of dissolution and death, in the positive a process of manifestation. Like everything else in Age Progression, this development depends on whether or not the individual concerned perceives the laws of growth within himself or herself and wants to live by them. It is the quality of consciousness that decides. In those who still have no concept of personal freedom and responsibility, the Age Point aspects have either a negative effect or none at all. The descending process during the second half-cycle then takes a negative course (i.e., one that is distressing and bound up with mental suffering) if the opposition has ushered in a collapse. In, on the other hand, a positive second phase the benefits gained can be consolidated.

• General Rules Governing the Sequence of Aspects

Only with planets on the Ascendant does the Age Point take an "ideal" course. Its journey can begin at any stage in the aspect cycle, but it will have to wait until it comes to a conjunction or opposition before the influence of a planet is fully felt. As already said, the AP aspects which precede a conjunction or an opposition have a preparatory effect.

The native does not yet feel directly involved, and can wait unperturbed until the conjunction is reached. Say, for example, we have the first effective contact with a planet as shown in figure 1.3.9 where there is an opposition to ninth-house Saturn from the third house at some age between twelve and eighteen as the AP transits the third house. Two aspects have already been formed since birth, a trine and then a quincunx. In general, these would represent a foretaste of something which will not become fully established until later. The experiences associated with them are divorced from practical matters, because the native cannot yet see how they apply to himself or herself. Therefore they leave no imprint on the character. This is the province of the primary contact when it comes. Where planets are close to the CD, this conjunction that makes such a clear impression on the character will not occur until the thirty-sixth year of life. Where the planets are in the twelfth house, the first primary aspect takes place at opposition when the AP is in the sixth house. In these two last-mentioned instances all five secondary aspects have already been made and have laid the groundwork for what is to follow.

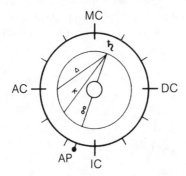

Figure 1.3.9. The Age Point in opposition to radical Saturn indicates the first effective contact between AP and Saturn between the ages of 12 and 18 years (third house).

● Primary Aspects in Childhood

In planets placed just after the AC or DC (see figure 1.3.10), primary aspects occur as early as the first or second year of life in either case. The effects are often traumatic. Since the child is as yet unable to have any conscious say in what is going on, he is completely at the mercy of the planetary influences. Taking this approach, we can read the formative events and traumas of childhood from the chart by tracing the course of the first quadrant from the AC to the IC. The first eighteen years of life may be taken as character-forming in general, although in some individuals the process is completed earlier while in others it lasts until the Age Point is well clear of the IC. During this period the native is strongly influenced and moulded by his environment. The character, which later arises from this, bears the stamp of the circumstances of youth in many respects. All oppositions and conjunctions in these first eighteen years serve to "bend the twig that will later grow into a tree." Whenever there are planets in the first and third quadrants, we have influences in the early years requiring careful investigation. (We shall return to this point later.)

It ought not to need saying that these impressions must not be regarded as inherently negative, although in the event of traumas there can often be severe inhibitions. By traumas we mean every character-forming experience of a planetary quality that leaves behind a strong impression which is hard to shake off, because the native feels he was a prey to circumstances. Circumstances can also throw up some special talent which then becomes fully active.

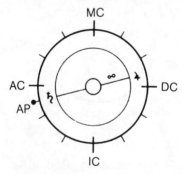

Figure 1.3.10. Traumatic aspects involving the Age Point and a radical planet may have long lasting effects.

Hints on interpretation

In interpreting youthful impressions, we have to run a check on the intensity of the conditioning, with due regard to whether or not the native has any freedom of awareness (age!), as well as considering his degree of dependence on his environment—whether he lives passively in the control of mother or nurse, say, or strives to develop interests and opinions of his own. As soon as this is known, we usually find a logical and straightforward interpretation of the native's problems or of his so-called compensations. Always there is that which is obvious or that which is concealed. The best thing to do is to ask the person concerned about what he has experienced. The rule is this: the person who compensates reacts unconsciously, the person who meets conflicts head-on reacts consciously. Thus whoever has suffered under hard primary aspects (and remembers his sufferings) has in some measure come to terms with them and is ready for further growth. But whoever compensates, that is to say suppresses problems and projects them into the world (laying the blame for them on others), is tormented by complexes or unconscious fears and behaves differently from what the planetary situations require. In instances like the latter there is often a very imperfect recollection of childhood. Before matters can be put right, a genuine effort must be made by the native to uncover the causes of his wrong attitude. True healing of a so-called disorder has to start with the uncovering of its root. In many cases this will require psychoanalysis.

• Beginning of the AP Cycle in the Four Quadrants

It will now be useful to see what happens when the aspect cycle begins in other regions of the chart. When the AP transits a planet that is not on the Ascendant (but in some other house position), the aspect sequence may begin with a secondary aspect. Alternatively, the process may start with an opposition should there be one or more planets in the third quadrant; in which case, the AP moves through the five minor aspects until it reaches the conjunction. Either way we have the same process of the perception, growth and realization of a capability. To recapitulate once more: at conjunction the half-cycle of construction begins, and at opposition the half-cycle of exploitation. The native's maturity in terms of age will naturally have to be taken into account when an analysis is made. All this will now be explained by dividing the chart into its four quadrants and looking at each in turn.

Quadrant 1: When the first contact (shown in figure 1.3.11) made by the Age Point to a planet takes place in the first quadrant, there is a corresponding process of growth in early life, even without any contribution from the infant consciousness. It goes without saying that external formative forces will be more influential in the first three houses (at ages 0-18 years) than in the later ones. In the former, the human psyche is still weak and unformed, and reacts with great sensitivity to seemingly insignificant events. There is no mature ego and therefore no properly aware response to the conjunction of Age Point and planet. Nevertheless, a powerful confrontation does take place with the planetary principle. If the planet concerned is an ego planet (Sun, Moon, Saturn), it is still not possible to handle it properly or to integrate the activated self-consciousness (the Sun) into the life. Attendant problems will not be finally solved until the opposition arrives. In the course of the aspect cycle the same set of themes is encountered at each stage (each aspect). By the time of opposition (after thirty instructional years) the problem and any traumas should have been overcome.

Quadrant 2: When a planet is standing in the second quadrant (see figure 1.3.12) life starts in the descending phase. Although the native profits by experience (perhaps gained in a former existence?), it is not until the conjunction of the AP with the planet concerned—at some age between eighteen and thirty-six—that he realizes that so far

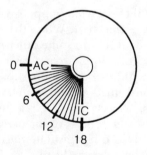

Figure 1.3.11. Age 0-18. The first, second and third houses.

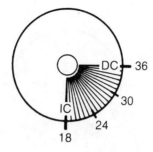

Figure 1.3.12. Age 18-36. The fourth, fifth and sixth houses.

he has not correctly understood or consciously mastered the planetary influence, even though behaving as if he had done so. The time of transit brings the first distinct awareness that much yet remains in the planetary position, and a new learning process begins. In the ascending cycle of trying and testing, the influence is brought more into consciousness; at the opposition, after thirty-six years, the native has managed to come to terms with the whole complex issue and can explore all its possibilities. Thanks to the wealth of experience acquired, the native is on a higher curve in the spiral of development, which then begins again at the conjunction (at an older age or perhaps in the next life?).

Quadrant 3: Figure 1.3.13 on page 74 illusrates the Age Point starting in the constructive half-cycle at a period in which the native's mind has been enriched by experience. Having passed through the minor aspects, he can apply some practical wisdom to the planet. His developmental phase began with an AP opposition in the first quadrant in youth. Nevertheless, the conjunction itself is not an end, but the beginning of a new process of learning and experience, usually at a more aware and at a higher level—by which we mean that the spiritual side of a planetary quality is promoted where possible. The individual who closes his mind at this point and assumes that he has no need for more experience and growth, because he already knows everything, will either be forced to develop further by inner or outer crises or be left stagnating. And stagnation is followed by resignation and senility, in that order. A conjunction of the Age Point with a primary principle requires the native to venture into new areas of experience. The planets enter with their

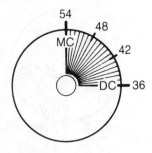

Figure 1.3.13. Age 36-54. The seventh, eighth and ninth houses.

full archetypal power into his consciousness and demand attention and promote participation in what is going on.

Quadrant 4: Figure 1.3.14 illustrates the hardest position—planets in the fourth quadrant; the native is then plunged into the building-up process at birth. A semisextile, sextile or square would be the first aspect encountered; therefore, root contact with the planetary influence is lacking—the native will attempt to deal with it this way and that and will be no more than semi-successful until the time of opposition when he knows what is really at stake. In the end he will see the planet in proper perspective against its background. From the vantage point of the opposition, he will be able to make a general survey of the planet's relationship to see how it functions. Although the native may previously (and for much of his life) gain insight in the sense of understanding into this planetary quality, he will not be able to use it much by way of development. It is too remote. People with many planets in the fourth quadrant are mainly "late developers."

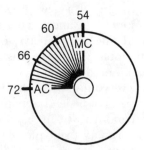

Figure 1.3.14. Age 54-72. The tenth, eleventh and twelfth houses.

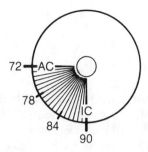

Figure 1.3.15. A second beginning

Only between the ages of fifty-four and seventy-two, when the AP comes into conjunction with one of the planets, can the latter be genuinely experienced in its deepest quality—generally through understanding. When the fourth quadrant is reached, "being" rather than "doing" is what matters. And so the fruit of past endeavors is usually "not of this world."

A Second Beginning in the First Quadrant: In figure 1.3.15 we see there is a chance that the native will be confronted with the influence of a planet he has encountered before, but on a higher turn of the spiral. He is now in a position to review past experiences, the childhood impressions and traumas. Perhaps he will discover the deepest meaning of the successes and failures, the joys and sorrows which have fallen to his lot. Even if he can no longer take a very active part in life during what is now a second ascending half-cycle, the seed is already being sown for the life to come. Should the native survive to the second transit of his first-quadrant planets, he can discover entirely new dimensions in them—the shores, so to speak, of other worlds. This is the great virtue of survival to an advanced age.

● Three Types of Aspect

It makes it easier to explain the aspects if we divide them into three types, which can be labelled with the colors red, blue and green. We will term the red aspects energy aspects, the blue aspects matter aspects, and the green aspects consciousness aspects.

Red Aspects

Conjunction: ♂
Opposition: 180° ♂
Square: 90° □

The red aspects (see figure 1.3.16) are invariably the expression of an inner dynamism, vitality, or motor energy. When the Age Point makes a red aspect with a planet, new forces are released in us in keeping with the planet concerned. Even the so-called "soft" planets (i.e., Moon, Mercury, Venus, Jupiter), have their functions intensified by red aspects. They release energetic processes in us and, often in our surroundings, too, thus bringing about the most significant changes in our manner of life.

The red aspects affect our attitudes rather than our readiness to do something positive. They act on the way we operate, not on our inner nature as the blue aspects do. For this reason we have to respond actively to such aspects; they give us an opportunity to overcome the fears and inhibitions which have so far held us back. Now we can rid ourselves of outworn conditions, either in our circumstances, in our occupations, or in ourselves. At the same time we must be prepared for possible conflicts with those around us, since any changes we make will frequently meet with their opposition. Fortunately, red aspects bestow the necessary courage to deal with the opposers.

However, if we allow ourselves to be beaten, and fail to do what needs to be done, the period can be one of suffering. And so the red aspects are classed as negative in traditional astrology. The native may willingly put up with suffering, may take excessive strain, when he ought to be reacting differently. He feels, perhaps, an

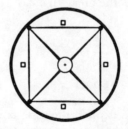

Figure 1.3.16. Red aspects: conjunction, opposition, square.

unaccountable disinclination to settle down to the work he should be doing and, because this gives him a sense of guilt, he engages in all kinds of hectic, but pointless, alternative activities. His strength is wasted—with nothing much to show for it. What is more, hastiness and a lack of proper control easily entail errors. How tempting then to say, "The red aspect has done this to me. Obviously, it is a bad aspect!" On second thought, however, the honest native would be compelled to add, "It was my fault, too. I jibbed at the challenge."

Where the red aspects are concerned, it is particularly important to determine what they require of us. The aspected planets should be closely studied to see at what points the personality needs refining. Then new actions can be broached intelligently, consciously and placidly, and positive results can be obtained in keeping with the nature of the planets concerned.

Further Rules of Interpretation for Red Aspects

Naturally, red aspects to the "hard" planets (Sun, Mars, Saturn, Uranus, Pluto) have a more powerful effect, since the planets and the aspects have much in common. Depending on the nature of the aspects in the natal chart, problems can become intensified. The individual either tends to become obdurate, or, in the best cases, to become confirmed in his essential strengths. Given the right approach, the same aspects can lead to putting one's abilities to work for the benefit of others, especially when they involve the spiritual planets (Uranus, Neptune and Pluto). A strain that would be too great for one person can prove to be an incentive to development for another—since he will appreciate the need to accept bigger tasks and responsibilities and, by doing so, to resolve his internal conflict.

Conjunction of and Opposition to the Age Point

As we have already mentioned more than once, conjunctions and oppositions are the most powerful of the seven aspects where the Age Point is concerned. Usually their ingress is marked by external events, which can bring about marked changes in behavior and life-style: in negative cases these changes take the form of mental blocks, repressions, depressions, refractoriness and aggression; but in the positive ones the change activates inner powers or the achievement of long-held ambitions—all according to the nature of the planets in question.

The Square to the Age Point

This martian aspect gives a great boost to further development. It activates us more strongly than does the opposition, but makes us more quarrelsome too. We are stirred by lively external and internal forces; and submerged wishes (and also problems, as the case may be) are brought to the surface, according to the planets and aspect configurations involved, and to the house and sign occupied by the AP.

At such times our aims and efforts may meet with opposition, but generally this will only incite us to strive the harder. A square often creates dissatisfaction with existing conditions, making us rebellious and more than ever ready to leap to the defense of our freedom and independence—but making us nervy and irritable, too, perhaps. This is especially true when the AP is aspecting "hard" planets. With aspects to "soft" planets, on the other hand, we have the temptation to intemperance and other excesses. It is not uncommon to find that the square lends a drastic character to what is going on around us.

With leading planets, i.e., those positioned near one of the main axes or standing out strongly in the aspect configuration, the four red aspects formed with each planet by the AP in the course of its travels (conjunction, square, opposition, square) can be clearly recognized during a cycle of circa eighteen years. Now and again they stand out as landmarks in life.

Blue Aspects

Sextile: 60° *
Trine: 120° △

The blue Age Point aspects (see figure 1.3.17) have to do with human "substance." Usually they inaugurate a process of change in our essential qualities. In other words, they rearrange us internally, making a qualitative, and often a quantitative, alteration in our potential. The blue aspects activate and mobilize latent capacities and release them for use. Not only do they envelop and mould us on the outside, they thrust themselves "under our skin" so to speak and

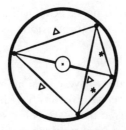

Figure 1.3.17. Blue aspects: sextile and trine.

set to work on making a radical alteration in us whether we will or no.

Because blue aspects penetrate to the roots of our being, it is next to impossible to escape their influence. At times their effects can be quite unpleasant; our bodies are drained of energy and we feel physically ill. And, once their influence pervades us, they will start attacking our ingrained habits and dissolving crystallized conditions. If we have been over-comfortable, have been living with a false sense of security, and are resting on our laurels, we shall have to start giving of ourselves once more. The "softness" of these aspects is deceptive; they can be very demanding. However, what they do to us will depend very largely on the planets being aspected and on the house and sign occupied by the Age Point.

The Sextile to the Age Point

A sextile between the Age Point and a planet will aid the solution of outstanding problems. Sextiles are venusian aspects, for which reason they often foster new relationships and the pleasanter side of life. The native becomes more adaptable and tolerant; he understands people better and can find excuses for their failures. The sextile frequently acts as a modifier and helps him to reach a compromise when involved in any dispute. His esthetic sense is heightened too. But this sense then causes discomfort if it is offended: in other words, depending on planet, sign and house, the native may over-react to petty annoyances, unwelcome events, and anything that is nasty or unpleasant. Having entered a state of harmony, he expects to be left in peace to enjoy it. Often he dreads conflicts and is ever ready to compromise—anything for a quiet life. Also, a type of assimilation process takes place during this Age

Point aspect. Often the time is now available to digest previous experience or to absorb new impressions.

The Trine to the Age Point

When we have acted creatively in some way or other, and have turned to account what certain planets have had to offer, a feeling of happiness rises within us, our reward being some solid achievement to enjoy. We can sit down and rest for a while, in the knowledge of having provided ourselves with a reserve for future needs. A new confidence in living emerges to compensate us for past strains and anxieties.

Yet there is also a risk that we will take things easy for too long and will lose sight of the fact that life is in an eternal state of flux, requiring new adjustments every day. If we have too little solidity about us, our lack will prove painful. All wrongs and errors ought now to be abandoned, so that our affairs can move forward in a happier vein. It should no longer please us to behave as if we were content with everything because a life of constant ease can end in satiety.

Trines may also lead to a continual hunt for perfection and to susceptibility to disease.

Green Aspects

Semisextile: 30° ⚺
Quincunx: 150° ⚻

Green aspects (see figure 1.3.18) act directly on our consciousness. They do not concern our human substance or demand of us any kind of activity or performance. Their effect is to make us wide

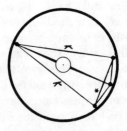

Figure 1.3.18. Green aspects: semisextile and quincunx.

awake and more keenly aware of what is going on around us. Through deeper reflection we come to realizations that promote our development. There is no need for our thinking to become rigorously logical at this time; more probably our conscious thought-life will be enriched by hunches and inspirations.

The term just used, "conscious thought-life," is a wider concept than "thinking"; it expresses what comes with the assimilation of all our experiences, and includes not only intellectual activity but sensory perceptions, together with those intuitive feelings that make hidden knowledge accessible to consciousness. Green aspects help us to be sensitive and open to new lines of thought.

Therefore the two green aspects have a special significance for the Age Point, being the main switchboards in our decision-making.

Decision-making possibilities peak during green aspects, by reason of the fact that not only is the Age Point primarily the focus of consciousness, but also these are the aspects which have to do with consciousness and thought. What is more, such aspects in the main promote not external performance but the activities of consciousness: clear thinking, the acquiring of experience, and decision taking. Squares are typical activity-incentive aspects, yet may encourage rashness and so lead to unfortunate results. When the green aspects arrive they help to correct such errors; they aid in the gathering of fresh information, and shed light on complicated situations. Although blue aspects allow scope for an individual's talents they can also lead to plethora and conceit. Green aspects, on the other hand, can make us aware of this fact that sometimes "virtue itself turns vice."

The Semisextile to the Age Point

At the semisextile we become desirous of learning, are eager to enrich our experience at the hand of the planet concerned, and many times commence a regular study of its properties.

When a semisextile is being interpreted, it is important to note whether the aspect is ahead or behind the conjunction. If we are looking at the second half-cycle, with the conjunction coming up, the native is usually absorbed in theory. He is still unsure of himself and is troubled by the notion that his practical knowledge of the quality represented by the planet is still deficient. Only at the following conjunction does he make the necessary identification with it. At the next semisextile (the one coming after the conjunction) it is easier for him to pass on whatever he has learned. He is communicative and keen to hear what others have to say on any subject. Therefore he can be found engaging in exchanges of opinions more frequently than formerly. He is more talkative and inquisitive and more intent on imparting his knowledge to others. As mentioned earlier, the Age Point traces out a continuous learning process, so that the action of one aspect forms a prelude to the next. Only at the opposition do we begin to reap the benefit of everything that is accessible to us through the aspecting planets.

The Quincunx to the Age Point

We would re-emphasize here what has been said before, namely that this aspect has a special significance in Age Point progression. We call the long green aspects the big stride forward in thought by way of contrast to a "little step forward in thought" (the semisextile). The long green aspect often creates uncertainty, due to a proneness on the part of the native to think ahead longingly to some distant goal. Therefore this is also known as the wistful or suspenseful aspect. Once again, it is important to determine whether the aspect comes before or after the opposition. Before the opposition, it is experienced as a yearning after some remote objective. In many instances it begets irresolution and crucial decision-making, and (after a long period of effort, of weighing up the pros and cons, and of looking for answers) can signify an acceptance by the native of the challenge to limit himself to a specific aim. When he does so, however, it will usually be after the opposition has been passed. The effect is to strengthen consciousness and will in keeping with the quality of the Age Point as a focus of consciousness.

● Three Stages in the Development of the AP Quincunx Aspect

There are three stages in the life of the long green aspect: In the first stage, the native is insecure and hovers between various thoughts and desires. He builds castles in the air and projects his innermost wishes on others, or on the far unknown. Without knowing what he really wants, he has the vague feeling that he was born to be a "somebody." He is easily influenced and will usually do just what he is told, gladly being subject to a stronger will—at least until he knows his own mind. He becomes a seeker, and an ill-defined longing drives him on.

In the second stage he is beset by doubts. Although his daydreams still please him, he is troubled by a nagging suspicion that things are not quite right. He now begins to think, to ask questions, to philosophize. A regular Faustian struggle develops with all its intellectual dissatisfaction and crisis of faith. Truth wears many faces for him, and the native sees so many possibilities that he tends to lose himself in the relative. Nothing he can do enables him to decide what is worthless and what worthwhile; he falls into a severe decision crisis.

In the third stage the native recognizes that everything depends on him; he must decide to restrict himself to a single matter, even if this is at the expense of his freedom, his fantasy life, or his ideal picture of himself and the world. Here is where the will is trained. Realizing that he will never achieve everything he would like to do, he settles for something less, even if it is not his first choice. And if he abides by this decision, he can be fairly confident that a day will come when his purpose will be gained and, what is more, that he will be a more resolute, maturer and wiser individual. The long and difficult way is also the way forward. Therefore we call these aspects development aspects.

But there are pitfalls. If the native defers making decisions that would benefit his inner growth, the long green aspect to the Age Point will make itself felt in some outer event corresponding to the planetary nature and will force him to face essentials. In the United States, the quincunx aspect is also known as "the finger of God" because it is often associated with the buffets of fate attendant on irresolution and a lack of sound judgment in the native.

It is wise to prepare for such quincunx aspects in good time—especially where the ego-planets (Sun, Moon and Saturn) are concerned. We must arrive at decisions which will lead to inner growth. What is more, it is important to recognize and, if possible, to solve EGO problems. Then, when the long green aspect arrives, we shall already know what is required of us. This is the very considerable help afforded by a knowledge of Age Progression in the horoscope!

Chapter 4

Age-Point Aspects
to the Ten Planets
and to the Lunar Nodes

Introduction—Age-Point aspects to the three personality planets—The Sun: AP transit (conjunction)—House position of the Sun—Aspects and aspect-cycle of the Sun—The Moon: AP transit (conjunction)—House position of the Moon—Aspects and aspect-cycle of the Moon—Subjectivity—Green aspects from the Moon—Sense of personal worth (sensitivity)—Contrasts existing in the emotional body—The child like Moon Ego: spontaneity—Saturn: transit (conjunction)—House position of Saturn—AP aspects and aspect-cycle of Saturn—Mercury, Mars, Venus, Jupiter: AP transits and aspect cycles—Uranus, Neptune, Pluto: AP transits and aspect cycles—The Lunar Nodes: AP transits and aspect cycles

● Introduction

In judging the aspects made by a planet to the Age Point, it is necessary to refer to the natal chart. We cannot properly assess an aspect or house position from the Age Point alone; the chart must be taken as a whole. A planet is found not only in a house and sign but also in relationships with other planets. All these together impart a characteristic—and permanent—coloration to the basic influence of each planet. Potentially this coloration can give lifelong problems, which are activated from time to time by the Age Point.

In order to evaluate the AP aspects as comprehensively as possible, we must be systematic and elucidate the following points in connection with the Age Point and planets:

A) Status of the Age Point:

   1. House position of the Age Point;
   2. Effect of the house;
   3. Stage of life represented by this house;
   4. Sign position of the Age Point;
   5. Aspect to Age Point (conjunction, semisextile, trine, etc.);
   6. Color of aspect (blue, red or green).

B) Status of the Planet:

   1. Number of aspects made by planet in the natal chart;
   2. Colors of these aspects;
   3. Sign position of the planet;
   4. Whether planet is strongly or weakly placed in the sign (strongest point 12°, weakest point 0° or 29°);
   5. House position of the planet;
   6. House region where planet is posited (cusp, invert point, low point, before or after the axis).

In judging an Age-Point aspect we must not assume that the native will make full use of the positive possibilities of the planetary position. When the radical position of the planets has some afflictions, difficulties of various degrees of severity can arise (compulsions, compensations). But this can be established only at an interview. During a counselling session with a client such potential problems have to be taken into consideration and evaluated.

• Age-Point Aspects to the Three Main Planets: Sun, Moon, and Saturn

In the aspects made between the Age Point and the Sun, Moon and Saturn, we see mirrored the development of personality into autonomous individuality. Our point of view is the human EGO anchored in three planes: the Sun representing the mental plane, the Moon the emotional plane, and Saturn the physical plane. The concerted action of the three EGO planets depends on their radical positions. From these we learn how the total personality is constituted and where its strengths and weaknesses lie.

It follows that, taken together, the Age-Point aspects made to the three personality planets are involved with 1) our ego, self-observation and degree of conscious autonomous thought (Sun), 2) our emotional liability and impressionability (Moon), and, 3) our physical safety and things "practical" (Saturn). Attention must always be paid, however, to the house region in which a planet is posited. On the cusp, the planet receives unlimited feedback, that is to say, it receives corroboration from the environment. At the Low Point, on the other hand, it prompts remoter, more uncertain and more subjective reactions. A person with planets at the Low Point is often totally unaware of any feedback. Here we find a distinction that makes it hard to lay down general rules for the AP aspects. In what follows we shall do our best to supply a comprehensive description of the effect of the AP aspects on the main planets; on the other hand, the leading indications only will be mentioned for the other planets.

• The Sun

The Sun is the symbol of the self-conscious mind, and of the logical thinker. Aspects between the Age Point and the Sun present a challenge to autonomous thinking that could lead to self-development. It goes without saying that it will help to increase independence and personal application. Events that support this trend tend to occur.

Transit or Conjunction

At AP-transit, the Ego's mental pole, or "solar" consciousness is activated. Generally, the native has a creative urge and a longing for adventure; he wants to "sit on top of the pile" and attract the attention of others. The Sun bestows the strength and courage to make his own decisions and to go his own way, even at the risk of a certain amount of failure. To enjoy a healthy self-confidence, he needs to trust his own ability and to accept responsibility for himself and others. This gives him more confidence to develop. According to the time of life of the native, and to the sign in which the transit occurs, there is a desire for freedom and self-determination.

House position of the Sun

When the Sun stands in the tenth house, for example, a transit through the fourth house brings us in opposition to it; then we have the strength of mind to make a conscious break with the aims of our community, our parents or other authorities. No longer do we need to wait for confirmation, permission or applause—we can get along under our own steam. On the other hand, when the Sun is actually standing in the fourth house, an AP transit will occur between the ages of eighteen and twenty-four. It is then the meaning of the fourth (not the tenth) house which has to be used in interpreting both Sun position and AP transit.

With a fourth-house Sun, we usually bow to community rules or family tradition whatever our initial objections. We gain in self-confidence by performing household duties or by accepting some function in the community or family.

Since the Sun also symbolizes the father (who is a key figure in the formation of our own self-confidence), it may also come about that—according to the aspects thrown to the Sun in the Radix—our self-confidence is braced or undermined by the father or by some father figure such as an employer of a government department. How this will work out in practice will depend on the situation as a whole, and is not easy to predict in advance. In consultation work, it is best to avoid concrete predictions and even to ask the client how he or she is experiencing this phase.

The aspects and aspect cycle of the Sun

As the solar aspects come and go, the native grows more practiced at using the force of his personality and at recognizing the strengths and weaknesses in his personal development. He can afford to smile indulgently at offers of encouragement and support from those around him and to make his own decisions without reference to anybody. Surprisingly enough, this is accepted by his fellows, even when (owing to a Low-Point position of the Sun in the radix) he himself has the uncomfortable feeling that he is being rather daring with them. In AP aspects to the Sun, the native experiences a greater inner and outer security and freedom in doing whatever he thinks to be right. Solar consciousness is autonomous and does not depend on consent. Independence and self-assurance will tend to be boosted every time an AP aspect is made to the natal Sun.

This theme is modified according to the nature of the aspect. By referring to the aspect cycle and its description, the reader will be able to trace the gradual development of self-confidence and.

possibly, of self-realization. As mentioned above, we have to allow for the Sun's radical aspects, since self-consciousness is largely influenced by associated planetary forces. These, too, are activated and brought into play by the Age Point aspects.

Thus with a natal Sun-Mars trine, Mars is co-aspected with the Sun when the Age Point transits the latter. The native then had the chance to show that he is as secure, strong and self-confident, as is indicated in his radix. Again, if the Sun is in conjunction with Venus or Mercury, these will share the transit with the Sun. With Venus, self-confidence will depend on harmonious surroundings, on personal esthetics, and even on whatever panders to the native's vanity. With Mercury, the intellect comes into play and may be brilliant at this time.

The above are no more than a few of the possible combinations. Every serious student of astrology should make sure of being able to define the qualitative effects of the basic planetary functions and should be able to work out their joint influences. (See also *Life Clock*, Vol. 1, p. 194, "Basic Functions of the Ten Planets.")

● The Moon

The Moon has to do with our emotional self, which puts us in immediate touch with our surroundings. Whereas the Sun's Age aspects enhance self-confidence and will-power, the Moon's Age aspects enhance the need for contacts, the capacity for love and sensitivity. In astrology, the planets and other elements of the horoscope may be considered from various points of view. So the Moon can be seen as representing the contactual ego, the juvenile ego or the emotional ego. These are merely different names for the same function, as we shall see. The Moon does not stand for the autonomy of the self as the Sun does, but for the perception of personal emotional responses to our surroundings. Through our relationships with people and with plants and animals, we receive confirmation that we possess a contactual or emotional ego, and that we are sensitive and responsive beings. Self-knowledge of the lunar ego is experienced in the following way: "I am being noticed, I am being understood," or simply, "I am being loved." These feelings are especially noticeable at Age Point conjunction or opposition at which times the heightened sense of personal worth brings happiness.

Human emotions predominately react on themselves, i.e. sub-jectively. Because of our human egocentricity, they work like a magnifying glass, enlarging all our impressions. But perhaps an even better comparison would be with a fairground "crazy" mirror, seeing that our subjectivity invariably distorts reality either positive-ly or negatively. Egocentricity also provokes rash judgments based on the current situation of the native, so that his one thought is, "This is good and that is bad for me." When the Moon "objectifies" or differentiates, it is into for and against, into sympathy and antipathy.

Transit (conjunction)

On direct transit there is a conscious experience of the emo-tional ego; usually through a closer knitting of relationships. This closeness is responsible, however, for emotional ups and downs: sympathy and antipathy, attraction and repulsion, can follow one another like ebb and flow.

The lunar conjunction causes an extra strain in our emotional structure; therefore the meaning of the Moon for our development needs to be examined in more detail. At the transit, we become more acutely aware of our personal wishes in respect to contacts, and seek to emerge from any comparative isolation to find satisfaction in proximity to our fellows. Whether or not we really get close to them will depend largely on how the development of our emotional life, as a whole, has been going. Anyway, we find it easier to surmount difficulties in handling others during this period, when we are honest with our feelings, since the Age Point activates all the emotional components relating to the Moon. If, in the meantime, we have suffered or are still suffering from emotional frustrations (a state of affairs frequently indicated by red, and occasionally by green aspects in the radix), this fact will now become painfully apparent.

House position of the Moon

As already mentioned, the interpretation of a transit of the Moon's place has to be guided by house position and by the age and maturity of the native. For instance, if the Moon is in the fifth house, the emotions will be stirred up at the age between twenty-five and thirty, either by some new love affair or by separation. In the fifth house, the Moon will retain a certain tendency to endorse childishness, and to some extent will make the native want to cling to what he already has. His sense of personal worth will depend on whether and on how much he is loved. Every readjustment will arouse jealousy and a struggle for possession; possibly the process of maturation will take place only through some painful loss, some rejection, some defeat in love, or a changed relationship.

Moon aspects and aspect cycles

In essence, there is a development of emotional qualities and values during all AP aspects to the Moon. The improvement of the capacity for making contacts, and for love, occupies the foreground, and frequently we even experience the very things that we need for our development: love won, love lost, and loneliness. Generally speaking the amplitude of the "pendulum swing" ruling this process is considerable, since our emotions are polarized between good and evil, love and hate, joy and sorrow, etc. For this reason the differences between the various aspect types are much easier to trace in Age Point aspects to the Moon than in Age Point aspects to the Sun and planets.

Responding to the qualities of the individual aspects, we work our way through change after change until we acquire emotional stability and become able to solve, with conscious intent, the problems arising from interpersonal relationships. Most folk suffer from emotional problems of one kind or another; but this is all part of being human.

To recapitulate, then, on what to expect from the aspects: Blue aspects bring reassurance and harmony, red aspects nearly always cause a certain amount of commotion, difficulty and hardship, and green aspects engender longings, undefinable states of the feelings and a sense of insecurity.

Green aspects to the Moon

The green aspects promote development through an increased capacity for comprehension. Our maturation is oriented toward the most relaxed and balanced emotional state as possible; for it is only composure and inner harmony that makes us capable of really making friends or of finding true love. With the quincunx, decisions often have to be made in matters of friendship and love. At that juncture we have the opportunity of achieving a certain neutrality or detachment in our feelings—so essential if we are not to run the risk of being swept off our feet into a relationship we shall later regret. As our maturity improves in quality, love will no longer be misused as a means of satisfying desires but will become ultra-personal in the sense of being all-inclusively open and sharing. What has to be encouraged is not quantitative emotion in the form of passionate outbursts but a consistent kindliness to all living creatures.

Feelings of self-esteem (sensitiveness)

Lunar feelings of self-esteem are dependent on experience, and are responsive to the environment. As the reflecting principle, the Moon enables us to perceive and react to contacts of every kind—it represents our sensitivity. It would therefore be a mistake to think that the Moon normally gives rise to a demanding ego. The causes of faulty reactions on the emotional plane are usually to be found in an overemphatic subjectivity, where all relationships are tied up with the emotional ego. But the ego-pole ought to have such a degree of detachment that, although there is still an ego-consciousness, this consists of an optimistic awareness that, "Yes, I am sensitive and always quick to react, but I am also able to identify and understand everything which stirs my emotions."

The end result is emotional security, and a feeling of personal value, combined with independence from the environment. We are no longer relying on confirmation from others that we are worthy of friendship and love; we have been set free to decide, without being under any kind of pressure, when to socialize and when to spend some time alone.

The sooner during the ascending half-cycle we release ourselves from selfish affections, the sooner we shall acquire a healthy neutrality, equilibrium and emotional stability. Then, with a more finely tuned emotional life, we shall find ourselves more sensitive in our reactions to our surroundings. At the same time, our perception of the objective world will become increasingly differentiated and our judgment of people and events will be more balanced and accurate.

Contrasts existing in the emotional body

The greater the swings of mood between positive and nega-tive—between love and hate say—the more powerful is the pull of the ego. This egocentricity embedded in the subjective side of our feelings becomes more apparent to us with each succeeding AP aspect, especially when it is a red aspect. During such aspects we can see for ourselves how keen we are to be loved. But the main thing is to beware of falling back into bad habits. Experience must already have taught us that understanding and love should be bestowed without any thought of recompense. Love means giving and taking freely; the compulsive urge to demand affection has nothing to do with it.

That is the one extreme in red aspects to the Moon; the other is when the individual lives for others in a self-sacrificing way and completely neglects his own interests. Egoism (but here a covert egoism) can lie behind this form of behavior, too, when the self-sacrifice is made in the hope of being loved. A vain hope this, because unrestrained giving and giving way to others is seldom rewarded as it would seem to deserve. Any extremes in our emotional life will lead to disappointments and instability. Nevertheless, during such periods, we learn a great deal about ourselves and others and about our relationships to them—especially during the green aspects.

The childlike Moon ego: spontaneity

A further effect of the Age Point aspect to the Moon depends on an essential quality of a well-developed Moon ego: spontaneity. In this respect the Moon is quite different from the Sun or Saturn. The Moon always encourages spontaneous reactions, because it represents the principle of changeableness. Such reactions cannot be planned in advance, but spring out of a given situation in the here and now. Spontaneity demands that we keep on our toes so to speak; it guarantees an optimal flow of information and brings increased learning capacity.

Children, who are so governed by the Moon, exhibit this spontaneity to a high degree, especially when in the care of their mothers. As is well-known, a child reacts in a direct and lively manner, is open in approach, and only gradually becomes more constrained under the guidance of its parents. The child's natural spontaneity is the proper attribute of the Moon, and will not be entirely lost during life. In spite of all demands and the struggle for existence, we can always rekindle our spontaneity and sensitivity if we set out minds to do so. This ought to be the aim of Moon-based development and it will enable us to remain capable of loving and of being surrounded by those who love us right down to a good old age. Of course, this will be easier for us to manage under green or blue aspects than under the red ones.

● Saturn

Saturn builds the physical pole of our personality. It gives physical reality, of which the vital instinct is this: I must survive, I must function properly. The supreme law of Saturn is security, and the struggle for security takes place on all three planes of human existence. Thus it is not only the body which craves safety; the soul and spirit long for it too. Looked at from another angle, Saturn is also our memory. It helps us to retain our experiences so that we can later interpret them. We gather them for future reference. The disadvantage is the ease with which anxiety arises out of all our gathering and hoarding of memories—and out of our security-mindedness; an anxiety lest something unfortunate should happen. And so we find the need to set up some form of protection. Saturn is the opposite number of the Sun. The latter as the active, expansive principle, and Saturn as the limiting principle, often counteract one another in us. Under the influence of Saturn, we are concerned not to spread ourselves but to keep a grip on things, people, or positions.

Transit (Conjunction)

It is chiefly the desire for security that is activated at the transit of Saturn. We are increasingly inclined to hang on to our gains—and also to lost causes. Owing to our own inflexibility, life is often turned into a sort of prison from which we may find it hard to break out, especially when anxiety gets the upper hand and we fight shy of changing. Then we cordon ourselves off and deliberately put ourselves out of bounds to the world at large. Such static blocking-up is the negative side of Saturn, and no concessions should be made to it. If we do fasten the shutters, so to speak, we are as good as buried alive, and are cut off from all the productive forces of nature. We expose ourselves to a risky state of dependency. We can no longer consciously take part in life. Events trample over us because we no longer have any control over them, and they leave us pressed down even further into our rut. To seek safety in non-acceptance is the wrong reaction to a Saturn aspect. Nature herself knows no complete standstill, but is borne along by continual rhythmic fluctuation and change.

At times, Fate seems to have us on the rack and it feels as if we are about to be broken. It is then that we have to behave accommodatingly. Some of our quite justified demands may have to go. Recognition of this principle is the essential step required of us at every aspect between the Age Point and Saturn. At the transit, we can learn to assume responsibility for our lives. Saturn, as an ego planet, bestows material competence, security, and inner competence—but only when we gain the insight that so much we encounter is already within us.

The house position of Saturn

The house occupied by Saturn frequently marks the area in which the native likes to complain he is having a bad time. If it is in the seventh house (or partnership) for example, he might make allegations that as soon as his wife married him, she tied him down, imposed her will on him, and has kept him at her beck and call ever since. But, when the Age Point transits Saturn, he may realize that his inherent weakness in the area of partnership has brought him a dominating spouse, and that he was half-wanting to be ruled by her. Armed with this amount of self-knowledge, he may find it possible to insist on his rights. Meanwhile, he still grumbles. Similarly, those with Saturn in the eighth house tend to blame society, those with Saturn in the sixth house will blame an employer or colleagues, and those with the planet in the fifth house will blame circumstances for faults partly their own. The same goes for the other houses.

The AP aspects and aspect-cycle of Saturn

As already mentioned, Saturn chiefly represents the physical ego or bodily consciousness. Therefore, with the advent of any Age Point aspects we should take extra care of our physical health and safety, and should cultivate the ability to sense how we are and what is the current state of the environment. In this way we shall improve the efficiency of our lives.

Even where the five intermediate aspects are concerned, it would be a mistake to view security as static, and to shut ourselves away behind stone walls as it were. The body's true boundary is the skin. When surrounded by other boundaries (other bodies) we instinctively grasp this fact and react accordingly. Boundaries also contain barriers, but it is possible to negotiate these by an elastic and sensitive response to the demands of life. Especially is this true of the mental realm, where a closed and static picture of the world brings spiritual death. But if we can overcome the trepidation felt from Saturn's aspects and are ready to accept what is endeavoring to grow within us, we shall gain in self-assurance—a self-assurance that will enable us to accomplish difficult tasks. The ability to mount a successful challenge to fate is perhaps the best gift of Saturn, and is something to which we should aspire. Our powers are brought into play, new doors open up, and we come aware of many things which were formerly out of range.

Red aspects will enable us to tear down old partitions, and to take stock of traditional opinions and cast them aside if necessary. During blue aspects, on the other hand, our reactions are rather rigid (due to habit) and there is a fairly high risk of suffering from anxiety states. Anxiety is typical of Saturn as a planetary influence and, what is more, it will only be aggravated by a determination to cling to things outworn. Of all the aspects, the opposition has the greatest braking effect on our activity and on the urge to forge ahead. Without some such opposing force however, there would be nothing to check the onward rush powered by the Sun. If we take a ride in a car with no brakes, our first outing in it is likely to be our last. It is the green aspects that provide optimum conditions for achieving an economy of forces.

Another fundamental function of Saturn is to promote economy in our expenditure of energy. We must learn how to employ our resources and to bring our energies into play as efficiently as possible—and when we speak of energies and resources we mean those that are mental and spiritual as well as those that are material. Whoever spends more than he earns, is behaving in a very un-Saturnian manner; he has no control over his means of subsistence.

The individual who has found it impossible to manage his energies can learn to do so during the Age-Point aspects. When we come up against limitations in the external world, such as impending insolvency, loss of face, illness, lack of encouragement, etc., we encounter that malefic quality attributed to Saturn in the literature. From this point of view, it is the "Dweller of the Threshold," which comes to exact payment and turn back the presumptive adept who attempts things beyond his ability. But when we learn to channel our energies effectively, Saturn brings us inner security, spontaneous confidence and a real joy in living. Younger patrons of astrology tend to see Saturn as a helpful influence which they welcome rather than dread.

● Mercury, Venus, Mars, Jupiter

When compared to the three planets of Personality, the Age Point aspects to the four planets Mercury, Venus, Mars and Jupiter appear somewhat less notable. Nevertheless, these planets do represent organs and functions in the native that are significant for his development. As already mentioned, we become more aware of the qualities of a planet when it is being transited. It is best, therefore, to cultivate an expectant attitude in order to be able to respond positively to the planetary principle and to grow in maturity. With a readiness to learn we shall develop true to pattern. Age Point aspects bring illnesses and material setbacks only when the opportunity for further development is deliberately ignored or rejected. To this extent we have a choice as to how the aspects will operate. We shall now discuss the most important effects of the AP transit (conjunction) and of the AP cycle in regard to the development of the individual planetary abilities. The intensity—positive or negative—of a planet's contact with the Age Point largely depends on the native's inner adjustment. There is no point in trying to make hard-and-fast predictions, since so much that happens to a person is determined by his character and by his conscious attitude.

● Mercury

During the AP transit, we are both eager and able to learn those things implied by Mercury's position in sign and house. Thanks to our mental nimbleness and curiosity, we are ready to explore new areas of knowledge and can glean a mass of interesting facts in the process. We may, for the first time, find that we have a good working knowledge of some subject; also that we can improve this knowledge considerably by conscious effort. The transit of Mercury improves our intellectual efficiency; professional and other successes are in the cards as we become more perceptive. The work of those of us who are still at school shows a marked improvement and lost time is made up with relative ease. For the rest, we may discover that people who once ignored us suddenly give us a hearing and take us seriously. The time is ripe for a change of job: we are ready for the new because the old has lost its fascination. In the past, perhaps, we were rather reserved, but now there are stimulating new people to meet with whom we can exchange ideas. Finally, we shall probably want to pass on our knowledge and may look for some calling in which it will be possible to do so.

During the aspect cycle a development takes place in our intellectual prowess. Mercury's medium is speech, and it gives the ability to clothe thoughts in well-chosen words that carry conviction. It also imparts a gift for languages. Its strength lies in the collecting, arranging and cataloging of ideas. Business sense, too, is displayed under its influence. Every aspect, as it arrives, will stimulate us to cultivate Mercurial characteristics, which is all to the good as long as we do not spread our interests so thin that we no longer have the energy to pursue our true path.

The negative effects are: talkativeness, sensationalism, false compromises, indecision, trying to bring everyone down to the same level, and trimming one's sails to every wind.

● Venus

When the AP transits Venus, we are more convivial and more prepared to indulge ourselves. We want to enjoy the good things in life and to avoid harsh realities. We may even fall over backwards to compromise with people. Where, in the past, we would have stuck to our guns come what may, we now seek to reach agreement. Enemies are won over and harmony replaces unrest.

Venus represents selectivity in human relationships. At the transit of the planet, we are usually acutely aware of who or what is congenial to us and the reverse. We become choosy about our friends and may want to have folks around us with whom we feel comfortable. Many of us will find that our former boon companions no longer appeal to us. In addition, Venus is the planet of the female libido. Age permitting, the transit of Venus can give a man an intense experience of the female sex. And, where a woman is concerned, she can become much more passionate and sexually demanding towards her partner. She could also get on better with other women.

As far as the AP aspect cycle is concerned, the chief point of interest is the development of our interaction with others (from mere politeness to genuine friendship) and of that esthetic sense which serves to smooth our rough edges. Venus embodies harmony and beauty, and each time she is aspected we have an opportunity to find pleasure—either in our loved ones or in material or spiritual things.

Venus takes part in all processes of selection and assimilation. At each AP aspect we are once more faced with the necessity of choosing between this and that, and will gradually improve our understanding of what our nature really requires. Many of us will have to learn when to say yes and when to say no. Others will be able to free themselves from feelings of guilt arising from faulty teaching which had hindered them from essaying anything good. Yet there is a distinct possibility (depending on the radical aspects) that we shall have to accept suffering. Venus seeks balance in all things and, where the equilibrium has been disturbed, she comes along with a counterweight to restore it. If we have been too absorbed in our little luxuries and personal comforts, the transit of Venus can make us aware of how soft and spineless we have become; we may even fall ill. And if, to avoid our responsibilities, we have abandoned independent thought in order to serve some idea, or are allowing ourselves to be ruled by a stronger personality, we shall have to face the challenge to take our destiny in our own hands again.

If on the other hand we have been self-reliant in the past, and have avoided close relationships, we shall become more approachable during the Venusian aspect. We shall start looking for friendship and love—and are quite likely to find the right partner.

The negative aspects are: indulgence, opportunism, presumption, lack of reliability, flightiness, excessive sexual demands in the female, poor sexual performance or effeminacy in the man.

● Mars

When the AP transits Mars our performance is improved. We perceive a new strength enabling us to do things which have needed tackling for a long time. Suddenly we have the courage to do what has to be done; our nervousness is gone. Those of us who are normally low on motivation gain an exhilarating sense of freedom. We venture into the unknown and set to work to gain our ends. At the same time, we are usually rather impatient and want to put our plans into immediate effect. Mars is the male libido planet and frequently brings women liaisons with the opposite sex. In men it helps to activate their potency and sense of machismo and so leads to more intense love-making. The transit is a positive period for our hopes and wishes.

Before making any rash moves, however, we should study the aspects in the radix. Perhaps we are overestimating our strengths, or flattering ourselves too much on our chances. After all, our resources may be great but they are not unlimited. Unless sign and house position decree otherwise, we are inclined to take an exaggerated view of things; our defense mechanisms and our pugnacity are increased, too, and should be checked for motivation.

During the AP cycle there is a development of our motor energy and such a blind willingness to get on with things that we are liable to go storming forward regardless of risk. During this cycle, therefore, we shall have ample opportunity to discover what we are really capable of doing—usually through crises arising at the various aspects. We learn from Mars by passing through the fire, by living experience, and not by mere observation or book knowledge. No doubt we shall burn our fingers more than once before we acquire wisdom. The goal of development during the martian cycle is to gain awareness of our motoric driving power. How long this will take depends on the planets associated with Mars. Alternatively, we can consciously employ the energy and executive power of the red planet to set things in motion again after a time of repose or relaxation.

The negative effects are: injudicious dealings, violence, a love of aggression and destruction, excessive carnal desire and male chauvinism, conflicts and schisms.

● Jupiter

Our powers of perception and observation are improved and we see the world and our own possibilities in a truer light. We have a clear appreciation of what is true and what false in ourselves and others. Jupiter represents the sum-total of all the senses; at conjunction it is stimulated and wide-awake. Discernment, a sense of values and an appreciation of quality are distinctly activated. Perhaps we shall be horrified by the knowledge of the mistakes we have already made. Things are often seen in their right proportions for the first time and our system of values may benefit by growing in scope. For Jupiter does indeed bring an extension of consciousness and allows the wider connections between things to be seen. The result is great assurance, spiritual growth, and a knowledge of inner motivations: all of which frees us of any doubts we may have had about our eventual success. We are now conscious of our best qualities and can turn them to good account. It was not for nothing that traditional astrology called Jupiter the "Greater Fortune."

During the AP cycle of Jupiter there is a development of our sense perceptions. In the ascending half-cycle the latter are sharpened; our powers of observation become better and more precise and we have a truer understanding of the realities of life. It is easier for us to recognize deceptions, illusions and untruths; we react to wrong attitudes in ourselves and others with greater awareness and do not labor under so many false impressions. What we do is more worthy of us, and we become wiser, more tolerant and more impartial. The clearer our perceptions, the more accurately we shall judge matters and, as the years go by we shall gain a clearer insight into the hidden "machinery" that rules appearances. This will give us more freedom in the way we express ourselves. The end of the cycle is often a time when everything fits perfectly into place, even those things which once bothered us or filled us with dread. For one of the functions of Jupiter is to release our self-healing powers.

The negative effects are: delusions and pride, an attitude of "I know best," boasting, arrogance, insubordination, light-mindedness, irresponsibility.

● Uranus, Neptune, Pluto

With the three more recently discovered planets we come to respresentatives of mental or spiritual faculties which are for the most part latent within us. During the AP cycle these can be developed. In figure 1.3.4 on page 55, we see these "newer" planets placed by themselves above the three main planets. This is because we regard them as "higher ego principles" or as organs of the so-called "higher self"—Uranus as the creative intelligence, Neptune as the higher love principle, and Pluto as spiritual will-power. In their purest form they are active only in a person who has largely succeeded in integrating his threefold personality and is unselfishly trying to help forward the evolution of the race. However, for the most part they operate as a collective fate, by which those who ignore the wider issues are often developed more harshly, and in spite of themselves.

During the AP aspect cycles of the three newer planets, we have opportunity for a gradual increase in our understanding of the true nature of these fundamental spiritual principles. They belong to transpersonal (suprapersonal) regions in which everything has to take place without the intervention of the ego; that is to say, without conscious purpose or self-assertion. If we are not calm and collected we shall not be able to handle them properly, and this is the reason why they so often exercise a disruptive effect, especially on selfish plans.

All AP aspects to the three spiritual planets, but especially the conjunction, perform transmutations on the elements that control our behavior. They mobilize forces within us that are inspirational and consciousness-expanding; forces that have a cleansing action but are often disrupting, too. It may well happen that, when the AP transits one of them, we begin to take an interest in spiritual topics and activities; or circumstances may take a hand in introducing us to transcendental dimensions.

● Uranus

Often, when the Age Point transits Uranus, we are visited by a spirit of unrest and have the feeling that something completely new is about to happen. We begin to wonder if the way we are living is as it should be. The very possibility that it may not be so can make us anxious and disturbed and open a door to new vistas, fresh concepts. We have a desire to investigate, and our creative intelligence is stimulated. There is a wish to know what lies beyond our everyday world. Therefore, at the time of transit, we are likely to come across some arcane volumes or some people who will introduce us to new thought structures (*e.g.*, to astrology). Such finds or encounters often impart a shock which upsets the values on which we have so far relied. Our old world sinks below the waves of life and a new world rises to view.

An important Uranian motive is to gain security through knowledge—not the narrow, personal security of Saturn, but a more spiritual and spacious type of security. The native wants to penetrate deeper into the secrets of life and to learn the laws of human, of planetary, and even of cosmic development. His attitudes undergo a transformation and a "Saul" may be converted into a "Paul." The life-style is altered and, maybe the traditional way of doing things is rejected out-of-hand in typical Uranian style. In a word, he experiences a revolutionary change of consciousness.

During the AP aspect-cycle we gradually become acclimatized to fresh, conscious attitudes. As aspects come along, we experience an urge of varying intensity to leave behind the frontiers of the known, to expand our consciousness, and to improve the running of our lives and our sense of security by an input of new knowledge. In the aspects succeeding the conjunction, we are still feeling our way and are ready to fall back on the tried and trusted at a moment's notice. The start of the spiritual path is beset by doubts, which are dispelled only a few at a time. Upon our first entry into spiritual dimensions, we are still unsure whether or not we are moving in the right direction. We take pains to make things secure for ourselves and, especially at the quincunx, tend to be tormented by spasms of doubt. These, however, serve to develop our awareness and our autonomy of thought. But by opposition at the latest we should have obtained clear indications of the reality of spiritual, impalpable things. As time goes by, we become more successful at integrating the effects of Uranus with our creative intelligence. This puts us in possession of a bubbling spring of inspiration: a source of originality and inner strength.

The negative effects are: willfulness and defiant behavior, nervous impatience, eccentricities, revolutionary notions, indiscriminate attacks on the establishment (terrorism), equating levelling with progress, technophilia, loss of compassion, know-it-all arrogance.

● Neptune

At AP transit over Neptune, our sensibilities are stimulated. We find ourselves able to participate in forms of communication in the external world of which we were hitherto unaware, even though they were always present. Therefore, such transits frequently cause indescribable feelings; we are uncannily open to the world around us, eavesdropping dreamily on our own thought processes and picking up the faintest signals coming from our immediate environment. Nepture wires us into the communications network linking every human being. Something like the mysterious ether, it is invisible to the eye, yet can be detected by a higher sense than sight. Often we experience through its agency the unity of all living creatures and, when Neptune is transited, our identification mechanism is put into operation. We can become so familiar with matters normally beyond our scope that we identify with them. And when, as may happen at such times, we lose ourselves in unrestrained love for another person, we step at that moment beyond the bounds of the ego.

From a different point of view, Neptune embodies the principle of ideal love: the highest we can conceive, and one for which we yearn our life long. This is a living force, which thrusts us past every barrier separating man from man and affords us a glimpse of the Other's inmost self. The Neptunian principle of universal love continues to unfold in us during the AP aspect-cycle, and it is by means of this that we come to understand—through empathy—the immeasurable universe, and to incorporate it in us in a certain sense. Once we begin to appreciate the extent of the unity underlying all things, we shall develop social and altruistic motives; which may well display some touches of extremism on occasion if we have previously been unduly self-seeking and materialistic. When we consciously unlock the true meaning of Neptune, every aspect made by the Age Point will bring a change in motivation, and often, in turn, a change of mind. With each aspect, our ideals, our humanity, and our social conscience are put to the test. In the ascending part of the aspect cycle, we can add further growth to our Neptunian qualities and, in the descending part, may be able to do much good to the underprivileged, to the disabled and in short to all who suffer.

Neptune, as the principle of all-inclusiveness, the transcender of limitations, has the power to evoke many strange and disconcerting emotions during the intermediate stages. As a primordial spiritual principle (along with the two other spiritual planets), it can provide the inner experiences we need to recognize the existence of something beyond the purely material. But it has to be remembered that, on leaving behind the substantial, we can go astray (if the aspects incite us) in realms of phantasy, in dreams or in the dark world of the unconsicous, and finally sink in a bottomless morass. In extreme cases we may fall at this time into the hands of deceivers who, disguising their bad intentions under a cloak of love or kindness and taking advantage of our susceptibility, will use us for their own ends, inducing us to make many sacrifices—even material sacrifices—on their behalf. Because we seem to lose our natural protection when exposed to the influence of Nepture, we come under the sway of trends of all sorts according to the aspects. This is why Neptune has a rather unsavory reputation in classical astrology. Numerous perversions and diseases, delusions and deceptions, are ascribed to it. Entering its influence is said to be like entering a poisonous fog; yet a clear light breaks once we have learned its lesson of identification with the highest love ideal, with Christ, with universal charity.

The negative effects are: deception, temptation, addiction to drugs of any kind, exaggerated sensitivity (hysteria), debilitated will, nebulous intellect, hallucination, anxiety, unreliability, fraud.

● Pluto

Pluto represents our prototype, our pneuma. Spiritually, it is the image of the higher man or overman to which we ought to be conformed. At the time of AP transit, we become capable and willing to make a change in ourselves. As the form-changing principle, it is initiating the tremendous metamorphoses going on in our times and in individual consciousness too. The hand of Pluto will often tear off any mask which is not representative of our true ego. Pluto is the harbinger of a higher stage of development and announces to our astonished ears that the world is different from what we thought it was; it pulls aside the surface of things to show us their inner workings. How significant it is, then, that the time of its discovery in 1930 also saw the splitting of the atom!

During the AP transit of Pluto it is not unusual for the native to be confronted with his "shadow." His compulsions and inadequacies become painfully obvious. Matters which have been put to one side half-finished now clamor for attention; repressions grow hard to live with. Perhaps the conscience wakes up and persuades the native to try and turn over a new leaf. Probably he will be able to see himself "warts and all" and will know what he has to do to improve. One thing at least is clear: old forms have to be abandoned and old rules scrapped; risks must be faced and anxieties overcome. In individual development, one frequently senses an influx of fresh energy, because Pluto activates the nuclear forces involved in one's deepest motivation. It impinges directly on the center of a person's being and releases the energies of the will; which then tend to bring him in line with his penuma—or image of his higher self. Far-reaching changes take place in the ego, changes spilling over into everyday life which may even alter the appearance. It is impossible to continue in the same old rut.

During the AP aspect-cycle, the degree to which we possess the experience and maturity required to cooperate with our higher self will depend on the quadrant in which we encounter this formidable Pluto-factor in our lives. A refined sense of purpose is the pre-requisite for overcoming the problems posed at every Age Point aspect. A contemplative approach to the alterations in the guiding imagery will often promote inner harmony. At each aspect we catch a partial glimpse of the sort of persons we ought to be, and of how we ought to be motivated in order to fulfill our task in life and grow to our true spiritual stature. Visions seen during Plutonian aspects should always be taken seriously, not treated as foolish fancies; even when we wonder whether we, with our modest talents, are capable of fulfilling them.

As the representative of our personal nuclear energy, Pluto is always endeavoring to bring us to perfection as soon as possible. Although perfection in this context is a relative term, each aspect to the planet does in fact bring us further forward along the road to it. At one time our characters need to have something trimmed off, and at others they need to have something added. Though the process can be painful, it is necessary to accept whatever Pluto brings. Our small wills have to be blended with the greater Will. With the advent of each aspect, we are confronted by opportunities we have not yet taken, opportunities we are not certain how to handle perhaps; but however much plagued by anxiety we may be, there is no further chance to shirk or pull back—Pluto's power is absolute. Pluto has to do with death and rebirth, with the transformation of one form of consciousness into another.

In all aspects of Pluto we are usually "on our own" and have to use our unaided will-power to achieve the goals we have glimpsed.

When we think there is nothing more we can do, that our affairs are out of control and that we might as well give up, it is then that the will-power of Pluto takes over the reins. And all activities which serve others, not self, have a positive outcome.

The negative effects are: manipulation of friends and associates, aggression in the name of higher authority, sexual magic, delusions of grandeur ("guru-trips"), destructive urges, premonitions of disaster, susceptibility to mass hysteria, death wishes.

• The Nodes of the Moon

The Nodes of the Moon are not planets, that is to say, they are not primary principles incorporated in bodies in space and radiating their influence to us, but they are in fact the points where the (apparent) orbit of the Sun and the orbit of the Moon cross each other. The point where the Moon appears to cross the Sun's orbit from south to north when travelling in its own path is called the ascending node (or Dragon's head), and the point where it crosses from north to south is called the descending node (or Dragon's Tail). We confine ourselves to marking the ascending node in horoscopes because, according to its placement in house (though not in sign), this node indicates the way of our spiritual ascent. It is particularly significant from the point of view of the Age Point, since that has so much to tell us about our development.

The AP transit often signposts the exit from blind alleys. Now it is the function of the ascending node to show the way forward, whereas the descending node (on the diametrically opposite side of the chart) shows the way back. Although the latter is usually more accessible, a fully aware person chooses the former. At the AP transit of the ascending node we have an understanding of what will aid our progress. We get into situations helpful to our spiritual destiny and meet people who can put us on the right track. It is not unusual, in fact, to find students of psychological astrology taking up their studies when the AP makes contact with one of the nodes in their charts.

With every aspect to the Dragon's Head, there is a notable opportunity for further development. At the same time, we discover what we must do to accelerate or round off our current development. In this connection we may need to gain a better understanding of the radical house position of the node. This indicates the area in which the significant activity will take place, the area in which there are lessons to be learned.

The above-mentioned opportunity for further development offered at each AP aspect can come to us either in the form of a fresh capacity for inner effort, or in the form of favorable external circumstances. Often we have a little idea of what is good for our development, but when the Moon's node is reached, our values may make a U-turn and things which were materially beneficial are seen to be damaging to our spiritual growth.

The negative effects are: avoidance of genuine effort, or a disposition to take the easy way out and to plod along in the same old rut in a self-satisfied mood.

Chapter 5

Age Progression in Professional Counseling

Introduction—The significance of the Lunar Node—The three personality planets: Sun, Moon, and Saturn—Age Progression and accurate timing—The impressions of early childhood—An example from consulting work—Five examples from our case books

● Introduction

Use of the Age Point is a great help in counselling. It provides us with an immediate understanding of the inner workings of questions involving education, employment and partnership, and of what lies behind life crises or turning points in spiritual growth. In psychological counselling the birth chart is already being used as a diagnostic instrument by many professional advisers; but now we have Age Progression as an outstanding additional analytical tool of incalculable worth for progressing a chart. It shows us, in an unequivocal manner, the exact mental and spiritual situation of an individual at a given point in time, together with a general survey of the whole course of his or her life with all its problems and potential for development.

Serious astrologers and psychologists often try to work with the classical methods of direction; but it is time-consuming to sort out the meaning of all the traditional transits and directions for a particular moment (that of consultation say). And yet that is what has to be done when these methods are employed, if the client's current situation is to be correctly assessed. Some consultants try to simplify matters by confining themselves to only one of the classical methods of direction, and by so doing fail to make a well-rounded judgment of the current situation of the person seeking their help. What they have to tell is necessarily sketchy, and it is all too easy for them to project their own thoughts and wishes onto the client for want of properly researched material.

Here the Age Progression system offers itself as a genuine alternative which, when properly understood, yields by the simplest means both the basic theme and the detailed structural patterns of the client's total character as it exists at a given moment in time. It is a tremendous asset to the counsellor to be able to identify the counsellee's situation from a glance at his or her radical chart. The psychotherapist, by tracing the course of the Age Point, can immediately spot acute problems and the duration of chronic depressions, etc., and can adjust his treatments accordingly. He can discuss with the client the influences and possibilities he has seen in the chart, and has the advantage of knowing when a depressive phase will end and when a "better" period will begin. Not only is time saved by this procedure, but it is possible to study the personality of the individual very intensively and to bring about the release of his constructive forces. Much more time would be required to achieve comparable results by the usual psychological techniques.

Once the trained counsellor or therapist knows how to read a client's chart correctly, he will now straight away why the latter has come to consult him. He will see the psychological reason for the given problem, since the Age Point reveals the current state of development in the horoscope. Also revealed are the main and side issues involved, the tasks which ought to be taken in hand, and the hindrances to be overcome. Advice can be given on the immediately available and quickest solutions.

It is important for counsellor and client to work together. A good therapist will go through the horoscope and the movement of the Age Point with the patient. The effect will be much more profound and there will be considerably less danger of transference on the part of the client. The horoscope is a neutral means of diagnosis, and its very neutrality greatly reduces the risk of transference. What is more, since it is not the counsellor with his or her personal opinions of the client, but the horoscope, measuring the problem against the constellations, that provides the key to the situation, the subjective approach is ruled out.

In any case, what is wanted in astrological counselling is not lengthy chart analyses so much as the cultivation of a genuine approach to the other person in order to begin the consultation on common ground. Then the client will not feel that he or she is being manipulated, but will become less nervous and will be able to relax in an atmosphere of frankness and mutual trust.

In the first place, our aim is to help the other person. This has to be the main motive in every attempt to give advice. To be successful, the counsellor must be a good listener, because people instantly detect whether someone is really interested in them or not. What is required is the wish to be sincere and the rejection of any impulse to model others according to some preconceived pattern.

A genuinely helpful approach is often crucial for the inner experience of the person being counselled: the horizon may be expanded and the viewpoint changed. With the help of the birth chart, the counsellor can make the client conscious of his or her deepest motivations and goals, can make them feel properly understood and recognized. Nevertheless, the horoscope is neutral: it remains an objective witness to the life situation of the individual. It does not take the place of the adviser, who can be selective in what he says, but is more in the nature of a "tide table" giving the ebb and flow of the psyche; as such, it enables the individual to view his problems more objectively and to set sail on fresh ventures.

● The Significance of the Node

Frequently we find people coming for advice just as their Age Point is transiting the Moon's ascending node. From an astrological psychological point of view, this is interpreted as the first step in further development. It is the starting point, the place of least resistance, which has to be activated and brought into consciousness because it is directly involved in mental or physical difficulties. People usually have some inkling of where this starting point lies, but need to have it positively identified for them before they can take action. The house containing the lunar node indicates the area in which current problems have to be broached, and the adviser must consider first the Age Point and then the node, if any real help is to be given.

• The Three Personality Planets: Sun, Moon, Saturn

The three personality planets (Sun, Moon and Saturn) are important, too, in astrological counselling, and represent the three poles of the ego. The Sun is the ego of the mental plane, the thought ego; the Moon is the emotional ego; Saturn is the physical ego or body consciousness. Many mental disturbances are due to the fact that one of these three poles is being over-stimulated and the body is not functioning as a unit. It is true, of course, that each of the three ego-poles has a characteristic time of development in a person's life: normally, the physical body develops in the first third of life, the emotions develop in the second third, and the understanding develops in the final third. In individual cases, however, one or another factor comes into prominence according to the positions of the three main planets in the horoscope, and so, during certain periods of the native's life (and sometimes throughout his or her life) the harmony between them is lacking. Thus hopes and wishes may not be in keeping with mental aims or with physical capacities. On occasion, the physical strength is stretched too far by the conflict between the various spheres of the ego, and the result is psycho-somatic illness.

When the person who comes for a consultation happens to have the Age Point transiting one of the three main planets in his or her chart, the problem is always to be found in the area of personal development and, depending on the planet involved, this problem has to do with material (Saturn), emotional (Moon), or mental (Sun) uncertainties and preoccupations affecting the ego. It is of the utmost importance that these factors be integrated within the characted as a whole. If there is a weakness somewhere in the ego— and, if so, the horoscope will show it—mental disorders such as depression or hysteria are possible, often because the native has not experienced success on any of the three planes.

In judging the Age Point aspects to the main planets, it is necessary to ask whether we are concerned with the development of the personality in the outside world, or are concerned with the growth of the spiritual man internally. Much depends on the age and mental development of the individual, of course, but, provided we know the answer to the above question when interpreting the aspects, we should be able to improve our understanding of our own situation and that of others.

Self-confidence is more or less marked according to the radical aspects and house positions of these three planets, even though, to begin with, we seldom possess as much self-confidence as we should like. The unfolding of our tripartite personality is an on-going process which is never complete. It is generally accepted that the key factor in the process is external success, or feedback from the environment. Often this is the only factor considered; the assumption being that the more recognition there is from the outside world, the stronger the self-confidence will be. Success is most important for creating a stable personality; because the individual feels more sure of himself, he feels that he knows how to handle himself in order to get the best out of any situation.

But, as already mentioned, in Age Progression we are concerned not simply with increasing self-confidence but also with the development of the "inner person" of those whose motives and actions are guided by a spirit of true humanity. The emphasis here is on the ethical side of astrology about which we do not know very much, although increasing attention is being paid to it in modern times. In the AP aspects to the three personality planets there is therefore always an opportunity for spiritual development, provided we gain a deeper insight into ourselves, our inner goals, and our spiritual guidelines. In the process of reaching a higher degree of self-awareness, the individual changes continuously: at each stage of life, in each house, at each Low Point in the signs, and with every increase in consciousness.

In brief, what we are looking at is the change from an egocentric individual to a consciously responsible, free individual who recognizes the Self as part of the Whole and is able to care for others. The integrated personality is freed from obsession with its own interests in order to concentrate on higher tasks benefiting the community. From a spiritual point of view, the individual outgrows himself or herself by making a creative contribution to evolution. Therefore we should take seriously in this sense all AP aspects to the main planets and should try to extract as much good as possible from the development of the personality and from the individuation process. It is extremely important to delineate with care the threefold structure of the personality in the radix, recognizing any weaknesses in the ego and any problems to do with parents or with superiority or inferiority complexes. The meanings of AP aspects to the three personality planets were discussed in the previous chapter.

● Age Progression and Accurate Timing

In considering the psychological application of the Age Point, it cannot be sufficiently stressed that the Age Point mainly indicates mental and spiritual development processes, which are usually initiated by internal and only seldom by external events. A further salient point is that these processes tend to be set in motion before the exact time of AP conjunction with a planet, sensitive point or cusp.

Frequently it is hard to tell when a certain period of development commenced; although many a time the first planetary contact or aspect has a causative effect, as we shall see later in the section on "impressions in early childhood." It is important to know that some events will not occur until certain changes have taken place in our behavior, our attitude to life or our mental attunement. From a psychological point of view, the exact date of an event is unimportant, as each new stage in life represents a process that has a beginning, a climax and an end, and lasts for a fixed time. Since this is a rather revolutionary concept, we shall illustrate it by means of an example (see figure 1.5.1.)

In our example, at the age of thirty-one, the Age Point transits a natal Sun posited just beyond the sixth cusp in the radix, and the

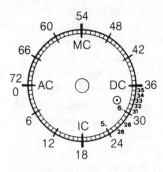

Figure 1.5.1. An Age Point transit to the radical Sun causes a confirmation of consciousness.

native may find that, during the preceding year, he has had to face the problem of self-determination with regard to his inner vocation, being much preoccupied, both before and after the transit, with what headway he can make in his job or profession. Moreover, in our example, the Sun has a great deal to do with self-confidence. Perhaps the acquisition of some special skill has given self-confidence a boost. Or perhaps the native's self-respect has been injured by slights or rebuffs when he has not been able to come up to the mark. In such instances, the connection between inner cause and outer effect is clearly exhibited.

Death of the father

Another example might be the death of the father. This traumatic event, with all its material and familial results, is likely to be indicated by Age-Point aspects in the charts both of the deceased and of the bereaved. The bereaved person will find it difficult to assimilate the event in a way helpful to his own development and maturity if he tries to dispose of it as quickly and as painlessly as possible. He should be thinking not simply that the father's "time had come," but that he himself is very much involved in this, the last step in the long and often heavy process of separation from his father. What was not achieved at the age of sixteen or twenty, in spite of all kicking over the traces, and later failed to occur "according to plan" owing to repression, is suddenly forced on the native by an external occurrence. If he can manage to see the death not simply as something distressing that has happened "out there," but as a challenge to further self-development, the sad event will be filled with more meaning than can be found in the elaborate ritual of a funeral.

Of course, such events do not keep on happening from one minute to the next but take time to be experienced. They build up slowly, reach their peak and then subside. The corresponding inner processes also continue over a period of months—as may be seen from the locus of the Age Point. Each aspect sits, so to speak, atop an intensity curve and, at the point in time indicated by the high point on the curve, an event of considerable importance can occur. Nevertheless, the Age Point starts to make its influence felt long before this. At the beginning of the slow rise, a flanking event may anticipate the main theme and bring interesting side-effects. Together with what is yet to come in the descending portion of the curve, the whole makes up an experience which is "greater than the sum of its parts."

Conclusion

To be able to use the Age Point Progression system, we do not need to know the exact timing of an event, but simply the year, the time of year or (at most) the month. We do not require to know the exact day because, as already explained, we are dealing with processes of development that extend over periods longer than a day. Usually, it would be impossible for us to tell just when there began to stir within us some feeling of unrest, some new idea, which perhaps took hold of our whole personality and radically altered our attitude to life and to other people. In handling Age Point Progression, we must learn to think in terms of a movement through time, of cycles and changes, instead of in terms of given moments as shown in figure 1.5.2.

Adopting the latter mode of thought was an error perpetrated by classical astrology, which was so preoccupied with pinpointing exact times that the very credit of the art came to depend on the ability to make accurate predictions. Being put to the proof in such an extreme fashion has done great damage to astrology, especially as many of the predictions failed to come true on time, and it cannot be repeated too often that we, with the advantage of today's psychological knowledge, ought to turn away from event-orientated thinking in order to concentrate on development-orientated thinking.

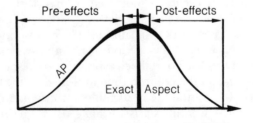

Figure 1.5.2. The intensity of pre- and post-effects of the Age Point.

● Impressions in Early Childhood

In recent decades, psychological researchers have discovered that experiences, especially those of childhood, will continue to exert a compelling pressure on our thoughts, emotions and behavior so long as they lie hidden in the unconscious. As soon as their memories are made conscious, their power is broken and we can set about counteracting their effects. Even our inherited or acquired characteristics govern us only until, however slowly, we manage to extirpate wrong attitudes. Naturally, the processes of self-recognition do not remove our innate or imparted flaws all at once, but they do enable us to distance ourselves from them and to adopt a new point of view. We are no longer sold into a helpless slavery to unconscious forces, but are in possession of the knowledge that could set us free.

It is here that Age Progression can assist us. All transits and oppositions affecting planets in the first quadrant (*i.e.*, affecting the first eighteen years of life) unequivocally point to such childhood impressions. In self-analysis and in therapy, it is essential to institute a thorough investigation of the events indicated, however small and insignificant they may seem to be. It is astounding to discover the close connection they have with later behavior patterns, patterns which can be gradually altered only through the release into consciousness and the mature understanding of these self-same events.

Age 0-18

The period when the environment makes the strongest impact on the character is from 0-18 years. In the natal chart this is represented by the first quadrant, running from the AC to the IC. Note that the whole quadrant is involved here, and that the environmental influence remains strong right up to the threshold of independence.

As a rule, planets posited in the first quadrant make a more powerful impression on the youngster and adolescent than do those distributed in other parts of the chart. In psychology, we speak of traumatic events: but by traumas we do not intend simply the unpleasant, negative occurrences; the positive ones are included, too. They are traumatic for the reason that our conscious mind refuses to have anything to do with them. Frequently they generate complexes and behavioral reflexes later in life without our being able to figure where the connection lies. Prolonged self-observation may be required before the link is found; unless, of course, we call in the services of Age Progression. Then it becomes relatively easy to see, from the planetary positions in the first quadrant, the operation of cause and effect, and thus to start making a change.

Even severe psychological complexes can be rooted in childhood's impressionable years. Almost any planet standing in the first quadrant points to a childhood trauma, positive or negative. However, a distinction has to be made between strong and weak effects. The planets are at their most powerful in this regard when in houses one and two, representing the ages from birth to twelve years old. This period of childhood finds the young person completely dependent on his environment because he is unable to look after himself. Since his will is still relatively weak and his ego undeveloped, his mother or surrogate mother is free to stamp her personality on him and to mould him in her chosen image. Yet, by the same token, she (like other factors in his environment) may be a source of traumas.

The presence of planets in the first and second houses in hard aspect to some other planet or planets, will suggest that the native was probably much under the influence of his environment at a certain period. If he was, then they will reveal the time of the formative experiences.

When there are no planets in the first quadrant, the question arises: "Were there not, during childhood, any impressions strong enough to give rise to traumas or complexes?" For the answer, we

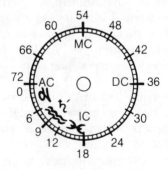

Figure 1.5.3. Secondary aspects involved in Age Progression.

have to take a look at the opposite section of the chart. It is practically certain that in the third quadrant there will be planets to oppose the Age Point while it is tracking the native's childhood phase. These have a formative effect almost as strong as that of planets transited by the Age Point in the first three houses. In other words, the third-quadrant opposition like the first-quadrant conjunction usually indicates events which have had a formative influence on character during the first eighteen years of life—influences which are responsible for certain behavior patterns later on.

The other aspects (for example, the square, trine, sextile and quincunx) are of secondary importance in this respect; though to some extent they prepare the way for, or perhaps weaken, the main effect according to the direction from which they are cast.

Figure 1.5.3 shows a planet situated at 20° Aquarius in the second house. The first house is empty; but 20° Capricorn in the first house is in 30° aspect to the planet in the second house. This point represents a preliminary impression as far as the planet at 20° Aquarius in the second house is concerned. Suppose, now, that the Age Point transits a planet (Saturn in our example) at 20° Aquarius; it is likely that at the age of nine years the primary impression will be experienced as an essentially psychological event. In addition, however, at the age of four (represented by 20° Capricorn) a secondary impression has already made itself felt. The child has been sensitized in advance by a somewhat similar experience, though not with such trauma as he will undergo at the age of nine.

Similar considerations apply if a planet is placed at 20° Leo in the same chart. The transit of 20° Capricorn in the first house makes a 150 degree angle (or quincunx) to this planet. Here, too, we are looking at a preliminary impression. The opposition at 20° Aquarius gives the time of the major influence. All other aspects from the following signs represent subsequent impressions which may help to resolve any problem that has arisen.

The square activates the problem. To stay with our example, an emotional experience can occur when the Age Point makes a square to 20° Aquarius from 20° Taurus. The problem refuses to be ignored any longer. Squares can have a shattering yet clarifying effect, but do not necessarily enable us to come to terms with our difficulties. Further information on this point will be found in the chapter on "Age Point Aspects."

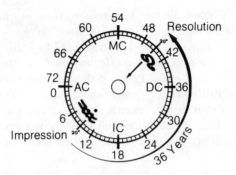

Figure 1.5.4. We need one half an Age Point (or 36 years) to overcome early impressions.

Generally speaking, the following points should be observed when judging the relationship of the aspects to early impressions:

1. The impression itself is made, not at the square but at the conjunction or opposition;

2. The solution of the problem does not appear until the AP has moved 180° on from the point marking where the problem arises.

3. In the intermediate aspects, the nuances of the situation become increasingly apparent and the problem starts to come within range of the conscious mind ready for eventual solution at the age represented by the opposition.

In our example, the actual solution of the problem indicated in the second house will not be possible until the age shown by the transit of the Age Point through the eighth house; that is to say at some age between forty-two and forty-eight or ca. forty-four years. (See figure 1.5.4.) Psychologically speaking it is interesting to note that usually we need thirty-six years (or half the full AP cycle) to extricate ourselves from the consequences of early impressions or to overcome a faulty reaction.

● **An Example from Consulting Work**

It is quite surprising what one finds when working through the chart positions for the first eighteen years of a client's life. "What experience did you have when you were seven years old?" we might ask, on noting the Age Point transit of the Sun (square Saturn) in the second house.

Figure 1.5.5 illustrates a case of this kind. The lady who consulted us did not take long in identifying her problem and soon volunteered the information that her parents were divorced when she was seven years old. As a result she was parted from her mother, because her father was awarded custody of her and of her brothers and sisters. The separation caused her a great deal of suffering; all the more so as she could not understand what was going on. Psychological-cum-astrological interviews elicited that she had secretly believed that it was on her account that her mother had gone away. Later in life, inexplicable guilt feelings would rise from her unconscious to stand in the way of any close relationship and to torment her with the dread that the loved one would desert her. This fear of loss went hand in hand with a fear of destitution, which became very acute at the age of twenty-nine when the Age Point was conjunct the Sun and square to Saturn. At that age she married and became the breadwinner of the family to enable her husband to continue his studies. It was not until the opposition was reached, when she was forty-nine years old, that her husband succeeded in his profession and she was set free from financial worries.

What really happened here was a development process undergone by her own personality, and enacted by two personality planets, the Sun and Saturn. Mostly under the pressure of circumstances, the client had done everything in her power to avoid loss and, by doing so, had developed her personal initiative and ability to cope with life. When, at last, she was fully self-reliant and had completed her development, she was released from her various

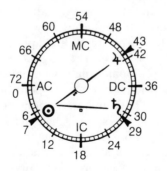

Figure 1.5.5. The horoscope of a client whose parents divorced when she was seven years old.

anxieties. The whole process lasted from the divorce of her parents when she was seven until her forty-third year. As a rule it is possible to trace any individual development cycle by Age Point progression in this way. The process usually begins at the opposition or conjunction and lasts for thirty-six years, or half-way round the chart from the starting point, by which time the capability implied by the planet concerned will be fully developed and matured. As in the above case, consultant and client together should be able to work out all the connections. The relief shown by the client when the real causes have been uncovered is often amazing. The following instances should help to exemplify this further.

● Case Histories

Our first example chart shows a client (figure 1.5.6) who was forty-seven years old when she came for advice. She wanted to know something about her destiny and about the childhood impressions which had formed her attitude to love and to professional life. When she was seventeen (AP at 25° Taurus in sextile to the Sun/Pluto conjunction), her father fell seriously ill and she was obliged to stop training as a hospital nurse because she was needed at home.

In order to understand the part played by the father, we must look at the radical position of the Sun. The latter stands at the Low Point of the sixth house in conjunction with Pluto, in opposition to the Dragon's Head and the Moon and square Mars (to give the triangle of performance). The sixth house has always been known as the house of work and of diseases; and here we see the father, whose disease created problems affecting the native's work (sixth house). The triangle of performance indicates, however, that the native will be compensated by her father's love and appreciation for what she has done. Prior to this he had never thought of praising her, but had behaved like a self-opinionated man who always had to be right.

Saturn in the second house was responsible for her strongest childhood impression. This must have gone very deep, because it influenced her subsequent behavior. Characteristically, the events of her sixth year of life were not easy to remember, and it was only after she had been told that the experience in question had to do with her female libido and love ideal (Saturn in opposition to Venus and Neptune) that the scales fell from her eyes. Visibly moved, she related the following incident: "Yes, I was playing at being nurse to a little two-year old boy from down the road and was giving him his physical examination, when my mother [Saturn] saw what I was doing, yelled at me and snatched me away. Father, too, happened by and he smacked me for the very first time. It was horrible. I could not understand why my parents were so upset or why my father had hit me."

From this time on, her mother was always able to manipulate her by making her feel guilty, as shown in the 2/8 axis of possession. Only when she reached the age of forty-two and the conjunction of Venus and Neptune on the cusp of house eight, was she able to throw off her mother's influence. Against her mother's will, she overcame all obstacles and took a trip to India. None of her parents' expostulations or reproaches were able to deter her—she simply had

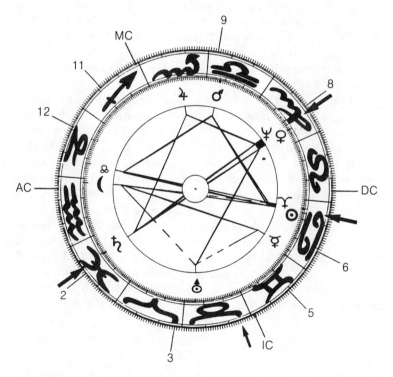

Figure 1.5.6. Horoscope of a female client born July 16, 1935, at 8:45 PM in Herisau, Switzerland.

to go. She made up her mind to climb out of her rut and to leave behind everything that stood in the way of her development. And so the eighth house challenge to make an inner change (death and transfiguration) was accepted. She had to face up to the things she had previously avoided, and endured considerable mental anguish until she had summoned sufficient strength and courage to release herself from the behavior patterns and unconscious compulsions of childhood.

In preparation for this individual development—a goal in life indicated by her Ascendant sign Aquarius—there was a transit of the Sun/Pluto conjunction at age thirty-three. She got to know a man at that time and experienced a love such as she had not thought possible. Her sense of personal worth was confirmed, not only because she was loved but because she had won the love of a man who was her intellectual and social superior. That was all to the good as far as her development was concerned, but there could be no consummation of the relationship since he was already married and did not want to hurt his wife. She had to suffer the pangs of renunciation, and this worked a change in the fundamental motivation of her life.

Pluto, with the Sun and North node (in opposition to the South node in the twelfth house), has a metamorphic power that thrusts aside false projections and modes of behavior in order to release the springs of the innermost being. What we learn from the Dragon's Tail is that the love of a man was not sufficient for complete restoration of her self-respect. As a point of ascension, the Dragon's Head is in individualistic Capricorn in twelfth house, implying that the native has to learn self-reliance and to free herself from dependence on a partner or on her environment. This development commenced at the age of thirty-four, just as the native's Age Point was entering Leo. At that time she enjoyed a busy and profitable year of learning, of travel, and of exploring her own abilities. And thus the way was prepared for the final break with her mother's influence at the transit of Venus/Neptune and the opposition to inhibiting Saturn.

* * *

Figure 1.5.7 is the horoscope of a client who expected astrological advice about her special abilities and on her chances of finding a partner. She was forty-six years old and her Age Point stood at 15°

Libra in quincunx to the Saturn/Mercury·opposition. Although ready to enter a fresh field of endeavor, she felt rather helpless.

The center of gravity of the aspect formation is in the first quadrant, and the detached Saturn/Mercury opposition to Neptune along the 2/8 axis immediately catches the eye. When asked what happened when the Age Point transited this conjunction, at the age of six and a half, the client said after a moment's reflection: "My mother threw away my favorite little doll because it was old and tattered. As far as I was concerned, this doll was a part of myself no matter that it was dirty and broken. I was so attached to it that I always took it to bed with me. Incomprehensibly, it was suddenly no longer there. To me, as a child, this did not make sense. I still remember how it stabbed me to the heart. I cried all day, was unmanageable, shut myself in my room and plotted revenge. My hatred of my mother lasted for almost two years."

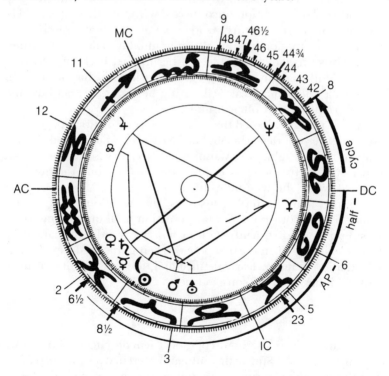

Figure 1.5.7. A female born on March 23, 1936, at 4:25 AM in Bern, Switzerland.

Then, came the Sun/Moon conjunction at the age of eight and a half, introducing another theme, namely a close relationship with her father. This relationship was very important to her at that time. When she was seven (with the Age Point practically half-way between Saturn and Sun/Moon) she fell behind at school and had to stay back in her third year. Her father was very supportive during this period of failure and did what he could to restore her self-confidence. Exactly at the transit of the Sun (when she was eight and a half years old) she passed into the higher grade with flying colors.

At the age of forty-three she married a man her mother could not endure. The Age Point was square Saturn and Neptune, the two planets representing her traumatic childhood experience. Her mother did everything in her power to prevent the marriage. But the greater the parental opposition, the more desirable did the man seem to the native. Later she came to realize that she had wed him to spite her mother. An opposition unconnected with the other aspects (here Neptune to Saturn/Mercury) works like an automatic mechanism and in stress situations betrays the individual into doing the wrong thing. Thus this lady wanted to pay her mother back for throwing away her doll so many years ago. But in reality she harmed herself, because she suffered a great deal during her marriage: her husband was self-centered and often brutal.

When the AP opposed the Sun/Moon conjunction at age forty-four and three quarters, she obtained a divorce, and felt as if she had escaped from a nightmare. Winning the decree was the counterpart of her success in the class examination at the time the Sun was transited when she was eight and a half.

As the above example illustrates, the Age Point will, in due course, transit both poles of an opposition and, on coming to the second pole, will frequently indicate a period similar in character to the one existing when the first pole was being transited—except that the situation is more clearly defined and, to some extent, has to do with a higher stage of consciousness.

* * *

Figure 1.5.8 is the horoscope of a female client who has the conjunction of the Sun with Pluto and Mercury on the cusp of the sixth house which turns our thoughts straight away to the client's profession. She is a social worker specializing in family therapy.

The personality planets in the sixth house are typical of an aptitude for work of this type.

The path of the Age Point is quite interesting. It transited the Dragon's Head when the native was in nursery school. To the enquiry concerning how this time had affected her, especially with regard to any anxiety or deprivation of love (opposition to Moon/ Neptune), she responded as follows: "My governess was very strict and I was afraid of her." She was asked: "Did she threaten you with anything (as seems likely in view of the fact that the opposition lies in the shadow of the 2/8 axis) or did she alternate threats with promises (since this axis suggests she probably employed the "carrot and stick" method)?" Her immediate reply was: "Yes, of course. There was something. My parents went away for four weeks, and my

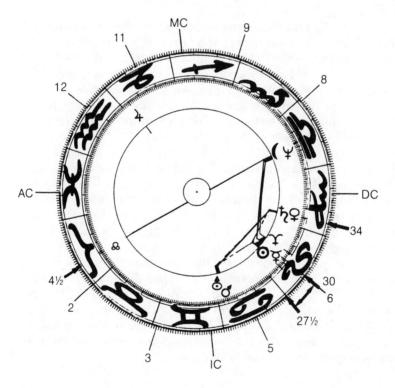

Figure 1.5.8. A female client born July 30, 1949, at 9:20 PM in Zurich, Switzerland.

younger sister and I were left in the care of our governess. During this period she would often say, 'If you don't behave yourselves your parents will die.'"

No wonder the client continued to be haunted by visions of the death of her beloved father and mother! Her chronic anxiety was the reason why, with the transit of Uranus and Mars and during almost the entire passage of the AP through Cancer (age 22-26), she underwent a course of psychoanalysis. The transit of the Sun (on the sixth house cusp at the age 30) marked a very good period, which had begun with the AP entry into the Sun's sign, Leo, when she was twenty-eight. Professional advancement, popularity and success were the key-notes of this phase. Everything offered by the Leo Sun by way of strength and qualities of leadership began to shine through.

When she came for advice she was thirty-three years old (at the Low Point of the sixth house). Her visit was on account of her man friend, who was some two years younger than she, and of whom she was very fond. He was a carefree fellow, a good dancer, and he gave her plenty of what made life pleasant. Yet it was this very thing which filled her with misgivings for, having reached the Saturn/Venus conjunction, she thought that her partner ought to be a much more serious person with a strict moral code. The counsellor pointed out to her that she needed to rid herself of her illusions concerning love and marriage. Her Moon/Neptune conjunction is not far from Low Point seven and the Dragon's Tail and signifies non-fulfillment of her dreams or illusions. With Virgo straddling her cusp of partnership and with and with Saturn/Venus so close to the seventh cusp too, it was advisable for her to look on marriage as a challenge requiring her devoted attention.

Previously she had believed that her partner should be someone who met her highest expectations and that all she had to do was to wait for "Mr. Right." However, she quickly recognized her error, because she had already begun to see a glimmering of the truth. Later she informed us that she had married her friend and was expecting a child. The latter was born just as the Age Point was transiting the Venus/Saturn position.

* * *

Figure 1.5.9 shows a horoscope with another instance of the conscious assimilation of early impressions: between the age of eleven and twelve the native had her tonsils out. The AP had entered Aries and was transiting the Moon/Venus conjunction with aspects to Uranus, Mars and Pluto. Her mother was heavily engaged in business and was not able to spend time with the child. The latter was left in hospital and felt deserted. Before the operation she had entered a new class and the teacher did not like her. The girl was mortified by the consequent neglect.

The Moon/Venus conjunction represents an intense need for love and tenderness, and the individual wants to be loved at all costs. Her sense of harmony demands style; she does not care to associate with uncouth individuals. The love she demands is always frustrated in the end however. Being left alone as a child threw her selection mechanism out of order. Because she did not experience affection during her formative years, she attracted men who punished her by

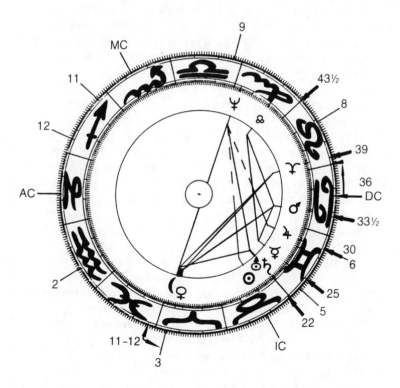

Figure 1.5.9. A female client born May 11, 1942, at 1:13 AM in Zurich, Switzerland.

either withdrawing their love from her or by becoming physically violent (Venus/Mars square). At the age of twenty-two, when the AP was close to the Saturn/Uranus conjunction, she married a childhood friend, but separated from him at age 25 (when the AP was conjunct Mercury). The marriage was contracted under the auspices of Uranus/Saturn (she was looking for security); the separation took place at the transit of Mercury square the Dragon's Head (a symbol of separation). At the transit of the rather isolated Jupiter, when the native was 30 years old, she married a wealthy man. She had a town house, a country house, and lived a life of dignity and luxury. Nevertheless, when Mars was transited (at Low Point 6, when the native was thirty-three and a half) the situation became intolerable and she divorced this man as well. Upon the transit of the DC, when she was thirty-six, she met a man-friend with whom she lived until the AP entered Leo. At this point, helped by the energy of Leo and Pluto, she came to herself. Shortly after the AP had reached the DC, she underwent a course of analysis and identified many of her YOU-fixations, illusions and projections, and freed herself from them fairly quickly.

*   *   *

Figure 1.5.10 illustrates another example of Age Progression. At the AP transit of the stellium in Virgo (age 9-18) this client experienced great difficulties within the family. She felt hemmed in and, although she had brothers and sisters, there was nobody in whom she could confide, nobody who took her seriously—she was alone.

The counsellor asked, "What was your relationship with your parents?"

"My parents? Oh, yes, they disappointed me. My mother, in particular, was absorbed in her own problems, and had no time for me or for my problems. Therefore, I was very much at the mercy of my environment and was tormented by guilt feelings."

"Well, it certainly looks as if what happened in your early impressionable years had a decided influence on your further development. Did you remain with your parents long?"

"Yes, until I went to America at the age of twenty-eight."

"I see. So at the Low Point of the fifth house, when the Age Point was in Sagittarius, you were finally able to break away from your old environment. But what happened to your childhood and teenage impressions? Were you also able to break free from your guilt feelings and your dependence?"

"Break free? No. It's true I had gone far away, but in myself I wasn't free; I was discontented and my guilt feelings were with me in America."

Exactly at the time of opposition to the stellium (age 46-54, when the AP was passing through Pisces), she lived through nearly seven years of severe upheaval. Having returned with her husband to the family milieu, she walked back into situations where she was not understood, just as she had not been understood as a child, and experienced the same old sense of frustration. Her self-confidence went completely. At the Low Point of the ninth house, the crisis reached its peak. Misunderstandings with relatives, financial losses,

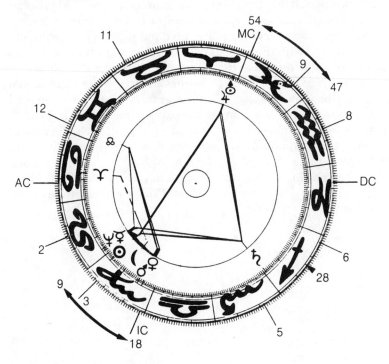

Figure 1.5.10. A female client born August 28, 1927, at 2:00 AM in Luzern, Switzerland.

conflicts with herself and with her partner all escalated. She felt universally misunderstood, lost her grip on reality and reached the verge of suicide. This was the typical crisis of consciousness and of transformation   at the ninth house Low Point, in which the individual feels that there is nothing left in life except to wander aimlessly in a kind of no man's land. Being thrown back on herself, "I AM" was the only thing to which she could cling. Eventually, after making a slow recovery, she took the decision to go abroad with her husband again.

When she came for advice, she was just turning fifty-four. After transiting the MC, the AP moved from Pisces into Aries: from the end to the beginning of the Zodiac. This invariably signifies a big change in the native's life, and we may be sure that, together, the MC and the sign Aries will help her to an inner rebirth and to a new start in life. She herself describes her existence in these terms: "My life has been full of stumbling blocks and false trails. I could never develop properly but was always the one to give and suffer. Office work did not satisfy me mentally, nor did the existence of a housewife. Life to me looked something like this: I was standing in a straight street. On each side of the street, herbs, bushes and trees were all in bloom (dreams, illusions, longings—or the real me?). Then the main road came to a dead end, but many small paths branched off it. I had to continue my journey without benefit of a signpost and without knowing the destination. The way was thorny in places; it was full of danger, and hateful and treacherous. Although my journey along it has been costing me so dear in physical and mental effort, I have not given up.... Nevertheless, I should like to return to my 'own street'—back to my better self."

Chapter 6

Life's Time Table: The Age Point in the Twelve Houses

● Introduction

In the following section, we shall be taking a look at the lessons to be learned, and the changes and problems to be faced at the various stages of life. Examples will be used to demonstrate problem positions and unusual Low Point experiences, and thus to elucidate the application of the Age Point.

The examples have been chosen at random and are merely illustrative. They should not be treated as definitive statements. We have been thinking about the best way to represent the special influences of the Age Point without having to confine ourselves to the basic effects of one house or period of life. For a while we hesitated, knowing the beginner's fondness for generalizing specific statements, and we would beg the reader to regard the examples as no more than teaching material. Even if he should find similar positions in his own chart, he will discover that the descriptions do not fit his own case in every respect. Much depends on the sign and house in which a planet is posited, also on its aspects—and this is a very individual matter. Correct interpretation involves a consideration of the part of the house where we find the planet: cusp, pre-cuspal area, Low Point, Invert Point, etc. And when we come to the aspects, we have to look not only at the overall configuration but also at their relative tension (that is to say, whether they are red, blue, or green aspects). It is also important to note cases in which planets have only one aspect—or none at all.

● Age Point in the 1st House (Aries)
Age 0-6

Development of bodily functions. Complete dependence on parents. Awakening of ego-consciousness. Stubborn phase.

During the first months and years of life, the individual is still not conscious in an egocentric sense. He or she is as yet unable to distinguish between the ego and the environment. At this stage, the child is simply there and requires love, nourishment, warmth and protection. It is completely identified with its surroundings and is therefore extremely open to the impressions that come from these. Everything encountered by the child at this time, and also the things it misses (such as tenderness and security) tend to mould its

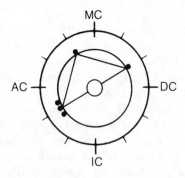

Figure 1.6.1. An example of the Age Point in the first house and extending into the second house because of the presence of planetary stelliums.

character. Only between the second and fourth year of life (Low Point of the first house) does the child begin to experience itself as an independent being. He becomes consciously aware of his surroundings for the first time. He begins to use the word "I." Impelled by this first stirring of the ego, the child enters the so-called obstinate phase, a period alleged to last no longer than two years in normal circumstances. It may even be briefer, covering no more than the time-span around the Low Point (age 3 to 4). If the obstinate phase continues into the second house (age 6), we frequently find planetary stelliums in front of or behind the second house cusp with hard aspects, as depicted in figure 1.6.1.

When we look at the aspects in this figure, we realize it would be useful for parents or teachers to know that this child will react defiantly when pushed too hard. He wants to defend his ego against any encroachments from his environment and, if he knew how, would express himself something as follows: "Here I am, and I have every right to my little bit of living space!" Above all, when the Sun or one of the other ego planets is after the Ascendant, this is always a sign of a preoccupation with the self so strong that it conflicts with the environment.

Some parents try to break the will of such a child and do all they can to make it fall in with their own plans and wishes. They demand instant obedience without any regard to the temperament of their offspring, and their attitude is frequently mirrored in difficult planetary positions lying under the shadow of the second axis. But if a "rebellious" child is always being disciplined every time it "gets out of line," this can store up trouble for later in life.

The better parental response is one of patience, which will be fortified if a glance is thrown at the AP to see how long the clash of wills is likely to last. In this, the strongest phase of ego-formation, the child normally begins to define its own living space. According to the dynamic theory of the houses, the second house influence starts to be felt at the Low Point of the first house when the native is three and a half years old. The child tries to file a claim it can defend against those with neighboring claims. This is the first constructive, social reaction of the EGO. At this crucial juncture the child becomes aware that other people also have personalities and that they too have staked out their claims.

Figure 1.6.2 on page 136 shows yet another approach to this phase. Saturn near cusp two and square the Sun in the collective

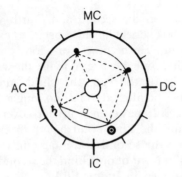

Figure 1.6.2. Another example of how the Age Point indicates stress that may affect future development.

area is usually an indication that the child has to win some of the living space owned by the family or by its father or mother. This creates an underlying anxiety that its own right to be one of the family might be in jeopardy, and could set a life-long pattern of defensive behavior—even when there is no longer any reason to be apprehensive. The individual always seems to be saying: "Halt, who goes there? This is private property." The first really effective method is then that of the second house: making one's own estate, one's own living space.

● Age Point in the 2nd House (Taurus) Age 6-12

Psychic development. Making one's own living space and habits. The distinction between "yours and mine." Ownership crises.

At the age of ca. six, the child begins to have his or her own possessions in the true sense of the word, and guards them like costly jewels. If anyone else presumes to touch them, there may be a sharp reaction. The real value of an item does not enter into consideration. Perhaps it is a broken car or a doll without arms or legs, but that does not matter—it is enough that the doll or car is the property of the child. Nobody has the right to throw an old doll away, "It is *my* doll!"

It is a serious mistake to clear out the child's toy-box during this formative period, or secretly to throw away its old bits and pieces while it is at school. By so doing, one shatters the basis of trust.

A typical example is an opposition along the second axis, or a performance triangle. From the planetary placement in the second house (or for that matter in the first or third houses) the exact timing of the formative experience can be calculated for the period between the ages of six and twelve. (For further information refer to Impressions of Early Childhood on page 117.)

Each unwelcome intrusion on the child's living space and sphere of possessions has an effect on the development of the ego. Its possessiveness is related to a sense of personal worth, and its typical "second house behavior" will determine the subsequent attitude to ownership. Parental admonitions against being a 'dog in a manger,' or continual hindrances put in the way of the child having its own property, usually lead to compensatory behavior in the adult where goods and chattels are concerned; to the extent perhaps of pathological envy, greed, cupidity and food mania, or of over-reactions against these such as asceticism, posing as an enemy of private ownership, etc.

This is the age at which children enjoy playing inside a small wigwam or house made of plastic sheeting. The game is all part of the process of securing living-space for the "I" in which it can shut out the interfering "YOU." Behavior learned now is most significant for later social deportment. Preoccupation with creating and maintaining one's own little environment clearly lessens at the Low Point (age 9-10). Of course, it does not disappear entirely, for everything we experience leaves its mark and becomes a part of our character, but its influence on conduct slowly fades.

When there is a planet under strong tension situated at the Low Point of the second house, especially if it is one of the ego planets (Sun, Moon or Saturn), the position of the child becomes awkward as soon as the Age Point reaches this position—at the age of ten years in figure 1.6.3. on page 138. Its struggle for possessions, living-space and protection does not meet with the same success as formerly. With this placement, the child is unlikely to receive much affection from its mother, and its situation does little to boost its self-confidence. In fact it is instinctively aware of becoming too set in its ways to the detriment of its general performance. Not that the realization is put in so many words; it is more in the nature of a deep but very positive feeling. Generally, at the Low Point of the second house (between the ages of 9 and 10) the environment is experienced as more powerful than the self.

Now it is true that the second house is not an angular house like the first, the Low Point of which (equivalent to the age of 3 and a half) introduces the obstinate phase; nevertheless the theme of this succedent house does undergo a comparable change in spite of its greater "fixity." The child recognizes that it must make a greater effort to enter into positive relationships with its environment. It has to learn that it must give in order to get. The difference between "yours and mine" begins to be understood. During this learning process it gravitates towards the cadent third house. The latter is not an activity house in the true sense of the word, but a house of discovery, perception, observation and experience. The child becomes increasingly interested in such possibilities during the period between the second house Low Point and the third house cusp (between ages 10 and 12). Hence that period is known as the "learning age."

For the first time in its life (at age 10 at the earliest), the child starts to learn of its own accord, and its classwork shows a marked improvement. It wants to find out as much as possible about everything and to understand what other people know. The child looks on those around it as cleverer than itself and therefore superior. Since it wishes to become one of these clever people, it tries to discover as much as it can about the world. That is the main

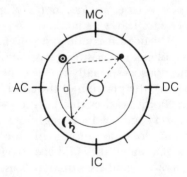

Figure 1.6.3. Planets under strong tension in the second house create problems with self-confidence early on.

reason for its eagerness to learn. What is more, the child enters puberty during this period and starts to take an interest in the opposite sex. In a way, this is a special form of the same principle: the individual wants to know and understand. And so the classical learning time in the intellectual sense begins at the third house.

An accurate analysis of the signs and planets occupying the space between Low Point Two and Cusp Three is particularly important if proper decisions regarding the child's education are to be taken—decisions having far-reaching consequences for its future life and profession.

● Age Point in the 3rd House (Gemini) Age 12-18

Development of the emotional and intellectual functions. The age of puberty; ambivalent shifts of mood. Idealistic notions, development of the will.

At the age of twelve—on the cusp of the third house—the young person enters the region of collectivity (houses three and four). The chief urge at this time of life is to be accepted into the community. The growing person begins to feel the urge to take wing from the confining family nest and to soar into the comparative freedom of society at large. The search for a wider community is led by idealism and accompanied by cricitism of the settled order (the family). The more strongly the family is identified with the standards and morals of the establishment, the more liable is the young person to have the feeling of being misunderstood and even "let down" by relatives. He or she looks for like-minded friends outside the family; and, in fact, groups of young peers with shared interests are easier to find in today's world than ever before. Many parents wring their hands over the fact that in this age of mass-communication (fast cars, the press, radio and TV etc., all closely connected with the third house) the family unit is less well able to cope with the competition from the street than it was some decades ago. A change is necessary in our educational methods too, if we are to keep pace with the altered conditions of modern times; blind authoritarianism has to yield to a more sympathetic understanding of the spiritual development of idealistic youngsters.

Between twelve and eighteen, children start using abstract thought. They try to absorb as much information as possible or have it crammed into them by their teachers or lecturers. Lessons are learned and the students are regularly tested, but their approach is piecemeal and frequently they fail to appreciate the bearing of one fact (or branch of knowledge) on another. Not before the LP of the third house at the earliest (15th to 16th year of life), and more often not until the age of eighteen, do young people begin to see the wider connections. This is the time for going to college or starting work training. What is being learned now is more vital and more related to other things. The next house (house four) is a water house, and, as it is approached, emotional qualities take the stage: the thinking is no longer purely cerebral but is enriched by a significant deepening of the emotional life At this age, the young person often displays an intense interest in philosophy or sociology, and in religious or political questions. For the first time, he or she may wonder if the world is really as it should be, and may enthusiastically espouse new ideas for changing it. Doubts concerning and criticism of the establishment can lead to revolutionary activities, from joining student protest movements to getting involved in terrorism.

When the native has Mercury or Saturn in the third house, as shown in figure 1.6.4, and Mercury or Saturn is square to Jupiter and in opposition to the ninth house—forming a thought-axis-based efficiency/performance triangle (traditionally the T-square) with its apex pointing to the "opposite number," the "YOU"—it is particularly important for the native to "stick to his or her guns"

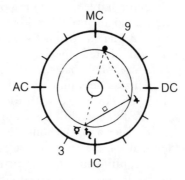

Figure 1.6.4. An aspect configuration showing the need to stick to ideals to get free from surrounding influences.

and not to let the thinking be dictated by those around. When there are planetary stelliums in the third house, those around will do their utmost to manipulate the young person into a "safe" situation where he or she will soon conform to the wishes of society. When this happens, the idealistic notions are usually abandoned pretty quickly.

The tendency of collectives to level their members arises from a natural desire for security and protection on the part of society, so this is normal, but it doesn't make the person who owns the chart very happy.

If there is an opposition along the thought axis, i.e, from the third to the ninth house as shown in figure 1.6.5, this always implies a confrontation between the collective way of thought and the personal world-view. The individual wants to emerge from the common herd and to rise superior to it by saying "No" to its dictates. When the Age Point makes contact with this opposition, the resistance of the environment will be experienced; he or she will feel misunderstood, and, in extreme cases, threatened by society. Conversely, by being disruptive or heretical, they may spread unrest. In school, especially, such trouble-makers face determined efforts to make them knuckle under quietly. Whether or not they can be made to do so will depend on the sign on and the planets in the third house. Even at this age, the conformists may be distinguished from those who think for themselves. The latter must reckon on always having to stand alone; for the interests of the two types are naturally very divergent.

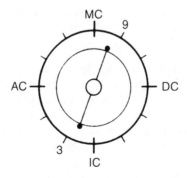

Figure 1.6.5. An opposition on the 3/9 axis shows a conflict between our goals and behavior.

When the LP is reached between age fifteen and sixteen, there is increased conscious awareness of sexual differences; and with it comes a conflict between the mind and the emotions that is profoundly unsettling to the adolescent, and often productive of considerable fluctuations of mood.

The period between sixteen and eighteen is also a difficult one for the parents. The young person is approaching the IC, the individual 4/10 axis, and wants to stand on his or her own two feet and to strike out an independent line. To most parents this is a thorn in the flesh, since they hope to keep control of their child and to choose its pathway through life. At this time they often find their children's behavior thankless; the children refuse to say where they have been or what they have been doing. It is hard for the parents to see the children slowly slipping out of their control. The adolescents come home to eat and sleep and that is about all. They feel compelled to "try their wings" and to get out and about in the world. It is best for parents to be very understanding at this time. In spite of everything, the children cannot be expected to be sufficiently mature to enter the struggle for existence on their own without suffering character damage. For the time being they are full of ideals, but these will have to be tested against the hard realities of life.

• Age Point in the 4th House (Cancer) Age 18-24

Separation from the parental home and traditions. Opting for one's own emotional attachments and affiliations. The tendency to "get up and go."

By the eighteenth birthday, the crisis of puberty is practically over. Due to the development of the sexual function, the parents should be appreciated more as adults, as man and wife, than as elders. An urge toward independent growth springs up in the teenager, who becomes aware that he or she is an individual with a taste for freedom. Until now, any sense of individuality has been rather hazy.

Figure 1.6.6 shows an opposition on the individual axis (4/10 or IC/MC). Each opposition on the individual axis joining the fourth and tenth houses indicates strong individual endeavor. If it crosses another opposition on the 3/9 axis, the native often clamors for personal freedom, wishing to break free from the common herd and, when the Age Point makes contact with this position, will want to brush aside all restrictions without more ado in order to pursue the most appealing course of action. Another possibility is that a sudden bid for power or fame will be made, especially when there is an ego-planet like the Sun or Saturn in the tenth house.

The fourth house signifies (for a young person) the effort to find a suitable place in society, offering a certain degree of status and room for action. With this in mind, he or she will try to join a congenial group of people. This personal group could be a football club, university, church or trade union, but, whatever the case, the motive will be enjoyment of a shared interest.

In general, the young person at this stage will turn more and more from the family, abandoning the old collective and identifying with one of his or her own choice or, if choice is out of the question, joining one that happens to be available.

When the LP of the fourth house is reached (age 21-22), the young adult begins to display a definite desire to leave home, inspired by a sense of the propriety and importance of possessing a place he can call his own—situated in some preferred locality. For various reasons (the length of time spent in vocational training being one of the most significant of these nowadays) this desire is not always so easy to fulfill. However, at the very least, the young

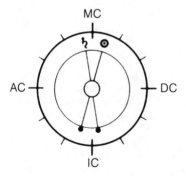

Figure 1.6.6. Oppositions create restrictions and a need for growth when the Age Point goes through the fourth house.

person ought to be provided with private living space (a room of their own) to be decorated and furnished as they wish, his or her creativity and longing for freedom being given as much scope as possible to manifest and unfold.

Figure 1.6.7 illustrates a fourth house heavily tenanted by the personality planets Saturn, the Sun, and Moon, and the parents may fail to comprehend these natural instincts, and may even have repressed them. When the Age Point transits these positions, traumatic processes of separation can be set in motion or relationships with father and mother can turn sour. If the aspect shape is a closed one or a so-called "bowl" (as in figure 1.6.7), the dependence can be so great that it clips the native's wings so to speak. Frequently the environment will hinder the development of self-determination.

At the latest after the LP has been reached in the fourth house and while the ascent is being made to the cusp of the fifth house (age 22-24), the young adult ought to have learned to take charge of life, to trade punches with the world when necessary, and not to creep nervously under the parental roof for protection. Parents whose children have so far failed to make their own way in the world, should seriously think of "stirring up the nest" a bit. It is important at this age to become a founding member of one's own group. Formerly this was achieved by marrying and having children. Today, the young sometimes gather in communes during the period the AP is transiting the fourth house.

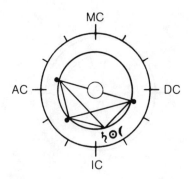

Figure 1.6.7. Age Point in the fourth house involving Saturn, the Sun and Moon.

● Age Point in the 5th House (Leo)
Age 24-30

Autonomous phase, progress in professional life and in building a family, love matches, creative self-development.

The fifth house is the most adventurous of all the houses. It is the house for proving oneself in the world, and involves contacts with the many individuals who cross our path. They and we are thrown together in the hurly-burly of life, and sometimes these confrontations (with the YOU) can prove to be extremely fruitful. The animated scene is often full of fierce struggles, with cut and thrust on both sides; hard knocks given and taken are all part of the learning process, which is not always easy. During this period of life, we are extraordinarily expansive and think we can conquer the world at one stroke. Such behavior is right and proper at this age, since it enables us to measure our capabilities against reality. More or less consciously, we discover our limitations.

Planets in the fifth house indicate special experiences at this time of life. If Saturn, the planet of restriction, is there, the native will be restrained or uncomfortable in his or her contacts. Things do not run so smoothly as with the Sun or Moon for example. If, on the other hand, either of the libido planets (Mars or Venus) is there, the love life will be strongly activated during the Age Point transit. (See figure 1.6.8.)

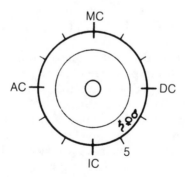

Figure 1.6.8. Planets in the fifth house indicate an important phase when the Age Point passes age 24-30.

In the fifth house, corresponding to the sign of Leo, it pays to be jovial and magnanimous in true leonine fashion; then we shall gain the hearts of our fellow-men and -women. Also, we shall learn the extent to which people can be won over by sympathy and liberality, incidentally discovering the strength and scope of our powers and how far we can go. In the process, a clearly defined form of behavior emerges by which we may well express our personality for most of our life. We become marked out by our bearing, our gestures, our clothing, and by our approach to people and things.

The planets in the fifth house have much to tell us about this. With Venus we easily win folk's sympathies. With Mars we are inclined to be too direct, too brusque. With Jupiter we are jovial, but invariably know how to take our advantage. With the Sun we can sway others. With Saturn we like to impose conditions, either consciously or unconsciously.

The period covering the ages from twenty-four to thirty is a very intensive phase. The potentials of the planets and the signs have to be worked out in actual experience where they will be hemmed in by reality. When the AP arives at the Low Point of the fifth house (age 27-28), a measure of failure is evident. The Low Point is particularly prominent in every fixed house, since the principle of fixity comes strongly to the fore. By analogy, the fixed house we are now considering has many of the qualities of Leo, and its Low Point makes itself distinctly felt. Anyway, we are cut down to size by people and things, and in the process come to know ourselves better. There is a risk that we shall be brought low, but may also climb to a new vantage point where vistas of hitherto hidden knowledge (not generally associated with the fifth house) will unexpectedly burst upon our gaze.

With the transit of the AP over one of the three spiritual planets Uranus, Neptune, or Pluto, we are likely to be brought into contact with religious movements, or with mind-changing ideas introduced to us by certain books or individuals.

In some respects, the Low Points of the houses on the right of the chart are the key to the opposite houses on the left. Thus the LP of the fifth house can represent our approach to the eleventh house. With planets in the eleventh house and an aspect pattern on the 5/11 axis, ideals will assume importance quite early on. Careful reflection should yield significant insights at the LP and help us to find the true balance between outer and inner reality. Individuals of this age frequently display intense interest in the spiritual side of life and

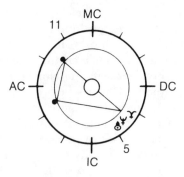

Figure 1.6.9. When the Age Point moves through the fifth house and touches aspects to Uranus, Neptune, or Pluto, the individual makes important changes.

its problems, especially if one of the spiritual planets is involved in any transits or aspects the AP may make. By so doing they have an opportunity for creative self-improvement and can enjoy the highest the fifth house has to offer. To some extent, all of us sow seed in the fifth house for a harvest to be reaped from the eleventh house between the ages of sixty and sixty-six. Whatever house is being transited, it is worthwhile looking at the axes, because one house sets the stage for another, and by allowing for this fact we can see the relationship between a given age sector and the whole chart. See figure 1.6.9.

● Age Point in the 6th House (Virgo)
   Age 30-36

Adjustment phase. Defensive life situation. Vocational crises. Mastering existence. Incorporation into the community.

If the fifth house is a dominant, active house, the sixth is subservient and passive—corresponding to the serving sign Virgo, so unlike ruling Leo. This difference comes out clearly as the Age Point crosses the boundary between the two houses: from the positive, even aggressive attitude to the world, there comes a retreat into suffering and endurance. We are thrown on the defensive—especially where the LP is located at the age of 28.

From an existential point of view, we each have to find our slot in the market place when the Age Point is passing through the sixth house. As seen by society, each of us has something to offer in the way of output or capability: some creative talent. We each possess personal qualities worthy of being developed in the situations into which we have been born. The task before us is to find our unique niche; a task that seems to become more urgent during this period. Now is often a time for refresher or re-training courses to enable the native to give of his or her best or to gain job satisfaction. Finding the right job or profession demands a very subtle play between skill and will, between wishes and possibilities. We have to place a realistic value on what we can do and we have to present it properly, demanding neither too much nor too little. Finding the happy medium is the task of the sixth house.

The sixth-house planets suggest how we shall have to exert ourselves and what requirements we shall have to satisfy. With the Sun or Pluto, for example, we shall possess the fund of vitality necessary for performing arduous tasks. We may even go in search of such tasks in order to prove ourselves. With Venus, Jupiter or the Moon, we are much more tractable and allow ourselves to be influenced or unsettled by our environment.

During this period of life, we must see how we can explore the options open to us in the light of our abilities. This is most important, as it guarantees, confirms and secures not only our outer but also our inner existence. Lack of success can lead to acute crises, especially in late starters who have yet to find their true path, for

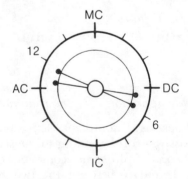

Figure 1.6.10. When the Age Point passes through the sixth house, natal oppositions may cause a crisis relating to self-support.

these people are ever searching and experimenting, and may already have abandoned one or more careers (perhaps due to setting their sights too high). This is the time to abandon all plans that are not in keeping with the personality. There the great uncertainty experienced by individuals who have so far failed to put their lives on a firm basis may easily be imagined.

Especially where there are hard aspects (oppositions) along the 6/12 existence axis (see figure 1.6.10), and even more strongly when two oppositions cross, problems to do with existence keep on recurring. As the Age Point transits such a position, a desperate crisis can arise affecting the very core of the being. The native's self-esteem may be shattered and he or she may be plagued by extreme doubt, thinking, "I'm good for nothing," or "Nobody wants me around, I'm no use to anyone," and oscillating between pity of self and bitterness against the world. The upshot could be full-blown depression, antisocial behavior or some form of psychosomatic illness.

There is always a danger of slipping into some form of disease in crises of this sort. If we snap under the strain, an inner despair may result which will cause us to be whisked away into a twelfth house situation—the twelfth house signifying, among other things, hospitals. We may wonder whether we are able to handle life and whether, indeed, life makes any sense at all. Here again the Low Point (age 33-34) is an essential factor in setting a new course. The individual may suddenly realize that the wrong profession has been chosen and so he or she will apply for retraining—the sixth house being closely associated with further education. For, because it shares many of the characteristics of Virgo, it presents us with opportunities to redress errors affecting body, mind and vocation. This is the house in which we concern ourselves with health matters, the cure of disease, and also with social duties. The problems of life are best solved by caring for others. "In helping others, we help ourselves," is the appropriate maxim for this house and this period of life.

And so, in the sixth house, one can set about making sure that one is in the right job or profession, not only for the sake of earning a living but for the sake of inner contentment. If, for example, as shown in figure 1.6.11 on page 150, there is a trine between Uranus (or some other planet) in the sixth house and the Sun or Jupiter in the tenth, and if a third planet forms with these trined planets a so-

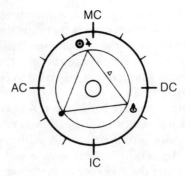

Figure 1.6.11. Planets in the sixth house can also inspire an active career when the Age Point moves here.

called big blue talent triangle, the chances are that either we know quite early on what we want to do in life or, when the Age Point transits Uranus, we become energetic enough to enter on a career in keeping with our abilities.

● Age Point in the 7th House (Libra)
Age 36-42

Formation of new connections, revision of life-style, partnership problems, life changes, high point of personal development.

When the seventh cusp is reached, a rather successful time begins. It is true that the influence of the sixth house very often continues for a further year or thereabouts, but generally speaking the effect of the seventh house starts to be noticed before the cusp.

Whatever the cusp, some sort of stress situation is encountered just prior to Age Point transit. We have the feeling of having to climb a steep mountain. Especially with the cardinal axes 1, 4, 7 and 10, the going is particularly strenuous. We experience an intensification of external and internal forces urging us on. Again and again, events start to snowball or we are drawn into matters beyond our control.

After the seventh cusp has been passed, success may suddenly be achieved on our own terms. Our chances for "being ourselves" improve; we get along better with our opposite numbers and are accepted for what we are. This is the theme of the seventh house. Now we can link up with those who are able to help our development: especially if Jupiter, Mercury, Venus or the Moon occupy the house. New paths can open up without any special effort on our part. Suddenly the realization hits us: "This is the way for me—this is the direction I can take!" Quite often the new decisions taken at this time are professional; but usually it is our personal relationships that take on a new aspect, since the seventh house is the house of partnership.

As the seventh cusp (the DC) is transited at the age of thirty-six, we enter the conscious sector of the chart. Since this is the day-time sector, we see many things in a fresh and clearer light. Factors that formerly over-influenced or troubled us can suddenly disappear. We can awake like Sleeping Beauty to things that until now we have not perceived or considered, whether they are external events or inner realizations. The process is one of becoming consciously aware, not only of ourselves but also of our partners. Such a process frequently has its painful side, particularly when we have lived under the spell of big illusions concerning partnership, spouse or contacts. Shortcomings on the part of our partners and ourselves are now found to be excessively disturbing. We can no longer tolerate or ignore them. There is also the chance that our partner will start finding fault with everything, and the shared life we have taken so much trouble to build up will no longer mean anything to him or her. Quite severe matrimonial crises can arise, usually lasting until the Low Point (40 years of age).

If an encounter axis joins the "I" with the "YOU," *i.e.*, if there is an opposition involving the first and seventh houses (see figure 1.6.12 on page 152), disappointments could mark the passage of the Age Point through the seventh house. Should the majority of planets be on the "I" side, we shall be too much inclined to impose our own personal ideas and wishes and too little inclined to make due allowance for those of others. Acute crises in marriage or partnership should result in differences being clarified or ironed out, and should bring fresh insights. With an opposition on the I-YOU axis it is difficult, however, to distinguish the different elements and to recognize the real cause of the crisis. We can not clearly see how and to what extent we make projections on one another. Consequently, we are amazed when we suddenly recognize that our partner thinks, feels, and behaves quite differently from the

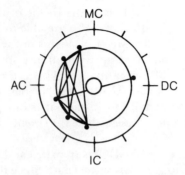

Figure 1.6.12. When the Age Point moves through the seventh house, it is a real encounter should planets be involved in an opposition between the seventh and the first.

way we have always assumed they did. In this confrontation of the I and the YOU, what matters is a mature, concerned relationship enshrining a nice balance between sharing and freedom of action. It is necessary to be constantly aware that both of these have contributed to the forming of the relationship and that both will determine its outcome. Perhaps there will be a separation or divorce. If a divorce is decided, several years will have to elapse before the process is complete, which will usually be at the Low Point (age 40) or even at the cusp of the eighth house (age 42).

Nearly all of us begin to entertain doubts as the Low Point is reached (between the ages of 39 and 40), wondering whether pulling together or 'go-it-alone' is the best policy for us. This incipient uncertainty can have the most varied causes. If, for example, the Age Point transits Uranus in the seventh house, and Uranus is involved in hard aspects from other planets, as shown in figure 1.6.13, the longing for personal freedom will be accentuated. The native will start thinking along such lines as, "My situation has become too stifling. I need to be myself again; I shall have to secure more room for my own development." With other planets, Neptune or Venus say, we are simply tired of our obligations. In which case, we look for a little bit of immediate freedom, and resort to various sly tricks to obtain it. With Saturn under difficult aspects in the seventh house, and especially when it is at the Low Point, we may find that our partner cannot be tied down. We must learn to give them their freedom even when it hurts to do so.

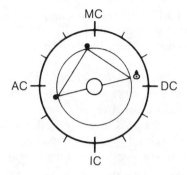

Figure 1.6.13. Uranus in the seventh house, for example, may force a relationship to re-evaluate itself when the Age Point moves through the seventh.

Another reason for crisis is the appearance of the first signs of the onset of old age in the form of certain small infirmities which can no longer be dismissed. The hassle and wear and tear of life are beginning to take their toll, although we are still not prepared to admit it.

• Age Point in the 8th House (Scorpio) Age 42-48

Change of life-style, death and transfiguration, social status, making sure of life.

During this phase of existence we are concerned firstly with stabilizing our position in society, and secondly with turning our attention to spiritual things. We feel the need to bestow some thought on the good of our souls. It is helpful if we can use our achievements to date as a sort of "fly-wheel" to keep us "ticking over" comfortably. Now is a time for drawing on our reserves and for reaping the benefit of former efforts; so that we can devote more time and energy to cultural, spiritual or philosophical pursuits. This fixed scorpionic house has long been associated with in-heritances, legacies and the possessions of one's "opposite number." Therefore the transit through the eighth house is a period in which we receive what we have earned—or get our just desserts. It is not unlikely that we shall be offered various positions in society, if we have gained a reputation for reliability. On the other hand, past frivolity and carelessness may lose us financial and social status now.

Because of the strong instinct for self-preservation, it is a natural reaction at this time to cling to what has already been accomplished, to fight against change, because we want security in the roles we have grown used to playing. But if we dwell too much in the past and persist in trying to re-enact the scenes of yesterday, we shall succumb to the death-and-transfiguration process of this Scorpio house. What has just been said almost seems like a contradiction, yet it lies in the nature of the transformation process that everyone has to undergo in one way or another during this period. Our passage through the eighth house forces us to adjust to the realities of life; we need to protect the roots of our life certainly, but also to grow spiritually. If we fail to do the latter, our materialism and clinging to dead forms will be purged by losses of all kinds. The things to which we are holding on so tightly will be snatched away from us. Our old world will suddenly crack wide open so that a new one may hatch out. In this connection it is interesting to note that the Low Point of the entire zodiac falls in the sigh of Scorpio (12-½ degrees). The name so often given to the eighth house—the house of death—would seem to find its explanation here. At this time of life we frequently lose things on which we have bestowed considerable love and care. Our parents may die, our children may leave home, or we may find ourselves stripped of some

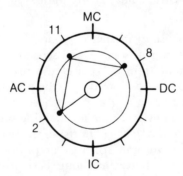

Figure 1.6.14. The passage of the Age Point through the eighth house will inspire an individual to try something new.

favorite office or function. Those who have applied themselves to building a career abandon it without warning or they break out of their familiar circle.

Eighth house crises have two main causes: in the first place we are seeking the path to the MC (the individualization point) and ever more independence and personal freedom, yet feel hemmed in by living conditions and the social set-up, or by the strong will of our partner. In the second place we may have to recognize that we made a mistake in our younger days and allowed ourselves to be guided too much by what the group thought and did. Now we are consumed by the desire to regain our liberty but are hindered by a hundred obligations and restraints.

Figure 1.6.14 illustrates an individual who has a performance triangle touching the 8th house, and the Age Point transit begets a wish to throw the past to the winds in order to take up something new. Usually we have allowed ourselves to be manipulated by life (or by our environment) into a fixed situation, but are now aware that we can no longer keep treating this as a passing phase. One possible reaction to this insight is resignation. We lose our last, fine illusions concerning how special we are, concerning our prospects of un-trammelled liberty or free love, and at that point we just give up. The reaction need not be negative. Instead of resignation we can assist at the birth of the spiritual person. Giving up or letting go are really no more than a change in life's motivation, a renewal in the spiritual sense. They are psychological counterparts of the eternal theme of death and transfiguration, and will help us achieve an inner rebirth during the so-called midlife crisis.

Here we have considered one manner in which the eighth house can be experienced. The reader may experience it entirely different-ly. Personal development has much to do with the case, and with whether the crisis affects the material, mental or spiritual side of life. Also, the signs occupied by the planets, and the part of the house in which the latter are posited (on or before the cusp, at the Low Point or Invert Point, etc.), all have a hand in this; as does the way in which these planets are involved in the aspect configuration.

An instructive example from our own practice is that of a young man who encountered a powerful aspect configuration just on the cusp of the eighth house when he was turning forty-two (see figure 1.6.15 on page 156). During the run-up to the eighth house, near the Low Point of the seventh house (age forty or therabouts), he felt completely trapped and looked on his whole existence as a prison from which there was no escape. He was unable to respond like a normal person to contacts and became neurotic. A defense mechanism had been formed when the Moon was transited around age ten, and it had interfered with his life for thirty-six years while the Age Point was traversing the empty space. Not until the opposition could the diverted vital energy break through. This demonstrates how serious such a life crisis can be.

As the Age Point reached the Saturn/Uranus conjunction, the young man attempted suicide because he was living at loggerheads with his father, his mother was dead, and a love affair (transit of Venus) had just ended. His world lay in ruins around him and he lost the will to survive. What had happened? What was the cause of his breakdown?

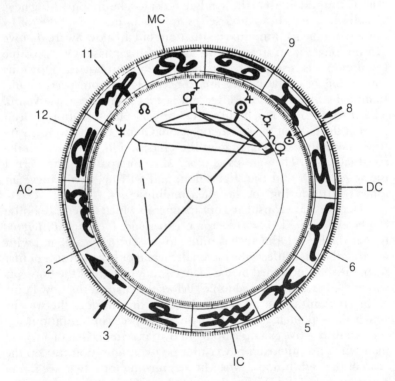

Figure 1.6.15. The chart of a male client who experienced a major transformation during the Age Point passage through the eighth house.

As a little chap of ten or eleven, just as the Age Point was transiting the lunar pole of the Moon/Mercury opposition, he had had his homelife disrupted by the war. The Moon-ego of childhood, with its need for love and security (2nd house) was replaced by a super-ego based on the fight for folk and fatherland. This was out of keeping with the child's nature, but helped him to come to terms with his fate as it was at that time. He continued to wear the same mask of bold confidence in the eighth house when he felt unable to cope any longer.

At this juncture two things happened. First he went back to his old job as a printer, and then—and this is what brought about the most far-reaching change—he became devoted to a mature older woman who mothered him and lent him her psychological support. She understood him and helped him to start a new life with her. What happened bears all the marks of the eighth house. He died to himself and was "reborn." That death is also rebirth is a lesson worth remembering in the time of crisis, if we are to move on confidently to the ninth house cusp.

• Age Point in the 9th House (Sagittarius) Age 48-54

Acceptance of greater responsibilities for the community, instruction of others, construction of a world of spiritual values, or else a sudden inability to make sense of life with resignation.

In this house of the expansion of consciousness (Sagittarian in character) we have the opportunity of taking up new and fascinating interests. We may well start delving into philosophy, religion or esoteric matters, start pondering the meaning of life or make a pilgrimage to some strange and distant shore, our choice being governed by the signs and planets in the ninth house. If we have managed to disengage ourselves from unnecessary tasks over the preceding few years, we shall now have more time to spare for the things we really want to do. The period between the forty-eighth and the fifty-fourth year of life is the so-called philosophical phase. Here it is wise to start occupying ourselves with the essential values and realities of life in preparation for the onset of old age.

At this time, we shall discover that the external world is not the be-all and end-all; worldly success, power, riches and fame may help to make life more settled and secure, but do not guarantee a fulfilled and happy life. The loosening of old ties in the eighth house has already been leading to this conclusion, but the ninth house brings it into clear view. And so there is an opportunity to see things in a new and more independent way.

Like the other cadent houses, the ninth is associated with questions of meaningfulness. We ask ourselves, "What is the meaning and purpose of my life? How best can I serve humanity?" Back of these questions is a desire to make sense of the whole workings of creation: the mind broaches philosophical and transcendental matters. Personal interests are no longer paramount. Actually, we should be bestowing our attention on problems of this sort as early as the Low Point between the ages of forty-four and forty-five, for if we do not we run the risk of coming to a dead-end in the ninth house.

Figure 1.6.16 shows ninth house planets in opposition to planets in the third house, so the native's opinions will not always be in line with the opinions of the group. This conflict will in fact already have arisen. If the opposition is aggravated by being part of a projection triangle (*i.e.*, of a triangle incorporating an opposition together with two long green quincunx aspects and a sextile), the Age Point transit can provoke a spiritual crisis, similar to the "Faustian" struggle for the ultimate truth, in which we are seized by a gnawing doubt.

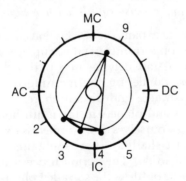

Figure 1.6.16. Planets in opposition in the third and ninth houses can force a crisis when the Age Point moves through that house (age 48-54).

The uncertainty crisis over the meaning of life as the Low Point of the ninth house is reached at the age of fifty-two, detaches us from the tried and trusted. We enter a so-called "null-sphere" where we should let go all egocentricity. In letting go, however, we are caught up to where our field of vision is widened to see things in their true proportions. This is in keeping with that saying of Socrates, "Wisdom begins only when we know that we know nothing."

As with Low Point transits in any other house, a new orientation is required here too. So many things appear to make no sense and we ask ourselves what the use is of all our knowledge and other accomplishments if we cannot pass them on. In this crisis it can be helpful to return to the ideals we had during the third-house period at age twelve to sixteen. As life widens out again we shall gain courage and renewed motivation.

When houses are above the horizon, it is always wise to take a look at the periods of the houses beneath them. The functions of two diametrically opposite houses, one above and the other below the horizon, are complementary. (See figure 1.6.17.) The poles of the axes are related in quality to a certain extent, and one house is the shadow of the other from whichever end we regard them. Each end makes its own contribution sooner or later.

In order to continue to enjoy life in the ninth house, we must leap out into the spiritual, into the transcendental—rather like a parachutist making a jump into the ocean of air. By so doing we gain the necessary distance from our little egos to operate more effectively. Since we are no longer so closely identified with events,

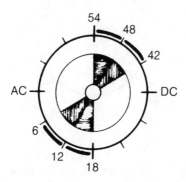

Figure 1.6.17. Opposite houses are complementary and one house is actually the shadow of the other.

we can work for the well-being of the whole. Especially when the Age Point is transiting the region of the Low Point, we have a chance to extend this distance and to behave more impersonally.

During the crisis of trying to make sense of life, and when there is a strong drift towards resignation, an opposition from Saturn in the ninth house along the thought axis can cast that planet in the role of "the dweller of the threshold before the spiritual gates." Saturn is a personality planet and as such represents the protective space surrounding the ego. For this reason, it is reluctant to release whatever it happens to be holding. But the ninth house demands expanded awareness and an abandonment of effete standards before we proceed on our way.

With Saturn in the ninth house (see figure 1.6.18) in opposition to the Sun in the third, it is not easy to place personal ideas and wishes in the service of the higher, ethical aims. At the Low Point at ca. fifty-two years and just before the M.C. at ca. fifty-three years when Jupiter is posited there for example, it is particularly important to see oneself set against the spiritual background of life as a whole. One will not then be so full of self-importance, but will make an effort to understand and help the rising generation and to accept the new world and advance with it. This tolerant attitude is essential for further development.

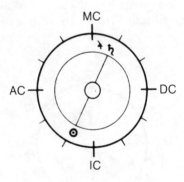

Figure 1.6.18. With Saturn in the ninth house, it is not easy to allow oneself to grow spiritually as the Age Point passes, but it is necessary to further development.

● Age Point in the 10th House (Capricorn) Age 54-60

Authority and individuation phase, identification with the calling, fulfillment of life's expectations, ossification.

Here too, as in angles four and seven, the impulse imparted by the MC (the 10th house cusp) is experienced as a strong incentive to be independent. At the age of fifty-four we have reached the highest point in the chart, where we and the world stand level. We see ourselves as we really are, and that is how we have to present ourselves. There is no longer any room for self-deception; we are obliged to show ourselves in our true colors. If we have something to offer, some skill or specialized knowledge, we shall be entrusted with greater responsibilities. It is impossible to hide behind others any more, and if we try to do so Fate will probably give us "a shove in the back" to force us into the open.

In the tenth house, the house of individual flowering, we have independent authority and the development of an inner vocation. Here is the place where experience and maturity can prove their worth. If the ripening process promoted by the ninth house has been successful, the native will find himself endorsed by his group around the time the MC is being transited. The group perceives that the native knows what he is talking about, that he is competent, and is therefore prepared to trust him with some of its affairs.

And so it often happens that people enter public life at this time, perhaps after previous attempts to do so have proved abortive. This usually occurs when a planet is not so powerfully placed in the tenth house (middle to Low Point)—but is now able to exert its influence.

Figure 1.6.19 on page 162 shows that this is true even of planets in the shadow of the axis: for example, Jupiter or some other planet just in front of the MC with the Sun in the tenth house on the Low Point. With an aspect formation predominantly on the ego-side, the native may never have obtained proper recognition, but now, with a transit by the Age Point the world suddenly sits up and takes notice of him. With this position, the individual does not strive for fame but endeavors to cultivate the ability indicated by Jupiter or one of the other planets. In which case, the motive is self-fulfillment not the pursuit of power.

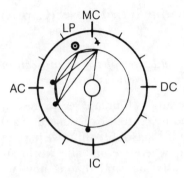

Figure 1.6.19. Jupiter in the shadow of the MC.

The period of life between the ages of fifty-four and sixty should be one of fulfillment if our special qualities are able to come to fruition. The environment often encourages this without any forcing on our part; the time is a particularly happy and satisfying one in which we reap the reward of past exertions. Yet here too there are problem positions requiring our attention.

Figure 1.6.20 shows an opposition along the individual axis from the fourth to the tenth house. Someone also having a stellium in the tenth house (especially one involving hard planets) can indicate tragic experiences or reverses at this time. If wrong means have been employed on the road to power and prestige, if corners have been cut unfairly, or if vaulting ambition and the lust for power have led us to kick others aside, we shall be repaid in the same coin when the Age Point makes its transit, and as likely as not will be rebuffed by those around us. Every sham authority that has not grown organically will be questioned and may be overthrown; every false claim on the service and respect of our fellows will be rejected sooner or later—at the latest when the tenth-house Low Point is reached.

Near the Low Point, in the fifty-eighth year, our juniors often begin to be seen as rivals. We become nervous of losing the position so dearly won and for some time oppose every internal and external change. The Low Point of house ten represents an important turning point in life. Standing, so to speak at a corner, we cast a backward glance on an active professional life, and also look ahead to a period when we shall need more rest for lack of energy or enthusiasm to face the hustle and bustle of the workaday world. As

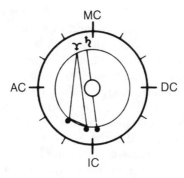

Figure 1.6.20. An opposition from the fourth to the tenth.

yet we do not know how we are going to shed our responsibilities or how we shall spend our new-found leisure. Our maturity is now put to the test—a maturity which does not depend on any outward success, but on integrity, inner strength, and creative imagination. Many a time we shall be shaken and shall need to fight to keep our balance, not so much by preserving our outward poise as by clinging to spiritual principles, inner values and experiences.

The tenth house is in a certain sense the last house of worldly joy. Already with the transit of the MC we have quitted the right side of the chart. All the energies flowing to us from close association with our fellows are on the ebb. Whoever wears the chain of public office in the tenth house may discover that he becomes progressively isolated and that his private life is affected too. For the most part, those who engage in public activities suffer an erosion of their private lives. They are under constant observation and cannot do just what they like.

- ## Age Point in the 11th House (Aquarius) Age 60-66

Digestion of life's experiences, ethics and tolerance, new friendships and relationships—or isolation and resignation.

The eleventh house usually brings with it a noticeable decline in contacts as compared with the number of contacts made from the fourth to the eighth house. At this time of life it is best to confine oneself to a small circle of friends, and to a few deep relationships. The years spent in the eleventh house from 60 to 66 are also suitable for taking stock. In the "more rarefied atmosphere" of the house corresponding to the air sign Aquarius, we are usually elevated above the world's feverish activity. This is the time to enjoy a more comprehensive view of things. For example, many people start writing their memoirs now, perhaps in a late bid for fame, although the main motive is to crystallize the essence of life's experiences. The years stretch back into the past. For a long time the native has been working hard to secure a good position and a comfortable retirement, and can now ease up. He will reflect on how insignificant his troubles often were, and on how often he squandered his energies on things that seemed important at the time but were really of little moment. Lessons are learned which would not have been understood twenty years earlier. The native also discovers that often it was not others who deceived him: he deceived himself by taking it for granted that his affairs were bound to develop in a certain way.

Here, then, is an opportunity to acquire a degree of wisdom, to see past mistakes in a clearer light, and to recognize what has to be altered and improved. Perhaps a circle of friends is formed for the exchange of opinions. A decision has to be made: since it is no longer possible to serve humanity in general, the native seeks out the people with whom he has something in common, people with whom he can share his thoughts and experiences, and deepen his philosophy. Contacts with youngsters tend to improve, because the individual is no longer fighting to keep ahead in life and has shed much of his dogmatism. There is an understanding of the problems faced by the young—who are always willing to accept advice given in a spirit of tolerance.

With one of the sensitive planets, Neptune, Jupiter, Venus or the Moon on the eleventh cusp, and this person will usually intuitively know who will form the most reliable friends. It is certainly important in the eleventh house, the house of friendship, to make friends who are genuine: not acquaintances who are there only when the going is good, but folk prepared to give loyal support during a crisis. When sensitive planets occupy the eleventh house, the native most likely had a good attitude towards others, even in youth, and will therefore be surrounded by loyal friends even at this stage—and will probably not suffer loneliness. To attract and keep friends, we need ethical behavior, kindness and a sense of fair play.

In the phase of life represented by the eleventh house, we generally wish to place our experience and our practical wisdom at the disposal of others, and so long as this is done with the right motives and in the right way (that is to say with a desire to be helpful without being condescending) others will profit by it. One of the most useful tasks of this period is to rid ourselves of one-sided ideas. If we fail, we may end up alone and friendless!

At the Low Point of the eleventh house, around age sixty-four, folk commonly discover that many of their acquaintances are no longer interested in them and even try to avoid meeting them. Their friends desert them; especially their younger friends, who somehow seem to be too busy to see them. Perhaps they have to face the deaths of old comrades—always a painful experience. Health problems or crises are also fairly frequent around Low Point eleven. Retirement lies just ahead, and this in itself can give rise to depression and anxiety. The less initiative the person has, the more he or she will be gripped by the fear of loneliness and old age. Failure to overcome the "little me" syndrome will leave the native with no road forward into a fulfilled life. If, by the time he has reached the eleventh house, he still has not shaken off the shackles of "poor little me," he will suffer from hypersensitivity. The least sign of neglect will mortify him deeply. He will stalk away sulkily and will cut himself off even from good companions; in which case there can be a negative crystallization of self-assertiveness in this fixed house, perhaps accompanied by senility.

Figure 1.6.21 on page 166 illustrates the possibility of counselling someone with a red square in the fixed houses 2, 5, 8, 11 or oppositions from hard planets like Pluto, Mars, Uranus or Saturn along the 5/11 axis. Health problems of some serious concern regarding friendships will undoubtedly occur. Usually, the problem is that the mind has lost its flexibility. Not all the fitness training, flashy ties, or showy hats in the world can magically restore the verve of youth. Endless stale reminiscences become a terrible bore to the listeners. And the causes of these things are usually to be found in earlier periods in the fixed houses.

In this connection, we should also mention the numerous causes of "pensioner's collapse." Individuals who have expended all

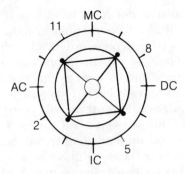

Figure 1.6.21. A chart showing a grand square in the fixed houses. The Age Point passage through the eleventh house will be very important.

their energies on the struggle for existence but have neglected to cultivate pursuits suitable for their old age find themselves suddenly out on a limb, not knowing where to start. Therefore it is extremely important to make preparations in the fifth or (at the latest) in the eighth house, for the big change to come.

Nevertheless, the eleventh house can also prove very enjoyable if we have the chance to be ourselves once more and possess the health and strength to spend our time well. This will bring fulfillment to us and will benefit those around in the bargain.

● Age Point in the 12th House (Pisces) Age 66-72

Completion of life, gradual cessation of personal effort, voluntary withdrawal or one forced by illness, self-finding.

The twelfth house is the last in the full circle, but this does not mean that life ends here; it merely closes the round. In keeping with its nature it produces a return from the outer world to the core of self. By the Low Point of the eleventh house at the latest (sixty-three and a half) we should begin to realize the meaning of this phase of life. As we already know, the Ascendant is the symbolic ego point in the chart, and its attractive power is felt as soon as the MC is transited. That is why the pivotal theme and task of the twelfth house is the return to the center of oneself. A certain isolation is required for this task and, if the native will not seek it of his own free will, nature will provide it for him.

Figure 1.6.22 shows a stellium of hard planets in the twelfth house (e.g. Saturn, Mars or Pluto with squares and oppositions). When this configuration exists, it often happens that the native is isolated at this period of life, being packed off to an old folks home, or abandoned by his family to live in a lonely room. The twelfth house theme is that of detachment from the external world to turn inwards for the purpose of exploring our own inner dimensions. The person who has passed through the earlier stages "correctly" will have no trouble here, but may anticipate a gracious old age, a time which enables him to see clearly both himself and the relationships between inner and outer. It will also be a time of gratitude for everything that has been experienced in the past and may yet be experienced in the future, of thankfulness for the riches of adventure and knowledge life has brought.

Since, in the twelfth house, we have little or no dealings with the world at large, it is possible to sit and meditate on self and the universe. We can become more detached since life has become much less demanding. The conditions are ideal to turn to higher things and to discover the treasures within; to learn how to be alone with ourselves.

After the Low Point, we enter the expansive sphere of the ego and the pull of the Ascendant can already be felt. In this phase from

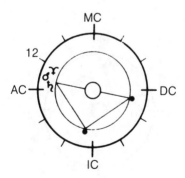

Figure 1.6.22. A stellium in the twelfth house shows mostly isolation in this life period.

age 70-76 (LP to LP) we are required to find our true selves and to become self-sufficient. This necessitates a release from everything external that would imprison the self, in order that a higher condition of soul may be born from the center of the being. At this juncture, a split is experienced between the wish to sit back and savor the ripe fruit of achievement and the impulse to forget the joys and sorrows of the past in order to embrace life again like a newborn and carefree child. The result is often a spiritual rebirth which will carry the life far over the Ascendant again, or else will produce mere second childhood. Unpleasant symptoms of aging, such as senility and physical degeneration, are retarded and even avoided by a mentally sound, vital attitude. Acceptance of life, the joy of living, affection, and sensible body care all contribute to an intact ego which will still function well physically in the twelfth house. If, in addition, we are free from everyday pressures, from the struggle to keep the wolf from the door, from obligations and debts, we can adopt the spectator's role and have fun joining in the game of life on the sidelines. For preference, the pensioners should not be solitary, but should remain in circulation and be given a quiet window seat from which to watch the world's comings and goings. And so the individual remains lively and awake; as, in fact, we see in Mediterranean lands, where old people sit at the window or in front of the house; they do not say much and usually are not conspicuous, but they share in everything going on around them, they study the world and their expression is one of content.

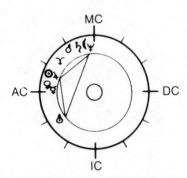

Figure 1.6.23. A well-aspected Sun in the twelfth house may inspire new creative potential when the Age Point passes through.

If the Sun is well-aspected (see figure 1.6.23) in the twelfth house and the whole aspect picture is framed by the fourth quadrant, natives may not realize their full potential until they are old. They will still be needed, perhaps as grandfathers or grandmothers. Grandparents are often good teachers, since they are able to pass on their experience. They are standing at the necessary distance from life and can offer the children understanding, whereas younger educators tend to project their own conceptions and compulsions to the children. For another thing, grandparents and grandchildren are pretty close to one another, because the elderly have an emotional rapport with the young.

With the transit of the AC (age 72) we are new-born in a certain sense, and receive a jolt of vitality something like that received at birth. Astrologically speaking, we have a new and quite conscious perception of any planets posited in the first house. We recognize dimensions which, although they are familiar to us, look new in the light of seventy-two years of earthly existence. When these planets were being transited in our infancy, we were in a passive position with regard to our environment and were not free to make our own decisions. There was no possibility of digesting and working on all our impressions. But now, in our old age, we meet these planets again and have an opportunity to use this fresh encounter to reach a deeper understanding of our destiny and of ourselves. A good example is available in the life of C.G. Jung, and in Part Two of this book we shall be describing in detail the Age Point Progression of his horoscope.

Publisher's Note: Age Point cycles repeat as our longevity increases. This new section has been added to explain how the Age Point may work when it goes through the first three houses for the second time.

• Return of the Age a Point to the First Three Houses

When the Age Point returns to the first three houses our "little ego" shouldn't really be all that important to us any more. It will be much more important to learn to identify with our immortal, indestructible soul. It will give us the opportunity to fathom the deeper meaning behind our whole life pattern and to get on more familiar terms with our Higher Self. We can also free ourselves from a lot of old patterning and false and misleading notions.

With a bit of luck we can now enjoy these added years of our lives, for they are given to us as a bonus. They don't have their individual specific characteristics, they tend to offer us a repetition of the original experiences, but on a higher rung on the evolutionary spiral. Many childhood memories will come back to us quite vividly, and we can "re-view" them from the point of view of our more mature consciousness. Many of us experience a new clarity of vision and understanding, and many a problem and trauma which had its origin in our early years (1st and 2nd house) can now be seen with more detachment, a different perspective, and may even find an acceptable resolution.

From an astrological point of view, we'll experience with a heightened degree of consciousness those planets which are placed in the first three houses. We sense interconnections vaguely familiar and yet novel to us. Because, of course, when the Age Point activated these planets in our early years, we had to react mainly defensively. We were entirely dependent on our surroundings and quite unable to make independent decisions. We did not have the ability then, or the know-how, to cope consciously with our experiences or to work with them.

Now we are given another chance to come up against these self-same planetary energies and thus gain a deeper understanding of our life pattern, and of our being. The life of C. G. Jung is a good example of this process. (See page 173 ff.)

• Age Point in the 1st House

Age 73 to 76
Our second "Birth," Cusp to Low Point of 1st House, renewed zest for life spontaneous Self.

In the 1st house we can experience rekindled confidence and a re-awakening of our *joie de vivre*, especially if we welcome our new lease on life with childlike innocence. Just as in spring the buds burst forth after a cold long winter, so Aries' cardinal energy

(continued on page 232)

PART II

Example Charts

Chapter 1

Age Progression in the Horoscope of C.G. Jung

Introduction—Description of Jung's life—C.G. Jung's birth chart with the most important Age Point data—Aspect structure in Jung's chart—The Leo Sun—Relationship with father and mother—Age Progression and life rhythm—Astrodata Age Progression Tables—C.G. Jung's Age Progression and Course of Life.

• Introduction

The following astrological study of the Swiss physician and psychologist Carl Gustav Jung (1875 to 1961) is offered as an example of the manner in which the AP can be used in practice. There are several reasons for the choice, the first being that Werner Stephan, who researched the Progression of the Age Point in the horoscope of C.G. Jung for us, has been involved in Jungian depth psychology for many years and so is a very reliable source of information on Jung's life work. In addition to studying his writings, he has prepared a didactic analysis of analytical psychology and has also been in contact with various individuals who knew Jung personally.

In his study, Werner Stephan has concentrated on the most significant periods in Jung's life and has worked as far as possible with verifiable data. Obviously, limitations of space prohibit reference to more than the salient facts, and therefore just a few periods of the great man's life have been sketched in—deserving though they are of fuller treatment. Werner Stephan has wisely placed the main emphasis on the Freudian period and on the following interim period, which are very revealing of Jung's thought and give the reader a deep insight into his understanding and into his system of analytical psychology.

● Description of Jung's Life*

In order to obtain as objective a picture as possible of the life of C.G. Jung, it is indispensable to read the book about his life: *Memories, Dreams, Reflections*. The reader will then be able to judge how Jung's preoccupation went hand in hand with whatever problems were currently being posed by the Age Point. The likenesses are amazing, even when no attempt is made to exaggerate them or to overrate their significance.

One of the chief reasons why I have chosen the life of C.G. Jung as an example of Age Point progression is that in Jung we have a man who, as a psychologist and psychiatrist, turned his attention on the inner life and had a unique gift for writing about the world of the soul. Now we know that the movement of the Age Point mirrors the movement of the inner, psychological life and is only indirectly suggestive of outer events; yet it is very difficult to garner adequate data on the interior life of famous people. Most biographies concentrate on external happenings and achievements, drawing a veil over what went on in the person's mind. Jung, quite exceptionally, made a point of stressing the significance of his inner experiences; so he meets our need perfectly. He said of his life that fate would have it that all the "outer" aspects of his life were accidental. Only the interior proved to have substance and a determining value for him. Eventually the memory of outer events faded, and he said that those "outer" experiences were never very essential, and when they were it was because they coincided with phases of inner development. Much of the "outer" manifestations of his life vanished from his memory—for the very reason that he participated in them with all his energies.[1]

---

*Contributed by Werner Stephan.
[1]C.G. Jung, *Memories, Dreams, Reflections*, edited by Aniela Jaffe, Pantheon Books, NY, 1961, p. ix.

Jung goes on to say in the *Prologue* to his autobiography that he was only concerned with his inner experiences, as these are the ones that he remembers best. Because he felt this way, and was willing to write about these experiences, we can easily study the course taken by Jung in his life and the path of the Age Point with its associated inner psychic attitudes and motivations.

Before taking a closer look at the Age Point progression, I want to present a brief study of Jung's natal chart, since this will show us the key to understanding the Age Point. Especially would I draw the reader's attention to the aspect pattern governing the native's motivation, for a knowledge of his motivation is indispensable to any attempt to interpret what the Age Point might trigger.

The aspect formation in Jung's natal chart (shown in figure 2.1.1 on page 176) falls into three main patterns or figures: Pattern 1 is a large trapezium formed by the planets Pluto, Jupiter, Mars and Saturn. The inclination of the trapezium to the Ascendant reveals the strong tendency to introversion in Jung's life, especially in youth and old age. Pluto in conjunction with the Moon serves as a point of contact with Pattern 2.

Pattern 2 is a scissors figure composed of the Moon, Uranus, the Lunar Nodes and Venus/Mercury. This is a clue to Jung's other and contrasting personality style, namely his Leonine readiness to star on the world's stage. Finally, Pattern 3 is a detached Sun/Neptune square embraced by the scissors constellation. This square under-lines the worldly nature but with the accent on dependence: recognition and positive feedback were vital to Jung and he was liable to be sharp with his critics. Also in this square we see his obvious feeling for transcendence: that equivocal aspect of his personality, which can neither be defined nor completely under-stood. What is more, the difficult relationship with his father has its basis here.

Presumably it was these different personality styles which induced the biographer P. J. Stern[2] to diagnose schizophrenia in Jung (supposedly cured through his own individuation process). According to our chart, there was no split in the personality styles, and according to Jung, an interplay between personality styles is normal to the growth of the individual. A constant interplay

---

[2]P.J. Stern, *C.G. Jung: Prophet des Unbewessten* ("Prophet of the Unconscious") R. Piper & Co. Verlag, Munich, 1977. (Publisher's note: As far as we know, this work is not available in English.)

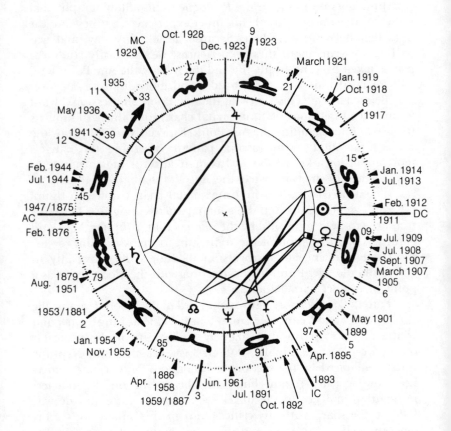

Figure 2.1.1. The horoscope of Carl Gustav Jung, born July 26, 1875, at 19:20h in Kesswill, Switzerland. This chart includes the most important Age Point dates that we will be discussing in the text. The reader should know that another birth chart exists for Jung, based on a birth time corrected to 19:32h. This may be found in the chart collection titled *Meine Begegnungen mit C.G. Jung und Hermann Hesse*, by M. Serrano, Rascher-Verlag, Zurich, 1968. (Publisher's note: We do not think this volume is available in English.)

Table 2. Astro-Data Age Progression for C.G. Jung

1875 Jul	27	HC	1	1886 Jul	28	□	☿
1876 Jan	27	□	♆	1886 Sep	17	△	♅
1876 Feb	**13**	☍	☉	1886 Oct	19	⚺	☾
1877 Jul	8	✱	☊	1887 Jan	25	□	♀
1877 Nov	9	⚻	☿	1887 Jul	27	HC	3
1877 Nov	10	IP	1	1887 Aug	2	△	♂
1878 Jan	11	☍	♅	1887 Dec	7	⚺	♇
1878 Feb	20	□	☾	1887 Dec	27	☍	♃
1879 Feb	14	✱	♂	1888 Jan	17	✱	♄
1879 Apr	11	LP	1	1888 Dec	27		♉
1879 Jun	23	□	♇	1889 Jun	25	☌	♆
1879 Jul	11	△	♃	1889 Jul	11	□	☉
1879 Aug	**4**	☌	♄	1889 Nov	10	IP	3
1880 Jul	22		♓	1890 Nov	24	⚺	☊
1881 Jan	22	✱	♆	1891 Mar	25	✱	☿
1881 Feb	8	⚻	☉	1891 Apr	12	LP	3
1881 Jul	27	HC	2	1891 May	25	□	♅
1882 Apr	26	⚺	☊	**1891 Jul**	**4**	☌	☾
1882 Aug	3	△	☿	1891 Nov	1	✱	♀
1882 Sep	22	⚻	♅	1892 Jun	18	⚻	♂
1882 Oct	24	✱	☾	**1892 Oct**	**24**	☌	♇
1883 Jan	31	△	♀	1892 Nov	10	⚻	♃
1883 Aug	7	□	♂	1892 Dec	3	□	♄
1883 Nov	11	IP	2	**1893 Jul**	**27**	**HC**	4
1883 Nov	13	✱	♇	1894 Mar	17		♊
1883 Dec	3	⚻	♃	**1895 Apr**	**8**	⚺	♆
1883 Dec	22	⚺	♄	**1895 May**	**12**	✱	☉
1884 Sep	28		♈	1895 Nov	11	IP	4
1885 Feb	25	⚺	♆	1897 Apr	11	LP	4
1885 Mar	8	△	☉	1898 Apr	16	✱	☊
1885 Apr	11	LP	2	1898 Dec	31	⚺	☿
1886 Apr	**20**	☌	☊	1899 May	12	✱	♅
1899 Jul	27	HC	5	1917 Jan	22	△	♆
1899 Aug	3	⚺	☾	1917 Feb	7	⚺	☉
1900 Mar	17	⚺	♀	**1917 Jul**	**26**	**HC**	8
1901 May	**26**	☍	♂	1918 Apr	26	⚻	☊
1901 Nov	10	IP	5	1918 Aug	3	✱	☿
1902 Jan	20	⚺	♇	1918 Sep	8	⚺	♅

Table 2. Continued.

1902 Feb	22	△	♃	**1918 Oct**	**22**	△	☽
1902 Apr	8	△	♄	**1919 Jan**	**31**	⚹	♀
1903 Apr	**11**	**LP**	5	1919 Aug	7	□	♂
1904 Jan	18		♋	1919 Nov	11	IP	8
1904 Dec	24	⚹	♆	1919 Nov	18	△	♈
1905 Jan	23	⚺	☉	1919 Nov	30	⚺	♃
1905 Jul	**27**	**HC**	6	1919 Dec	2	⚻	♄
1907 Mar	**11**	□	☊	**1920 Sep**	**28**		♎
1907 Sep	**5**	☌	☿	1921 Feb	23	⚻	♆
1907 Nov	11	IP	6	**1921 Mar**	**8**	⚹	☉
1907 Dec	5	⚺	♅	**1921 Apr**	**11**	**LP**	8
1908 Feb	1	⚹	☽	1922 Apr	20	☍	☊
1908 Jul	**27**	☌	♀	1922 Jul	28	□	☿
1909 Apr	**11**	**LP**	6	1922 Sep	16	⚹	♅
1909 Jul	**2**	⚻	♂	1922 Oct	18	⚻	☽
1910 Jan	4	⚹	♈	1923 Jan	25	□	♀
1910 Jan	30	□	♃	**1923 Jul**	**27**	**HC**	9
1910 Mar	5	⚻	♄	1923 Aug	2	⚹	♂
1911 Jul	26		♌	1923 Dec	6	⚻	♈
1911 Jul	27	HC	7	**1923 Dec**	**24**	☌	♃
1912 Jan	27	□	♆	1924 Jan	17	△	♄
1912 Feb	**27**	☌	☉	1924 Dec	26		♏
1913 Jul	**8**	△	☊	1925 Jun	25	☍	♆
1913 Nov	9	⚺	☿	1925 Jul	11	□	☉
1913 Nov	10	IP	7	1925 Nov	10	IP	9
1914 Jan	**11**	☌	♅	1926 Nov	23	⚻	☊
1914 Feb	**20**	□	☽	1927 Mar	24	△	☿
1914 Jun	23	⚺	♀	1927 Apr	11	LP	9
1915 Feb	14	△	♂	1927 May	25	□	♅
1915 Apr	11	LP	7	1927 Jul	3	☍	☽
1915 Jun	23	□	♈	1927 Nov	1	△	♀
1915 Jul	11	⚹	♃	1928 Jun	18	⚺	♂
1915 Aug	4	☍	♄	**1928 Oct**	**23**	☍	♈
1916 Jul	**21**		♍	1928 Nov	9	⚺	♃
1928 Dec	3	□	♄	1949 Nov	10	IP	1
1929 Jul	26	HC	10	1950 Jan	11	☍	♅
1930 Mar	17		♐	1950 Feb	20	□	☽

Age Progression in the Horoscope of C.G. Jung 179

Table 2. Continued.

Date	Day			Date	Day		
1931 Apr	8	⊼	♆	1951 Feb	14	✶	♂
1931 May	22	△	☉	1951 Apr	12	LP	1
1931 Nov	10	IP	10	1951 Jun	23	□	♈
1933 Apr	11	LP	10	**1951 Jul**	**11**	△	♃
1934 Apr	16	△	☋	**1951 Aug**	**4**	☌	♄
1934 Dec	31	⊼	☿	1952 Jul	22		♓
1935 May	12	△	♅	1953 Jan	22	✶	♆
1935 Jul	27	HC	11	**1953 Feb**	**8**	⊼	☉
1935 Aug	3	⊼	☽	**1953 Jul**	**27**	HC	2
1936 Mar	17	⊼	♀	1953 Apr	26	⋎	☋
1936 May	**26**	☌	♂	1953 Aug	3	△	☿
1937 Nov	10	IP	11	1953 Sep	22	⊼	☽
1938 Jan	19	⊼	♈	1953 Oct	24	✶	☽
1938 Feb	22	✶	♃	**1954 Jan**	**31**	△	♀
1938 Apr	7	✶	♄	1955 Aug	7	□	♂
1939 Apr	11	LP	11	**1955 Nov**	**11**	IP	2
1940 Jan	18		♒	**1955 Nov**	**18**	✶	♈
1940 Dec	24	△	♅	1955 Dec	3	⊼	♃
1941 Jan	23	⊼	☉	1955 Dec	22	⋎	♄
1941 Jul	26	HC	12	1956 Sep	28		♈
1943 Mar	11	□	☋	1957 Feb	23	✶	♅
1943 Sep	5	☍	☿	1957 Mar	8	△	☉
1943 Nov	**10**	IP	12	**1957 Apr**	**11**	LP	2
1943 Dec	**5**	⊼	♅	**1958 Apr**	**20**	☌	☋
1944 Feb	**1**	△	☽	1958 Jul	28	□	☿
1944 Jul	**27**	☍	♀	1958 Sep	17	△	☽
1945 Apr	11	LP	12	1958 Oct	19	⋎	☽
1945 Jul	1	⋎	♂	1959 Jan	25	□	♀
1946 Jan	3	△	♈	1959 Jul	27	HC	3
1946 Jan	29	□	♃	1959 Aug	2	△	♂
1946 Mar	5	⋎	♄	1959 Aug	7	⋎	♈
1947 Jul	26		♒	1959 Dec	24	☍	♃
1947 Jul	**27**	HC	1	1960 Jan	17	✶	♄
1948 Jan	27	□	♆	1960 Dec	27		♓
1948 Feb	13	☍	☉	**1961 Jun**	**25**	☌	♆
1949 Jul	8	✶	☋	1961 Jul	11	□	☉
1949 Nov	9	⊼	☿				

between an outer personality (No. 1) and an inner personality (No. 2) is discussed by Jung, for he said that the play and counterplay between personalities No. 1 and No. 2, ran through his entire life, and had nothing to do with a "split" or dissociation in the ordinary medical sense. He further states that it is indeed played out in every individual.[3]

The Leo Sun

Jung's powerful Leo Sun is described very aptly in *Words and Image*, by Professor Adolf Portmann. He said that to get to know Jung, and to experience this man, was a great honor. Jung's mind was incessantly productive—to watch him grasp new insights was an incredible process. Meeting over the course of ten years at the Eranos conferences, Jung appeared as a powerful natural force, a person who had an extraordinary capability of brining out a spiritual way of functioning in all those who attended the meetings.[4]

Nevertheless, Jung's personality also had its dark side. Without doubt, the Leo Sun gave him an appetite for power and, through the isolated square to Neptune, an allergic reaction to criticism whether justified or unjustified. His arrogant nature brooked no contradiction. The emotional side of his make-up, characterized by the Moon at the Low Point (LP) square to Uranus and with Pluto near by, was blunt and irascible and from time to time expressed itself in a devastating tirade directed against his children, friends or even patients. The placement at the Low Point made these reactions puzzling and unpredictable to those around him. However, his quick mind (Venus/Mercury conjunction in the 6th house) re-interpreted the outbursts as a "necessary part of becoming conscious or of therapy."

Relationship with father

A few words are in order here about the father-and-son relationship as indicated by the detached square linking the Sun and Neptune. This position indicates that the father was out of touch with the life of the child, paying him scant attention and probably often thwarting him. To Jung, his father seemed more like a part of

---

[3]C.G. Jung, *Memories, Dreams, Reflections*, edited by Aniela Jaffe, Pantheon Books, NY, 1961, p. 45.

[4]See C.G. Jung, *Word and Image*, edited by Aniela Jaffe, Bollingen Series XCVII:2, Princeton University Press, Princeton, NJ, p. 187.

the outside world than one of the family (Sun on the Descendant) and, of course, his father's calling as a minister of religion must have had something to do with this.

In *Memories, Dreams, Reflections* we read that between the ages of 17 and 19 he had engaged in many intense discussions with his father on religious questions, but that these had been unable to dispel his nagging doubts.[5] Because his father, although a parson, was tormented by an inner conflict of belief from which the church was unable to save him, Jung's mistrust of theological thought was stirred up even more and he was confirmed in the decision to turn away from theology and to take up medicine and natural philosophy. Nevertheless, these early religious questions and doubts haunted him throughout his life and were laid to rest only in his last works (*e.g.*, in the *Answer to Job*).

In January 1896 came the premature and unexpected death of his father. Jung was 21 years old (AP in the fixed sector between the IP and LP of the 4th house) and was only a year into his medical studies in Basle. His father's death left the problems of their relationship unresolved until it was relived and integrated in his connection with Sigmund Freud, 19 years his senior (when the AP reached the Sun, as we shall see).

The death of his father is not indicated by any direct aspect from the Age Point, although the theme of the fourth house (through which it was passing at the time) has to do with relationships within the family, and especially with the parents. The transit of the Low Point of the fourth house will always loosen the ties to the parental home. The death of Jung's father set this process in motion. Since the father's death occurred without any direct pointers from Age Point aspects, we may surmise that inwardly Jung had already severed himself emotionally from his physical father.

This does not mean that Jung did not grieve for his father, or that he was through looking for a "father image" that he could relate to—it merely means that his father's death was not a terrific "jolt" to his psyche.

Relationship with mother

Jung's relationship with his mother, who, in her role as teacher and protectress is represented by Saturn, was full of problems, too,

---

[5]See *Memories, Dreams, Reflections*, p. 91 ff.

though these were rather more concrete than were those occasioned by his Neptunian father relationship. In *Memories, Dreams, Reflections*, Jung discussed an experience with his mother when he was twelve: she always called after him to give him advice when he was invited out somewhere—saying he should give his parents' best regards, he should wipe his nose, wash his hands, etc. He was bereft of self-confidence by the time he reached the house he was to visit, and refused to carry his parents' regards, or he became shy, losing self-confidence, feeling unworthy, and becoming timid. In his forlorn states, he would have to draw upon the energy of his "other," the No. 2 personality, in order to overcome the lack of confidence his mother unwittingly engendered in him.[6]

Students should read this passage directly from *Memories, Dreams, Reflections*, as it will give insight into Saturn in Aquarius in the first house for an image of the mother; the embarrassment he felt from his mother shouting after him in the streets indicates the AC in Aquarius, the Sun in the DC with Venus not far away. When he was overcome by the power of the people he was to visit, and became timid, he was reacting to Pluto square Saturn, and the Mars in Saggitarius sextile Saturn influenced his feeling insignificant when he made his contact at the house he was to visit by ringing the bell.

Taking the horoscope as a whole, I should like to lay emphasis on the Plutonian fear of the Collective with its powerful establishment, a fear which engendered obstinate resistance (Mars sextile Saturn) and kept Jung hacking out new paths for himself (Mars in Sagittarius) right down to extreme old age. In the process, traditions (Saturn in Aquarius) were studied, attacked and, if possible, overthrown (Mars in the eleventh house, the natural house of Aquarius ruled by Saturn).

● Age Progression and Life Rhythm

Let us now make a closer examination of Age Progression. Life, seen and unseen, is governed by inherent rhythms causing it to flow from one pole to the other. We breathe in and we breathe out, we sleep and wake, in the same pattern as that of night and day of ebb-

---

[6]See *Memories, Dreams, Reflections*, p. 26.

tide and flood-tide. The whole natural world around us is established on such rhythms or, shall we say, runs by such "internal clocks."

As explained in earlier chapters, our psychic life itself is guided by inner rhythms according to a preset plan. This idea of cycles in the psychic life, has to some extent already been mooted and described by Jung for he described how, in childhood, our consciousness progressively emerges from the great undifferentiated stream of life into a state of illumination and a sense of personal power. Our objectives in this first half of the life-cycle are those of finding a niche in society, and of seeing what we can accomplish in the workaday world.

Then in mid-life—which Jung also puts at the age of 36—the mature psyche gradually changes direction. The outer world with its aims, dreams and wishes slowly retires to be replaced by confrontation with fundamental questions springing from higher sources in the being, questions concerning the meaning of life, concerning birth and death, and concerning growth and maturity. The second half of life is the road back to the realm of the mother; a road back to death—which may be regarded as a new birth into life on the other side.

This basic rhythm of the psyche's development, given here in its ideal form, seldom proceeds so smoothly, and this can give rise to many neuroses. Exaggerated introversion in teenagers can segregate them from the outside world and push them into isolation; older people sometimes grow so materialistic that they become fossilized and impervious to the higher frequencies of life and wisdom.

According to Jung, extroverted individuals have an easier time in the first half of life, but are severely tested in the second half when they see death approaching; introverted individuals, on the other hand, suffer considerably in the first half of life from the lack of understanding in the world for their dreams and phantasies, but get on better in the second half.

The Age Progression Method developed by the Hubers provides a key to the study of this psychic rhythm in fine detail and helps us to detect something of the laws behind the course of human fate. The reader is now invited to trace the movement of the Age Point in the horoscope of C. G. Jung and to compare this with Jung's own words. A prior knowledge of his life and works will certainly be very helpful; to those who are unfamiliar with them I would recommend

Jung's autobiography, *Memories, Dreams, Reflections,*[7] for here he speaks freely of what went on inside of him during the growth process—something very important to understand when using the Age Point. Jung's *Word and Image*[8] shows us a great deal about his professional life, so you can use this material to also understand the events of his life. Some readers may prefer to read the horoscope details straight through, so as to get the feel of how Jung's life unfolded, and then go back to see how it appeared in the Age Point Progression, Table 2 on pages 177-179.

• Age Progression and Course of Life of C.G. Jung

The exact dates of the Age Point as calculated by the Astrodata computer (see the Age Progression Table on pages 177-179) have been placed in bold type in the text, whereas dates of the "actual" events just appear in the text.

• Age Point in the 1st Quadrant (Age 0-18)

Childhood and youth

Jung was born on July 26, 1875 at 19.20 hrs in Kesswil, Switzerland and when he was only six months old (**2/1876**) the family moved to Laufen near Schaffhausen by the Falls of the Rhine. Some four years later came another move (**Aug. 1879**), this time to Klein-Hüningen near Basel. On each occasion the related aspects (opposition Sun and conjunction Saturn) indicated that these early changes of residence created in Jung a certain lack of confidence in the security of the family nest.

In the spring of 1886 (**4/1886**) Jung entered the secondary school in Basel. The conjunction with the lunar nodes appears to

---

[7]C.G. Jung, *Memories, Dreams, Reflections,* edited by Aniela Jaffe, Pantheon Books, NY, 1961. Also available in paperback in the U.S.A. by Random House, and in the U.K. by Collins Publishers.
[8]C.G. Jung, *Word and Image,* edited by Aniela Jaffe, Bollingen Series XCVII:2, Princeton University Press, Princeton, NJ.

show here that the commencement of this new phase of life was accompanied by ambivalent feelings, and his memoirs confirm this. At this time he wanted very much to take refuge in his "No. 2" personality, which had so much to offer for the future.

The whole period was marked by the awakening of the conscious ego-personality, accompanied by dreams, day dreams, intuitions, and confrontations with the disagreeable outer world.

Until the age of 16 (**July 1891**) the No. 2 personality held a certain priority, but this was gradually lost to the No. 1 personality in a change of direction (**Oct. 1892**) coinciding with the conjunction with Pluto. What is more, the Age Point entered the shadow of Cusp 4 (**1891-92**) at that time (near the individual axis 4/10), and this introduced the theme of individuation and of thinking for himself— a development that found its outlet mainly in the study of philosophy. As the Age Point made its way from the Moon to Pluto (**1891-91**) there was a conscious awareness of what had previously been experienced in a more visionary manner and between the age of 16 and 19 (from LP 2 to Gemini with transit of the Moon) he said that the fog of his dilemma slowly lifted, and the depressive states of mind gradually improved. His No. 1 personality emerged more distinctly, while increased knowledge took over his world of intuitive premonitions. In order to develop more systematically, Jung read an introduction to the history of philosophy to get an overall view of everything that had been thought in the field.[9]

• Age Point in the 2nd Quadrant (Age 18-36)

From medical student to head physician

The No. 2 personality certainly displayed an interest in religion, philosophy, paleontology and history, whereas the No. 1 (or everyday personality) was interested in science. As No. 1 came to the fore, Jung commenced the study of medicine. He said that as the tensions of this moral conflict increased, No. 2 personality became more and more doubtful and distasteful, and he could no longer hide this fact from himself. He tried to extinguish No. 2, but could not succeed

---

[9]See *Memories, Dreams, Reflections*, p. 68.

with that either. He could forget No. 2 in school or while keeping company with his fellow students, but as soon as he was alone, the interest in such philosophers as Schopenhauer and Kant and "God's world" would return.[10]

In April of 1895 (**AP April 1895, as well**) he successfully passed the school-leaving examination (**sign change into Gemini**) and took up his medical studies and was soon initiated into the "Zofingia" fraternity, where his Leo nature began to shine (**May, 1898, AP sextile the Sun**).

● Age Point in the 5th House (Age 24-30)

At the end of 1900, Jung completed his studies and joined the Bürgholzli University Psychiatric Clinic in Zurich as an assistant (**May 1901**).

With the **transit of the AP over the Low Point**, an important event occurred in Jung's life: on February 14, 1903 he wed Emma Rauschenbach, whom he had known in his youth and who at one time had rejected him. The fact that LP 5 (**April, 1903, LP 5**) was strongly involved indicates that Jung must have been laboring under strong internal pressure. Jung solved the problem posed by the intimate side of partnership at this time by making a hasty marriage.

Perhaps the fact that this marriage was contracted under an unusually strong inner complusion was the deeper reason why his relationship with his wife Emma, except in the early years when Emma respected her husband as if he were a father, grew increasingly difficult and stormy (cf. what is said about T. Wolff on p. 190). After a while Emma became more of a saturnian, sheltering mother-figure, while the other side of womanhood—that of the seductive mistress—was embodied for Jung in T. Wolff.

Now Jung set out (**July 1905, Cusp 6**) on the long road of professional and social advancement. In August, 1905, the Age Point reached the cusp of the 6th house. The two-year phase in the shadow of the 6th cusp gave way to a period of break through. In H. F.

---

[10]See *Memories, Dreams, Reflections,* pp. 74-75.

Ellenberger's book, *The Discovery of the Unconscious*,[11] we read that 1905/6 was a very fortunate period for Jung. First, he was appointed head physician; second, he was put in charge of the out-patients department, in which there were greater opportunities for him to cultivate his interest in psychotherapy; third, the University of Zürich conferred on him the position of private unsalaried lecturer. External good fortune of this kind can attend us at the 6th house cusp, if we have worked hard to earn it.

At this stage, Jung seemed assured of a secure career as a physician and lecturer and of an equally secure, if average, financial future. That Jung's life took a rather different turn, we own to another man who had already been blazing a trail in Vienna and was striving for recognition of his revolutionary theory: the nineteen years senior Sigmund Freud.

• Age Point in the 6th House

Sigmund Freud, the fatherly friend

Owing to the early rupture in the father-and-son relationship Jung still had an open psychic wound which needed healing. He seemed already to have found a father-substitute of sorts in Eugen Bleuler, his chief at Burghölzli. But when he became acquainted with the writings of Freud in 1906, he was so inspired by their content and the force of expression that he initiated an exchange of letters with Freud, and eventually adopted him as a new father figure in place of Bleuler. After some correspondence, the two men had their first meeting in Vienna in 1907. Jung was invited to visit with him in February, and Jung says of that first encounter, "We met a one o'clock in the afternoon and talked virtually without a pause for thirteen hours."[12] Jung said that Freud was the first man of importance that he had ever met up until that point in his life, and he found him to be extremely intelligent and not in the least trivial.

This initial encounter took place on March 3, 1907 (**exactly when the AP was making a square with the Lunar Nodes**). The

---

[11]H.F. Ellenberger, *The Discovery of the Unconscious*, Basic Books, NY, 1970.
[12]See *Memories, Dreams, Reflections*, p. 149. The reader should really investigate the complete chapter, pp. 146-169.

aspects suggest that the meeting would have far-reaching results for both men (or for Jung at least). The fact that squares were involved is an indication of the tension and dynamism that lay in the meeting and the subsequent relationship with Freud. These squares kept Jung busily engaged in the relationship for a long time.

Lunar Nodes in the second house demand fertility, the exploration of all possible avenues and the utilization of one's personal abilities and of all the powers accruing to one from within and without. That the meeting with Freud took place under a square aspect to the Moon's Nodes shows that Freud managed to throw Jung back on his own resources: through the method of dream analysis, Freud placed in his hands a means of understanding his first childhood dreams, which came to him along with other information from the "greater No. 2."

Contrary to the commonly held opinion, Jung differed from Freud in his theoretical ideas right from the start. Thus, even before their first meeting, Jung made statements to that effect. In a letter written to Freud on December 29, 1906, Jung mentions that he "understands" that Freud cannot be pleased with his book (*The Psychology of Dementia Praecox*) and discusses the fact that they do not see eye to eye. He writes that his material is totally different from Freud's, his working conditions are totally different, and here Jung states that he is working with uneducated insane people, implying that Freud is working with a different kind of patient. He also states that his background and environment are totally different, as well as mentioning that his experience is limited in comparison to Freud's. At the end of his dissertation about why they are so different, Jung is deferential by saying that Freud must have more talent than he, and that he, Jung, was bereft of having a chance to study with Freud himself, and therefore his training was, as Jung puts it, "regrettably defective."[13]

The significant fact, that from the outset Jung did not go along with Freud in all his views (thus sowing the seeds of their future discord and separation), is overlooked by many. Freud found in Jung not some poor parrot of a pupil, but someone with whom he could confer, someone with a mind of the same caliber as his own. It was precisely the spontaneously occurring polarity between the two

---

[13]*The Freud/Jung Letters*, edited by William McGuire, translated by Ralph Manheim and R.F.C. Hull, Bollingen Series, XCIV, Princeton University Press, Princeton, NJ, 1976, p. 14.

men in regard to their different religious (!) views that set in motion a dynamic interaction out of which the psychoanalytical movement eventually sprang. I venture to suggest that their differences arose from their religious opinions, because I regard sexuality mainly as a religious and not a scientific phenomenon (which certainly does not prevent us from approaching the subject from the scientific angle, as has been done for hundreds of years to a noteworthy degree by the tantric Yogis and Buddhists of India and Tibet, and by the Taoist sages of China, all of whom have left us writings and teaching which are full of wisdom).

The conjunction of the AP with Mercury (**September, 1907**) seems to be double-edged in its effect: 1) Officially Jung presented himself at the International Congress for Psychiatry and Neurology as a spokesman for Freud in the heated discussion about hysteria (September, 1907), and two months later he read a report on psychoanalysis to the Zurich Medical Association. It is to be remembered that, at this time, psychoanalysis with its daring new theories was a highly controversial subject, and all those who advocated these theories were lumped together (just as astrologers are today). 2) In spite of his official sponsorship of Freud, Jung was already expressing profound doubts. In a letter dated August 19, 1907, Jung asks a number of veiled questions regarding Freud's concept of sexuality.[14]

Jung vacillated between doubt and conviction during that time—which is typical of the versatile, analytical nature of Mercury. That eroticism and sexuality dominated his thought processes is clearly defined by the presence of Venus (conjunct Mercury).

● Age Point Moving from LP of the 6th House to Cusp 7 (Age 33-36)

Life crisis

With the transit of the AP over Venus and over LP 6 (**July, 1908**), various interesting events occur. Venus in Cancer understandably gives a wish for a house of one's own and the position at

---

[14]For further details, see *The Freud/Jung Letters*, p. 79.

the LP points to withdrawal and settling down in a private sphere; hence it is not surprising that Jung had a house of his own design built for himself at the lower end of the Lake of Zurich.

One year later (**April, 1909**), two months after the **exact Low Point 6**, he resigned his position at the Burghölzli in order to go into private practice as a psychotherapist in Küsnacht. At this time (July, 1909) there was also a quincunx to Mars, which has a highly sensitive placement in Sagittarius, indicating rich erotic urges, but in the eleventh house these were held tightly in check by his puritanical upbringing and morality (his father was a clergyman!).

And so a phase began in the shadow of the next house with its doubts, anxieties and motives for changes of direction—and Jung entered that stage of practical psychological experience through which every budding analyst and therapist must pass, even today, if he is not to remain one of those cerebral theorists we all too often encounter. In a letter Jung wrote to Freud on March 7, 1909, he recounts such an illuminating experience, for he discusses a problem that is often confronted by serious therapists. Evidently an old patient that he once treated created a scandal because Jung denied himself the pleasure of making her pregnant. He was very hurt because his intentions were honorable, he was a gentleman with the lady, and because of the doctor/patient relationship, he was forced to look at an old complex. He says, "Meanwhile I have learnt an unspeakable amount of marital wisdom, for until now I had a totally inadequate idea of my polygamous components despite all self-analysis."[15]

In the same year, 1909, when he was thirty-four, Jung made the acquaintance of a female patient, Miss T. Wolff, who was to play an important part in his later life. T. Wolff was a shy and reserved young woman of twenty-one who had recently lost her father.

In the beginning, Jung was fully aware of the complexes that gripped him so strongly, although the sensitive Venus in Cancer at the Low Point, over which the AP was moving, shows that he must have been experiencing a powerful life crisis (**LP 6**) aggravated by an erotic crisis (Venus). His polygamous components surfaced in subsequent years to the extent that T. Wolff was increasingly accepted into Jung's family and became his semi-official mistress.

---

[15]Readers may wish to read this letter. See *The Freud/Jung Letters*, p. 207.

It is specifically in this sector (**stretching from LP 6 to cusp 7**) that Jung was compelled to accept, assimilate and integrate an irruption into his world of personal relationships, and this led to a temporary diffusion of his concepts of existence.

Obviously, a second relationship like the one with T. Wolff would entail, in years to come, a conscious confrontation in partnership matters (**passage of the Age Point to the DC**). This point represents the opposite number, and the transits to the seventh house, which have always been associated with relationships with the partner in marriage and work.

● Age Point in the 7th House
(Age 36-42)

The break with Freud

In **February 1912** the AP transited the Sun and then the problem of the father relationship came to a head and demanded a solution, especially as the square between the Sun and Neptune entered in as a disturbing factor.

That Freud, Jung's senior by nineteen years, was elevated to the rank of father-figure seemed only fair to the latter and Freud encouraged this state of affairs to the extent that he called Jung his "crown prince" who one day would spread psychoanalysis still further when Freud was dead and gone. Others regarded this as a very privileged position and many might have striven hard to attain it. No so Jung.

Jung's psyche, which was seeking wholeness, simply had to integrate the father-figure projected on Freud. For this purpose, the father-figure had first to be detached from the object, *i.e.*, from Freud; in other words, the relationship with Freud had to be severed. Admittedly, the very patriarchally inclined Sigmund Freud helped to promote this process of detachment by demanding "absolute obedience and toeing of the psychoanalytical party line," which incited the rebellious Leo Sun in Jung, with its craving for freedom from restraint, to thrust him still further from Freud's side. And anyway, Freud broke with other disciples who would not kowtow to him (first of all A. Adler). Therefore it was not so much the differences in their psychological theories, as the realities of personal development and egotism, that precipitated the break between these two pioneers of the psyche.

In astro-psychology the Sun stands for the principle of self-consciousness. With the transit of the AP over the Sun an individual can and must be himself; the will to engage in independent thought and action is strengthened, as we see in letters written by Jung to Freud.

Six months after the transit of the Sun by the AP, Jung wrote (on December 18, 1912) to question Freud's behavior with his students. The letter is basically an attack, for Jung says that he is being straightforward and ambivalent now that he has discovered a particular behavior pattern of Freud's. It seems that Freud surrounded himself with psychoanalysts and in meetings with them brought out certain weaknesses that he then used to keep everyone in their place. Jung stated that this behavior would only produce "slavish sons or puppies" and not good thinkers. He questioned Freud's behavior, saying, "For sheer obsequiousness nobody dares to pluck the prophet by the beard and inquire for once what you would say to a patient with a tendency to analyse the analyst instead of himself. You would certainly ask him: *'Who's* got the neurosis?'"[16]

This was only one of a whole series of "confidential letters" showered upon Freud. For the partriarchally-minded founder of psychoanalysis, this pugnacious letter was a shot that slipped through his guard (Jung had Mars in Sagittarius, the Archer!) and it left Freud no option but to climb down from the seat of authority to meet his colleagues unconditionally on equal terms, or to purge the psychoanalytical movement of such rash and mulish spirits.

To my mind, this demand for partnership is an essential expression of Jung's Age Point progression through the seventh house, which is also the house where his Sun is posited. Therefore, we are looking here at a central problem in Jung's life. It is plain to see in the letter discussed above how partnerships are regarded by the Leo Sun, which would rather rule than serve: "You and I are equal partners, and I am telling you how our relationship must develop," says Leo.

Six months later (**July, 1913**) there is a trine to the Moon's Node, that is to say, another aspect to the Lunar Node under which the relationship between the two men had begun: the relationship

---

[16]*The Freud/Jung Letters*, pp. 534-35.

was commenced under the square aspect, and was dissolved under the trine.

So much for the traditional teaching that the trine is "good" and the square is "bad." The square showed strength and initiative and promoted active behavior, while the trine to the Lunar Node represented the first step toward self-realization. In this it was possible for Jung to break free and extricate himself from the involvement with that external object, the projected father figure.

Another way of looking at it is this: under the square aspect Jung was fated to attend to unfinished business; he used the unresolved father problem as a dynamic component. The transit of the Sun activated his complex and the approaching trine to the Moon's Node enabled him to explore for himself, and to profit by, the rich experiences of the previous few years. This he had to do on his own without some father-figure breathing down his neck. The break with Freud was therefore unavoidable, and what occasioned it was not so much their differences of opinion as the striving of Jung's psyche after integration and self-development.

● LP of 7th House to Virgo

The interim period

This digging into his resources turned out to be much more difficult than Jung had anticipated. After his break with Freud, he made a veritable journey into the underworld, which H. F. Ellenberger has called the "interim period," or even the "creative illness."[17] As the AP entered the area of consciousness (above the horizon in the horoscope), Jung commenced a self-analysis of the images and phantasies that gushed from his unconscious with ever increasing force. That these images were also warnings of collective events, namely an anticipation of the happenings of World War I, did not become clear to him until very much later. Since his self-analysis provides the key to Jung's whole system of psychology, we shall share one of his dreams with you. Note that during this period the **IP was in the 7th house,** and the **AP would move to a conjunction with Uranus in January 1914.**

---

[17]H.F. Ellenberger, *The Discovery of the Unconscious*, Basic Books, NY, 1970.

During this period one of his profound dreams involved a sinking to the depths. Jung had a vision on December 12, 1913, as he was sitting meditatively thinking about his fears. He let himself drop and found himself plunging into dark depths. He could not fend off a feeling of panic, but that was soon averted as he landed in some sort of a sticky mass. His eyes became accustomed to the gloom of the darkness and he was able to make out the entrance to a cave. Inside the cave stood a dwarf, which Jung describes as looking mummified for his skin was very leathery. He squeezed past this dwarf and got inside, wading knee deep through icy water to the other end of the cave. There he sees a glowing red crystal, and he grabbed the stone, finding a hollow underneath. Then he saw running water. The water must have changed in depth, for it carried a corpse—a youth with blond hair with a headwound, followed by a black scarab, followed by a red and newborn sun that rose out of the depths of the water. He was overcome by the light and wanted to replace the stone upon the opening in the cave, but he found that when he did this, some kind of a fluid welled out. Looking closer, he saw that the fluid was blood, and he became nauseated. The blood seemed to keep coming out for a very long time. Finally it stopped, and his vision was over.[18]

This dream occurred six months after the trine to the Lunar Node, almost exactly when the AP was conjunct Uranus. What is more, Uranus itself was transiting in the vicinity of the Ascendant at this time, and was moving between 3-7° Aquarius.

When we leave Uranus behind there is a considerable stretch in the chart before we come to Jupiter. Jung's "descent to Avernus" can also be seen as the long journey through the empty space. The inner significance of an empty phase like this is, generally speaking, to cultivate and harvest the fruit of the soil broken up by previous transits of planets.

Now one of the things Uranus is good at helping us to do is building bridges into infinity, in order to leave behind the known, and to press forward into the untried. Metaphorically, Jung slithered into the depths down the radical trine between Uranus and the Lunar Node, and down the square to the Moon into the great Deep, where he encountered the brute force of the archetypal images and made his way across the great trapezium and up to the holistic realm of Jupiter.

---

[18]See *Memories, Dreams, Reflections*, p. 179.

In addition (**February, 1914**), the square of the AP to the Moon churned up his emotions, and these were investigated and interpreted with Uranian scholarly ardor. Jung made forceful reference to this process in *Memories, Dreams, Reflections*, where he discusses releasing an incessant stream of fantasies, and that he had difficulty trying to understand what was happening to him. In this work he states clearly that he felt helpless, the world felt alien to him, everything seemed hard to understand. He lived in a constant state of tension. He felt a strength that was close to demonic when he needed to find the meaning in his experiences and he endured the assaults of the unconscious because he was also convinced that he was obeying a higher will. This feeling helped give him the endurance he needed to follow through. By continuing with the imagery, he was able to actually find the images that were concealed in the emotions, and when he could do that, he felt more calm and reassured. He talks about the challenge—he could have left the images hidden in the emotions, but felt that he might be torn to pieces by their very existence—or he could succeed in splitting them off and then would have developed neuroses that would have destroyed him anyway. By experiencing this encounter with the unconscious images in a personal way, he learned how valuable it was to find the images that lie behind the emotions. While pursuing this stage of his life, Jung speaks of his commitment to the future of his patients, for by knowing that he would someday be able to help others, he was able to endure the pain of his own experience.[19] This is typical of Jung's Moon placement: in the radix, the Moon as the emotional self is flanked on each side by the so-called spiritual planets Pluto and Neptune, and these lend their support to the Moon as the "purest of motives," as selfless impulses and as suprapersonal goals.

● Age Point at Cusp 8 and in the 8th House (Age 42-48)

Process of transformation

Jung's journey through the unconscious continued until about 1919, and with the entry of the AP into Virgo (**July 1916**) a change began to make itself felt. In *Memories, Dreams, Reflections*, he

---

[19]See *Memories, Dreams, Reflections*, pp. 176-79.

discusses the fact that an inner change was taking place within him. He felt (1916) an urge to give shape to something, literally compelled from within. The work was pushed through in the midst of some parapsychological phenomena, and was named *Septem Sermones ad Mortuos*, a privately printed work subtitled "The Seven Sermons of the Dead written by Basilides in Alexandria, the city where the East toucheth the West."[20]

The torrent of phantasies abated, and as the AP passed through the shadow of the eighth house cusp, he began analyzing and organizing the imagery that had emerged. The unconscious pushed him to face the death-and-becoming processes of the eighth house, and has to be seen as one of the most difficult stages in the journey of life. A rather aggressive period following the transit of the seventh cusp and the radical Sun had now given way to inner seeking and to inner renewal.

In December 1916 (that is to say just before the exit from the shadow of the eighth cusp), Jung delivered a lecture in Paris on "La structure de l'inconscient" (The structure of the unconscious), out of which developed his extremely important and foundational work, *Two Essays on Analytical Psychology*, which was published twelve years later (when the MC was transited). In this lecture and the subsequent elucidations, he expounded his own concepts of the unconscious, and commenced to develop his ideas about the collective unconscious and about the stages in the individuation process (persona, shadow, animus/anima, the self or mana-personality). With this step into the eighth house (in which, as we know, there is a recognition of structures and their changes), the step beyond Freud was fully taken. With the concept of a collective region of the psyche, that is to say of a region of the psyche common to the human race, he laid the foundation stone of an edifice to house his ideas on the transpersonal—an action very much in keeping with the character of the eighth house.

AP halfway between two figures

In Age Point research, a regularity has been discovered which is plainly perceptible in Jung's chart. If the AP leaves one aspect figure and travels through empty space, a kind of switch over from old to

---

[20]See *Memories, Dreams, Reflections*, pp. 189-91.

new takes place halfway between two figures. In Jung's case the halfway mark is circa 19° Virgo. This corresponds to **April, 1919.**

Now Jung describes how two events signaled the end of his journey through the unconscious: in the winter of 1918/19 (in October, 1918, the AP made a trine to the Moon and in January, 1919, a sextile to Venus) he severed his connection with a lady who tried to persuade him that the pictures in which he painted his phantasies from the unconscious possessed artistic merit and wanted to sell them. Secondly, he began to draw mandalas which, so to speak, as "cryptograms of his Self," indicated his growth into wholeness.

● Age Point at Cusp 8
(Age 45)

In 1921 he published, in German, the book *Psychological Types*,[21] in which he presented a new way of looking at depth psychology. It was his first major work since separating from Freud. The Age Point was making a sextile with the Sun in March 1921, and this suggests a degree of public success. Soon afterwards, in April 1921, the AP made contact with the LP of the eighth house, a significant point for psychological change in the sense of death-and-becoming: something old, on which he had worked hard until it finally materialized in this book, was completed, and something new, which was already present in the germ, could and indeed should begin to grow.

It is an interesting fact that the book on psychological types is still relatively unknown even today and its statements on the psychology of the conscious mind are for the most part neglected. Presumably this is because the Age Point was transiting the Low Point of the eighth house. This point ushers in a time when the native turns inwards, winds up an old course of action and manages to change direction.

Psychological Types represents the breakthrough into the outer world after his tour of some eight years through the "underworld."

---

[21]C.G. Jung, *Psychological Types*, published in English by Harcourt, Brace & Jovanovich in the U.S.A., and by Routledge & Kegan Paul in the U.K.

In the next few years the Age Point in Jung's chart drew nearer and nearer to the other great trapezoid figure and the No. 2 personality began to coalesce with the No. 1 personality. The father-figure was integrated into the self as the trapezium unfolded its whole wealth of potential.

● Age Point in the 9th House
(Age 48-54)

Travels, expansion of consciousness, energetics

With the entry of the Age Point into Libra (September 1920) there were several trips to Tunis and Algiers. Now here is a typical case in which the planet Jupiter and the cusp of the 9th house (both of them having to do with journeys and both in Libra) start to exert a powerful action as soon as there is a change of sign. Further information on the significance of changes of sign will be found in Chapter 2 of Part I.

In **December, 1923** the AP/Jupiter conjunction was exact. Shortly afterwards he visited the Pueblo Indians in Arizona and Mexico (1924/25).

The year 1928 was another fateful year. The AP reached the **opposition to Pluto in October of that year**, and this had already brought about a radical change when it conjuncted in 1892. Pluto symbolizes the higher self and its powers of metamorphosis and, with the opposition to this planet, Jung placed a paper before the public which indicated his contemporary views ("On Psychic Energy," 1928).

Jung felt a great need to understand the libido, for he conceived it as a psychic analogue of physical energy. He felt that it should be judged in quantitative and not qualitative terms, for he wanted to escape from the then prevalent concretism of the theory. He did not wish to speak of the libido as an instinct of hunger or aggression or sex, but rather wanted to regard all of these instincts as a form of psychic energy. If libido was considered as an energy form, an actual understanding of libido would allow the observer to let sexuality, power, or hunger recede into the background, while allowing the libido to be observed in a more scientific view. His paper, "On Psychic Energy," was an attempt to express this idea.[22]

---

[22]See *Memories, Dreams, Reflections*, pp. 208-09.

Another event occurred to help Jung along. Richard Wilhelm sent him the manuscript of a Chinese treatise, *The Secret of the Golden Flower*, and through this manuscript he came in contact with alchemy and oriental mysticism which held a powerful attraction for him from that time forward. The spiritual penetration of alchemy and its reinterpretation from a psychological point of view is probably one of Jung's greatest and most gratifying gifts to posterity. He rescued this important empirical material produced by generations of seekers for the "stone of the wise" from the musty past. Quite incidentally he founded a new method of unlocking both individual psychic contents and old texts through the technique of amplification.[23]

• Age Point in the 10th and 11th Houses (Age 54-66)

Success, recognition and peak of activity

In July, 1929, in collaboration with Richard Wilhelm, he issued the book, *The Secret of the Golden Flower*,[24] at a time when he, himself, was in the flower of life. As he wrote in retrospect that after he reached the central point of his thinking and understood the basic concept of the *self*, he was able to go back to the world. He lectured and travelled a great deal. The lectures and writing formed a counterpoise for the years commited to the search within. They also contained questions and answers that were brought up by both readers and patients.[25]

---

[23]While it is true that Jung introduced the subject of alchemy to the psychological fraternity, and while it is also true that several of his books reproduce many valuable alchemical illustrations (some of which it would be hard for the general reader to find elsewhere), we should not imagine that he salvaged the material single-handedly. A renewed interest was being shown in the old works before Jung came on the scene, and a number of them had been republished. Indeed, he can be accused of distorting their meaning quite unscientifically, by lacing them with the jargon of twentieth century psychology instead of coming to terms with the thought of the various periods in which they were written. *Tr.*

[24]*The Secret of the Golden Flower*, translated by Richard Wilhelm, with a foreword and commentary by C.G. Jung. First published in England by Routledge and Kegan Paul, London, 1931.

[25]C.G. Jung, *Memories, Dreams, Reflections*, p. 208.

The transit of the tenth and eleventh houses thrust Jung into the public eye. He found recognition of his work and was honored an an eminent specialist in the psychological sphere. It is amazing how well his life at this time fits with the tenth house theme. Readers should also note that he put in a great deal of work in the earlier years, and the work bore fruit at this time.

● Age Point in the 12th House (Age 66-72)

Myocardial infarction and other diseases

We are now making a leap forward into the twelfth house. LP 12 occurs in November of 1943, and the next important stage of Jung's life is in complete accord with the dicta of classical astrology: in December of 1943 the AP made a quincunx to Uranus in Leo, which traditionally indicates problems with the heart. And in fact, at the beginning of 1944 Jung suffered from a serious myocardial infarction (after breaking a joint) and began to see visions. As life approached its limits, he saw himself flying away from the earth and had the same sight of our terrestrial globe as that enjoyed by a modern astronaut. Nowadays we would classify these visions as a genuine trans-personal peak-experience. Since A. Maslow made them accessible to psychological research we know how transforming such experiences can be.

The impact made by this imagery must have some connection with the **trine to the Moon** that occurred in **February 1944**. The visions persisted for three weeks, until Jung was off the danger list.

It was not until half a year later (July 1944, to be precise), that Jung resumed active correspondence (**AP in opposition to Venus**). Therefore, the period between Invert Point and Low Point in the twelfth house was a time of inner separation from the world. This is characteristically a time when many people give up and begin to withdraw from life.

In the shadow of the Ascendant, in November of 1946, Jung suffered another coronary embolism, and was once more confined to bed. The exact timing of this embolism, like that of the infarction at the beginning of 1944, is not shown in the Age Progression. This can sometimes be predicted by progression, but not necessarily always. The cause of disease lies deep below the surface and can sometimes be avoided, or it may rise earlier in life, and not be taken care of.

Thanks to his indomitable Leo nature, Jung recovered from this setback, too, and a month later he wrote to his friend Father V. White to share how he felt. It is really moving to read a letter in which Jung states that the *aspectus mortis* is a lonely thing, for "one is stripped of everything in the presence of God." He tells of a dream that he had, where he saw a bluish diamond-like star in heaven, and it was reflected in a pool—heaven above, heaven below. He related himself to the *imago Dei* in the darkness of the earth, and said that the dream was a great personal consolation. He mentions that he is ready to die, but there are still powerful thoughts coming to him— not his, but belonging to God. And at this phase of his life he feels that everything worth mentioning really belongs to God, or the universe.[26]

This description of Jung's experience when he was having a close encounter with death bears witness to the marvelous things that can happen to people when they enter the shadow of the AC. He had gained access to his true self, to his source, and, with the transit of the AC, underwent a new beginning, until the transit of Saturn brought a return of the illness.

● Age Point in the 1st House (Age 72-78)

Answer to Job

In the early summer of 1951 Jung suffered from a disease of the liver. On this occasion he concerned himself not with death but with the pressing problem of God and of the true content of religion, which has already been broached in his letter. Although he strove to preserve a scientific and empirical point of view, one cannot help noticing that he abandoned this and trespassed on the preserves of the theologians. This was taken very much amiss by many, and he was subjected to a great deal of criticism (conjunction with Saturn).

---

[26]*Selected Letters of C.G. Jung, 1909-1961*, selected and edited by Gerhard Adler, in collaboration with Aniela Jaffee; translated from the German by R.F.C. Hull. First Princeton/Bollingen Paperback printing in 1984, pp. 69, 70.

It was a hard and lonely time full of mental wrestling over the true nature of man.

Once more (as in 1879 when he was very young) the transit of Saturn signalled uncertainty about his "home," but this time there was no external situation unsettling him through changes of residence, nor was he being bullied by a dominating mother-figure; he was worrying about his spiritual home, and about the form in which God may be experienced. The book that came out of his search for God, *Answer to Job*,[27] can be seen as one of Jung's most significant works.

A newly awakened inner motive force had taken hold of him after the transit to the AC. He said he had to overcome a great internal resistance before he could write *Answer to Job*. He felt that the external root of this work lay in his environment as many questions from public as well as patients obliged him to express himself more clearly over the religious problems of modern man. He hesitated for years because he was aware of the storm it would raise. But in the end he couldn't refrain from coming to grips with a problem so urgent. It never crossed his mind that anyone would think he was proclaiming a metaphysical truth, but the theologians did not understand his psychological thinking.[28] And Jung experienced again the restraints of Saturn as criticism and doubt, and had trouble taming his Leo nature.

● Age Point in the 2nd House (Age 78-84)

Memories, Dreams, Reflections

Early in 1953 (**February**), T. Wolff died very suddenly at the quincunx to the Sun, as Jung's AP was approaching the cusp of the second house. Then some two years later his wife, Emma, died (**November 27, 1955**) with the AP exactly at Invert Point 2 and sextile

---

[27]C.G. Jung, *Answer to Job*. First published in German as *Antwort auf Hiob*, Zurich, 1952; first published in England in 1954. Available in the U.S.A. in the Bollingen Series, *Psychology East and West*, Princeton University Press; in the U.K. by Routledge & Kegan Paul.

[28]See *Memories, Dreams, Reflections*, pp. 216-217.

Pluto. There now followed a time of loneliness and retirement, and the strength of his own integration was repeatedly tested. He wrote to Erich Neumann on December 15, 1955 (quincunx Jupiter, semisextile Saturn), that the shock he experienced was so great that he could not concentrate or recover the power of speech. He said that two days before his wife's death, he had what he called a great illumination which lit up an old secret that had been embodied in her, and which exerted a tremendous influence on his life. Her quick and painless end, plus the transformative experience, were of great comfort to him. But the stillness, the audible silence, the empty air and the infinite distance were hard for him to bear at this time.[29]

And yet, in this vacuum, Jung prepared his last great work, which many have regarded as the key to the Jungian world of ideas—his autobiographic *Memories, Dreams, Reflections*. People had often spoken to him about having a biography written, but he had consistently refused to entertain the idea until, in the spring of 1957, he finally overcame his reluctance just as the AP reached LP 2 (**April, 1957**).

It is interesting to note that the publication of *Psychological Types* is associated with the Low Point of the Eighth house, and this new and important work with the Low Point of the opposite house.

Aniela Jaffe, the editor of *Memories, Dreams, Reflections*— without whom it would certainly never have seen the light of day— recollects how it was to work with Jung on this volume. The book was begun in the spring of 1957, at the request of the publisher, Kurt Wolff, and it was to be done as an autobiography—in Jung's own words. She asked him questions and recorded Jung's replies. At first she reports that he was reticent, but he soon got involved in the work, talking about himself and his development. At the end of the year, she noted that Jung, himself, noted a connection between images of his childhood and works that he had written in his old age.[30] One can see here how the years of childhood represented by the first two houses (and the AP moving through them for the second time) are brought back afresh—to be regarded in a new light.

In **April, 1958** Jung ended the three chapters on childhood and school years. This date coincides with the conjunction of the Lunar Node, which had played such an important part in Jung's life.

---

[29]*Selected Letters of C.G. Jung, 1909-1961*, pp. 145-46.
[30]See *Memories, Dreams, Reflections*, p. xiii.

The following year, as the AP traversed the region between the Lunar Node and Neptune, Jung concentrated on letter writing and on finishing his "memoirs." He also wrote a contribution to *Man and His Symbols*, in which he strove to present his system of psychology as clearly and as simply as possible, since he realized that he was addressing the lay public to a much greater extent than he had previously supposed. The "memoirs" are free from the aggressiveness and impulsiveness of former years. They are a circumspect work full of inner life, in which Jung expresses one or two personal convictions, conscious of the "jester's license" granted to old age.

Ms. Jaffe describes the final phase of the book with additional insight, for as the book took shape, a certain transformation and objectivization also took place in Jung. He was able to see himself and the significance of his life in an impersonal way. He said that if he was asked the value of his life, he would only be able to measure himself against the centuries and that he would definitely say it meant something. But if his value was only measured by contemporary ideas, it would mean nothing.[31] This impersonality becomes obvious more and more as one continues to read the book.

On **June 6, 1961**, Jung died peacefully at the very time signified by the conjunction of the AP with Neptune, and escaped from this world in order to travel in another realm. He left behind many volumes containing the results of his investigations into the human psyche, and these were to have a fruitful influence on Western psychology for decades to come.

---

[31]See *Memories, Dreams, Reflections*, pp. v-viii.

Chapter 2

Example Horoscopes

● Introduction

In this next chapter, with the help of three more example charts, we shall be taking a look at the meaning of the Age Point as it traverses a limited sector. We shall choose one moment in the life and describe the situation found at that time. This will reveal the positions in a chart which one needs to consider in order to understand the life situation as a whole.

● Chart 1

Calculation of the Age Point

We shall first give a quick way of calculating the degree reached by the Age Point shown in figure 2.2.1 on page 207. If we allow six years per house, the Age Point will be in the ninth house when the native is fifty-one (because when he was 48 the AP crossed the ninth cusp). But to pin-point the house position of the AP on the native's fifty-first birthday we need to know the size of the house. By inspection, we find that there are 17°29′ in the ninth house in figure 2.2.1. We now need to work out how many degrees the AP moves in a year in a house of this size. There are two methods of doing this.

One is to divide the number of house degrees by six: 17°29′ : 6 = 2°54′50″. The other is to turn to the AP-LP-IP table in *Life Clock* Vol. 1, pp. 38-39.

Find 17 in the House Size column and run your finger along to the Per Year column	2°50′
For the remaining 29′ take 30′ in the House Size column for "minutes" and find the corresponding Per Year value	0°05′
By addition, the annual Age Point progression is	2°55′
For three years (48 + 3 = 51) this comes to 3 × 2°55′	8°45′
These 8°45′ are now added to the position of the ninth cusp in Capricorn	+ 16°31′
	= 25°16′

And so, on the fifty-first birthday (November 18, 1973) the Age Point stands at about 25° Capricorn. The next step is to look in the radix for any planets in the region of 25°. The Sun is 25°32′ Scorpio and the Dragon's Head is 26°33′ Virgo. Since the AP moves very slowly in such a small house as this one, the permissable orb is 1°. In a larger house, it would be half a degree.

Therefore at this age there is an exact sextile to the Sun, and in a few months the AP makes a trine with the lunar node. Each AP aspect, however, must be seen and interpreted not in isolation but in relation to other aspects past and future. This is especially important when the AP is contacting, in quick succession, planets linked by aspect in the radix. In the present example, the sequence running up to the Sun began with the sextile to Mercury. This was followed by the square to Saturn (15°), the quincunx to Neptune (18°) and the sextiles to the Moon and Sun. Finally there was a trine to the lunar node, at which point the process more or less came to an end.

In figure 2.2.1, the Moon is conjunct the Sun (the new-moon position) in the sixth house, the house of coping with life. These are ego planets (the Sun representing self-awareness, the Moon a more

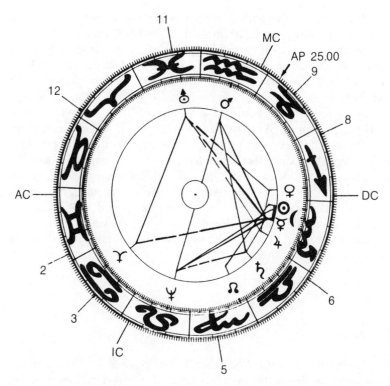

Figure 2.2.1. Chart 1 is a male born on November 18, 1922, at 17:00h in Teufen, Switzerland. At age 51 the Age Point will be in the ninth house at 25°16′ Capricorn.

emotional sense of self), and in the sixth house they manifest themselves mainly in the areas of profession, work and duty. When the AP aspects the Sun, the Moon is implicated, too, because of their conjunction. The native has a solar standpoint but, in the process of achieving relative independence in the ninth house, cannot entirely avoid childish modes of behavior or unconscious anxieties about life. These need to be dealt with by the conscious mind. Since the Age Point aspect was made from the ninth house, the native had to think for himself about striking a balance and about reaching a decision on whether he ought to be working just to earn a living and to get on in the world, or whether he ought to be striving for idealistic and less selfish goals.

Accordingly, the native decided to become heavily involved in community affairs, and although this absorbed much of his time and energy it gave him more satisfaction than anything he had ever done. He managed to overcome his sense of insecurity and occasional fear of failure (sixth house) and, by accepting public responsibilities, was able to mature and to become stronger both in self-awareness and in sense of self. His life and work took on a deeper significance. What helped to make this possible was that the sextile formed to the ego planets by the Age Point from the ninth house served to distance the native somewhat from his personal problems, and added a whole new dimension to his awareness. He himself created the conditions for self-improvement. The planets below the horizon became effective and he gained a better understanding of his self-consciousness in all its weaknesses and strengths. By making the right decision he was able to take an essential step in his further development.

● Chart 2

In figure 2.2.2 the Age Point is not posited at the beginning of a sign or on a house cusp, nor is there a planet near it, so we need to look at any aspects; in this case a trine to Pluto. In addition, everything we do with the current situation has to be carefully weighed. We must not miss the fact that the AP has recently made a sextile to Mars. We have also to check what is going to happen next, since this is often significant for the current situation. The Age Point is in Scorpio in the region of experience we call the eighth house. This is the predominant theme. Pluto is in Cancer and just approaching the fifth house. Mars and Venus are in opposition to Pluto, and these three planets work together as a functional unit; their individual qualities being stimulated one after the other by AP aspects. The color of the aspects is blue, so we may safely assume an absence of struggle at this stage and an effortless learning process arising from a harmonious experience of the properties of the three planets. There are no hard or awkward circumstances with which to deal. The influences of the 5/11 axis can be met and mastered with calm confidence. Since the native is not being pressured, he is much less likely to react ill-advisedly.

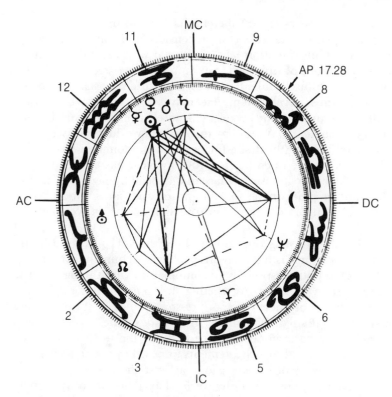

Figure 2.2.2. Chart 2 is a male born on January 19, 1930, at 10:30h in Baar, Switzerland. On his 44th birthday, the Age Point is 17°28′ Capricorn.

Age Point aspects are effective for about one degree on either side of the exact position, depending on the house size. All AP aspects to the house cusps, except transits, are found to be inoperative, but changes of sign are very powerful.

We must now define the successive positions of the AP. The theme of the third quadrant is the confrontation between the ego and its opposite number, between the external world and the individual who seeks his freedom. Half-way round this quadrant, in the fixed (*i.e.*, succedent) house, the native encounteres those structures that weld human beings into communities. The eighth house issue is joined not (as in the seventh) with separate persons, but with the organization of the community, with its laws, rules and conventions and, in a higher sense, with the laws of nature.

In these years (42-48) the emphasis is on the native's psychological reactions: he seeks comprehension, and wants to undergo a process of transformation. His emotional world is liable to suffer a certain amount of upheaval. Structures he has erected are broken; perhaps he himself pulls them down because they stand in the way of his further development. He may see them as a burdensome obligation and may try to release himself from them or else starts living a double life. A peculiar inconsistency evidences itself: on the one hand there is the desire for personal freedom and on the other hand there is the intention to profit by what has been achieved so far. He looks for an assured place in the social framework, and, from this vantage point strives for recognition and status. But in Scorpio his treatment of society is controversial; a new answer has to be found.

The Pluto/Mars opposition along the 5/11 relationship axis, when viewed in this light, reveals problems in human relationships. The eighth house, especially in combination with the sign Scorpio, raises certain doubts as to whether the commitments made in the seventh house or under external pressure (shown by the opposition) were truly desired. The blue trine and sextile aspects tend to encourage a harmonious balance between the inner need for personal freedom and the requirements imposed by society. There are a number of ways of offsetting one against the other.

With an opposition along the 5/11 axis there is always a chance that the native will get himself trapped in some confining relationship. But where there are blue aspects in the eighth house, any problem-relationships (whatever their origin) can be tackled afresh with better prospects of solving them. In the present instance, the problems are particularly pressing, since the Sun, Mercury, and Venus are all in the eleventh house. There is an earnest desire to find true friendship, the right group, the ideal society; the native seeks congenial company. This theme now occupies the center of the individual's attention.

In Pluto we recognize a strong super-ego function. Here is an imposing, very capable person (fifth house) with obvious patriarchal qualities which would be exercised in a thoroughly philanthropic (Cancer) manner. This leading tendency stands in stark contrast to the eroticism signified by Mars and Venus. The latter planets make for idealism whereas Pluto makes for realism—and there is a constant conflict between the two. There is a powerful tension between the two poles, not only because they are in opposition but also because of their house position. Mars and Venus would have been better placed in the fifth house, and Pluto ought, for preference, to have occupied the cusp of the eleventh. Neither Mars/Venus nor Pluto can develop as they should, even with blue aspects in the eighth house. To know this may not be comforting but, like all true insights it has a liberating effect, is beneficial, and promotes a more balanced outlook. Indeed, the tension can be sublimated in creative work given the right motivation. That was what happened here—the native liked helping people and never stopped learning. As a lay medical practitioner he was always looking for new ways to solve physical problems, methods he could put to immediate use for the benefit of his patients.

As long as the Age Point was moving through the relatively empty space of the eighth and ninth houses, nothing much happened in his life. It was not until the LP of the ninth house and the run-up to the MC that the professional body to which he belonged approached him and asked for his active participation in various projects. And only at the MC (cusp of the tenth house) did he start to play a leading role, working since then in his official capacity just as progressively as he used to do in his small practice. To sum up, the aspect configuration centered on the planets at the top of the horoscope is very suitable for someone who takes a lead; especially in this case, where Saturn promises a sense of responsibility and Mars gives the necessary energy.

● **Chart 3**

Figure 2.2.3 on page 212 shows a momentous transit: the crossing from a ruling into a serving situation. The difference between the two signs is seen in a marked change in the attitude to life. In our example it is more marked than usual because Saturn on house cusp ten points clearly either to a ruling position or to the Leo wish to domineer. Shortly after the MC and Saturn are transited, the Age Point enters a serving sign—while still in the tenth house.

The owner of the hororscope in figure 2.2.3 was a dominant female, a matriarch who knew how to make herself obeyed. Her Virgo demands greater concern for humanity. The native takes an increasing interest in need and suffering; it is no longer possible to ignore them. The desired power must be renounced—or it will be taken away. The aspect configuration that indicates her ability to govern includes all three main planets. Her influence spreads itself over the thoughts and emotions of anyone under her physical control. The Sun is particularly well placed just inside the ninth cusp, and is very strong by sign. Saturn and Venus, the two classical female planets, are not far away. However, there is a small gap between them separating the two configurations to which they belong. The transition of the Age Point from one aspect configuration to the other signifies abandonment of the mothering role to return to pure femininity, Venus being female charm, and Saturn wifely care. The role-playing represented by Saturn is certainly much to the fore in the present case, because Saturn is on the MC in

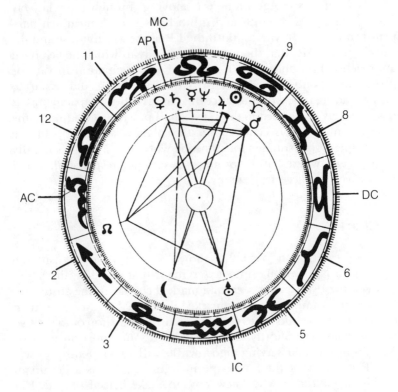

Figure 2.2.3. Chart 3 is a female born July 23, 1919, at 15:00h in Langenthal, Switzerland. The Age Point is crossing from Leo to Virgo at age 55.

Leo, the sign in which role-playing is an aid to increased self-awareness. (Incidentally, the maternal function as an archetypal role is not limited to any given sex or age. It can also be assumed by men.) But at the transition point the maternal role is left behind and femininity *per se* comes to the fore together with a genuine helping function (Venus in Virgo). In Virgo this can mean a sympathetic response to the poor, the suffering and the weak—it can mean what we think of as "the woman's touch." The form taken by this response will depend on the situation and its possibilities, and on those around, but invariably there will be the desire to help or heal. The opposing Uranus points to welfare work and (assisted by the lunar node) could inaugurate changes when aspected. This could work out in such a way that opportunities for dedicated social service will offer themselves. After the change of sign, Uranus, the dragon's head, Mars, Venus and Pluto are all aspected in quick succession. Hence we have a veritable transformation or metamorphosis (Pluto on cusp 9 producing a change in outlook) and a renewal of the personality from the mind outwards.

In the tenth house, this lady experienced a thorough reshaping of her life. Opportunities suddenly arose for using to the full her gifts for healing and relief work. She was highly successful in combining advisory and medical activities. Many people were able to thank her for helping them when they were in distress and she became a popular figure both inside and outside her own country.

Appendix

Age Point Calculation

Written by Michael A. Huber
Translated and edited by Michael P. Munkasey

Quick calculation explanation—Age Point movement and calculation—Mathematical calculation techniques—Time calculation in the houses—Examples using timing questions—Examples using zodiacal questions

● The Age Point Method and the Horoscope

The horoscope acts like a clock in one sense, and it is through the use of the horoscope as a clock that the position of the Age Point (AP) can be measured. The process of measuring the AP through the houses of the horoscope is called Age Progression. The speed of the AP through the horoscope can be compared to the speed of a car which a person is deliberately driving along a road. The road is like the zodiac, and the number of miles along the road that the driver moves can be compared to the distance in degrees of the zodiac that the AP advances as life continues. Just as the speed of the car along the highway is not always the same, the speed of the AP also varies as life's circumstances (*i.e.*, house sizes) change.

The speed of the AP changes every 6 years, as a new house is entered. The size of the house (the number of degrees that the house occupies) determines the speed, in degrees, that the AP progresses. The larger the house the greater the speed of the AP in degrees. The smaller the house the smaller the speed of the AP in degrees. The speed of the AP is constant through any one house, but the speed changes abruptly at the Koch house cusp. This change occurs every six years as the AP passes through each of the twelve houses of the horoscope.

As the AP passes through the house it makes contact with the planets and the Nodes in the house that it's in, as well as making aspects to the other planets and points in the horoscope. The AP will also encounter sign changes. As each of these aspects or contacts are made, the person will experience certain events in the real world which will be related to the nature of the horoscope event that has just occurred.

Here are the important things to remember about calculating the Age Point (AP) as it moves through the horoscope:

1. The AP passes through each house in six years, regardless of the size of the house.

2. Only the Koch House System is used with the Age Progression method.

3. The size of each house, in degrees and minutes, must be measured accurately.

4. The speed of the AP as it moves through each house is expressed in time units (*e.g.*, years, months, days, etc.). Therefore, to calculate the important times of life as determined by the AP, degree distances within the house must be converted to time units using the methods described later within this appendix.

Considerations

Because each house represents six years of life, the following numbers can be used as constants for all of the following AP calculations:

● One solar year   =   365.25 days

● 72 solar years   =   One Horoscope cycle   =   26,298.0 days

● One House   =   6 Years   =   2,191.5 days

● The Low Point of a House is reached 1,354 days after entering a house.

• The Invert Point of a House is reached 837.5 days after entering a house.

You may find that using a pocket calculator will be helpful for the following calculations. A small calculator that can add or subtract hours or minutes directly is the best type to use. However, any small calculator can be used to do these calculations. To find the daily speed of the AP through a house, perform calculations like these in the following examples:

1. Measure each house size, Koch cusp to Koch cusp, in degrees and minutes. For instance, if the Koch cusp of the 4th house is 20°00′ Libra, and the Koch cusp of the 5th house is 10°05′ Sagittarius, then the number of degrees in the 4th house is the number of degrees from 20 LIB 00 to 10 SAG 05. To measure this distance in degrees we measure from 20 LIB 00 to zero degrees of Scorpio, then measure 30 degrees for the sign of Scorpio (because Scorpio is intercepted in the 4th house), and then finally add the remaining 10 degrees and 05 minutes of Sagittarius that are left. Doing this we get:

Distance from 20 LIB 00 to 00 SCO 00	=	10°00′
Interception for the Sign of Scorpio	=	30°00′
Distance to 10 SAG 05	=	+ 10°05′
4th House Size	=	50°05′

Similarly the size of the 2nd house, which goes from 1 VIR 18 on the 2nd house cusp to 25 VIR 37 on the 3rd house cusp is found by:

3rd House Cusp placement is 25 VIR 37	=	25°37′
2nd House Cusp placement is 1 VIR 18	=	- 1°18′
Subtracting one value from the other	=	24°19′

Therefore the 2nd house size is 24°19′, while the 4th house size is 50°05′. Each of these degree distances will be travelled by the AP in exactly six years, or 2,191.5 days.

Take the following horoscope as an example:

Date of Birth = May 10, 1942
Time = 11:30 AM; Location = Zurich, Switzerland.

(This Chart) Location		Koch Cusps	(For all charts) Age (Years)	Age (Days)
1st House Cusp (AC)	=	7 LEO 06	0	0
2nd House Cusp	=	1 VIR 18	6	2191.5
3rd House Cusp	=	25 VIR 37	12	4383.0
4th House Cusp	=	20 LIB 00	18	6574.5
5th House Cusp	=	10 SAG 05	24	8766.0
6th House Cusp	=	11 CAP 37	30	10957.5
7th House Cusp	=	7 AQU 06	36	13149.0
8th House Cusp	=	1 PSC 18	42	15340.5
9th House Cusp	=	25 PSC 37	48	17532.0
10th House Cusp	=	20 ARI 00	54	19723.5
11th House Cusp	=	10 GEM 05	60	21915.0
12th House Cusp	=	11 CAN 37	66	24106.5
1st House Cusp	=	7 LEO 06	72	26298.0

VENUS at 4 ARI 41 in the 9th house

Notice that the zodiacal sign of Scorpio is intercepted in the 4th house, and that the zodiacal sign of Taurus is intercepted in the 10th house.

• Calculation of the Year Point

A "year point" is the location of the AP on a person's birthday. Each house gives six birthdays or year points. Each of the birthdates can be measured as an exact number of days from each house cusp, because the number of days in a year and in each house always remains the same. It is the speed of the AP that changes through each of the houses. Each year consists of 365.25 days. The first calculation we can then perform, once the house sizes (in degrees) are calculated, is to find out where the year points are in each house. Each house will have six year points within in. For example, the 3rd house will have the year points: 12 (at the cusp), 13, 14, 15, 16, and 17. The zodiacal position of the AP for each of these year points can be calculated once the size of the house is known. To calculate the size of the 3rd house, proceed as before:

Distance from 25 VIR 37 to 00 LIB 00	=	4°23′
Distance to 20 LIB 00	=	20°00′
3rd House Size	=	24°23′

Each of the year points will occur at a distance of 1/6 of the house size from the house cusp. In this example for the 3rd house, each year point will be alloted 1/6 of the 24°23′, or:

$$24°23′ \div 6 = 4°03′50″ \text{ or } 4°04′ \text{ approximately}$$

Using Table 1 on page 220 these calculations can be performed and broken down into different parts, as follows:

$$23′ = 0.38333333° \text{ (From Table 1)}$$
$$24° + 23′ = 24° + 0.38333333 = 24.38333333°$$
$$24.38333333° \div 6 = 4.06388888°$$
$$4.06388888° = 4° + 03′ + 50″ = 4°03′50″$$

The calculations to determine the year point intervals in degrees could have also been performed using a hand calculator in the following manner:

$$24° + (23 \div 60)° = 24.38333333°$$

(The degree part and the fractional minute part are added.)

$$24.38333333° \div 6 = 4.06388888°$$

(The sum is divided by the 6 years.)

This is equal to 4° plus 0.06388888°

(Taking the fractional part of this number)

$$0.063888888° \times 60 \text{ minutes} \div \text{degree} = 3.833328′$$

(The number to the left of the decimal point in this answer gives the MINUTES part.)

Subtracting the "3" part out, gives 3′ as the MINUTES answer, and, leaves

0.833328 as the fractional part; multiplying this fractional part by 60 (seconds ÷ minute) again we get

49.99997 which is close enough to 50 when rounded off.

(This number is the SECONDS answer.)

Therefore, the answer (using a hand calculator) is the accumulation of all of these parts, or: 4°03′50″ (which, rounded, is: 4° 04′).

Table 1. Equivalences

Minute and Degree Equivalences		
1′ = 0.0166666°	21′ = 0.3500000°	41′ = 0.68333333°
2′ = 0.0333333°	22′ = 0.3666666°	42′ = 0.70000000°
3′ = 0.0500000°	23′ = 0.3833333°	43′ = 0.71666666°
4′ = 0.0666666°	24′ = 0.4000000°	44′ = 0.73333333°
5′ = 0.0833333°	25′ = 0.4166666°	45′ = 0.75000000°
6′ = 0.1000000°	26′ = 0.4333333°	46′ = 0.76666666°
7′ = 0.1166666°	27′ = 0.4500000°	47′ = 0.78333333°
8′ = 0.1333333°	28′ = 0.4666666°	48′ = 0.80000000°
9′ = 0.1500000°	29′ = 0.4833333°	49′ = 0.81666666°
10′ = 0.1666666°	30′ = 0.5000000°	50′ = 0.83333333°
11′ = 0.1833333°	31′ = 0.5166666°	51′ = 0.85000000°
12′ = 0.2000000°	32′ = 0.5333333°	52′ = 0.86666666°
13′ = 0.2166666°	33′ = 0.5500000°	53′ = 0.88333333°
14′ = 0.2333333°	34′ = 0.5666666°	54′ = 0.90000000°
15′ = 0.2500000°	35′ = 0.5833333°	55′ = 0.91666666°
16′ = 0.2666666°	36′ = 0.6000000°	56′ = 0.93333333°
17′ = 0.2833333°	37′ = 0.6166666°	57′ = 0.95000000°
18′ = 0.3000000°	38′ = 0.6333333°	58′ = 0.96666666°
19′ = 0.3166666°	39′ = 0.6500000°	59′ = 0.98333333°
20′ = 0.3333333°	40′ = 0.6666666°	60′ = 1.00000000°
Second and Degree		
10″ = 0.00277777°	20″ = 0.0055555°	30″ = 0.00833333°
40″ = 0.01111111°	50″ = 0.0138888°	60″ = 0.01666666°

This tell us that each year of life, for a house of size 24°23', takes up 4°03'50' of zodiacal arc. Adding this to the 3rd house cusp we can get the year point locations:

Age 12 = 25 VIR 37 (the 3rd house cusp)
Age 13 = Age 12 + 4°03'50" = 25 VIR 37 + 4°04' = 29 VIR 41
Age 14 = Age 13 + 4°03'50" = 29 VIR 41 + 4°04' = 3 LIB 45
Age 15 = Age 14 + 4°03'50" = 3 LIB 45 + 4°04' = 7 LIB 49
Age 16 = Age 15 + 4°03'50" = 7 LIB 49 + 4°04' = 11 LIB 53
Age 17 = Age 16 + 4°03'50" = 11 LIB 53 + 4°04' = 15 LIB 57
Age 18 = Age 17 + 4°03' 50" = 15 LIB 57 + 4°03' = 20 LIB 00

20 LIB 00 is also the cusp of the next house, the 4th house.

The last year point calculation used 4° 03' instead of 4° 04' because the actual degree interval of 4° 03' 50" was rounded up to 4° 04'. The last line of the calculations above was lowered one minute to compensate for that rounding.

Taking another house as an example, let us do the same set of calculations on the 4th house:

The 4th house size is 50°05'; 1/6 of 50°05' is 8°20'50".

Therefore, the age arc for the 4th house, which has a size of 50°05', is 8°20'50". The individual year points can be calculated as before:

Age 18 occurs at the cusp of the 4th house which is at 20 LIB 00
Age 19 = Age 18 + 8°20'50" = 20 LIB 00 + 8°20'50" = 28 LIB 21
Age 20 = Age 19 + 8°20'50" = 28 LIB 21 + 8°20'50" = 6 SCO 42
Age 21 = Age 20 + 8°20'50" = 6 SCO 42 + 8°20'50" = 15 SCO 3
Age 22 = Age 21 + 8°20'50" = 15 SCO 3 + 8°20'50" = 24 SCO 24
Age 23 = Age 22 + 8°20'50" = 24 SCO 24 + 8°20'50" = 2 SAG 45
Age 24 = Age 23 + 8°20'50" = 2 SAG 45 + 8°20'50" = 10 SAG 5

Age 24 also occurs at the cusp of the next house, the 5th house.

Similar types of computations will produce the year point arcs for the other ages in life. Using these year point arcs is a useful way of determining where in the horoscope your AP is for the year. This type of computation should be performed for each year and once these calculations are done you will have a list of the zodiacal positions where your AP is for all your birthdays.

● Calculation of an Aspect to a Planetary Position

In our example, Venus is in the 9th house at 4 ARI 41. The cusp of the 9th house is 25 PSC 37 and the cusp of the 10th house (the MC) is 20 ARI 00. Since the 9th house will be the same size as the 3rd house, and the years will be symmetrical about the house points, we can copy our information from the 3rd house that was calculated on page 221 and modify it for the 9th house by inserting the opposite signs of the zodiac:

Age 48 = 25 PSC 37
Age 49 = Age 12 + 4°03′50″ = 25 PSC 37 + 4°04′ = 29 PSC 41
Age 50 = Age 13 + 4°03′50″ = 29 PSC 41 + 4°04′ = 3 ARI 45
Age 51 = Age 14 + 4°03′50″ = 3 ARI 45 + 4°04′ = 7 ARI 49
Age 52 = Age 15 + 4°03′50″ = 7 ARI 49 + 4°04′ = 11 ARI 53
Age 53 = Age 16 + 4°03′50″ = 11 ARI 53 + 4°04′ = 15 ARI 57
Age 54 = Age 17 + 4°03′50″ = 15 ARI 57 + 4°03′ = 20 ARI 00

20 ARI 00 is also the cusp of the next house, the 10th house.

Since Venus is at 4 ARI 41, the conjunction of the AP with Venus will be reached between the 50th and 51st years of life. The number of degrees in this year has already been determined to be 4°03′50″ (see page 000). It will take 365.25 days for the AP to travel this number of degrees. **The number of degrees that the AP travels in one day** can be determined from the following calculation:

4°03′50″ = 4.06388888° (determined before)
4.06388888° ÷ 365.25 days = 0.0111263° per day, or 0°00′40″ per day (using the same type of calculation logic as shown on page 19)

Thus, the AP moves at about the rate of 40″ of zodiacal arc per day while travelling through either the 3rd or the 9th houses. Now we must determine the distance from the nearest point to Venus, and then divide that arc distance by the movement of 40″ of arc per day to get the number of days it will take for the AP to travel from that year point date to Venus. The procedure is:

$$\begin{array}{rcl} \text{Venus} & = & 4 \text{ ARI } 41 \\ \text{(subtracting) Age 50} & = & -\ 3 \text{ ARI } 45 \\ \hline \text{The arc difference} & = & 0° \qquad 56' \end{array}$$

This tells us that these is 0°56′ of zodiacal arc between the point where the AP will be on the 50th birthday and where Venus is natally located. Since we have already determined that the AP is traveling at the rate of 40″ per day, we can convert the 56′ to seconds by multiplying it by 60. Doing this we get:

56 minutes of arc = 3360 seconds of arc

Dividing 3360 seconds of arc by 40″ of arc movement of the AP/day, we get:

$$3360 \div 40 = 84 \text{ days}$$

Adding 84 days to the birthday, which is May 10th, we will find the date when the AP is conjunct natal Venus. We know that May has 31 days, and therefore there are 21 days left in May after the birthday. June has 30 days, and July has 31 days in the month. The total of 21 + 30 + 31 is 82 days. We have to stretch to 84 days, which is two more beyond July 31, so the date that the AP would reach Venus is August 2, in the 50th year of life.

• Calculation of the AP on a Particular Date

Suppose we wish to know where the AP was (*i.e.*, the sign and house position) for September 14th, 1960. Going back to the calculations that we have done previously (see pages 218 and 221), we first determine that this date, September 14th, 1960 occurs in the 18th year of life. Therefore the AP will have just passed the 4th house cusp (the IC) on the previous birthday, May 10th, 1960. We can see that the AP will have just passed the IC which is at 20 LIB 00. We must count the number of days from the birthdate to September 14th. Doing this we find the date of September 14th, 1960 is exactly 21 days (for the rest of May) + 30 days (for the month of June) + 31 days (for the month of July) + 31 days (for the month of August) + 14 days for the September portion away. Adding these days we get:

$$21 + 30 + 31 + 31 + 14 = 127 \text{ days}$$
That is, September 14th is 127 days away from May 10th.

Since the AP moves through the 4th house at the rate of speed of 8°20′50″ (see page 221 for this calculation) we can get the number of degrees per day that the AP is traveling through the 4th (or 10th) house. Doing this calculation we get the following result:

$$8°20′50″ = 8.3472222°$$

Dividing 8.3472222° by 365.25 we can get the number of degrees a day that the AP is moving through the house, which is:

$$8.3472222° \div 365.25 = 0.0228534° \text{ per day}$$
or 0°01′22.27″ per day of travel by the AP through the 4th house

Multiplying this daily rate of travel by the number of days between the birthdate and the target date we get:

$$0.0228534° \times 127 \text{ days} = 2.9023818°,$$
or 2°54′8.5″ motion in 127 days

This is the arc distance that the AP has moved in 127 days in a house of this size. Adding this distance (rounded) of 2°54′ to the AP location on the 18th birthday we get: 20 LIB 00 + 2°54′ = 22 LIB 54. Therefore, the AP is at 22 LIB 54 on September 14th, 1960.

• Determining When the Zodiacal Sign Changes Occur

Suppose we wish to know on what date the AP changes from the sign of LIBRA to the sign of SCORPIO. We can follow a set of calculations very similar to the ones used for determining when the AP would reach the planet Venus. In this example we realize that the AP must travel from the 4th house cusp, which is at 20 LIB 00 to 00 SCO 00. This is a distance of 10 degrees, exactly. In the 4th house we have already determined that the AP is traveling at a rate of 8°20'50" per year, or 0.0228534° per day (see previous example). Since the sign of Scorpio will be reached between the 19th and the 20th year, we know that we have to measure between 28 LIB 21 and 6 SCO 42 in the 19th year of life. See page 221 for these numbers which have been previously explained. The distance, in zodiacal degrees between 28 LIB 21 and 00 SCO 00, is found by subtracting the two values: 00 SCO 00 - 28 LIB 21 = 1°39' of arc difference.

Converting this (as before in the Venus example) to seconds of arc, we get: 1°39' = 5940 seconds of arc. Dividing the number of seconds of arc by the daily arc travel in the 4th house, which is 1'22.27" (or 82.27" of arc travel per day for the AP through the 4th house) we get:

$$5940 \text{ seconds of arc} \div 82.27'' \text{ of arc/day} =$$
$$\text{(about) } 72 \text{ days of time}$$

Therefore the sign of SCORPIO will be reached about 72 days after the 19th birthday. Calculating the days (as in the example before) we get 21 days for the rest of May, and 30 days for June. This has used 51 days. If we add the 31 days for July we will have used 82 days, which is more than we are looking to use, so the date the AP reaches 00 SCO 00 must be in the month of July in the 19th year. Since May has contributed 21 days to us, and June has given 30 days, then we have 72 - (30 + 21) = 72 - 51 = 21 days yet to account for. Therefore, on or about the date of July 21, in the 19th year of life, 1961 in this example, the AP will cross from LIBRA into the zodiacal sign of SCORPIO.

• Conclusion

At first glance the calculations seem a bit more formidable than they really are in practice. The calculation of when the AP reaches and activates the different parts of the chart is not very difficult or time consuming. With a little bit of practice you can easily master the techniques for doing these calculations. The following layouts and reviews of these steps may be of further help to you. Use them for your own practice.

House Size Calculation

1. Cusp of the 2nd House - Cusp of the 1st House = 1st House Size
   1st House Size = _____ - _____ = _____

2. Cusp of the 3rd House - Cusp of the 2nd House = 2nd House Size
   2nd House Size = _____ - _____ = _____

3. Cusp of the 4th House - Cusp of the 3rd House = 3rd House Size
   3rd House Size = _____ - _____ = _____

4. Cusp of the 5th House - Cusp of the 4th House = 4th House Size
   4th House Size = _____ - _____ = _____

5. Cusp of the 6th House - Cusp of the 5th House = 5th House Size
   5th House Size = _____ - _____ = _____

6. Cusp of the 7th House - Cusp of the 6th House = 6th House Size
   6th House Size = _____ - _____ = _____

7. Cusp of the 8th House - Cusp of the 7th House = 7th House Size
   7th House Size = _____ - _____ = _____

8. Cusp of the 9th House - Cusp of the 8th House = 8th House Size
   8th House Size = _____ - _____ = _____

9. Cusp of the 10th House - Cusp of the 9th House = 9th House Size
   9th House Size = _____ - _____ = _____

10. Cusp of the 11th House - Cusp of the 10th House = 10th House Size
    10th House Size = _____ - _____ = _____

11. Cusp of the 12th House - Cusp of the 11th House = 11th House Size
    11th House Size = _____ - _____ = _____

12. Cusp of the 1st House - Cusp of the 12th House = 12th House Size
    12th House Size = _____ - _____ = _____

Year Point Calculations

1. Determine the House Size in degrees and minutes   _____

2. Convert this number to whole degrees   _____

3. Divide this house size by 6   _____

4. Convert this answer to degrees, minutes and seconds   _____

5. Add the result (line 4) to the cusp to get the six different year points, as shown in the examples before:

Year Point #1 = House Cusp + the number from line 4 above

_____ + _____ = _____

Year Point #2 = Year Point #1 + the number from line 4 above

_____ + _____ = _____

Year Point #3 = Year Point #2 + the number from line 4 above

_____ + _____ = _____

Year Point #4 = Year Point #3 + the number from line 4 above

_____ + _____ = _____

Year Point #5 = Year Point #4 + the number from line 4 above

_____ + _____ = _____

Year Point #6 = Year Point #5 + the number from line 4 above

_____ + _____ = _____

Aspects to Planets, Points, IP, Sign Cusps

1. When you wish to know when an aspect will be exact, determine the arc distance from the nearest Year Point to the point or planet that you wish. Always measure ahead in the zodiac. Let us use a planet in the text here, but remember that the IP, a sign cusp, etc., will substitute equally well in this example.

Planet Position   =   _____

Year Point next previous   =   - _____

Distance to move   =   _____

2. Determine the speed that the AP is moving through the house: House Cusp at far end of house - House cusp at near end of House = Number of degrees in the House:

_____ - _____ = _____ (degrees in House)

3. Number of degrees of daily travel for the AP is the answer from No. 2, above. Divide this by 365.25:

_____ ÷ 365.25 = _____ (degrees AP moves/day)

4. Distance to move (from step 1), divided by AP speed in degrees (from step 3, above) gives the number of days from the birthdate to the target date:

_____ ÷ _____ = _____ (days from birthdate)

5. Add this number of days to the birthdate to get the target date.

Determine For Any Date Where The AP Is

1. When you wish to know where the AP is on any particular day, determine the number of days from the last birthday to this target date.

_____ + _____ = _____ (days from birthdate)

2. Take this number of days from #1 above, and multiply it by the speed that the AP is moving through the house the AP is in:

_____ × _____ = _____ (arc to move from birthdate)

3. Find the AP year point position on the birthdate: _____

4. Add 2 and 3 answers (from above) together:

_____ + _____ = _____ (AP position on target date)

Days in Life When the Cusps, IPs and LPs are Exact

		Days after Birth		Days after Birth
1st House Cusp	=	0	7th House Cusp	= 13149
IP	=	837.5	IP	= 13986.5
LP	=	1354	LP	= 14503
2nd House Cusp	=	191.5	8th House Cusp	= 15340.5
IP	=	3029	IP	= 16178
LP	=	3545.5	LP	= 16694.5
3rd House Cusp	=	4383	9th House Cusp	= 17532
IP	=	5220.5	IP	= 18365.5
LP	=	5737	LP	= 18886
4th House Cusp	=	6574.5	10th House Cusp	= 19723.5
IP	=	7412	IP	= 20561
LP	=	7928.5	LP	= 20177.5
5th House Cusp	=	8766	11th House Cusp	= 21915
IP	=	9603.5	IP	= 22752.5
LP	=	10120	LP	= 23269
6th House Cusp	=	10957.5	12th House Cusp	= 24106.5
IP	=	11795	IP	= 24944
LP	=	12311.5	LP	= 25460.5

Worksheet for Your Natal Chart

Zodiacal Location		Zodiacal Location	
1st House Cusp = _____		7th House Cusp = _____	
IP = _____		IP = _____	
LP = _____		LP = _____	
2nd House Cusp = _____		8th House Cusp = _____	
IP = _____		IP = _____	
LP = _____		LP = _____	
3rd House Cusp = _____		9th House Cusp = _____	
IP = _____		IP = _____	
LP = _____		LP = _____	
4th House Cusp = _____		10th House Cusp = _____	
IP = _____		IP = _____	
LP = _____		LP = _____	
5th House Cusp = _____		11th House Cusp = _____	
IP = _____		IP = _____	
LP = _____		LP = _____	
6th House Cusp = _____		12th House Cusp = _____	
IP = _____		IP = _____	
LP = _____		LP = _____	

(continued from page 170)
brushes aside anxieties, grief, depression, and unwarranted worrying. We can say YES to life with renewed zest, feel more enterprising, and also healthier. Many of the worries of the past no longer have power over us; we can break through old restrictive habits and maybe even branch out into new territory. We can plan to do what it is we want to do, and realize some of our long-held dreams. Some of us no longer want our lives to be ruled by other people's opinions, we energetically reject their advice as interference, develop an unexpected degree of courage, and can even become foolhardy. Only when we reach the Low Point do we come to our senses, because our show of energy then finds itself confronted by the greater realism of the 2nd house.

Age 76

Low Point in the 1st House of Cardinal Fire: Defiance.

Needless to say, by rejecting all advice as unwarranted interference and restriction, we come into head-on conflict with the outside world. At times the oldies of this age group can be as stubborn and unreasonable as children, and it can be quite impossible to have a rational argument with them. They will insist on making their own decisions regardless, and simply ignore their physical limitations. More often than not, it is their own children who are the receiving end of this defiant attitude. In order to demonstrate that they are still a power to be reckoned with, some old people resort to threats of disinheriting their children, which can lead to a full-blown power struggle between the generations. But alas, eventually defeat is unavoidable, and they have to concede that they really aren't as young as they used to be. The 2nd house need for security is beginning to make itself felt.

Age 77 and 78

Low Point of 1st to cusp of 2nd House: renewal of family feelings.

This is a calming phase. We have to face up to our limitations and connect again with other people. Many of us become painfully aware of our dependence on other people, and prepare ourselves to hand over eventually. The 2nd house is already showing its influence; we want to make sure of our comforts and our security, and cherish the feeling of belonging somewhere, and so we learn to compromise and to become more amenable. Some of us in this phase of our life are thrown back onto our own resources, and we may also have to reap the consequences of past financial excesses.

Lessons to Be Learned in the 1st House (Aries)
Age 72-78

Experiencing a new start and a new way of being. Reawakening of the enterprising spirit and *joie de vivre*, struggle against restrictions, misjudging our available energies.

The urge to manifest, which is the key concept of the 1st house, can now be used creatively and to great advantage. It is, after all, a positive energy that enables us to carry on courageously, and to overcome limitations. It helps us tackle weaknesses, lethargy, and defeatism. We'll know that we've made real progress once we can accept that even our most painful experiences—rejection, failure, or humiliation—were exactly what we needed at that time for our inner growth, by being shaken out of our old attitudes, by being forced to some hard thinking. Now we have the chance to become consciously aware of our own inner core, of our own worth, without the need to have this affirmed by other people.

But during this phase of their lives many people yield to the temptation of letting themselves go, of falling back on their little egos, loathe to change anything at all. Of course, this only causes them to stagnate, and it stops any chance of further development. Others may tend to overestimate their resources, they make the most wonderful plans but then have to concede that after all they are no longer young and will have to ration their energies. As the Age Point crosses the 1st house for the second time, it should be quite possible for us to see our egos from a more realistic perspective, but frequently this view will still be somewhat egocentric. Many people become defiant, want to demonstrate their individuality, and those who lack any concept of the Higher Self will insist on competing with everyone around them. Obviously this is bound to fail, younger people have a physical advantage over them. It is well known that in an old people's home, for instance, some residents can be most obstreperous and cantankerous, unwilling to abide by the most basic regulations or unwilling to consider any helpful advice which may come their way.

The learning potential of the 1st house, on the second rung of the spiral, demands of us a conscious awareness of the reality of our soul and our spirit. No longer is it all-important for us to assert our egos, to outshine everyone else, to be seen to be the biggest and best. Instead, we now have to aim for self-awareness and for confirming out knowledge of our Higher Self. We should ask ourselves the question: "Who am I? What is my true reality? How can I best use the span of life left to me?" Maybe we can then tap into a higher source which will guide our spiritual destiny. True, we may experience a new zest for life, but it is important that this surge forward doesn't come from our little temporal self, but from our soul.. Then we can do no other but to yield to its bidding. This can best be summed up in the words of the old saying "Thy will be done O Lord, not mine." And we'll then come to the conclusion that we have been given free will in order to affirm our Higher Self, and the Higher Will, and this is most appropriately expressed in religious or philosophical terms. Jung demonstrates this very clearly in his book *Answer to Job*, written when he was 76, which deals with his search for God.

• Age Point in the 2nd House
Age 79–82

Cusp to Low Point of 2nd House; Letting go, dreams and memories; working with our childhood experiences.

This phase of our life can bring back our preoccupation with material possessions. Those of us who are of a materialistic frame of mind will surround ourselves with all our goods and chattels, will become tight-fisted and, just like children, unwilling to part with anything at all. We'll be dead scared to be short-changed, won't share our belongings, quarrel over trifles, become jealous, and take all possible precautions lest anyone deprive us of our dues. All manner of anxieties can raise their heads in this phase— fears of material, mental, or spiritual loss.

Age 82

Low Point of 2nd fixed earth house; crisis of loss; detachment from possessions.

At the Low Point of the 2nd house it is quite usual for us to experience a crisis through the unavoidable process of continuing detachment and loss; either by the loss of one of our loved ones, or by a feeling of diminishing security, or by having to move away from familiar surroundings. Now we have to face up to the unpalatable truth that nothing lasts forever, neither possessions nor, indeed, life itself. Only a spiritual view of life can now help us to cope constructively with the 2nd house Low Point. Only this can point the way for us to detach voluntarily from everything which up to then symbolized material security for us. Many people will insist on hanging on to old habits; they stubbornly continue with their old ways, reject any sort of change out of hand, while they could be much happier if only they'd let go. But they have become far too fearful to face change and uncertainty.

Age 83 and 84

Low Point of 2nd house to cusp of 3rd; fading of vitality.

This is the time when a spiritual perspective on life really will be most useful to help us to carry on meaningfully. It is a time in which we can gain new knowledge and awareness, and find new interests which can give a new impetus to our lives. Our physical energies may decline, we may no longer be able to take part in everything that's going on around us, but it is all the more important to keep an active mind, not to allow it to go to sleep. The stress zone leading up to the 3rd house actually can stimulate intellectual capacities. We can still be wide awake, and take an active interest in all manner of topics without actually having to use any physical resources. It is well known that a lively interest in local affairs, in the news and views of those around us, is the best possible medicine to prevent deterioration.

Lessons to Be Learned in the 2nd House (Taurus)
Age 78-84

End of the phase of expansion, adapting to reality, relying on inner resources, working through childhood experiences, learning to detach from the need for possessions and relationships, diminishing life energies.

In the 2nd house we have to learn to deal sensibly with our available energies as well as our material goods. Many of us may learn to make do with less and less, perhaps by restricting our living quarters, and by shedding, voluntarily, anything we do not really need. We may find ourselves obliged to cut down on our belongings, and to restrict ourselves to the bare minimum. The possessions which we have accumulated over the years are no longer a joy to us; they are fast becoming a burden. We also now have to part with many a memento which used to be dear to our hearts. This applies not only to material objects, but also to some of our nearest and dearest. It is the time to say our goodbyes, and to withdraw into our inner core. Many of our erstwhile friends may die before our eyes, and we grieve for past companionships and feel deserted. This, in fact, is the very point which the 2nd house wishes to teach us, to become aware of the impermanence of our physical existence. Material concerns lose their importance, when death beckons we can't take them with us anyway. Indeed it would be a wise move for us to use this phase in our lives to distribute our knickknacks and our valuables among our heirs; then they can't squabble about them later on. It is our task to manage to part with them with good grace. But some people will stubbornly hang on to every bit of their belongings and refuse to part with any of them. They do so with grim determination, become meanspirited, and hide behind their legal rights. Some even engage in power games. If they feel they have been slighted by someone in the past, and they haven't yet worked through this experience, they may now make a point of paying them back in kind.

That's also the reason why, at this time of life, some people make a point of disinheriting their dis-favorite relatives, by way of punishment. Needless to say, this kind of conduct is not exactly conducive to peace of mind. Quite to the contrary. The 2nd house is the house of karma. The principle of cause and effect is directly related to the law of economy of the possession axis (2/8). "As you sow, so you shall surely reap," supply and demand, give and take, are concepts which are especially meaningful and appropriate here.

Just as in the 8th house, we here receive what we have earned or previously set in motion. And that's why, for many people, this phase has a distinct karmic flavor, everything that happens to us seems to follow the law of compensation. It demonstrates a boomerang effect, and peace of mind eludes us until we have balanced our karmic books. This may consist in settling old scores with erstwhile adversaries, for others it can be the reward for good deeds done. Frequently this law uses our physical bodies for demonstrating this effect, possibly via physical "dis-ease."

When the Age Point conjoins a planet in the 2nd house, we may well relive some of our childhood experiences. Some older people turn these over and over again in their minds. They keep on talking about them, and repeat themselves endlessly. Actually this very repetition may give them the chance to come to terms with their traumas. But those around them very often find the whole process rather burdensome, only very few may find themselves able to listen to the selfsame story time and again. But from the point of view of growth and development, this phase could be most fruitful to help to unravel old complexes and hangups. Therapy could well prove useful here, but then, who has the chance to tackle it at that time, and which therapist would be willing to undertake such a task?

It could be most beneficial during this phase to look out for such occasions, and to use them to try to bring about a reconciliation where there may have been disharmony. For instance, relatives who care for the elderly can do a great deal to bring about a harmonious solution to a karmic parent/child conflict. And role reversals are quite common here. Now it may be the parents who become weak and helpless, while the "children" have to learn to parent their parents. Observing their parents' deterioration into helplessness and dependency demands a great deal of understanding from children, and a genuine wish to be of help, but, at the same time, a degree of detachment from their parents' condition, and a letting-go of powerful father or mother figures which were previously so important.

• Age Points in the 3rd House
Age 85-88

Cusp to Low Point of 3rd House; Musings, transformation, restitution; forming of ideas.

It is quite possible that in this phase of life some people become more open to new ideas than they were beforehand. Some even want to embark on a new course of instruction and learning. We knew a husband and wife team of this age group who regularly attended our classes in Germany. They both were very open to new ideas, and grasped the deeper meaning of our methods much more quickly than the younger participants, although they had practiced classical astrology for some forty years previously. Between ages 12 and 16 we are busy attending school; we are given a similar opportunity during the second passage of the Age Point through the 3rd house. Some elderly people begin to study a new language at this stage.

Age 88

Low Point in the 3rd House of mutable air; identity crisis.

The year of the Low Point can create an identity crisis, because our sense of our selfhood is beginning to dissolve. We may have intellectual interests, but the volatile nature of this house tends to be detrimental for the personality. Many lose short-term memory, the days seem to merge into each other, we lose our powers of discernment, and our notion of the passage of time.

Age 89 to 90

Low Point of 3rd to cusp of 4th House; dissolution of our sense of selfhood.

The volatile principle of the 3rd house, the house of Gemini, can, for many people, dissolve their feeling for space and time. Similarly the approach of the 4th house cusp can dissipate their sense of the self, to be engulfed by the collective. Many an event which used to be deemed really important now just vanishes into the mists of time, it is totally forgotten. And it doesn't seem to matter greatly whether it concerned our Self, or maybe someone else instead. The cardinal IC/MC axis had been the beginning of our individuation process, but now it erodes the meaning of selfhood. Some people are able to drop any further demands and expectations from life, and prepare quite consciously for the process of dying. (If they have come to terms with the concept of reincarnation, they can use this time to prepare for the next life.)

Lessons to Be Learned in the 3rd House (Gemini)
Age 84–90

Making friends with dwindling time, dissolution of the sense of identity, the possibility of approaching senility, realizing the ephemeral nature of life, becoming unsure of everything, preparing for death.

Many people in this phase of life have moments of true illumination and intuition. They suddenly seem to fathom the deeper meaning of events and surprise others by their wisdom. At the same time, they often forget everyday affairs, because they no longer matter so much anymore.

Others react to their 3rd house feelings of uncertainty and ambiguity with a kind of cold optimism an indifference to any attempt to plumb the depth of meaning. The just live from day to day without much serious thinking; everything that used to be of value just evaporates. In the 2nd house of realism and economy, they may have been frugal, steadfast, and even stubborn; now all these traits can just dissolve away. Many even may give the impression that they are no longer the selfsame person. The change from the fixed to the mutable way of being is much more pronounced at this stage of life than in youth.

During the identity crisis at the Low Point of the 3rd house, the ego can either become more ephemeral for the Higher Self to use, or it can ossify. Those who have managed to develop awareness of the spiritual nature will take this opportunity to prepare consciously for the forthcoming transition. The majority of people, however, don't cope very well with this challenge as they are insufficiently prepared for it.

Unfortunately our culture does not deal with the process of laying down our physical life with dignity. The personality, instead of becoming more fluid, often may harden because of its overwhelming fear of death. Then people are no longer open to new learning, their consciousness is already clouded while bodily functions are still comparatively intact. And the nearer they come to the IC, the more they are beyond caring.

Quite often people may have to be uprooted from home and familiar surroundings, if, for instance, they have to move into an old people's home because they are no longer capable of taking care of themselves. For some this may very well be the end, as they cannot cope with such drastic change.

The transformation of our ego into the Higher Self demands conscious cooperation. That's why, in the 3rd house, we should make sure that we are well acquainted with the process of dying and the nature of life after death, so that we know what to expect. Nowadays there are many books available on this subject, notably books by Elisabeth Kübler-Ross and by Alice A. Bailey. We especially recommend Bailey's *Esoteric Healing: The Process of Restitution*, pages 460–485, and *A Treatise on White Magic: Salvation from the Fear of Death*, pages 492–507.

Bibliography

Bailey, A. *Esoteric Astrology*. NY: Lucis Trust, 1979.

Brunton, Paul. *The Quest of the Overself*. York Beach, ME: Samuel Weiser, 1970; and London: Rider, 1970.

Ellenberger, H.F. *The Discovery of the Unconscious*. NY: Basic Books, 1970.

Erikson, Erik. *Childhood and Society*. NY: Norton, 1964.

——. *Identity and the Life Cycles*. NY: Norton, 1980.

Freud, S. and C.G. Jung. *The Freud/Jung Letters*. Edited by William McGuire, translated by Ralph Manheim and R.F.C. Hull. Bollingen Series, XCIV. Princeton, NJ: Princeton University Press, 1976.

Huber, Bruno and Louise. *The Astrological Houses: A Psychological View of Man and His World*. York Beach, ME: Samuel Weiser, 1984.

Huber, Louise. *Reflections and Meditations on the Signs of the Zodiac*. Tempe, AZ: American Federation of Astrologers, 1984.

Jones, Ernest. *The Life and Work of Sigmund Freud*. NY: Basic Books, 1961.

Jung, C.G. *Selected Letters of C.G. Jung, 1909-1961*. Selected and edited by Gerhard Adler, in collaboration with Aniela Jaffe. Princeton, NJ: Princeton University Press, 1984.

——. *Memories, Dreams, Reflections*. Edited by Aniela Jaffe. NY: Random House, 1965.

——. *Word and Image*. Edited by Aniela Jaffe. Bollingen Series, XCVII:2. Princeton, NJ: Princeton University Press, 1970.

Krishnamurti, J. *Freedom from the Known*. Krishnamurti Foundation, 1973.

Levinson, Daniel J. *The Seasons of a Man's Life*. NY: Alfred A. Knopf, 1978.

Ruperti, Alexander. *Cycles of Becoming*. Reno, NV: CRCS Publications, 1978.

Russell, Bertrand. *The Autobiography of Bertrand Russell*. London: Allen & Unwin, 1978.

Index